BACK OF THE PACK

An Iditarod Rookie Musher's Alaska Pilgrimage to Nome

DON BOWERS

Publication Consultants

PO Box 221974 Anchorage, Alaska 99522-1974

ISBN 1-888125-24-1

Library of Congress Catalog Card Number: 98-65166

Copyright 1998 by Don Bowers
—First Printing 1998—
—Second Printing 2000—
—Third Printing 2003—

Manufactured in the United States of America.

Dedication

This is Everyman's Iditarod, a tribute to the dedicated dreamers and their dogs who run to Nome in the back of the pack with no hope of prize money or glory. This is "the rest of the story" of the Last Great Race on Earth.

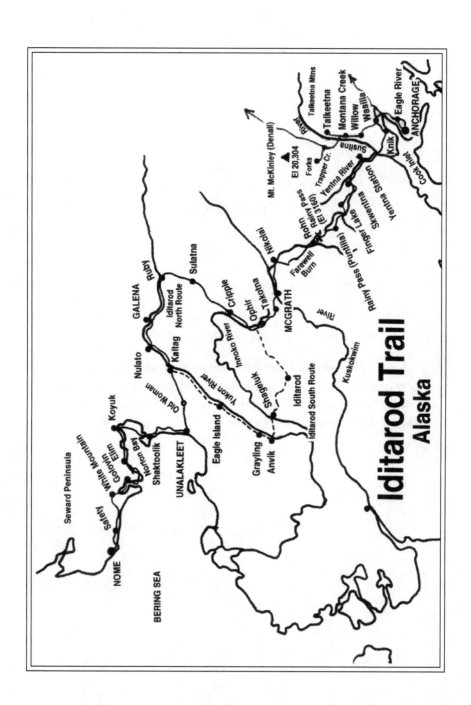

Iditarod Trail
Alaska

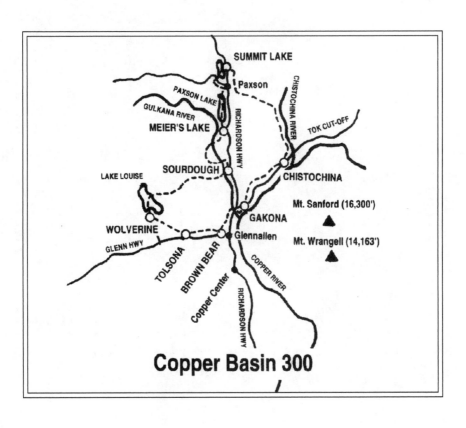

Copper Basin 300

Foreword
Martin Buser
Three-time Iditarod Champion
Big Lake, Alaska

Back of the Pack is a fabulously written account of the Iditarod experience and the long and difficult path of just getting to the race starting line, and of the incredible amount of work and determination it takes. Don has put in words what many of us have experienced over the years but always kept to ourselves.

As you join Don in his Iditarod epic, you will gain a new respect for the land and the dogs. You'll meet Socks, Pullman, Buck, and Maybelline as they are getting themselves and their owner ready for the world's longest sled dog race, Alaska's Iditarod — a challenge of body, mind and soul. Don and his team encounter numerous obstacles on their long way to the burled arch finish line in Nome. Their account will enlighten, educate, and amuse you, as you become one with their motley crew.

Back of the Pack is great adventure on the way to Nome. Travel up the trail and join Don and his huskies as they are chasing their dream of reaching the finish line. Back of the Pack is a must read for all travelers of any mode.

Introduction

To those who are unfamiliar with it, the Iditarod Trail Sled Dog Race is probably one of the more exotic sporting events in the world. In reality, though, it is much more than a race—it is the culmination and commemoration of a lifestyle that is unique to the North Country, and whose roots extend more than a thousand years back into the prehistory of Alaska.

On the one hand, modern mushers on the 1,150-mile run from Anchorage to Nome travel in the footsteps of the freight and mail mushers of the early part of this century. In another and deeper sense, they are carrying on the tradition of Alaska's earliest inhabitants, who perfected the use of dog teams more than a millennium ago. Indeed, the race is a remarkable journey into the past, passing through legendary frontier gold-rush mining districts as well as some of the very Native villages where mushing was born.

When I decided to run the 1995 Iditarod as a rookie musher, after many years of flying for the race as a volunteer pilot, I resolved to keep a journal of what I thought would be an interesting adventure on a par with my flying exploits. However, this account rapidly became much more than I expected as I found that becoming a musher was far, far more than learning to stand on the runners of a sled, and was a world apart from seeing the race from the air.

I learned that to drive dogs in anything more than a recreational mode is to adopt a lifestyle centered around the dogs themselves. I also discovered this way of life is addictive beyond imagination—there is virtually no escaping once hooked. The dogs become a second family, and the affection and devotion given to them is easily equal to that given to any human family.

This alternative lifestyle has a payoff which few people outside it fully appreciate. Unlike a house pet or even a hunting dog, a team of sled dogs is a finely tuned machine that is a passport to—and a permanent link with—another world. A dog team in Alaska in winter is the ultimate instrument of discovery. Nothing can compare to a run along wilderness trails under a full moon and the shimmering aurora behind a ghostly silent, smoothly pulling team— actually a team of friends—that you've trained yourself.

To run the Iditarod is the ultimate goal of almost every dog musher. It is a daunting test for both team and driver, but it is also the most profoundly rewarding journey imaginable. No one who has ever run the race will ever forget a moment of it, nor the incredible range of emotions and experiences it represents.

I regret that mere words cannot adequately convey the intensity and spirit of the Iditarod and everything leading up to it. This journal is at best an imperfect log of a two-year voyage of discovery. I hope it will paint at least a partial picture of what it is like to prepare for and run the Last Great Race on Earth.

Note: A background of the Iditarod—both the trail and the race—and a brief introduction to dog mushing can be found in the Appendix.

March 20, 1994
Front Street, Nome, Alaska

I'm standing on Front Street in Nome under the burled arch at the end of the Iditarod Trail. It's early Sunday evening. The cold sun is just setting over the Bering Sea to the west. Wind is gusting from the north and snow is whipping from every cross street. At the far eastern end of the street, where the road from Safety Roadhouse and Cape Nome turns off the beach, I can see a police car with its red and blue lights flashing, escorting a solitary musher and his team back into civilization after the long, lonely journey from Anchorage.

The musher is Ron Aldrich, whom I've known for 20 years and who is my next-door neighbor at Montana Creek, 100 highway miles north of Anchorage. In addition to being one of my oldest friends in Alaska, he is also one of the group of dedicated mushers who helped rescue dog mushing from its snowmobile-induced near-extinction in the 1960s and 1970s. He ran the first Iditarod in 1973, and the initial Yukon Quest almost a decade later. He's always had good teams, placing in the top 10 in the late 1970s, but he was never a real contender.

This is Ron's first Iditarod in 15 years; it is his seventh trip to Nome. Remarkably, next month Ron will celebrate his 69th birthday. He ran the inaugural Iditarod when he was 46—my age—after a full career in the Air Force that began as a B-17 pilot in World War II and included a number of years in Alaska in the late 1940s. Ron retired to Alaska in the early 1960s and ran a commercial dog team, hauling freight in the Susitna Valley. He still lives in a cabin with no electricity and no running water—and swears he prefers it that way.

His reasons for running the race this year are several. One is that Dorothy (or Dottie, as we all knew her), his wife of almost 50 years, passed away a year or so ago after a long illness. Ron probably won't admit it, but preparing for and running the race have been a helpful focus to get him through a difficult time.

Just as important, Ron is a serious dog musher. In Alaska this carries a special connotation, denoting a kind of addict, someone who is always planning for next winter, always dreaming of trails yet to explore and races yet to be run. Mushers may outwardly resemble ordinary human beings, but there is something not far beneath the surface making them different. They know another way of life, an alternate existence at cross-purposes with modern civilization, which they can never completely shake. They may break away from the dogs for months or even years, but they almost always come back in one way or another. Once infected with the mushing virus, there is no cure—there is only the trail.

Musher Ron Aldrich and his team work their way up the chute to the finish line in the 1994 Iditarod after two weeks on the trail.

I became aware of the Iditarod Trail Sled Dog Race in 1975, soon after I arrived in Alaska from a tour in Southeast Asia. In fact, I pulled into my new assignment, a C-130 Hercules pilot at Elmendorf Air Force Base in Anchorage, just before the third Iditarod got underway. The race wasn't much known outside Alaska then, but when I met Ron not long afterward, my interest was piqued. A couple of years later Ron loaned me three dogs for my cheechako (beginner's) race at the Montana Creek track. I finished second and couldn't believe it.

I began volunteering for the Iditarod in the late 1970s, flying amateur radio operators along the trail in my venerable Cessna 170. Every year,

I became more intrigued by the race and the heritage it represented—and by the mushers who ran it and the army of volunteers who supported it. My Air Force flying reinforced my interest in the race, sending me to countless villages and remote locations around the state. I became fascinated by the unending variety and vast solitude of the Last Frontier, as well as its astonishing array of ancient cultures.

After completing my tour, I endured a five-year absence from Alaska while the Air Force steered me to warmer climes and higher headquarters. I flew my Cessna back to Alaska every summer on leave, eventually returning for another tour at Elmendorf in 1985. I quickly resumed my involvement with the race, which had grown into an internationally famous event. By then, the Iditarod volunteer pilots had coalesced into the Iditarod Air Force, a more or less formally organized group donating their flying skills as well as their own planes. The IAF—already becoming something of a legend in its own right—carried everything from dog food to sick dogs to dog doctors among the 20-odd checkpoints.

I reluctantly left Alaska once more in 1988 for another Outside engagement (this time in the Pentagon), during which I traded my old Cessna 170 for a heavy-duty Cessna 206, which I continued to fly north every summer. After several interesting but intensely frustrating years inside the Beltway, I retreated to Alaska for a last assignment and subsequent retirement. I promptly reenlisted in the IAF once I was back in Anchorage, fully intending to fly for the race well into the next century.

In 1991, I was trapped at Unalakleet, with several other pilots and numerous mushers, by the ferocious storm that swept the coast during the race. I almost wrecked my airplane at Shaktoolik in 20-below zero temperatures and hurricane-force winds while trying to pick up 11 sick and injured dogs. At the same time, the maelstrom threw the entire front end of the race into chaos less than 100 miles from the finish. When Rick Swenson incredibly pushed through the howling blizzard to gain his fifth victory, with Martin Buser not far behind him, I started to wonder what kind of people would willingly put themselves through such punishment year after year—and why.

In 1992, I worked the rear of the race while Martin Buser blazed a new record. Then I waited in Nome for the tail-enders while one of them, Bob Ernisse, whom I'd helped sponsor, almost died in a storm not 40 miles back down the trail. He finally made it in—not with his team but aboard a medevac helicopter. When I got a chance to see him I was shocked by his frost-ravaged face and bandaged, frostbitten hands. He broke down in tears because he hadn't completed the race, and swore he'd do it again and finish it. As I talked to him, I could only ask myself, "Who are these people?"

In 1993, I helped fly out dogs of another acquaintance who scratched at Finger Lake. I then hunkered down with my plane as yet another raging storm battered the coast and pinned down the last half of the race. I watched in awe as a pack of never-say-die drivers and their dogs banded together and finally pushed through everything to pass under the burled arch in a grand 17-team parade, even though they all finished out of the money. I looked on as my friend (and former Iditarod Air Force chief pilot) Bert Hanson plodded into Nome with his dogs after two and a half arduous weeks on the trail. He was followed a day later by rookie Lloyd Gilbertson, dead last, but with a smile a mile wide as he carried his Red Lantern across the finish line. My overriding question was, "Why do they do it?"

Nome, the City of the Golden Beaches, lies on the north shore of the Bering Sea. More than 20,000 people lived here at the turn of the century during the height of the gold rush. For a year the beaches themselves yielded gold to anyone who could wield a shovel.

This year I was the only IAF pilot who stayed with the back of the pack all the way from Anchorage. Martin Buser rewrote the record book for a second time, thundering into Nome even as I watched the last-place musher, Lisa Moore, toil into Galena. I flew overhead as Lloyd Gilbertson was evacuated from a lagoon at the foot of the Blueberry Hills north of Unalakleet, 1,000 miles into his second Iditarod, after he spilled his sled and broke his leg; he said he'd be back. I also looked on as my friends Bruce Moroney and Diana Dronenburg conducted a nationally televised courtship while both of them ran the race—he for the first time, she for the sixth. And only a couple of hours ago I hugged Bob Ernisse after he finally fulfilled his promise of two years ago, finishing 43rd after a fortnight's journey.

But I've been following Ron, and several other mushers I know, with more than casual interest. I met Ron at several checkpoints along the trail and managed to overfly him a dozen more times. As I watched his slow, steady progress, and talked to him along the way, the impossible thought of running the race myself slowly began to germinate.

Now I'm standing in the swirling snow on Front Street waiting for Ron to make the last few blocks to his 45th-place finish. There aren't many people here because the huge awards banquet has been under-way across town for two hours. Almost everyone in this end of the state is there. In the finish chute with me are only a handful of race officials, the odd bystander, and Martin Buser. Martin is personally greeting every finisher under the arch, no matter the time of the day of night, and he has left the banquet—his banquet, really—to come out here in the blowing snow to welcome Ron.

As Ron's team pulls into the fenced-in chute for the last 100 feet, there's no more doubt in my mind: I can no longer stand here and watch others complete this journey. I must do this myself, no matter what it takes.

Martin Buser (right), winner of the 1994 Iditarod, greets Ron Aldrich (bib number 14) after his finish. Ron, a veteran of the first Iditarod, finished his seventh trip to Nome in 45th place—at the age of 68.

April 10, 1994
Amber Lake, Alaska

Today I've dropped in on the annual Iditarod Air Force post-race party at a remote cabin northwest of Anchorage belonging to one of the pilots. As I'm exchanging flying "war stories" of the recent race with other pilots and a few mushers who showed up, I mention my intention of running the race to Diana Dronenburg (now engaged to become Diana Moroney this June). She immediately offers me four dogs and I don't know what to say, since I haven't even thought about building a team yet.

I only talked to Ron a few days ago to seek his tutelage and assistance. I hadn't even thought about getting dogs this soon. But I can't turn down an offer like this—Diana has good dogs, as attested by her 19th-place finish this year. These are older second-stringers, of course, but still superb sled dogs. I agree to pick them up in a few days when I can get into Anchorage. At least Ron has already said I can keep my dogs at his place, along with his kennel of 50 or so.

As word of my folly becomes generally known at the party, other pilots seek me out to shake my hand and congratulate me, although I'm not quite sure for what. After all, my total mileage on a dog sled can be counted on the fingers of one hand.

I fly back home later with mixed emotions. On the one hand, I see a grand adventure about to begin; on the other, I'm not sure how I can ever carry through on my brave resolution. Only time will tell.

April 25, 1994
Montana Creek, Alaska

Quite unexpectedly, I've become caught up in the fever of mushing. Until a week ago I hadn't been on the back of a sled since my cheechako race in 1978. I wasn't even worrying about getting a full team together until this fall. Now that's all changed and I can't wait to get going.

Last week I took the four dogs Diana gave me on a 10-mile run over our local trails. Ron loaned me old Smith, his main leader, and I couldn't have gotten lost if I'd tried, but it seemed like a glimpse into a magical world I'd only heard about. To watch and feel the dogs running smoothly and silently through the soft spring snow was like nothing I'd ever known. It seemed my odyssey to Nome was beginning on an auspicious note.

And now, just like that, I have a complete team for next year. My friend Bert Hanson, a longtime Iditarod pilot, has run the race twice (in 1990 and 1993) and is looking for a place to board his dogs for the next year or so. He's not planning to run in 1995 because of an injury, and he has offered me the use of his dogs if I will look after them at Montana Creek. Ron agrees to this arrangement, since the dogs will technically be in his kennel.

Bert's only proviso is that his daughter, Kim, can pick 10 of them to run the Junior Iditarod the week before the Iditarod itself. I readily agree, since the Junior Iditarod will serve as an excellent training run in its own right. Besides, Kim and some of her friends will come up on weekends to help with the dogs. Bert also agrees to help me out with sleds, ganglines, and lots of other important accoutrements I can't even identify yet. I'll still drop 6,000 bucks or so over the next year (maybe a lot more), but it could be worse: some people willingly pour 20 or 30 grand into a run to Nome.

But I have a sneaking suspicion I might be in this for more than one trip. I already look at the four dogs Diana gave me—Weasel, Blues, Eddie, and Bear—as something of a family (I'm not married). Everything is rapidly becoming much more complex than I first thought. It's obvious I didn't figure on my relationship and commitment to the dogs themselves. Nobody warned me about this, but I can't see turning back now.

The coveted Iditarod belt buckle is awarded to mushers when they finish their first Iditarod. Mushers receive only one buckle no matter how many times they make it to Nome. The buckle cannot be bought or acquired anywhere else. There are many more Super Bowl or World Series rings than Iditarod belt buckles.

Every musher who makes it to Nome receives the distinctive Iditarod finisher's patch. Unlike the belt buckle, mushers receive a patch every time they finish the race and can buy more if needed. However, only Iditarod finishers can receive or buy the patches.

May 25, 1994
Iditarod Headquarters—Wasilla, Alaska

For better or worse, I'm putting my money where my mouth is. I've told everyone I'm going to run, and now it's time to make it formal.

Ron and I made the trip to Iditarod Headquarters in Wasilla this morning for the first day of sign-ups for the 1995 race. Ron has agreed to run the race with me; he said he had so much fun he wants to do it again. However far into his cheek his tongue may have been, we're both in line now with our $1,750 entry fees because we want to commit ourselves before we change our minds.

We're in good company: Martin Buser is here, as are Diana Dronenburg and many top finishers from this year's race. When I walk up to fork over my money to race director Joanne Potts, with whom I've worked for many years, she does a world-class double take: "I didn't think you were really going to run!" she exclaims, as I produce the hard cash to back up my intentions.

As I pocket my receipt, it dawns on me I've really stepped off the deep end. Joanne certainly isn't alone in her disbelief. I'm the last person anyone thought would run the race. In fact, I'm the last person I thought would run the race. But on the ride back to Montana Creek with Ron, the reality starts to sink in. I'd better learn how to spell m-u-s-h-e-r, because in a few months I'm going to have to be one.

June 2, 1994
Anchorage, Alaska

Diana and Bruce are getting married today. I've known them both for a number of years and I wouldn't have missed this for the world.

They both ran the race this year, he with a team of her second-stringers mixed with some of Bert's dogs, the same ones I'm now starting to train. Bruce ran the four dogs Diana has given me and they did quite well. Of course, Diana finished 19th and Bruce finished somewhere around 55th, but that wasn't the point.

About halfway through the race, after Diana had pulled far ahead of Bruce, he proposed marriage to her on his knees on the runners of his sled—in front of a CNN camera team. His bended-knee plea became the talk of the race and got national news coverage for several days.

Diana was still on the trail and didn't find out about it until she got to Nome a couple of days later. The CNN folks played back Bruce's televised proposal for her in the finish chute under the burled arch. On national TV she accepted, and sent Bruce a fax at Unalakleet, 250 miles back down the trail, that simply said "YES!"

Since Bruce was an Iditarod Air Force pilot for some years, those of us in the IAF contingent at Unalakleet tried to think of something appropriate to do with Diana's fax when we saw it come in. We considered dropping it to him while he was still on the trail from Kaltag, and even thought about changing the "yes" to "maybe" or something equally tantalizing. In the end, though, we just put it up on the bulletin board in the checkpoint, carefully folded to conceal its contents, and put Bruce's name on it.

Anyway, today is the big day and the church is full of mushers, pilots, and other race people—a good cross-section of the Iditarod "family." A Channel 2 news team is here and they get their camera's worth when Diana comes down the aisle preceded by Ruby, her lead dog, who is decked out in a frilly lace harness. During the vows, Ruby steals the show as she wanders through the audience to everyone's great amusement, apparently more interested in finding a handout than watching her owner get married.

The ceremony is over quickly and most of the wedding party repairs to the reception. The balance of the celebrants—namely, the race pilots—head for Lake Hood airport and seaplane base, where a multi-ship fly-by is quickly organized. I hop aboard a friend's plane as a passenger since my big Cessna is based all the way across town. Once everyone is airborne and assembled into a loose formation, we head for the new municipal golf course, where the festivities are underway in the expansive clubhouse. As we roar over the tees and greens (scrupulously maintaining the appropriate altitude required by FAA regulations, of course) I can see a score of jerked putts, shanked drives, and one-finger salutes.

We zoom past the clubhouse in a manner to suitably arrest everyone's attention and then pull up into a reasonable facsimile of the Air Force Thunderbirds' "bomb burst" maneuver. After we return safely to terra firma (or aqua firma, as the case may be) and put the airplanes away, we rush back to the reception. A good time is subsequently had by all.

I'm not planning to get married out on the trail, but this is the kind of thing that has drawn me ever closer to the race over the years. I've heard people say the mushing community can be a tight-knit one, almost a big family. What I've seen today certainly hasn't done anything to disprove this theory.

July 20, 1994
Montana Creek, Alaska

Ron and I now agree we can't pull this off by ourselves. I must begin student teaching in a few more weeks at Mount Spurr Elementary in Anchorage in order to finish up my Master of Arts in Teaching. Since the dogs are a two-hour drive north at Montana Creek, I'll only be able to run them on weekends and holidays, if then. Ron originally thought he could help me out by running my dogs during the week, but we both realize it's not feasible.

Ron put out the word on the musher grapevine a few days ago we might need a live-in dog handler. Earlier today the solution to our problem drove up in a battered Chevy pickup. Twenty-year-old Barrie Raper has worked in dog lots in the Big Lake area for a couple of years. She knows Martin Buser and other mushing luminaries and she even has a team of her own.

In fact, she began mushing dogs in Wyoming in her early teens. After high school, she headed north with 15 hand-me-down dogs, a beat-up pickup truck, and her parents' blessings. Her goal was Alaska and ultimately the Iditarod. Now she will help us in return for a place to live and help in running her own dogs.

Ron has an old cabin on his 120-acre property Barrie can use, and Ron and I commit to food for her dogs as well as some spending money. We also agree to pay her entry fees in some of the local races like the Knik 200. There is no mention of her running the Iditarod, but Ron and I secretly agree to help her enter the race this fall if things work out.

So now we have what amounts to a co-op kennel, with all three of us planning to run the Iditarod, even if one of us doesn't know it yet. Ron and I understand we'll be operating on the thinnest of shoestrings, but there's nowhere to go but onward. I think to myself the adventure has truly begun, and now I'm going to be like every other musher I've ever met: permanently broke.

Dogs are hooked up in tandem in front of the sled. The central gangline has a core of aircraft cable and is made in two-dog sections 8 to 10 feet long that can be linked together for any number of dogs. Each dog is attached to the gangline by a tugline at the rear of its harness and by a thin neckline attached to its collar. There is no gangline for the leaders—their tuglines are attached to the previous section, and they are hooked together by a double-ended neckline called a doubler. There are no reins or lines connecting the leaders to the driver—the musher controls the team by voice commands only.

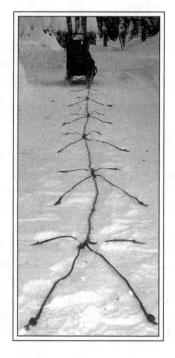

August 15, 1994
Montana Creek, Alaska

There are no shortcuts to the City of the Golden Beaches. The dogs require months of training, beginning well before the first snowflakes fall. Ron estimates we'll need to put at least 1,000 miles on the dogs before the Iditarod, preferably more. So, the sooner we start, the better.

We've been running our teams for a couple of weeks with ATVs on unpaved local borough roads. (Alaska has boroughs, not counties.) This early in the season the runs are very short, only three or four miles long, and serve mainly to get the dogs back into the swing of things after their summer layoff.

The ATVs provide excellent training and the gravel toughens the dogs' feet, but we must be very careful not to overheat the dogs in the late-summer warmth. We don't even consider hooking up unless it's raining or the temperature is below 60 degrees. Naturally, many of our runs are early in the morning or late at night, which greatly amuses our neighbors and the inevitable tourists.

My conveyance for these snowless safaris has so far been a beat-up three-wheeler I got really cheap earlier this summer. My first few excursions were sufficient to reveal why the machine's previous owner didn't ask more for it. On my first run, I hooked up half a dozen dogs and careened out onto the trail not knowing quite what to expect. I met approximately the same fate as a raw graduate of a driving school on a Los Angeles freeway.

I quickly discovered the thing is about as stable as a greased unicycle. Moreover, it's not heavy enough to seriously impede the dogs when they're in the "go" mode. Even six of them were more than powerful enough to overpower it, capsizing it on the first sharp turn and dragging it 25 yards while I observed helplessly from my sudden perch in the trail-side bushes.

Now I look on the infernal contraption with the same regard as a Bangkok pedicab I once tried to drive after knocking off a bottle of Thai whiskey. Luckily, I've managed to convince Bert to loan us a couple of four-wheelers, which are much less likely to assume the inverted position with no prior notice.

Anyway, another use for the ATVs is to establish the dogs' speed. We help them with the engine until they start to lope and then try to hold them to the fastest possible trot. Loping is faster, but the dogs use more energy. The accepted method to master the endless miles of the Iditarod is a steady, energy-conserving trot, and the art is to set the trotting speed as high as possible. While we might accustom our dogs to trot a steady 10 miles an hour or so, the fast movers like Martin Buser get their number-one teams to trot at 14 or 15.

> *Speed isn't really necessary for back-of-the-packers like us. Our dogs aren't world-class trotters, but they'll get us to Nome if we can keep everything else intact.*

Dog trucks are among mushers' most important pieces of equipment. They can vary from aging pickups with homemade plywood dog boxes on the back to professionally constructed heavy-duty machines. Dogs can be hooked to chains hung around the truck at races or for enroute stops. Regardless of size or cost, the truck has room for dogs, sleds, and all of the miscellaneous gear necessary to take a dog team on the road.

September 25, 1994
Mount Spurr Elementary
Anchorage, Alaska

I've been student teaching for about a month, about the same time we've been seriously working the dogs. I'm finding it's not always possible to completely separate the two activities.

In fact, I often can't tell much difference between my class of 31 third and fourth graders and my dog team. Occasionally I even catch myself admonishing a boisterous kid as if he (or she) were one of my recalcitrant dogs: "Eddie, Sit!" On the other hand, I wonder on weekends if the dogs haven't learned the kids' tricks when they tangle up and generally act like jerks.

The kids, of course, are nuts about my dogs and my participation in the Iditarod. Our first read-aloud book of the semester is Gary Paulsen's *Woodsong*, his young-adult version of his preparations to run the 1983 Iditarod. (According to the principal, Paulsen has visited our school more than once; indeed, the school library has virtually a complete autographed set of his books.)

There's only one problem with a book like *Woodsong*—some of the passages are so emotional I have to stop reading aloud in mid-sentence and regain my composure, to the kids' great consternation. They can't understand how strongly I'm becoming attached to my own dogs, and the events Paulsen describes sometimes strike painfully close to home. Fortunately, my host teacher sympathizes, even if he often has the same problem I do. Only half-joking, he tells me our next book to read will be *Where the Red Fern Grows*; I respond he'd better find somebody else to help him read the last couple of chapters, because I'll break down completely.

My growing obsession with mushing and the Iditarod is seeping into every facet of my life. I'm not sure what to think, probably because I'm so totally involved in it all. When I confide my thoughts to Ron, he just smiles as if he's seen this all before. At least the kids have an uncanny ability to bring me back to earth when I get too far out in left field. Come to think of it, so do the dogs....

Village children—and their dogs—are omnipresent spectators at Iditarod checkpoints in the bush. Most towns along the race route let students out of school when the race teams come through.

September 30, 1994
Montana Creek, Alaska

The period after the fall equinox is the darkest time of year in Alaska. It's also one of the most critical times for training, and we must cope with darkness as best we can.

Unlike November and December, there's no snow on the ground to increase the albedo and multiply the light from the stars, moon, and aurora. The Northern Lights rarely come out much before midnight, and the waning harvest moon rises later and later each evening. With an overcast to shut out starlight, darkness at nine or ten in the evening becomes nearly absolute.

Now, at the end of September, days are growing shorter with dramatic rapidity. We lose six or eight minutes of daylight every 24 hours and our headlamps become ever more important. We lay in stocks of D-cell batteries and six-volt bulbs and resign ourselves to wearing the belt-clip battery packs like holstered pistols and the headbands with their attached reflectors like the crowns of some peculiar arctic royalty.

But inconvenience is quickly forgotten. The musher's headlight is actually a magic scalpel to probe darkness and reveal things from another world—the nighttime world—in which man has never been more than a barely tolerated visitor. It's not like donning high-tech night-vision goggles that bathe everything in green daylight. It's not even like a car's headlights, with their high-wattage halogen-enhanced highway illumination.

Rather, the musher's headlamp presents its own view of night, strangely different and more focused than the wide-screen panorama humans are used to. It is a pencil of light that follows the gaze, constantly moving and dancing with the slightest head movement. The narrow beam creates an alternate reality in a series of thumbnail images as it dissects the blackness bit by bit. Perspectives alter, shapes mutate, shadows become real.

Easily the most arresting beacons in this parallel universe are the dogs' eyes. Everyone has seen a cat's eyes catch light and hurl it back. But not everyone realizes many dogs see as well in the dark as their feline antitheses. Dogs' eyes in the headlamp beam can be unnerving in their intensity, perhaps because they are often so unexpected.

Most sled dogs have superb night vision and their eyes are among nature's most efficient reflectors. However, they are keenly focused so they can be seen to best effect only when the illuminating beam originates virtually at the eyes of the viewer.

The dogs in the wheel position, just in front of the sled, are very important in steering. On sharp curves, they keep the sled from cutting across the corner. On twisting trails, they also do most of the actual pulling when the gangline is not straight enough to allow the power of the dogs up front to be transmitted efficiently to the rear.

The link between human eyes and canine eyes is established only when the beam forms a bridge of light directly between them. The headlamp becomes a luminous connection between minds, a direct communication pathway between different species in this alternate world of the night.

At the other end of the mind-link, the crystalline intensity of the dogs' eyes is astonishing. It is startling to those who are used to seeing dogs only in daylight, or in indirect illumination when eyes can at best catch a stray sparkle in their brown or bluish or amber depths. At night the dogs vanish in the probing beam of the headlight, to be replaced by pairs of diamond-bright, prismatically pure lasers radiating with the brilliance of the very brightest stars.

Colors are glimpses into the dogs' inner beings. Ordinary brown eyes by day become piercing blue or green flames at night. Malemute and husky genes—whether or not they yield the familiar blue eyes—can reflect ruby red. But eyes of gold, glowing amber gems, signature of the wolf and its descendants, seem to shine brightest. They are like distant, powerful, mysterious quasars penetrating from beyond the edge of our familiar, neatly ordered, domestic universe.

Only at night do the dogs' true selves emerge. Their eyes, in the revealing beam of the headlamp, are their pedigrees, their family trees. Indeed, their eyes are windows to their souls, and it is the rare musher who is not just a little awed by the rainbow-hued constellation of eyes in the night.

It is hard not to feel a primeval tremor from dozens of pairs of radiant eyes staring intently back from the enfolding darkness. It is an echo of our earliest forebears who saw the same gleaming eyes hovering just outside the mystic protection of their new-found fire. And there is no doubt these eyes are focused on us, marking our every move. They are waiting for us to bridge the gap and reestablish the age-old partnership between humans and dogs, waiting for us to renew the mutual bonds of trust and respect without which the lights in the night will remain as enigmatic as they were to our ancient ancestors.

October 6, 1994
Montana Creek, Alaska

I'm amazed how much progress we've made in barely a month and a half of serious training. It's astonishing how quickly dogs get back into shape.

We have almost 300 miles on the dogs now, and they can easily average 10 miles an hour or better on runs of 10 and 15 miles pulling the small four-wheeler. They have completely shed their summer lethargy and are rapidly metamorphosing into first-rate athletes.

Barrie is running my dogs during the week, and I'm trying to hold my end of the bargain by making the long drive north up the Parks Highway every weekend. My Friday-night runs with the team are always late because it takes me so long to get out of town after school lets out for the week. This means I'm out on the roads and trails with eight or ten dogs sometimes well past midnight.

I always run with the four-wheeler lights off, using only my six-volt headlamp. It seems pitifully inadequate to guide a powerful dog team along narrow trails with sharp turns. The narrow beam usually vanishes in the utter blackness not far ahead of the lead dogs. It's not even much good to illuminate the dogs themselves, and it's sometimes difficult to see if a dog is having a problem, or if a neckline has broken or a dog is running on the wrong side of the gangline. I have to remind myself their night vision and their noses and their ears tell them far more than I can ever hope to experience even with the finest light.

Hanging on to the little four-wheeler as it bounces crazily through smothering blackness past overhanging brush and across roots in the trail becomes a challenge as the dogs come to understand their own collective strength. Their sense of triumph as they crest a difficult hill is palpable, as is their exuberance as they surge down the other side at 20 miles an hour.

I find it hard to believe I'm part of it, and I must remember I don't have as much control over the dogs as I'd like to think. If they feel in the mood, they can easily drag the small four-wheeler even in gear with the parking brake set, with or without me on it. They can crack the whip on sharp curves and I swear they laugh when they do it. It is downright scary to think what they will be able to do with a sled, which pulls much more easily than the four-wheeler.

I can use the brakes to suggest to them to restrain themselves going down steep hills or around the sharpest curves, but everything else depends on my ability to talk to them, to communicate with them on a much more direct level. If I don't have the dogs' trust, if they won't listen to me when I tell them to gee or haw or whoa up, I'm not much more than an unwilling passenger on Mister Toad's Wild Ride.

This is a partnership in every sense of the word, and it demands much from all involved. The team is a finely tuned machine, a thinking organism that can operate with a will of its own. Its individual components require my support for food and training and maintenance, but once assembled and in motion, it is a creature of a very much higher order whose total greatly exceeds the sum of its parts. If I'm very good, I will learn how to become part of the brain of this magnificent entity and thus make it whole.

It's a sobering experience, but also profoundly satisfying and exhilarating. I may finally be starting to understand how mushers become so completely hooked, and why one-time Iditarod runners are a distinct minority in the Official Finisher's Club.

October 10, 1994
Montana Creek, Alaska

As the dogs get back into shape in the fall, they expend prodigious amounts of energy. Without a healthy diet to provide the necessary calories and vitamins, all of our training would be meaningless, if not impossible. Therefore, we feed our dogs only the best.

Indeed, we cook for them, which not many mushers do any more. It's more work, but the result is cheaper, more nutritious, and more appetizing (to the dogs). Even by human standards it would probably provide excellent nourishment, and might even be appealing if it weren't for the inevitable smell from using fish guts and beef innards.

The vehicle for this culinary venture is a so-called Yukon cooker, which is a 55-gallon drum cut in half. A fire of spruce and birch is put in the bottom half (we'll use a big propane burner later on in the winter) while the upper portion is inverted to hold maybe 25 gallons of food. The meat or fish is cooked first with water to make a steaming soup. As weather turns colder, additional fat goes into the mix to fuel the dogs' runaway metabolic furnaces, and it forms a rich gravy whose aroma carries all through the dog yard. When the meat and fat are cooked, rice is added as a filler. Rice absorbs several times its volume in water and turns the meat soup into a thick stew.

One cooker load will yield a day's food for 100 dogs. An hour or two before serving, dry dog food is added to the mix along with more water. The dog-food nuggets provide needed vitamins and absorb still more moisture. The result is a sort of pilaf of meat chunks, fat, rice, and commercial dog food which the dogs find irresistible. (Of course, they also find popcorn, tree roots, old bones, road kill, and even their own harnesses irresistible at times.)

The finished product contains a high water content. This is critical because some dogs won't drink enough on their own to prevent dehydration when they're working. This will be especially important on the race, where it will be necessary to ensure they take in water. By eating this moist food, they build good eating habits for the trail.

We're feeding about 2,000 calories per dog per day, and that will go way up for the 60 or so first-string dogs we'll start to focus on by the end of November. The folks at Costco and Sam's already recognize me as a regular; I'm in there every few weeks for a quarter-ton of rice and several jumbo-size boxes of dog biscuits. Ron hits one of the feed stores back down the highway for a dozen, 40-pound bags of high-grade dog food on about the same schedule.

Ron also makes periodic trips to the slaughterhouse at Palmer. Their unfit-for-human-consumption by-products are perfect for the dogs and cook up very well. An average trip to the abattoir will yield half a dozen 60-pound boxes of the kind of stuff you usually find only in hot dogs. Occasionally we'll also get the results of a freezer cleanout or maybe even the leavings from somebody's yearly moose. (Moose rem-

Many mushers operate do-it-yourself butcher shops to feed their dog lots. Ordinary band saws make excellent meat slicers, but electric circular saws, recipro saws, and even axes work just as well. Most mushers buy frozen meat in blocks of up to 50 pounds to supplement their commercial food, and this must all be reduced to dog-sized pieces. In preparation for the Iditarod, mushers have to slice up as much as half a ton of frozen meat.

nants are especially good—the dogs can gnaw contentedly for weeks on the huge bones.) No matter. It all gets sliced up and tossed into the cooker and it all comes out looking the same. I've learned protein and fat come in many different forms and the dogs don't care a bit.

Feeding time in the dog yard is an explosion of happy frenzy. The dogs can sense we mean to feed them, even if we make no overt move to do so. They must make a complex association between time of day, elapsed time since last feeding, smell of food in the cooking barrel, and our subtle but unintentional body language. For all I know, they may read our minds as well. I wouldn't put it past them.

Feeding time in the dog yard borders on pandemonium. The pups are especially frantic, since they don't yet understand they all will get their share sooner or later.

We often feed at night since we don't like to run them on a full stomach. Besides, we want them to understand finishing a run means food, and they seem to appreciate this cause-and-effect relationship. If the dogs think the time is right, all we have to do is walk toward the cooling cooker and a chorus of barks and yelps and yips and howls instantly erupts. Ron's dogs will even key on the creaking of his front door, which they must hear from 200 yards away.

As soon as we reappear with buckets of food in hand, the canine concert rises to a crescendo. Every dog has his or her own excited way of greeting us. At night, of course, the dancing, glowing eyes are all focused on us. They all want to be first. Little Penny at the far end of the line bounces at the end of her chain like a crazed popcorn kernel. Pullman hops up and down on a stump next to her house and barks as loudly as a dog three times her size.

Bear, whose demonic red-reflecting eyes belie his affectionate, playful nature, crouches like a tightly coiled spring with forelegs spread, ready to leap. His brother Chewy has the same eyes and frantically friendly disposition but his shorter legs give him the appearance of a demented bulldog; he is barely a blur as he races back and forth. Silvertip, my personal pet (and surprisingly good sled dog) who is three-quarters wolf, stands on his hind legs at the end of his chain and jumps two feet straight into the air, turning a flip and coming down facing the opposite direction, barking and yipping all the while.

Demure Blues hardly moves, carefully watching everything and

Some mushers cook for their dogs when they are at home. Big propane crab cookers are the weapon of choice, although wood-fired "Yukon cookers" made from 55-gallon drums work just as well. Ingredients include commercial dog food, fish, frozen meat, meat scraps, rice, fat, and anything else the dogs might eat. Cooking is an especially good way to safely use waste meat and wild game such as caribou which might harbor parasites.

giving only an occasional ladylike bark. Her half-sister Bea sounds like a siren and looks like a dervish as she circles her post. Socks, the wise old veteran who knows he is The Lead Dog, takes a watchful but silent stance. And pups on the outskirts keep up a chaotic racket; they don't yet understand they will all eventually get fed and still treat feeding time as a live-or-die, zero-sum contest.

As each dog gets its pan full of food, the din gradually subsides. After the last morsel is ferreted out and the last dish is licked clean there is always a period of complete silence. The dogs are quietly looking at us. It seems as if they are making mental notes, recording who we are, and that we have brought them food and affection once again.

And later—always—comes the thank-you song. One dog will start it with a howl and the rest will join in. Those who can't howl, bark. Slipper, the old but still excellent leader who spent many years with Libby Riddles, has more than a touch of hound in her family tree. She has an unmistakable comical throaty bellow somewhere between a bay and a bark, and she sounds as if she has a raccoon treed deep in the Georgia woods. Silvertip is her counterpoint, throwing his head back and making the forest echo as hauntingly as his not-so-distant wild cousins.

The wave of sound reaches a climax and continues for several minutes. The effect is other-worldly. Every musher will always stop to listen and none will ever make any move to disturb the purity of the moment.

There's no doubt the dogs are talking to us, thanking us for their food and care, telling us we are part of their pack. They are reaffirming the age-old bond between humans and dogs that seems to reach its culmination in the dog team.

October 22, 1994
Montana Creek, Alaska

At last I'm back on the runners. Thanks to last week's storm, we decided to hook up the sleds today for the first time this season. There really isn't much snow, maybe only a couple of inches, but it's enough. After playing musher on a four-wheeler all summer and fall, I'm finally back to the real thing.

About mid-afternoon, I hook up five dogs to Bert's Bernie Willis sled, the same one he used on the 1993 race, and which Bruce Moroney used this year. Willis sleds are very flexible and are built to give; in fact, they give a lot, and seemingly feel like they're about to fall apart. This is my first time to ride one and I'm not at all used to its very tippy nature.

The dogs are beside themselves with anticipation. They know this is the first run on snow with the sled and are positively supercharged. When I pull the slipknot in the tie-off rope the sled shoots out of the lot like it was fired from a cannon. Unfortunately, our outbound trail makes a tight S-turn, which I impressively don't negotiate. The sled flips instantly and I drag through the brush with a death grip on the handlebar, yelling "Whoa!" at the top of my lungs.

Old Socks is leading. He's done all this before to more mushers than I can count. He knew the sled would whiplash and spill on a turn like this, and I'm sure he's been laughing to himself from the moment we started hooking up. Of course, he also knows to stop the team when the sled goes over on its side, but he makes sure he goes just far enough extra to make me think he's going to leave me behind.

I manage to hang on somehow and get everything upright in a few seconds. As soon as my feet touch the runners, Socks is off again. We tear across our backyard, half-mile-wide swamp at breakneck speed, and I have no doubt the neck in question is mine. There isn't nearly enough snow to make a smooth trail. It's like riding a bicycle over railroad ties at 20 miles an hour as the sled flies from one crest to the next with a knee-buckling series of crashes and thuds. At least twice within a half mile we hit boulder-size bumps while I'm off balance, leaving me looking up at the south end of my northbound wheel dogs and imploring them to stop in my very best and most authoritative "playground voice."

We finally roar off the swamp onto the overland trail. Unlike the four-wheeler, I don't have a lot of choice about which side of the trail the sled uses. Almost immediately one runner settles into a deep rut on the right side; I'm suddenly up close and personal with every overhanging branch and limb. On the outside of one turn a particularly thick clump of willow bushes literally rips me from the sled. Fortunately I have the tie-off rope wrapped around my wrist and am only dragged 20 yards or so before Socks figures he's made his point and stops the team.

I realize I have to learn to ride this sled. All I can do is hop back on and wait for the next face full of snow. After a couple more belly dances with Mother Earth, I begin to get the hang of it. The Willis sled does have a good feel to it, but it's an acquired taste, sort of like single-malt Scotch whiskey or sushi. It leans and sways, but if I can control it, it's like riding a pair of cross-country skis. As I figure out how to shift my weight and play the brake and the drag (a piece of snowmachine track tied behind the brake), and I find I have a lot more control than I think, particularly on turns.

> *After 10 miles, we sweep back into the lot. I haven't gone down for the last four miles, and I begin to think maybe this dog-mushing thing will work out after all. Whether my battered body will survive long enough to see the payoff is another matter, however. I wonder if Martin Buser and the other Big Names went through a stage like this?*

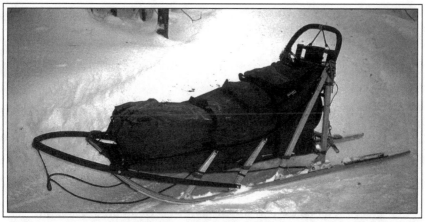

Basket sleds are constructed to be relatively lightweight, flexible, and maneuverable, with an elevated "basket" supported on stanchions several inches above the runners. The handlebar is an integral part of the basket structure. Most Iditarod mushers run variants of basket sleds for the latter part of the race. This is a Bernie Willis model.

Sprint sleds are built to be as lightweight as possible. Some barely weigh 20 pounds. The basket on a sprint sled is very small and the handlebar is located close to the midpoint of the runners to better spread the driver's weight.

October 29, 1994
Montana Creek, Alaska

As if to celebrate the first real subzero night of the season, the northern lights come out.

All evening they teasingly show themselves in the north, each wave venturing ever more southward and hinting of glories to come. After a break to visit the local lodge for dinner, Barrie, Ron, and I return to finish running the dogs.

About 11, before we get back on the trail, the display begins in earnest as the northern sky begins to glow from horizon to horizon. A bright band of green hovers low, just beneath the Big Dipper. Sensing the show is about to start, I walk out to the road for a better view.

I don't have long to wait. Within a few minutes soaring spikes and swirls materialize overhead, creating the effect of a Gothic cathedral with iridescent columns of light reaching to the zenith. Simultaneously the northern band of luminescence grows steadily brighter and broader, starkly silhouetting the delicate tracery of the bare birch branches. The intensity continues to increase until I can actually see shadows on the snow-packed road.

Then about 11:30 the northern sky explodes in one of the most amazing displays I've ever seen. For 10 minutes, frantically shifting curtains tipped in brilliant crimson race in all directions. The northern third of the sky is completely chaotic, seething and swirling like some glowing, ghostly thunderstorm. Fully formed multi-hued curtains suddenly appear and disappear, tumble and stabilize, careen apart and randomly collide.

The sky is alive and seems to be churning perceptibly closer to me. Now I begin to understand why some traditional Inupiats fear the lights can steal their souls: if I were alone on the winter tundra without the comforting 20th-century knowledge of what really drives the auroral displays, this writhing creature of light might be utterly terrifying.

Scientific theories notwithstanding, I am totally lost in the spectacle until a car horn blasts in my ear. A pickup has come down the road behind me with its lights on, but I completely failed to notice it. I sheepishly hop back into the driveway and the driver eases his truck by with a friendly wave.

I am reminded of my first-ever encounter with the lights, early on a cold February morning 20 years ago, somewhere along the Glenn Highway in Chickaloon Pass northeast of Anchorage. I was headed to my new assignment after returning from Southeast Asia and didn't have the faintest idea of what I was getting into. I'd just come up the Alaska Highway and had been on the move for a week on highways I'd never traveled before, through country I'd only imagined in my dreams, and in winter conditions I had only seen in my nightmares.

My attention on that long-ago night was suddenly attracted by glowing movement to the north, outside my headlights. I stopped and stepped out into the 20-below cold and came face-to-face with a first-magnitude display. I'd heard of the lights but had never seen them. No description could ever have done them justice. For an hour I stood next to the car transfixed while the lights danced and raced, faded and reformed. No tour company could have arranged a more profoundly impressive introduction to Alaska.

Back in the present, I imagine what this would be like out beyond the Alaska Range, with just me and the dogs and the trail and all of the vast emptiness of interior Alaska. I've seen the lights while flying for the race and have watched them from checkpoints along the trail, but I've never seen them from a sled. Many experienced mushers have told me all of the months of work and hassle and hardship can be erased by one clear night on a sled on the trail, cruising under the lights behind a smoothly pulling team, headlamp extinguished, and the only sound the hiss of the runners on the crystalline snow.

I remember standing on the river bank at the Galena checkpoint during the 1994 race, waiting for the last-place musher to straggle in from Ruby. A small group of us had watched the bobbing speck of her headlamp for what seemed like hours as she worked her way slowly down the darkened, mile-wide Yukon. At the same time, we were listening on the radio as Martin Buser closed in on the finish line at Nome. As much as I respected and admired Martin, I couldn't identify with him; he was—and is—on another level from me when it comes to driving dogs. I was with that lonely musher far out on the ice, who could just as easily have been me.

As the long minutes crawled by, a magnificent display of the lights began to build in the northern sky, over the distant and unseen Brooks Range. They intensified and expanded, shading from green to yellow, and finally danced from horizon to horizon, tinged with deep red. I was transported to the pinpoint of light still miles away on the river, wondering what it would be like to be out there with my own team under those same shimmering curtains, making my own way across the vastness of the Last Frontier.

Now, less than a half a year later, I might get my chance. The lights fade as quickly as they came and I return to the more mundane business at hand. But another piece has fallen into place. I have yet another experience to anticipate and savor on my pilgrimage to Nome.

Without good feet under them, the dogs can't do their job. Every musher spends inordinate amounts of time checking dogs' feet for everything from cuts to broken toenails to sore wrists. Martin Buser calls the process "praying to the dogs"; by this standard, mushers might be considered among the most religious people in the world.

November 5, 1994
Montana Creek, Alaska

The past week brought a decent dump of snow and we've got at least eight inches on the ground. Our nearby trails are finally in fairly good running condition with most of the bumps smoothed out. I decide to try the 20-mile loop for the first time.

The sun is well down by the time I'm ready to go. I've seen the long trail from a four-wheeler during the day in the summer, but it's an unknown quantity now. I have an ace in the hole, though—Socks. He will undoubtedly make me work for the roundtrip ticket, but he will ultimately get me through, just as he has Bert and other mushers on the Iditarod in conditions more like Antarctica than North America.

This is the first time I've really realized how much I will have to depend on and trust the dogs. This trail isn't really remote, but it has enough hidden dangers and is sufficiently isolated to leave me on my own for at least a couple of hours while everyone figures I'm late and then mounts a search party. The temperature is hovering down around zero as well, so any mistakes on my part will be magnified by the cold. I'm doubly glad Socks is up front for this particular run. He may have some fun with me, but he's as reliable as they come. In any case, I have little choice but to trust his proven trail sense.

Socks doesn't waste any time showing me who's really running the team, nearly ripping the sled out of my hands as he launches us out of the yard. Somehow I get around the infamous S-turns and out into the swamp without crashing. After a few minutes I pick up my bearings and start to get the feel of the sled and the trail. The dogs continue at a dead run for a full mile, across the swamp and up the hill on the far side.

At the top of the hill the trail opens into a driveway and then crosses a borough road. When we burst out into the driveway I see the taillights of a truck completely blocking the narrow cut through which we must run. I stomp on the brake and yell to the dogs to hold up, but not much happens because the snow is still too thin and too firmly packed. Then I notice there are maybe a dozen people standing around. I don't have the faintest idea what they're all doing out here. We're by in a flash and the last thing I think to do is initiate a casual chat with them.

Meanwhile, the driver of the truck must have seen my headlight bearing down on him because the taillights suddenly turn out onto the road barely 30 yards before what I thought would be a calamitous collision. Of course, Socks would have stopped, but you couldn't have convinced me. We whistle across the road and over a two-foot snow berm tossed up by the road grader. The sled goes airborne, with me in loose formation, and returns to earth 15 feet down the trail. I follow shortly, miraculously still aboard.

The dogs really have steam up now and it's all I can do to keep the sled upright. The heavy, sticky snow has bent over every bush and sapling and some really big trees as well and the trail resembles a sugar-frosted obstacle course. The dogs are streaking merrily beneath everything, intent on exploring the new world of snow. In my slightly more lofty perch, I'm getting pummeled by every branch. I try to crouch down and hide behind the handlebar but there is no escape, and I repeatedly get whacked hard enough to raise welts.

The first four miles of the trail are like this and I feel like a long-term guest of the Singapore penal system by the time we tear out of the end of the back trail onto upper Montana Creek Road. Quickly we sweep onto the unmaintained portion of the road, which is now a newly packed snowmachine trail.

We hit the first hill almost immediately. It's a 10% grade with maybe a 100-foot rise, but the dogs hardly hesitate. It's the biggest hill they've seen so far this season but their instinct to pull carries them up and over with speed to spare. Triumphantly they surge down the other side as I step on the drag to keep the gangline taut and avoid overrunning the wheel dogs on the downgrade.

There seems to be a change in the team. They realize this is a major watershed. This is what the endless boring training in front of the four-wheeler and on the short local trails has been about. Now we're doing some real mushing and they're even more anxious than I am. The next several hills are bigger and much steeper than the first one but the dogs need no urging to conquer them. They have united to become a powerful engine capable of surmounting anything in its path.

After another five miles we climb one last brutal hill to the halfway point of the run. Eventually, instead of turning back at this point, we will continue up through the thinning birch and spruce along the South Fork of Montana Creek onto the wide-open uplands of the Talkeetna Mountains. That trail ends maybe 15 miles farther on at the 3,000-foot level, about the same altitude as Rainy Pass on the Iditarod. It's as close as we will get to the Alaska Range until we actually head out on the race, but it's a reasonable approximation, especially for being right in our back yard.

Training runs with smaller teams occupy many weeks before the first races. Most mushers prefer to have at least 600 or 700 miles on their dogs by New Years.

Tonight, though, I stop the dogs at the top of the hill and give them each a biscuit while I look out over the valley to the west. There are only a few lights along the Parks Highway and the Talkeetna Spur Road seven miles away. Otherwise the blackness is complete. Even though it's dark I can half-see, half-sense the 20,000-foot bulk of Denali looming barely 70 miles to the northwest, faintly silhouetted against the starry night sky. Beyond it lies the great interior of Alaska with Nome beyond.

Most Alaskans have never seen the other side of the Mountain, either literally or figuratively. I've been lucky enough to see much of the state from the air over the years, but the thought of seeing it from the back of a sled like the old-timers did is overwhelming. Tonight the black void beyond the tenuous thread of lights along the highway looks vast and mysterious, a world I've seen and taken for granted before but now will experience in a completely new way within a couple of months.

Socks figures I've taken enough time to admire the view and signals his impatience by yanking the snow hook. I grab the handlebar as the sled shoots by. We run for three miles on an easy trail down an unfinished road. Then we reach the end of the improved section and plunge into a narrow winding corridor of willow and alder.

Barrie has told me there's an open stream where a temporary culvert has washed out, but before I can figure out where we are the black gap of rushing water yawns ahead and the dogs have launched themselves across it. I yell "On by!" to Socks and hang on while the sled crashes into the foot-deep water and slithers across the rocks of the creek bed. I manage to stay upright as we slam over the two-foot bank on the far side and the dogs gleefully haul on up the next hill.

Fortunately I've waterproofed my new boots and my feet stay dry. Bert has told me about his numerous misadventures with the wet stuff on the Iditarod, including one time in Dalzell Gorge when he went in up to his chest to keep a dog from being dragged under an ice ledge. Ron has amplified these tales with his own, and I've resigned myself to seeing flowing water on the trail. I know I've seen open water all along the Iditarod from the air even at 40 below, so this is only a slight taste of what's to come. I guess I'm starting to pay my dues, but so far it's nothing I can't handle.

The trail winds on for another half mile and then all I can see in front of me in the headlight beam is yawning blackness. This must be the hill I vaguely remember from my trip through here on the four-wheeler this summer. By the time my memory banks dredge up the information this is the longest and steepest hill on the whole trail, I realize I'm rocketing down it at a high rate of speed and the dogs are yelping in delight as they continue to accelerate.

I don't dare yell to the dogs to whoa up because I'd overrun the team before I could get the sled stopped. So, I jump on the drag and shift my entire weight onto it to try to slow down the juggernaut and keep the gangline taut. But in doing so I sacrifice what's left of my balance, and the deed is completed by a snow-covered rut and the Willis sled's inherent tendency to go with the flow.

In a flash the sled tips and I flail behind it as it slides off the near-vertical embankment and down into the bordering brush. The quick-release cord still wrapped around my wrist keeps me from flying off into the deep ditch, but at the price of several pulled muscles in my arm. The dogs stay up on the trail but they have so much momentum they drag me like a sack of potatoes for what seems forever through the scrub and over the rocks. Sometime in the 15 seconds or so before things come to a grinding halt I bang my right knee against a rock and the pain is almost enough to make me yell something ungentlemanly, which I'm sure Socks would enjoy.

However, the old pro knows to stop when the sled tips over and he finally gets around to doing it. I lie there for a minute or so getting my bearings and catching my breath. Slowly I get myself and the sled untangled from the grabbing branches. As I lever the sled back up onto the trail, I can see Socks looking around and I swear he's smiling. As usual, he's moving the instant he thinks I'm reasonably upright and we tear off down the trail again.

Half a mile later we come to another hazard Barrie warned me about, a tree down across the trail that is outflanked by a contorted makeshift bypass winding for several hundred yards through the forest. The sled capsizes a couple of times in the deep snow but the dogs are barely moving so nothing untoward happens. Then we pull up a sharp incline back onto the road. Socks veers to the right and then stops; I see he's turned us back into the downed tree from the opposite side. I sigh and tell him to come haw (double back to the left).

After a minute he pulls the team around and heads down the trail in the right direction, but the wheel dogs, Weasel and Bear, are hopelessly tangled. I stop the team and go up to sort things out. I must completely unhook Weasel's neckline and tugline for a few seconds—and at this exact instant the team jerks and I lose my hold on Weasel, who darts off to one side.

Weasel is one of my favorites, a pure white female who's run the Iditarod a couple of times and has even been from Nome to Russia on the international Hope race. She has a bouncy and lovable disposition but also displays a mind of her own at times. She won't come to me when I call and darts out ahead of the team as if daring us to follow. I don't have much choice but to head on back to the lot. I'm reasonably certain she'll tag along; she's smart and is a good trail leader in her own right, so I know she'll find her way home if she gets separated. Still, the thought of having a loose dog on the trail is a musher's worst nightmare, and losing a dog is the most fundamental sin a musher can commit. If this is paying dues, I'm writing big checks tonight.

Socks treats it all as a game and streaks after Weasel, who dances ahead like a pale ghost. I occasionally get a glimpse of her glowing green eyes as she pauses to check where we are. After another half mile I realize I've still got a few dog biscuits in my pocket. Weasel is a pushover for a biscuit, and I think there's a chance I can lure her back. I stop the team, set the snow hook around a log, and then creep out in front of Socks. Quietly I call to Weasel, who is about 20 yards ahead, watching me with what must be amusement.

As soon as she senses the biscuit, she bounds over and nuzzles me. I give her the treat and hug her like a prodigal daughter. Then I realize Socks has also smelled the biscuit and has dragged the team and the sled and the log with the snow hook wrapped around it to get his rightful share of the spoils. But all is forgiven as I toss him a snack and hook Weasel back into the team. We're off in a flash, homeward bound and happy.

I have plenty of time to reflect on the errors of my ways as the team pulls steadily back to the lot. I remember almost every word of Gary Paulsen's *Winterdance*, in which he describes his preparations for the 1983 Iditarod. By his account, he made every rookie mistake possible, and a few more for good measure. I read the book just after I decided to run the race and half the time I couldn't decide whether to roll on the floor laughing or just forget the whole thing and seek competent psychiatric counseling.

Now I see what he was talking about because I'm going through many of the same trials and tribulations. Taken in context, the individual events aren't as bad as they might sound to someone who hasn't been there. I've been a human weed-whacker, eaten bucketfuls of snow, imitated a Pachinko ball, gotten bit, sorted out dog fights, and nursed sick dogs. I've untangled Gordian knots of dogs, sleds, trees, and me. I've had to figure out how to keep always-amorous males away from unexpectedly amorous females. I've learned how to rearrange dogs within a team to keep harmony and a sense of purpose. In short, this has been more fun and ultimately satisfying than anything I've ever done before, and I can't wait to see what happens next.

To look at the individual parts of the picture, any non-musher would question my sanity for continuing such a quixotic quest. But any veteran dog driver will nod knowingly and smile, and I'm starting to understand why. As Paulsen said, it's a fine madness, this getting ready to run the Last Great Race.

November 6, 1994
Montana Creek, Alaska

The 20-mile trail beckons again. But if last night could best be classified as a learning experience, this evening is something altogether different.

I take another eight-dog team out with Slipper in the lead. She's 10 years old, the oldest dog on my team, but still a marvelous runner. She spent five years with Libby Riddles and several more with Bert and has run tens of thousands of miles.

However, she's what we call a trail leader, and is not a very good command or "gee-haw" leader. She will follow a trail instinctively and will set a blistering pace, but to turn her takes a somewhat different technique from what most people imagine. The usual method involves waiting to see which way she will go when we come up to a turn and then stomping on the brake if she takes the wrong one, accompanied by a loud "Whoa" or "No."

Actually, it doesn't matter what I shout, as long as it gets her attention and lets her know I don't want to go that way. When she finally starts to go the direction I want, I reinforce her decision with a "There you go!" or something equivalent. It's not a perfect system, but it's quite sufficient when we're out on the trail and away from other dogs or congested areas.

Sometimes, though, she can be incredibly stubborn and won't make a turn no matter what I say. Usually this devolves into a contest of wills while I stand on the brake and try to coax her in the proper direction. Often as not, I have to set the hook and physically lead her the way I want to go. Sometimes even that fails and I simply have to switch leaders, which almost always works. That's one reason I try to run with several dogs who will go up front, even if they're not all good leaders.

Regardless, the oldest rule in dog mushing is you can't let the leader get away with not following your commands. In Slipper's case, this can sometimes require the patience of Job. But tonight she is responding well enough to get us through the more complicated parts of the trail with only a few near-detours. I keep the sled upright the whole way up to the top of the trail and actually start to enjoy myself a bit.

Like last night, I stop at the top of the hill and admire the view. Tonight, however, I feel much more a part of the team. Without really realizing it, I've been able to guide Slipper and the team easily and to handle in stride all of the little distractions. I seem to have crossed a psychological divide that has kept me from feeling secure with the team. As I gaze at the team and out over the silent mountains, I understand I can take the dogs practically anywhere. The team has now become a powerful and exotic instrument of travel and discovery, not just a collection of dogs I must herd over the same trails night after night.

Mount McKinley, called Denali (the Great One) by Alaska Natives, dominates the skyline of central Alaska. The highest mountain in North America, it towers in solitary grandeur to 20,320 feet above sea level. It can often be seen from more than 200 miles away, and is visible along the Iditarod Trail in many places from Anchorage to beyond Takotna.

Instead of returning to the dog lot tonight, I could just as easily keep going up the mountain or on toward Talkeetna. Slipper, for all her quirks, can take me to places most people will never see except in photographs. She and her teammates have turned the winter, which chills more conventional spirits, into a beckoning wonderland for me. I pity the snowmachiners with their noisy, smelly engines, and even the cross-country skiers with their limited range. I have never fully realized how uniquely suited the dog team is to the North Country. It represents freedom of a kind I've never experienced before, even with my airplanes.

The ride back to the dog yard is a study in perfection. Slipper, in her special wisdom, seems to know that I, too, now understand and leads flawlessly as if to reward me for my belated insight. I hope there will be many more nights like this.

November 10-30, 1994
Eagle River, Alaska

Be careful what you wish for: it might come true. I'm sitting awake at four o'clock on a Monday morning because I can't get to sleep, attempting to reconcile the incredible events of the last few weeks. As I review them in my mind I don't think anyone would believe me if I swore everything was true on a stack of Bibles.

First there was the snow. Lots of snow, even for up here. To be sure, ever since Labor Day we were hoping for enough of the white stuff to start serious training. But we must have punched the wrong buttons when we entered our modest request at Weather God Central, because after our initial few inches we were smacked by a series of major storms that left us with four feet on the ground in barely 10 days.

Of course, our carefully marked and packed trails were inundated until even the most intrepid snowmachiners wouldn't give them a shot. The dog lot was completely cut off by the first dump (almost two feet in 24 hours) because Ron's narrow half-mile-long driveway was hopelessly blocked.

Since we didn't have an operable snowmachine, we hitched up a few teams just to get between our houses and cabins. A couple of vehicles were parked close enough to the borough road so we could extract them and keep them parked on the plowed public right of way, although access to and from them was only by dog team. On top of everything I had to keep driving back and forth to Anchorage during the week to teach; at least the big state plows kept the main roads open.

After the fluffy deluge eventually quit, I was able to unlimber my snowblower to clear my own 300-foot driveway, but Ron's stayed

51

blocked for a week. It took two days with a front-end loader to get his opened up and in the process his phone line was cut and we couldn't repair it.

The snow we'd been hoping for ended up cutting our training drastically. We were up to daily 30-mile runs before the heavy snows and were actually ahead of the power curve for the Iditarod. However, limited strictly to the plowed local roads and the sporadically groomed Montana Creek Dog Mushers Association 10-mile track, we were lucky to get 15 or 20 miles every few days.

Then the snow was followed by a 40-below cold snap. While we'll certainly hit comparable temperatures out on the trail, we didn't see any point in intentionally risking the dogs in extreme cold weather without a good reason. The dogs can handle it just fine when the time comes for real, but it's not good training at this stage of the game. We made a policy of not running the dogs unless the temperature was above 25 below—still plenty cold.

I spent so much time outside during the cold snap trying to get things cleared I came down with a vicious cold. Monday and Tuesday before Thanksgiving, Anchorage schools were closed because of more heavy snow and my student teaching was on hold; I felt so bad I just stayed in bed. Wednesday the schools were open and I went in to teach my kids. My host teacher repeatedly warned me I looked like I should have stayed in bed, and after school I finally headed over to the hospital emergency room to see if they knew something I didn't.

The physician on duty took one good look at me, sent me down for a quick chest X-ray, and the next thing I knew I was laid out on a bed with IVs in my arms and a breathing mask over my face. Pneumonia, she said, with a temperature of 102 degrees, spiking as high as 105. Some cold, I thought. After six hours of medical ministrations, the doctor said I could go home as long as I took it easy for several days. She prescribed a new antibiotic that only required six pills over five days to knock out just about anything, and sure enough it worked like magic, deep-sixing my fever within a few hours.

I spent Thanksgiving in bed recuperating, but I couldn't stay away from my dogs. I felt well enough to take them 30 miles yesterday (Sunday) and both they and I came through with no apparent ill effects. On the way back to Anchorage late last night, though, I smacked a 1,200-pound moose at 50 miles an hour after it darted out from a huge snow berm. My minivan was virtually totaled, but its sturdy construction—and the seat belt—protected me from suffering even a scratch. The moose wasn't as lucky and the state trooper had to dispatch it. All of the meat went to charity, although I had a passing regret I couldn't even keep a hindquarter for my trouble.

It took me three hours to nurse my battered and windowless but still drivable vehicle back to town, with great clumps of moose hair and oceans of broken glass filling the seats and littering the floor. When I finally limped into my driveway I was so tired I just wanted to crawl under the covers and not come out for about a month.

Now I'm about to go to bed in hopes of even a short nap because I've got to be back in the classroom at eight. I suppose all of this will be good practice for the trail, where I'll have to weather equally traumatic experiences. I guess it's just been my turn to be tested, to make sure I can "take a licking and keep on ticking" just like the dogs.

Most sleds are of two types: toboggan and basket. This is a toboggan sled, consisting of a rigid piece of plastic firmly bolted to two sturdy runners, with a handlebar braced upright at the rear. Toboggans are strong and good for deep snow, but they tend to be heavier, less flexible, and less maneuverable than basket sleds. Many Iditarod mushers start the race with toboggans and run them until they are through the sled-battering trails of the Alaska Range.

December 15, 1994
Montana Creek, Alaska

My student teaching is finally completed and I'm living full-time at Montana Creek. I'm running the dogs every day and looking forward to the racing season, which begins day after tomorrow with the Sheep Creek Lodge Christmas Classic, just a few miles down the road.

I decide to take out my "A"-team of 12 dogs this afternoon. I want to give them 30 miles and rest them tomorrow before the back-to-back 40-mile heats in the Sheep Creek race this weekend. I'm not worried about the dogs handling runs of this length; we're back on line with our training after the heavy snows and the team is in good shape.

In fact, they're positively jumping to go somewhere today and I intend to oblige them. First I secure the sled's quick-release to a telephone-pole-size post and set the snow hook for insurance—I'm still awed by the brute power of 12 dogs and am not anxious to let the team do something unplanned. Then I add a couple more sections to the gangline to accommodate all the dogs and lay the harnesses out.

Harnessing and hooking up goes surprisingly quickly. The dogs are quiet until they see me put on my windbreaker and gloves, then it's like someone turned on a master switch. They have obviously zeroed in on my habits, which include not putting on all my outerwear until the last minute to avoid overheating while I run around hooking up. They also understand hooking up a bigger team usually means an interesting run.

As I pull the snow hook and get ready with the quick release, the dogs strain into their harnesses and set up a deafening chorus of barking, yipping, and whining. The dogs who aren't going help drive the noise to rock-band levels. There must be a formula to explain why adding dogs to a team increases the noise geometrically. Hooking up an eight-or ten-dog team is noisy, but getting ready to go with 12 or more probably exceeds OSHA standards. People who live in musher country can tell you in a heartbeat when one of their neighbors is hooking up for a run, and likely how many dogs as well.

As I let go the quick release, I stomp on the brake. It's like trying to stop a moving freight train by dragging a stick. About the best I can manage is to slow the team down enough to keep me from being flung from the sled as we thread our way out onto the main trail.

When we hit the wide, hard, manicured Montana Creek club trail, I turn them loose. It's like mashing the accelerator on a Trans-Am. The dogs are in full frenzy and we tear around the mercifully gentle turns at 20 miles an hour or more. The first mile goes by in just a few minutes and suddenly I realize we've overshot our turnoff for the 20-mile trail.

I stand on the brake and yell to Socks to stop, but he's gone 10 yards past the turn. Without thinking I tell him to haw and he and Weasel immediately jump into the waist-deep snow and start to flounder over to the correct branch of the Y. Unfortunately, the dogs behind them don't have to go through the deep snow. The swing dogs win the race to the new trail, resulting in a dog-ball of epic proportions.

With a sigh I set the snow hook as best I can and move up to untangle everybody. After I get the first few deciphered, Socks decides it's time to go again and jerks the team forward. I catch the gangline just in front of the sled and hang on, shouting between mouthfuls of snow for Socks to cease and desist.

He finally slows down and I'm able to lever the sled over onto its side, which creates enough drag to convince the team to stop. I shove the hook into the too-yielding snow again and go forward to finish the untangling process.

After five minutes I've got everyone ready and am rather pleased with myself for restoring peace and harmony. At that exact instant the team shoots forward, popping the sled upright and ripping out the useless snow hook like a bent safety pin. Rank rookie that I am, I'm caught completely by surprise and miss the handlebar as the sled rockets by. I shout at Socks to whoa up but he's not listening to me or anyone else. He and the team are heading down the trail like they're supposed to, with or without their inconsequential human baggage.

This is the unthinkable thing I've always feared—I've lost the team. Dumbfounded, I stare after them for a minute or so. Then I start walking down the trail. There's nothing else to do. I know Barrie is out on this trail somewhere and my best hope is she will see the runaway team and stop it, and maybe even hook it to her sled and lead it back.

Failing that, I know Socks will probably continue around the 20-mile loop and I can grab the team as he brings it back by in a couple of hours. Of course, there are also any number of less pleasant possibilities. He might make an impulsive wrong turn or chase a moose and wrap everyone around a tree. Even on the main trail, the sled could overrun the team on one of the steep hills and injure the wheel dogs.

There's also one thing I don't even want to think about. The trail is partly on the borough road system and there is a chance the team will meet a vehicle. Fortunately, the roads we use don't see much traffic, and most of the locals are used to seeing dog teams. In fact, a concerned motorist might even stop the team and tie it off—it's happened plenty of times before. Still, the thought of a vehicle running into my team is too frightening even to think about.

I trudge up the trail and onto the road. After a few hard miles and an hour or so I finally flag down the first vehicle I meet. The driver says he hasn't seen the team; since he came up from the highway, I assume Socks has kept to the 20-mile trail and hasn't turned down toward the heavier traffic.

I impose on my surprised Good Samaritan and ask him to run me up to the end of the plowed road to see if the team has made it that far. We race the three miles to the end of the road; my team isn't there, but Barrie is just coming down off the back trail. She says she met my team almost an hour ago on the borough road only a couple of miles past my unscheduled debarkation point. She tried to grab the leaders as they shot by and missed them. Then she turned her team around and chased the runaway train back up the trail for several miles.

Because my team was only dragging the empty sled, she knew she didn't have a prayer of catching them unless they tangled up. She says they stayed lined out and just kept moving, widening their lead. She finally turned around when it looked like they would make the whole loop before she could get back to cut them off on the lower road.

I decide to wait and see if my team reappears while Barrie takes hers back and picks up my van. If my team doesn't show up by the time Barrie returns with the car, we'll try to go find someone with a snowmachine to backtrack up the trail. As I stand there by myself in the overcast twilight I feel totally helpless and utterly stupid. I play the scene over and over in my mind—Why didn't I realize Socks was going to go as soon as I finished untangling everyone? Why didn't I let them continue 100 yards or so where I could have tied the team off on a swamp spruce alongside the trail? Why didn't I see the turnoff coming in time to keep the tangle from happening in the first place? I promise myself and any deities who might be listening never to lose the team again if I ever get it back in one piece.

In the end, something like this is the musher's fault and I know it. The dogs only do what they're trained to do—run. A few mushers have the luxury of a leader who will stop and check to see if the driver is still aboard, but Socks doesn't work that way. It's strictly up

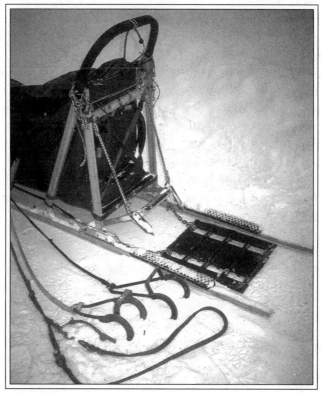

All sleds have some kind of brake; usually, the musher steps on the brake bar to drive metal points into the snow or ice. Most also are equipped with a drag, a piece of old snowmachine track that can be dragged behind the brake when needed. The musher steps on the drag for varying amounts of braking action. The snow hook is used to anchor the team when the sled is stopped. Many mushers use two hooks for insurance, as well as a snub line with a quick-release snap that can be looped around a tree or rock.

to the musher to stay a step ahead of them and anticipate things like this. There is no excuse, and I call myself every name in the book and worry myself sick about my team as a light snow starts to fall.

After maybe 15 minutes I catch a glimpse of movement up on the hill that materializes into a team. In another few seconds I can see there is no driver, and I can make out Socks and Yankee and Silvertip and all my other misplaced puppies. They're running as if nothing has happened, lined out smartly and making at least 15 miles an hour over the soft trail.

I'm so overjoyed I almost forget to catch the sled as it comes by. As the dogs slow a bit to go over the berm where the plowed road starts, I swing aboard the sled like a tourist grabbing a San Francisco cable car. As we continue down the road I see to my astonishment absolutely nothing is amiss. I've been incredibly lucky. (I find out later our neighbor John Barron and son Will were out with their teams and got mine turned around almost 10 miles up the trail.)

A few of the dogs casually look back to acknowledge my presence and immediately refocus on the run. For a minute I feel they could do everything without me. It's a chilling realization. Then my gathering depression is replaced by a certain pride—I've apparently trained them well enough to function smoothly even when I'm not around to oversee their every move.

As we head back to the dog lot, I realize I've just learned an extremely valuable lesson for the long races which are rapidly approaching. The dogs will keep moving even if I get tired or disoriented or injured, and I can trust them to do so even if I'm not capable of controlling them. Their built-in autopilot will see the team—and me—through all manner of problems. After all is said and done, I understand we really are a team and the dogs are equal partners in this enterprise, even if it has taken a profound blow to my ego to drive home this fundamental fact.

December 17-18, 1994
Sheep Creek Lodge, Alaska
The Sheep Creek Christmas Classic

Today is my first real race as a reasonably serious dog driver.
I've been looking forward to this—and dreading it—for weeks.
In a manner of speaking, this is my semester exam, and if I can
get through it in one piece I'll consider myself to have passed
with flying colors.

The Sheep Creek Christmas Classic is staged by the local lodge every year as a sort of prelude to the regular long-distance racing season in Southcentral Alaska. It's not a lengthy race, only 40 miles or so on Saturday with another heat over the same trail the next day. However, it usually draws some of the top mushers in this part of the state and is a good opportunity to see how my dogs will react around other teams and lots of strange people.

Naturally I don't expect to win anything. I know my dogs aren't even remotely a match for some of the big names who usually enter, or even for most of the smaller names, for that matter. All I want to do is finish honorably, with the dogs all intact, and without taking so long as to require a search party. Hopefully I'll learn something from watching the other mushers and from talking with them between heats.

Things aren't starting auspiciously, however. We've had another big dump of snow within the past 48 hours and we got Ron's big van—our main dog truck—stuck in his driveway trying to get it out last night. Since we couldn't get any other vehicles back into the dog lot, we decided I would hitch four of my dogs to the sled and run them over to my place for the night, with Ron and Barrie bringing the remaining eight over in the morning.

I'm up by eight o'clock preparing soup (hot water flavored with dry dog food) for the team when Ron and Barrie show up with the rest of the dogs. Barrie's truck is already at my place with Bert's small eight-dog box precariously balanced on old tires in the back. We rope the sled onto the box, fill the box with dogs, strap down the box, and load the remaining four dogs into my replacement minivan. It's not exactly a professional operation, but it'll serve.

As we convoy the 10 miles down to the lodge for the 10 a.m. musher's meeting, I ponder everything that can go wrong. After a few minutes of steadily increasing panic, I manage to reassure myself there's no point in being pessimistic. I have to start somewhere to try to conquer the doubts. In all likelihood, the dogs will run just fine and all I'll have to do is hold onto the sled until everything settles down. In any case, I'm committed, and besides, I don't think I could get my $100 entry fee back.

As we pull in I see several other Iditarod rookies; I'll be in good company. I also see some of the real heavyweights of Alaska dog mushing. Since this race is short enough for the sprint racers, there are several of them, including Roxy Wright-Champaine, the many-times-over world champion of the sprint circuit. Her dogs are blindingly fast and are trained to go 20 or 30 miles at top speed; they'd probably have a tough time doing this all the way to Nome, though.

Martin Buser is here, as are Vern Halter and Diana Moroney, both top-20 finishers in the last Iditarod. Many of the dogs in my team came from Vern's kennel, and like all mushers he'll certainly recognize his former proteges when he sees them. Diana, whom I've known for years, gave me several of my dogs, so I'm glad she'll see them running. Her husband Bruce, a longtime Iditarod pilot like me, is also here; he ran to Nome last year using many of the dogs I'm now using. It seems most of my dogs are better known than I am.

At the musher's meeting we find out there are 23 teams in all, a very good turnout for this relatively minor race. Everyone is in good spirits and there is a real feeling of "cooperate and graduate." Of course, everyone can pretty well predict who the top finishers will be. That being all but settled, the rest of us will perform our function as the Greek chorus and get a good training run out of it, which is really why we're here.

I draw the number three starting position, which I don't want. This just means I'll be passed by faster teams, which is practically every-body behind me. Barrie and Ron and I linger over coffee and then go out to prepare for the 11 o'clock start. The parking lot is now full of dog trucks of all descriptions, from humble, rusted pickups with homemade dog boxes thrown on the back—like Barrie's—to the heavy-duty rolling palaces of some of the professional dog drivers.

We get the dogs unlimbered and harnessed up and immediately have a fight on our hands. Doc and Rocky, normally best friends and running partners, are apparently stressed out by the race atmosphere and have a brief go at each other, fortunately with no damage. We do some fast rearranging and restore order, at least until the first team moves up to the starting line. Then the entire parking lot erupts in a crescendo of howls, barks, whines, and general bedlam.

Sprint mushers usually hold races every weekend at their local track (in this case, at Montana Creek). They run dogs for distances of up to 10 or 20 miles in 4-dog, 6-dog, 8-dog, and open classes. Distance mushers will often run their dogs in these races for fun and to expose younger dogs to the frenzied race atmosphere. Sprint teams pull lightweight sleds with no loads and can easily average better than 20 miles an hour for up to 20 or 25 miles. This is usually enough to leave distance teams far behind.

This is one of the phenomena I want my team to experience so I can see how they react. Sled dogs have a sixth sense that alerts them when something important is going to happen. Race starts are always incredibly frantic events and the dogs are in a state of terminal excitement to get moving. My dogs seem to be average, which means it takes half a dozen people to hold them back as we move up to the starting line even while I'm riding the brake as hard as I can.

In the starting chute, some of the more volatile dogs jump around and get tangled, which Ron and Barrie get straightened out with maybe 30 seconds to spare. Then the starter counts down the last five seconds and we're off—the first real race of the season for the dogs, and my first serious mushing competition ever.

Socks is leading and he explodes up the trail with the team in a full run. I'm riding the brake as hard as I can to keep the speed down because I don't know this trail and I've heard there are some bad moguls on it. I keep the team down to five miles an hour for the first mile, by which time I realize the trail isn't as bad as I'd heard. I let up on the brake and we speed up, the dogs running in the pure ecstasy of a new trail and a real race.

We scream along for another mile along the beautiful spruce-lined trail, which eventually opens out into a flat swamp as it approaches the powerline right-of-way along which most of the race route is laid out. As we pull off the swamp and over a small rise studded with clumps of willow, we hit the first series of moguls. At full speed, the leaders sail over the crest of the first one and almost disappear down the other side. Before I can get on the brake they are up and over another and yet another. In a sort of delayed reaction I see coming and can't do anything about, the sled crests the first mogul and crashes almost three feet straight down. Then the suddenly-slack gangline pops taut as the speeding team yanks it taunt, slamming the sled into and over the next mini-mountain.

After a couple of teeth-rattling repetitions I finally get the brake to work and drag the team down to walking speed. If this were a ski slope, it would be marked "Expert" and the Ski Patrol would be doing a land-office business picking up the casualties. Fifteen minutes later, we reach a flat stretch and I let the dogs resume their pace.

About then I turn around and see another musher—whom I don't recognize immediately but finally identify as Martin Buser—charging up behind me. I find a wide spot in the trail and stop the team while he passes. His dogs step smartly by and accelerate rapidly out of sight like an expensive European luxury car. My team can't even begin to catch up and I resign myself to being passed by everyone else before the lap is over. I suppose this is what they call character building. I feel a little better knowing many of those who are passing me are either sprint racers or will finish in the top 20 in the Iditarod.

The next two hours are a jumbled mix of moguls, soft punchy trails, being passed by everything including the kitchen sink, and to top it all off, a gathering snowstorm. I refuse to let the dogs go faster than a walk over the moguls, even though I see other mushers hitting them full speed. They must know something I don't, but until I learn their secret I won't risk injuring my dogs a couple of weeks before my first real Iditarod qualifying race.

By the time I'm on the track back inbound, everybody who's going to pass me has done so. The snow is heavy and stings my face unmercifully. Like a fool I've left my goggles in the car; another lesson learned—never get on the sled without all the equipment I might need. I also left my headlamp behind, and this run is taking so long I won't be back until well into twilight.

The last hour is a plodding journey through thickening snow into deepening darkness. Finally we pass a few remembered landmarks signaling the end is only a few miles away and the dogs suddenly break into a lope. Somehow the team knows we're coming to the end; I hang on as we whip through the last stretch of trail. I get in dead last, but the team has finished very strongly and everyone says so. Barrie and Ron help me put the dogs away and we all head into the bar for a cup of coffee.

The second day goes much better. In most multiple-heat races, the order of finish determines the next day's start positions. This means I'm starting out at the tail end, so I have nowhere to go but up. The weather is near-perfect and the trail is in great shape, fast and hard. Besides, I know it well enough now to let the dogs roll a bit. They respond admirably and we actually pass a couple of teams within a few miles after we start. On the way in I note the goggles and headlamp I carefully included won't be necessary today, even though I started an hour later. The dogs are actually running flat out for the last five miles; it seems they are thoroughly in the spirit of the race and enjoying themselves.

We storm across the finish line an hour faster than yesterday, cutting more time off our first day's run than anyone else. I thought for awhile we might get the red lantern for being last, but we've done so well we move up a position and are instead recognized as "most improved," which I find infinitely more satisfying.

I've survived my first race. I still can't believe I'm actually running dogs with the same mushers I've watched for years while flying for the Iditarod. More important, it seems I've actually learned something. But I also know this is only the beginning. I've just graduated from dog-driver grade school, and I have two months to earn what amounts to a Ph.D. in mushing before I can run the Iditarod.

December 31, 1994—January 1, 1995
The Knik 200
Knik to Skwentna and Return

The Iditarod requires rookies (meaning anyone who hasn't run the race before) to qualify by finishing one or two races totaling at least 500 miles. Iditarod hopefuls in Southcentral Alaska frequently run the Knik 200 as their first race, and either the Copper Basin 300 or the Klondike 300 a couple of weeks later as their second one. Barrie and I have chosen to do the Knik 200 and the Copper Basin 300. Race day for the Knik 200—New Year's Eve—is on us before we realize it. For me, this will be by far the longest run I've made, even though it will probably be a yawner for the dogs, most of whom have been to Nome at least once or twice. So, the test is not so much for the dogs but for me, and how well I can keep the team focused on the task at hand.

As distance races go, the Knik 200 isn't particularly difficult, consisting of a 100-mile run out the first section of the Iditarod Trail to Skwentna, followed by a six-hour layover and a return over the same route. On the other hand, it is the first real distance race of the season in this area. Anything from 200 to 500 miles is considered "mid-distance" in the world of dog mushing, although most mortals would consider 200 miles on the back of a dog sled to be a Really Long Trip, official nomenclature notwithstanding.

Ron will run with us on the Knik as a sort of advisor and to put the miles on his dogs for training. So, while normal people are watching bowl games on television, we're trucking our teams 80 miles down to the tiny settlement of Knik, across Turnagain Arm from Anchorage.

I've gotten virtually no sleep the night before the race. In fact, I haven't had much more than a nap since our practice run over part of this trail two days ago, when we ran 35 miles out to Flathorn Lake and back. I've drawn number 28, which lets me leave well toward the rear of the 40-team pack. At least I won't be overtaken by too many drivers and I can let the team settle into its stride without a lot of interruptions for passes.

Before the race start of any distance race, an official must check the loaded sled for all of the required equipment: ax, cooker, sleeping bag, snowshoes, booties, and (for the Iditarod) a mail packet. All of these items must be in the sled at all times until completing the race.

The weather is astonishingly mild. It's been above freezing the past few days thanks to a big low pressure system in the Gulf of Alaska pumping in Hawaiian air. This will be great for the mushers but the dogs might flag a little more easily, since they've been training in considerably colder temperatures and are permanently dressed for the "real" Alaska winter.

As we mainline coffee before the race and nervously await the time to start hooking up, I stop to think about Knik's prominent position in the history of mushing. With its tidewater dock on Cook Inlet, it was the main starting point for teams on the original Iditarod Trail. Beginning about 1910 and lasting until airplanes started to take over in the 1930s, as many as 120 freight and mail teams a month started from this exact spot headed for the gold fields of interior Alaska, with many going ultimately to Nome.

Those intrepid drivers sometimes had 20 big dogs hauling two or three long freight sleds laden with a ton of everything from gold dust to gasoline engines to paying passengers. They'd stop every evening at a roadhouse or village after traveling perhaps 25 miles, most of which was spent walking or wrestling the heavy sleds. The Iditarod—and distance mushing in general, for that matter—is really a recreation of the world of the freight and mail mushers, a time when winter transportation in most of Alaska was via dog team. Of course, our light sleds and 100-pound loads are nothing compared to what the old-timers sweated and fought along the trail. I'm a little awed just to be following in their footsteps for a bit on this race.

With 40 teams signed up, the cramped starting area in front of the Knik Bar is the usual madhouse of eager dogs, frantic mushers, scurrying handlers, and wandering spectators. There are more than 600 dogs in an area about a third the size of the average Wal-Mart parking lot. Many teams are running 16 dogs, the maximum; Barrie and Ron and I are only taking 14, which we feel is plenty to get out and back while maintaining a measure of control.

To put this in perspective, every two-dog section of gangline is eight to 10 feet in length, which stretches a 16-dog team plus the sled to 75 or 80 feet. That's as long as a full-sized semi-trailer rig, except the musher is standing all the way at the back of the trailer with little more to control the canine diesel tractor than dragging his (or her) foot on the snow and hoping the dog at the steering wheel will follow commands. The Iditarod limit this year will be 16 dogs; it was formerly 20, which resulted in more than a few teams becoming unguided missiles early in the race when the dogs were fresh and frantically eager to run. All things considered, 14 dogs are plenty for us rookies, at least for now.

As every straining team is hooked up and wrestled out to the starting line by as many as 10 handlers, the dogs on the remaining teams ratchet a notch higher on the excitement scale. As chaotic as it seems, this is really nothing compared to the Iditarod start, which is probably the biggest collection of screaming dogs in the world in one small area.

My start goes smoothly, at least until about 30 seconds before the starter says "Go!" Somebody helping hold back my surging team casually asks me whether I intended to hook up the gangline so it runs over rather than under the brush bow at the front of the sled. Obviously I didn't, because the gangline will be rubbing on the hard edge of the brush bow and could start to fray, which in turn might lead to the line breaking and the team running loose down the trail.

I feel like an idiot, but there's nothing I can do except get out on the trail and find a place to stop the team, undo the dogs' tuglines, anchor everything on a tree, and then make the 10-second fix. I wonder what else I've forgotten to do as the starter counts down and we rocket out of the chute.

Things settle down quickly out on the trail. Surprisingly, I'm only passed by one or two teams, and actually overtake several myself. I

The Knik 200 is traditionally the start of the distance racing season in south central Alaska. It follows the route of the Iditarod from Knik out to Skwentna and back. For the 1995 race, 40 teams made the journey.

keep a close eye on the mis-rigged gangline, but it seems not to be chafing so I push on, not wanting to break the dogs' rhythm.

The first few hours go like clockwork, partly because we've seen this stretch of trail before. I even get the gangline re-routed with no trouble during a five-minute pit stop. About 20 miles out of Knik, we come to a hand-painted wooden sign at a fork in the trail. Over a prominent left-turn arrow it says in gold letters, "Nome 1049 miles." We're not going to Nome, at least not this trip, but I get a thrill as I realize I'm actually running my own team over a part of the real, honest-to-goodness Iditarod Trail in a serious race leading to the Iditarod itself. After months of work and training, I can finally see something tangible to mark my progress from rank civilian to aspiring dog musher, and it's very gratifying.

At the 45-mile point we roll onto the broad, frozen Susitna River as night falls and then swing up its main tributary, the Yentna. Although I've flown this river so many times I can recite waypoints in my sleep, everything is different on the ground. The first thing I have to learn is to adjust to life at 10 miles an hour, for hours on end. It's really not that bad, and there are plenty of reminders of substantial movement and progress. On the other hand, in the middle of a half-mile-wide river things can seem to be frozen in time, and the next bend always seems to take forever to arrive.

I spend a lot of time running without my headlamp. On the white nighttime expanse of the river, this yields a peculiar sensation of floating. The team and the sled and even me seem to be suspended in midair, on a magic carpet of sorts. I flip on my Walkman and the music I've carefully selected for just such a situation adds the soundtrack completing the illusion. It's a shame I can't bottle these moments and save them. If I could sell them, I'm sure I'd be rich beyond avarice.

On the upper reaches of the river, after we've passed most of the cabins, I'm traveling with Ron and Barrie on the last 35-mile leg into Skwentna. Rounding one isolated bend, I'm surprised when the dogs suddenly all look to the left, at the south bank of the river. They make no noise and don't speed up as they would if they scented a moose. I stab the bank with my headlamp but see nothing. The dogs keep staring as they run, until after a few minutes we're back to normal. Barrie tells me her dogs did the same thing, and so do several other mushers.

An experienced driver later tells me it was wolves, which are definitely not an endangered species in this area. For me, the feeling was primitive and mysterious; my dogs sensed something from another world, another time, something from which I was excluded. I was being silently watched by eyes from what amounts to another universe, being evaluated by intellects totally alien to my understanding.

In two decades I've flown planes all over Alaska and hiked many miles as well, but here on the Yentna River, with my dogs running silently in front of me, isolated from the modern mechanical world I've always taken for granted, is the first time I've actually felt the undiluted primeval soul of the North Country. I can begin to understand what other mushers have told me: driving dogs is the only way to see the "real" Alaska.

Finally the long hours in the darkness and now below-zero temperatures bring us to Skwentna, where we pull in just after 11 p.m., less than 12 hours after leaving Knik. We've actually made pretty good time, considering our periodic breaks to tend to the dogs. Soon after we arrive and begin to feed and bed down the dogs, we hear fireworks going off through the trees. The New Year has arrived. If someone had told me last year I'd be spending this New Year's Eve at Skwentna tending to my dog team, I'd have collapsed laughing. I'm not laughing now, although I'm so tired I might collapse anyway.

I start feeding the team, Silvertip and Yankee first. They are my biggest dogs and have happily run beside each other in wheel all day. However, like many sled dogs after a long run, they've become grouchy now that we've stopped and immediately begin to quarrel over a chunk of frozen lamb I carelessly toss between them. Without thinking, I lunge into the fray and grab Silvertip's collar; Yankee obliges by taking a chunk out of my little finger as he tries for Silvertip's ear. I manage to pull them apart with help from a nearby musher who wades in swinging her aluminum feeding dipper, which does no harm to the dogs but certainly gets their attention.

Yankee has managed to puncture Silvertip's left front foot, which is bleeding and is obviously causing some pain. Silvertip, although younger and inexperienced, seems to be learning his trade and has gotten in his licks, opening cuts on Yankee's ear and muzzle. I can patch Yankee up with no trouble, but I don't want to force Silvertip to run on his foot. I reluctantly lead him over to the dropped dog area. He'll get a quick look from the vet tonight, a plane ride back to Knik in the morning, and will be waiting for me when I return.

His injuries are quite minor, but I'm a bit shaken because he is my personal companion, whom I raised from a puppy before I ever decided to get into mushing. I never intended him to be a sled dog, but he has become one of my best—a true "walk-on" of whom I'm inordinately proud because I trained him myself. At least he's pulled well coming out, and he'll be ready to go again in a few days.

After leaving Silvertip with the vet, a sharp pain in my left hand reminds me I've sustained a worse wound than either of the dogs. My little finger has a one-inch gash ripped completely out of it, almost to the bone, and it's bleeding profusely. I shake my head at my own stupidity in jumping into the middle of a brawl between two 70-pound male dogs in top combat trim.

The approved solution, of course, is to prevent fights in the first place. For obvious reasons, no sensible musher will keep a habitual fighter. Likewise, any driver who has a dog that attacks other teams is quietly asked not to enter any more races with it. But even non-fighters will occasionally not get along, and quarrelsome combinations must be separated within the team. And without proper supervision, even best friends can quickly revert to atavistic behavior during the critical feeding period, especially when they are tired or stressed.

Often an authoritatively shouted "Knock it off!" can defuse a developing situation. Failing that, more drastic measures are needed to separate the combatants before they hurt each other. However, the occasional squabble is a part of mushing nobody likes and everyone tries to prevent, but which sometimes happens nonetheless. Dogs (and particularly male dogs) will, after all, be dogs. I suppose I'll have to chalk this up as another learning experience and do my best not to let it happen again.

I wander over to the New Skwentna Roadhouse (the original, 10 miles up the Skwentna River, was abandoned decades ago) to get my finger bandaged up enough to let me get back to Knik. Inside, most of the mushers are eating, talking, or sleeping. After I get my finger patched, I realize I'm ravenously thirsty and head for the nearest pitcher of ice water. Ron intercepts me and suggests I try Tang instead because it will quench my thirst better; he says it's long been a favorite of distance mushers.

Half an hour later, after two quarts of the stuff, I have to admit he's right. For no reason I think of the old Tang astronaut commercials; I can't think of any activity farther from the high-tech space program than dog driving. I wonder if the Tang company has considered a spot featuring mushers, or what the astronauts would think about this rather more traditional form of voyaging.

I talk with other mushers for awhile until the leaders' six-hour layovers start to expire. John Barron, a longtime contender in the Iditarod and other races (and previous winner of the Knik 200), whose trails we share around Montana Creek, was the first in and is the first out. We count him and his mushing family, which includes wife Kathy and sons Jason and Laird (both Iditarod veterans) and up-and-coming Will, as good friends. In fact, John has given Barrie and me several fine dogs and lots of advice on mushing that has proven its worth to us over and over. We wish him luck as he heads back down the trail. To me, he—like Ron—personifies the people who make mushing such a worthwhile endeavor, and I am honored to be accepted into such a worthy fraternity (or is it properly also a sorority these days?).

Ron and I finally decide to go out about eight in the morning, which will give us and our dogs a couple of extra hours on top of our mandatory six. We stretch out on the roadhouse floor in front of the stove in a living room full of snoring mushers. We sleep like babies despite the all-night comings and goings of 50 or more people, waking quite refreshed about seven.

Barrie has already hit the trail; Ron and I roll out right at eight. It's still dark, but the eastern sky already shows a hint of dawn. The run down the river is beautiful as the rising sun gleams through layers of wind-driven clouds over the Chugach Mountains behind Anchorage. Ron eventually stops to readjust his team and tells me to move on. Besides, my dogs are pulling well and I don't want to interrupt our progress.

About three hours out I pass Barrie, whose team has stopped. Her main leader, Bambi, was cut up pretty badly by a dog in another team only a few miles into the race; she carried Bambi all the way to Skwentna rather than turn around and risk a major catastrophe meeting a fast-moving outbound team on the narrow tree-lined trail. As a result, she's been running one of her yearlings in lead; as young dogs will do, he finally lost interest and decided to stop, which meant none of the other dogs wanted to go, either. I ask her if she needs any help but she says she'll just camp and wait them out, continuing on when they're rested.

My team moves smoothly on down the river into the gathering day. About 40 miles down the river I pull over to the side of the trail and pass out food to the dogs, after which I give them time to lie down and catch some rest. I stretch out on top of my sled bag in the balmy 20-degree temperature and warm sunshine. Before I realize it, almost an hour has gone by. It's amazing how comfortable sleeping on top of a sled can be; it's a good thing I'm not really in the competition or I'd have just blown my lead.

Refreshed, we continue down the wide Yentna River at a good clip. However, I notice Socks is limping; it's probably just a sore paw, but rather than risk something major I unhook him and load him in the sled bag, where he very much does not want to be. As soon as we cross the Susitna and start over the hills and swamps, I have to divide my time between helping the team haul the sled over the hills and pushing Socks back down into the safety of the bag.

By the time we pass Flathorn Lake, 35 miles from the finish, the dogs realize they've been over this trail before and speed up. We pass half a dozen teams and continue to accelerate. When we start up Nine-Mile Hill (so named because it's nine miles out of Knik) the dogs roar up it and down the other side as if they had just left the starting line. By the time we hit Five-Mile Swamp, they're in a dead run, even with

55-pound Socks riding as excess baggage. All I can do is hang on and marvel at their strength and spirit after almost 200 miles on the trail.

As we gain the final ridge above Knik Lake I can see the lights of the finish line through the trees, and so do the dogs. They hit 20 miles an hour

The author finishes the Knik 200, his first distance race, in 20th place.

headed down the last hill to the Knik Museum, where the trail turns out onto the lake for the final 200 yards to the finish. I catch a glimpse of a team just ahead of us; we're gaining rapidly until I spill the sled rounding the final corner onto the lake. The 15 seconds it takes me to right the sled and get moving again costs me 19th place, and I finish barely 50 feet behind the other team.

To finish 20th out of 40 in a race like this, especially after I took a couple of extra hours' layover at Skwentna, is beyond my hopes. Race Marshal Bobby Lee, a friend from my Iditarod flying days, congratulates me on a super run and tells me to go on into the bar, where the awards banquet has just started and a turkey dinner with all the trimmings is waiting with my name on it. Before I do, I toss the dogs a chunk of frozen lamb and hug each one. They've shown me and everyone else they've got what it takes to do the long haul.

And finally, I go check on Silvertip. He loves riding in little airplanes and probably had a lot more fun on the way back than I did. He's bouncing with glee to see me, and his injured foot is apparently a thing of the past. I probably could have just left him in the team and run him home from Skwentna, but it wasn't a call I cared to make.

So ends my first real distance race. I'm tired beyond caring and know I'll ache for days, but the feeling of satisfaction and accomplishment, as well as pride in my team, is beyond measure. I still have a lot to learn, but now I'm confident I can at least keep things intact during the learning process.

January 7, 1995
Montana Creek, Alaska

Let me tell you about moose. That's right: those big, lovable, half-ton cows of the forest everyone thinks are so cute and can't resist photographing. Well, to a musher, moose are the spawn of Satan himself (or herself, if we must scrupulously hew to political rectitude).

Every musher has at least one horror story about these ungainly ungulates (and most have several) ranging from the merely scary to the truly tragic. It seems mushers and moose are doomed by fate to dance forever in a kind of mutually destructive embrace. Indeed, mushers have a perspective on moose shared by few others.

Lots of people have never seen a moose in other than its typical roadside shrub-munching mien. In reality, an outwardly amiable moose can suddenly turn into a 1,500-pound herbivorous transformer toy run amok. Annoyed moose can run at greyhound speeds, knock over fair-sized trees, and tap-dance automobiles into tinfoil for what would seem to be the slightest of provocations. They can also mercilessly stomp animals and even humans: fatalities occur every winter in Alaska, even in downtown Anchorage.

One part of the dilemma arises because Alaska's moose population is kept artificially high to accommodate hunters, particularly in the Southcentral part of the state. In the old days, bears and wolves kept the moose population to a small fraction of its current bloated level. Nowadays, most of these predators are scarce where they are needed the most. In built-up areas where hunting is prohibited and natural carnivores are all but absent, moose become positively bothersome. Within the environs of urban Anchorage, for instance, more than

1,000 moose wander about like sacred cows in Calcutta, causing problems ranging from shredded shrubbery to tangled traffic to stomped citizens.

The situation is complicated when deepening winter snows restrict moose to the paths of least resistance—which also tend to be the same paths used by snowmachiners, Nordic skiers, and of course, mushers. The problem is worse later in the winter when browse grows scarce and undernourished moose become ornery. Toss in the age-old genetic enmity between moose and wolves (and thus dogs) and the complete scope of the Moose Menace becomes clearer.

For many mushers, moose present probably the single biggest ongoing threat to peace and tranquility. A moose can wreck a dog team in any number of ways. The most obvious, of course, is for a moose to wade directly into a team on the trail and physically abuse or even kill dogs. The harnessed dogs can do little to avoid the flailing hooves and antlers and the musher often as not has to shoot the moose to save his team and very possibly himself. The normally placid creatures can do the same thing if they wander into a dog lot, although this is much less likely because moose usually won't intentionally venture around barking dogs. Besides, the dogs—even though chained—can at least hide behind trees or in their dog houses.

Moose can wreak woe on mushers in less direct ways. A team scenting a moose will try to break into a run, even if the moose isn't in view. If this occurs at an inopportune time, the driver can lose control. If the dogs actually see the moose, they will go crazy. In the atavistic frenzy of pursuit, brakes and drags are often insufficient to stop the team despite the musher's best efforts. The entire team may actually chase the moose off the trail and into the woods, resulting in no end of unpleasant possibilities.

The most insidious moose-generated problems don't even require the perpetrator to be present. A moose walking on a trail tends to punch through the hard crust with its hooves. These holes become traps for fast-moving dogs, who can dislocate shoulders and even break legs by stepping into a foot-deep moose print. A musher whose team has barreled into a mine field of moose tracks can easily make the saltiest sailor blush with his (or her) language.

Any musher would much rather scare a moose off than try to blast it out of a team. To this end, everything from flare pistols to whistles to fireworks has been pressed into service with varying degrees of success. Some drivers carry pepper spray or mace, although these devices aren't effective unless the moose is almost on top of the team, and then there is a real risk of gassing the dogs as well.

So, most mushers carry some sort of firearm as a last-resort moose defense. Some pack a rifle or a large-caliber pistol, while others tote a shotgun loaded with slugs and buckshot. No musher wants to get into a situation requiring heavy artillery, but once in a great while there's no choice when a run with the dogs turns into a combat mission.

This winter we've had more than a few close calls with moose around Montana Creek. Thanks to the very heavy snow before Christmas, moose took to the lowland trails much earlier than normal. Even our half-mile driveway from the road to the dog lot

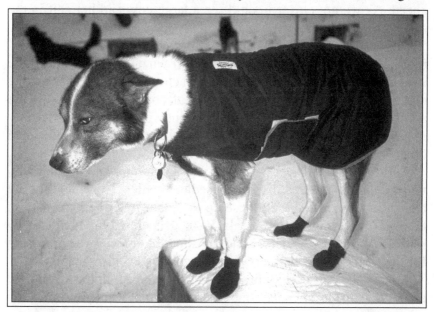

Some dogs are more susceptible to cold because of thinner coats. Special dog coats provide protection in extreme conditions. Booties protect the dogs' feet from abrasion and trail hazards. Most dogs are bootied on longer races such as the Iditarod. Booties can last from 20 to 200 miles, depending on type and trail conditions.

has turned interesting. A young cow moose has come to regard it as her own and is often grazing there when I drive through in my minivan. Usually she will turn and run up the driveway until she nears the dog lot and hears nearly 100 dogs barking at her. Then she will stop, lay back her ears, raise her hackles, and make a couple of bluff charges at my car. At that point, I'll turn off the engine and the lights and wait. After a minute or two she will think the car is dead and no longer a threat and will charge by it like a four-legged freight locomotive.

At night it's not a little unnerving to sit there as an angry 800-pound stomping machine materializes out of the dark and thunders by within inches of my car window in a pass that would earn an ear for any torero. At such times, even the car doesn't feel very safe.

Out on the trails, I've been lucky so far and haven't had to draw down on an errant moose. I've had a couple of close encounters of the frightening kind, though. One night a few weeks ago the dogs were trotting down the borough road (which we now call "Moose Alley") on the way home when I saw a pair of brake lights repeatedly flashing ahead. As we got closer I could see a large cow and her calf in the truck's headlights.

The cow had her hackles up and was yielding ground only grudgingly. Because of the very high berms thrown up on either side of the road by the snowplows, the calf couldn't climb out of the road and the cow wouldn't leave her calf behind. Of course, the dogs saw the moose about the same time I did and went wild. The brake was only marginally effective on the icy road and I could only keep the team down to a slow trot.

Fortunately the driver of the car was a neighbor and musher who understood my predicament. She used her vehicle as a shield for my team, slowly herding the moose up the road. After perhaps half an hour of this strange rodeo barely 50 feet separated the increasingly irate cow from my leaders. I had my shotgun out and was preparing for the worst if she charged past the truck to get at my team.

Finally the calf darted through a fortuitous gap in the seemingly endless berm; the cow made one false charge that scared me out of my wits and then clumped off the road in high dudgeon after her offspring. Somehow I maneuvered the team past the gap and we got back to the dog lot in one piece, although I had sweated completely through my parka. Too close, way too close.

This afternoon I'm in almost the same location as the previous incident. I'm outbound with eight dogs I haven't run in a few days and they're really rolling as we round a corner. Suddenly I see a blur of brown above me on the six-foot snow berm. A young bull moose has been using the hard-packed berm to reach some higher branches and we've surprised him. He jumps clumsily down from his perch and I'm sure he's going to land right in the middle of my team.

I jam on the brake with everything I've got and manage to slow the team almost to a walk for a critical half-second. The moose lands sprawling perhaps 10 feet in front of my surprised leaders, scrambles back to his feet, and for a moment stands glaring at my team with his ears back and hackles up. I can literally smell his breath and am completely convinced the end of the world is at hand. It's deja vu all over again, only without my vehicular angel of mercy. It's probably the longest five seconds of my life.

Then young Bullwinkle decides discretion is the better part of valor, turns, and lumbers off up the road. The team chases him, of course, but with only eight dogs I'm able to keep their speed down sufficiently for the moose to steadily gain ground. After half a mile we reach our planned turnoff and the moose continues straight on down the road. The dogs reluctantly acknowledge I'm not going to let them keep after the moose and they swing onto the side trail. I belatedly realize I never even tried to get out my shotgun, which is a good thing because I'd probably have blown off my own toe or clipped one of the dogs in my haste.

But too many other mushers have had dogs crippled or killed by moose attacks, even on major races such as the Iditarod. Susan Butcher was knocked out of contention on one Iditarod by a moose that killed one of her dogs. Diana Moroney, who gave me several of my dogs, lost her world-class leader for several months earlier this winter after a moose attacked her team practically in her own back yard. John Barron had to shoot a moose out of his team a couple of months ago, luckily with no major injuries to his dogs or himself. In the ultimate case of self-defense, a musher on the Yukon Quest a couple of years ago who was armed only with an ax went "mano-a-mano" with a charging 1,200-pounder; he won, but just barely.

As a matter of practical necessity Alaska permits dispatching a moose to protect life and property—or a dog team. And the moose isn't wasted: the musher is required by law to take steps to keep the meat from spoiling and notify the authorities. This applies even in the middle of a race and following drivers must help before they can continue. The meat is later recovered and is given to local charities for distribution. However, it's safe to say any musher would much prefer to buy a truck full of groceries for the needy than use a dog team to troll for charity meat on the trail. As for me, if donating to the local food bank will somehow keep the moose out of my team, just tell me where to drop the goodies.

January 13-17, 1995
The Copper Basin 300

It's finally time for the Copper Basin 300. This is the second of the two qualifying races I must run (and finish), and its reputation precedes it. The course describes a 300-mile circuit around the Copper Basin, 150 miles northeast of Anchorage. The checkpoints are all on the highway system, but many of the trails between them cut across some of the most remote territory in Alaska. The race is widely known for its variety of terrain and trail conditions, its propensity for open water and overflow, and above all its cold temperatures. Experienced mushers have told me running the Copper Basin is the best practice I can get for the Iditarod, but not to be too upset if I don't finish.

This well-meant advice hasn't exactly done wonders for my mental state, but there's not much I can do now. Barrie and I are on the road with dogs, sleds, and what's left of our self-confidence. Ron and our neighbor Steve Adkins, a veteran Iditarod musher himself, will be our handlers, cleaning up after us at the checkpoints and giving us timely advice. About the only bright point is the weather for the race will be only in the 10-to 30-below range, somewhat better than the 40-below deep freeze we've had at Montana Creek.

At any rate, I've settled into my fatalistic mode, resolved to see what happens and try to make the best of it. This is rapidly shaping itself into the biggest physical and mental challenge I've had in many years, and I'm thinking thoughts about my own capabilities I haven't thought in decades. After all, I'm 46 years old, not exactly a world-class athlete, starting from scratch in an extremely demanding sport, and about to run one of the toughest races in the state. I'm really beginning to wonder if this time I haven't bitten off more than I can chew.

My confidence isn't helped at the musher's meeting the night before the race when I draw number three—again. I know absolutely nothing about the trail, which means I'll have to take things cautiously and slowly for awhile. Also, I know my team isn't as fast as most of the others in the high-powered field, which comprises some of the biggest names in mushing, including Martin Buser and Jeff King. It's a lead-pipe cinch I'll be waving to them and a lot of others as they pass me within a few hours after the start.

To complete my pre-race preparation, I only get two hours of sleep at Paxson Lodge the night before the start. After a couple of cups of coffee while my long-suffering handlers get the dogs watered and fed and into the truck, we push back down the highway to Meier's Lake for the start of what I fear may be a long, hard journey to frustration.

The mental carnage is almost complete when the veterinarians checking my dogs at the pre-start vet check tell me they won't let me run Wild Thing, one of my best pullers, who they say is too thin. Even though I know this dog is naturally thin and is in great shape, I'm not experienced enough to argue with the vets, so I have to use Kona, a spare dog I'd brought along for just such an eventuality.

> So with the stage thus set, I hang on for dear life as Pullman and Bea lead 10 other uncontrollably enthusiastic bundles of energy out of the starting gate like an unlimited class nitro-fueled dragster. Mentally, I'm a vegetable along for the ride through the Cuisinart, and I only recall the race as a series of snapsots from here on.

Copper Basin Snapshot — The First 15 Miles of the Trail from Hell

From the starting line, the trail climbs almost immediately 500 feet up the side of a mountain, then down the other side and up yet another equally brutal incline, followed by an even steeper downgrade. Then it threads through a mile of trees with turns so sharp and frequent I cannot even see the lead dogs most of the time. Finally it crosses the frozen Gulkana River and settles into a merely hideous stretch laden with sidehill slopes and soft shoulders and icy stretches where trickles of water have made mini-glaciers which make control of the sled virtually impossible.

I am practically in shock and almost numb with exhaustion trying to keep the sled upright, but it keeps slipping down the cross-hill slopes and into the soft snow on the downhill edges of the trail, where it usually collapses on its side. This requires me to jump off into the thigh-deep snow and lever it upright while urging the dogs to go on.

Usually I can jump back on the runners as the sled careens back onto the trail, but more often than not, I find myself hanging onto the handlebars with my feet trailing out behind as the excited team charges on down the trail. My stiff, heavy arctic gear makes it almost impossible to regain my feet while the sled is moving, so the only thing I can do is yell at the dogs to whoa up and try to tip the sled into the snow so I can try everything all over again.

By now other, faster teams behind me have begun to pass me with some regularity. On one particularly gruesome sidehill pitch I spend the better part of 100 yards dragging behind the sled until I can get it toppled into the snow and stopped. As I lie there in the snow catching my breath I realize there are several teams behind me who have been waiting to pass during this whole episode. Without getting up I motion for them to come on by, which they do, trying somewhat unsuccessfully to conceal their amusement at my rookie antics. The driver of the last team to pass slows for a moment and asks solicitously, "Are you all right?" I answer "No-o-o-o problem!" before I realize it is Martin Buser. At least he isn't laughing, although I certainly wouldn't blame him if he were. My mortification is complete as I watch Martin's world-class team speed him up the hill and out of sight.

I cannot understand how all of the other mushers have so little trouble controlling their teams and sleds over what is—to me anyway—the Trail From Hell. I still have a lot to learn about this business of dog driving. It's a good thing I have 285 more miles to bone up in this open-air classroom before I get my report card.

Copper Basin Snapshot — Night Trail Under a Running Moon

The dogs have rested a couple of hours at Sourdough Roadhouse, the first checkpoint, and I've actually gotten a few minutes' nap in the crowded mushers' warm-up cabin. I finally realize the sun has set and I've got to get moving. After I finish the 45-minute process of bootying and hooking up the dogs, Steve Adkins leads the team through the crowded lodge grounds to the outbound trail.

The dogs come alive and pull with renewed eagerness into the moonlit spruce forest. I've noticed , the dogs always seem to like to run better at night, and especially under a bright moon. Some old-timers call it a running moon, and under conditions such as we have tonight it can make for a rare experience. For this leg, 65 miles across the virtually uninhabited heart of the Copper Basin over to Lake Louise and Wolverine Lodge, the groomed trail is like a superhighway: hard, smooth, and level. Under the flood of moonlight, the dogs settle into a 10-mile-an-hour trot I know they can hold for as long as I want to let them.

Now the race has taken on a whole new dimension, and I have time to take in the stark beauty of the ghostly wilderness washed by light from the misty full moon. Like a sailing ship of old running with a fair wind through unexplored seas, we cruise across endless flat lakes, float over eerie swamps, and thread our way through silent stands of snow-laden spruce. The diffuse moonlight is easily bright enough to obviate the need for my headlamp.

Without the lamp there is no color. The palette of this phantom world spans only the spectrum from the softly glowing white of moon-bright snow to the deep shadowy black of brooding spruce thickets. I adjust my senses to this alternative dimension and am completely disoriented when I flick on my headlight to check out a shadow that might be a moose. I quickly retreat from reality's harsh glare to the land of the night without realizing I've become a creature of this world with the dogs—endless snow and moonlight.

After an hour I come to understand silence is the true denominator here. The dogs make almost no noise, and their footfalls on the trail and the swish of the runners are not so different from the soughing of the wind through a full set of clipper-ship sails and the soft wash of the sea against the bow. The creaking of the sled could just as easily be oaken timbers and taut rigging. Like a ship under sail without the constant throb of engines to remind one of progress, forward motion seems almost negligible; only a glance behind the sled reveals the trail receding at a satisfying six minutes a mile.

There are only a couple of teams on the trail with me, and we pass and repass each other quietly and as quickly as we can, almost embarrassed to intrude on each other's journeys through this nether realm. We turn on our headlamps for the actual overtaking and then turn them off as soon as is decently possible, retreating to our personal voyages across the snowy sea.

I'm sure the old wooden-ship sailors would have made good dog drivers, with their appreciation of a good, steady pace and the patience to enjoy the voyage for its own merits. Or maybe I

*would have made a good seafarer. I guess that's something else
I'll have to try someday.*

Copper Basin Snapshot—Wolverine Lodge Checkpoint

After a near-perfect run over from Sourdough, the Wolverine
checkpoint is a madhouse, with 40-odd teams bedded down in a great
arc on the snow-covered ice of Lake Louise in front of the lodge. I
arrive about five in the morning and there will be a mass restart at 10,
in which everyone who is ready will make a wild simultaneous dash
for the outbound trail. This is the real beginning of the race, inasmuch
as whoever is in front after the restart is the actual leader.

I have already decided not to try to make the restart, since I am not
really racing; besides, I'm not sure what my dogs would do in such a
chaotic situation, which I won't see on the Iditarod in any case. Every
veteran musher I've talked to has advised me not to push things
because I'll get plenty of chances to excel just trying to finish. I get the
dogs fed and bedded down on the straw we've shipped out and then
wander up to the lodge about seven for some shut-eye.

The musher sleeping room in the lodge is full of snoring drivers, so
I find a nice patch of floor in the bar and stretch out with my parka for
a pillow. This is pretty much normal for a checkpoint, where tired
mushers can be found snatching a nap in all manner of unlikely
locations and positions.

Sometime during the morning the big-screen satellite television is
turned on for the NFL playoff game, and I subconsciously absorb the
49er massacre of Denver as I fitfully sleep. As the restart approaches,
the lodge fills with spectators, most of whom don't even notice me or
the several other mushers who are still racked out in odd corners of the
lodge and adjoining restaurant.

I stir myself long enough to watch the madness out the window as 25
teams beat a confused path to the outbound trail; then I collapse back to
the comfy carpet, satisfied my dogs are still sleeping as soundly as could
be expected amid the mayhem. Shortly after, I find the musher room
now has a few slots available and I stagger in for another hour or two
of quality rest, but discover I really can't get back to sleep.

If the dogs didn't sleep any better than I did, they won't be very
happy when we get ready to go. Sure enough, when I hook up about
noon several of them are grouchy and snapping at each other and I
have to break up a small fight. It takes me another couple of hours to
get everyone sorted out and calmed down before I can finally get back

on the trail for the 28-mile run to Tolsona Lake, four and a half hours behind the leaders.

It seems checkpoints aren't necessarily the havens I had hoped. Some mushers avoid the hubbub and plan their real rest stops for the less frequented locations; a few just camp out on the trail. Whatever the case, I can see I'm going to have to pay more attention to resting, or even on a short race like this one neither I nor the dogs are going to be able to keep up the pace.

Copper Basin Snapshot—The Diarrhea Express to the Gulkana River

Aside from an unexpected patch of open water and a quarter-mile of ice going up a ravine, the run from Wolverine to Tolsona goes well. However, several of the dogs are developing diarrhea. Illness is a problem on the bigger races where dogs from many kennels get together, and especially for teams at the back of the pack that must "eat the dust" and other stuff of teams ahead.

I know there's a nasty canine virus making the rounds in a couple of areas of the state. If my dogs are coming down with this, I may well have to scratch because I wouldn't dare push them over a tough trail in such a condition. At Tolsona, the vet says she thinks it's just a strain of diarrhea that seems to be affecting a lot of teams and gives the dogs some antidiarrheal pills (the same as humans use). I push on quickly for the 21-mile night run to Brown Bear, just outside the town of Glennallen.

The trail is good and running conditions are ideal, with a full moon and temperatures dropping to perhaps 35 below. The dogs are moving well, but more and more of them are showing signs of diarrhea. Some of them must let fly every 15 minutes or so; this results in a general slowdown of several miles per hour in our average speed. I notice lots of other teams have apparently had the same problem, judging from the quantity of frozen residue on the trail. If nothing else, I won't have any trouble keeping on the race trail—it's marked very well in addition to the regular trail markers.

I know the dogs will probably be okay, but I'm going to have to give them extra rest and lots more food and water to make up for what they're losing. At Brown Bear the vet and I have to give all 12 dogs a mass of pills, including some antibiotics. I spend eight hours there to give the team time to rest and to allow the medicine to take effect.

As I'm getting ready to leave, I talk to another musher who has had to scratch because his dogs have what is coming to be called the "black virus." Dogs with this malady recover after four or five days, but they're in no condition to run in the meantime. Several other teams also have this scary infection, but it's now clear my dogs have something else, much gentler.

At 5:30 in the morning we finally pull out to run the 23 miles up to Gakona, with the diarrhea apparently mostly under control. As it turns out, the dogs are in very good shape and have a lot more resiliency than I give them credit for. They seem to be enjoying the predawn run that takes us first through sleeping downtown Glennallen and then up the Trans-Alaska Pipeline right-of-way.

On the other hand, I don't realize it but I've gotten almost no real rest because of worrying about the dogs' condition. I haven't eaten any decent food for a couple of days and I'm more than a little dehydrated myself. I'm running on nervous energy that can't last forever and my judgment is probably becoming as impaired as if I'd slugged a six-pack of beer.

My wake-up call comes about five miles short of Gakona where the trail crosses the frozen Gulkana River. In the pre-race trail briefing we had been told there were some rocks on the final drop down to the river, but not to worry about it. I'm half asleep as the team roars up on the river bank and don't think to slow them down as much as I should, even though I see the multiple crossed trail markers signaling a "double-X" hazard ahead.

Before my fuzzy brain can process what's happening, the dogs have bounded down an impossibly narrow rocky chute in the boulders placed there to protect the nearby highway bridge. The drop is a dozen feet, virtually straight down over bare rocks the size of microwave ovens. There may have been snow to cover everything for the earlier teams, but now it's like I've become some kind of bouncing ball in a giant pinball game as the sled slams and bangs against the rocks on its uncontrolled fall to the river below.

At the very bottom is a rock the size of a railroad tie sticking half out into the mouth of the chute. The dogs have easily jumped it and swung sharply to the right to follow the trail downstream under the bridge. As the sled careens down the bank, the right runner hits the obstruction and flips, flinging me into the rocks.

It is a major wreck-crash-and-burn, due in part to my slow reactions and poor judgment. The dogs have stopped and are looking back at the carnage with what I swear is amusement. The sled bag hasn't spilled, but the plastic track has been partially separated from the right runner, part of the brake has been broken off, and everything has been generally loosened up. The sled will still go, but I'll have to fix it at Chistochina on my mandatory six-hour layover, 40 miles up the trail.

My middle-aged body has taken a few hits as well. My left shin feels like it's broken, although it turns out to be only a deep bone bruise. I think I've also cracked a rib or two, judging from the piercing pain in my side. I lie there for a minute trying to sort out what's happened. I finally determine I'm not dead or crippled and the dogs are okay. As soon as I get everything upright and climb back on the runners the dogs roar off down the river, no doubt wondering what the silly two-legs behind them thought was such a big deal.

For me, it's been another hard lesson learned. The dogs are tough, much tougher than I realize. I must spend more time watching out for myself. If I don't keep my own physical condition up to par I'll make more dumb decisions that can have even more drastic consequences. On the Iditarod, I'll have to go for two weeks, not a couple or three days, under conditions that can be much more dangerous than what I've seen here. If I'm not fulfilling my role as the brains of this outfit, we can all be in serious trouble. The dogs are doing their part—I've got to make sure I do mine.

Copper Basin Snapshot—Following the Old-Timers Up the Eagle Trail

After Gakona, the trail abandons the highway for the first part of the 31-mile run to Chistochina and climbs out of a deep canyon via the old Eagle Trail, built around the turn of the century for freight sleds and pack trains traveling from Valdez to the Yukon River gold fields. The trail snakes up a very steep mountainside out of the gorge to the plateau above, climbing 500 feet in less than a mile. It's barely five feet wide at best, with only willow bushes and scrub spruce for guardrails against the drop into the chasm below.

I've been warned about a particularly bad area where water flowing from a spring on the uphill side of the track has created a mini-glacier across the trail. The trailbreakers say they've cut away the worst of it with chain saws, but I'm still apprehensive. After half an hour of steady climbing and threading around switchbacks we finally reach the problem zone.

It's a sharp bend set into the mountainside with timber retainers underneath the downhill part of the trail. The 60-foot-long team pulls quickly into and out of the bend, leaving me looking at a straight shot across the void. I desperately lean the sled to the right with all the strength I can muster, but it's too late. I slip on the ice and the left runner drops over the lip. The sled flips and rolls over. Off balance, I follow it over the edge of the 70-degree slope.

The sled quickly stops, anchored by the gangline and the dogs, who are still on the trail with good traction and pulling hard. I finally regain my footing on a ledge under the soft snow and climb carefully back on to the trail to survey things. The sled is still in one piece but it's upside down and the brush bow is wedged against a willow bush. The dogs are holding it firmly enough and everything seems stable for the time being. However, there's no one behind me for more than two hours and there's no way I can leave the team here to hike back to Gakona for help. I only have one choice—somehow get the sled back on the trail and get going again.

It's really just a matter of finding a good point from which to pull so I can get the sled upright to take advantage of the team's tremendous tractor power. I believe it was Archimedes who said, "Give me a fulcrum and I can move the Earth." It takes me a while to find a good Archimedean point, but I finally get the sled more or less stood up after 20 minutes of straining and slipping. I climb up to help the dogs pull the heavy sled past the obstructing willow bush . After another five minutes of pulling and jockeying, the sled groans up off the verge and onto the trail.

> *Once we're safely back on the right of way, I take a breather and look down at the 400-foot drop. It would have been quite a ride if the gangline had snapped or the dogs had been dragged over the side. I wonder to myself how the old-timers handled this with their 15-foot-long, half-ton freight sleds and 20-dog teams. My admiration factor for the old pioneer freighters goes up a few notches as my dogs, who think this has all been a rest break, tear on up the hill as if nothing has happened.*

Copper Basin Snapshot—Journey to the Top of the World

The crown jewel of the race is the leg over a 4,000-foot summit between the Chistochina and Gakona River drainages, on a 71-mile wilderness run from Chistochina to Summit Lake. The summit is a rounded mountain peak surmounting a ridge, well above timberline.

The leg begins as the most beautiful and trouble-free run of the race for me. After watching a spectacular sunrise as the team sweeps up the smooth trail above the Chistochina River, I snack the dogs and rest them for half an hour. I even get a chance to stop and chat with Emmitt Peters as he rests his team. He won the 1975 Iditarod—the second Native to do so—and is a good friend of Ron's. Emmitt was also a race judge in the Iditarod just past and I flew him extensively in my plane.

Leaving Emmitt and passing a couple of other teams, we reach the foot of the east approach to the summit after seven hours on the trail from Chistochina. The ascent begins abruptly as the trail climbs straight up out of the Excelsior Creek valley, running directly up a forbidding slope. We charge into it and the dogs settle into their steep-hill mode, digging in and shifting into "granny low" gear. I help by pedaling (pushing with one foot while holding on to the handlebar) and occasionally even by jumping off the runners and walking alongside the sled to lessen the load.

After 20 minutes and maybe a mile we reach the top of the first big ridge, 1,000 feet above the valley floor. We run along the ridgeline for awhile and then suddenly drop back down into another valley, surrendering much of the altitude for which we've fought so hard. At the same time I notice the temperature has risen dramatically, from 20 below at Chistochina to several degrees above freezing here atop the ridges— almost a 60-degree temperature rise. There's a big low pressure system in the Gulf of Alaska pumping warm air in over the top of the Copper Basin, and we've climbed up into the southerly breezes.

At the foot of the second hill, which is the dauntingly steep final climb to the summit, the dogs quit. Socks, my number-one leader, turns and gives me a look that says, "I'm willing to go, boss, but I can't convince the others." I know they're probably overheated, and I know they need a rest. However, there's no way I can stop them here or they'll balk at every hill from here on. Somehow I've got to get them to the top of this mountain before they stop and rest.

After half an hour of shuffling dogs, I find a combination that will allow me to gently pull them up the hill as they drag the sled. This final 800-foot ascent to the summit is a numbing half-mile slog on a slope almost too steep to walk up. We start up with me leading and the dogs following. The big horses at the back of the team are still raring to go; they think this is all a joke and pull the sled up abeam the more fatigued dogs at the front end.

And I'm not exactly a paragon of athletic competence myself, plodding up the incline like an out-to-pasture draft horse. I have to take a break every few minutes, since I'm still in my full arctic gear and am overheating even more than the dogs. I resign myself to taking the hill a step at a time and just try to put one foot in front of the other. As I crest every little knoll, however, I see yet another stretch heading on up the seemingly endless mountain.

After maybe half an hour of stop-and-go snail's-pace progress, the dogs start following me without my actually pulling on the leaders' necklines. Eventually the slope gentles somewhat and the dogs continue past me without my urging. I hop on the sled as it trundles by and the dogs pull me the last few hundred yards to the top as I heap praise and exhortations on them.

Once we finally gain the summit, I stop the team and give them food and let them wolf snow at the side of the trail for moisture. My forced march up the mountain has left me unspeakably thirsty and I slug at least a quart of water from my Thermos after I rip off my parka and hat. Then I lean back on the sled bag to see what we've earned.

We're on top of a windswept peak in the foothills of the Alaska Range, with a 360-degree view of the most spectacular scenery in North America. To the south I can see all the way to the Chugach Mountains on the Gulf of Alaska, and over to 20,300-foot Denali more than 150 miles to the west. To the southeast are the great ancient volcanoes of the Wrangells, topped by 16,300-foot Mount Sanford and backed by the somewhat lower but gently steaming Mount Wrangell. To the north, the 13,800-foot peak of Mount Hayes looms much closer in the great arc of the Alaska Range enfolding the vast Copper Basin across which we've spent the past three days traveling. From this lofty perch, I can almost trace our entire path across the distant lowlands.

> *It is a sublime moment, fairly won and profoundly appreciated, and over all too soon. But underlying all is the knowledge that I've learned how to get the team over a seemingly insurmountable obstacle in good order, a skill that will certainly stand me in good stead on the Iditarod seven weeks hence.*

Copper Basin Snapshot—Under the Aurora to the Finish Line

I'm only a few miles from the finish line on the final 30-mile run south from Summit Lake to Meier's Lake, traveling with Wayne Curtis, another Iditarod rookie musher and friend I overtook back on 11-mile-long Paxson Lake. He's running just behind me and we're talking back and forth as we tick away the last miles of the race under the clear night sky studded with a million glittering stars. After a period of silence while I half-doze watching the trail ahead, Wayne shouts, "Look up!" I glance to the east, where the full moon has been slowly rising above the hills for the past hour or so.

In an instant I forget the fatigue and worries of three and a half days on the rugged trail. The northern lights are exploding in a luminous, undulating arc across the eastern sky. Curtains of iridescent green and yellow, their lower fringes tinged with red, perfectly frame the brilliant, bone-white moon. The tableau is punctuated by a handful of the very brightest stars glinting like diamonds through the shimmering veils. I feel I am in the midst of some revelatory medieval vision that can only be imperfectly related to those who have not actually experienced it.

As the dogs run smoothly on, Wayne and I watch the display in unabashed awe. It continues for perhaps 10 minutes, waxing and waning and then fading away almost as quickly as it came. The timing was too perfect, the impression too profound to be easily dismissed. It is impossible to escape the feeling that this display was meant just for us, to emphasize that there truly can be treasure buried amid the work and sweat and cold and aching muscles of mushing.

Almost immediately after the aurora fades we round one last clump of swamp spruce and catch a glimpse of the lights of Meier's Lake Lodge and the finish line. My dogs pick up my excitement and break into a run. Within a few minutes we surge onto Meier's Lake itself for the half-mile sprint to the finish.

After 300 miles spanning three days and nine hours on the trail, we roar into the chute and under the banner marking the end. The awards banquet has just concluded and dozens of people are waiting to welcome us in. Every musher in sight shakes my hand and congratulates me on finishing, because they've all been where I am and they understand that this has been a voyage of personal discovery. Merely finishing is more than enough reward. For me, it's especially satisfying because my hard-won 33rd-place finish—even though it's well out of the money—officially qualifies for the Big One, the Iditarod. But there's no time to reflect on that. The dogs must be fed and bedded down and then I'm going to have a well-earned steak dinner and a beer. And then I'm going to sleep for a week.

February 1, 1995
Iditarod Headquarters—Wasilla, Alaska

When I was flying transports for the Air Force, we used to say only half-jokingly the airplane wasn't allowed to take off until the gross weight of the paperwork equaled the gross weight of the pilot. The Iditarod seems to have a similar rule, and I'm starting to wonder if all the paperwork could be stuffed even into one of the old-time freight sleds.

The avalanche of cellulose begins every year at the original sign-up with the forking over of the $1,750 entry fee. In return, mushers receive a package of forms to do any bureaucrat proud. Lurking inside the plain blue folder are the detailed entry application, a biography sheet, and a sponsor list, not to mention a public relations release form, a local contact form signed by someone in the Anchorage area who will be responsible for dropped dogs during the race, and a certification of a $200 deposit with a veterinarian to treat returned dogs if necessary. And of course there's the Nome housing form, designed to match every musher with a host or hostess on arrival in Nome. Every rookie also has to get a picture (some call it a mug shot) taken as quickly as possible.

Every rookie musher must also view a four-hour video of the previous year's pre-race rookie seminar and sign yet another document attesting thereto. Rookies must also provide proof they have finished the appropriate qualifying races in the form of certificates signed by the marshals of the races in question, but which many rookies (including me) often fail to get in the fatigued, confused hours after the finish of races like the Copper Basin.

During the months leading up to the race, ITC Headquarters sends out multiple editions of the seemingly ever-changing race rules, policies, and regulations, each of which must be examined carefully for some modification which might require frantic compliance action. These are accompanied by periodic updated lists of the mushers and their sponsors. The ITC also issues a steady stream of letters, instructions, booklets, and pamphlets on everything from dog care to preparing for the food drops to what kind of vet services will be available on the trail.

Race Director Joanne Potts punctuates this torrent of type with periodic reminders to tardy mushers to catch up on their paperwork—or else. As the deadline for forms submission approaches, her gentle memos grow ever more forceful. I'm sure more than a few drivers have wondered if she ever worked for a collection agency at some time in the past.

The dogs generate their own blizzard of paper. As race day draws near, every dog must have a valid rabies vaccination certificate, proof of inoculation against parvo, distemper, and corona virus, and a signed record of having been dosed with a special race-provided worming medicine. Every canine must also receive an electrocardiogram with the ensuing printout (all free of charge), as well as a complete pre-race vet check and certificate of health (also provided by the race organization).

Finally, the week leading up to race day is consumed by meetings and briefings, with still more handouts and notes. Rookies must also endure the real-life edition of the interminable video they viewed months before. And then everyone goes to the mushers' banquet on the Thursday before the race to draw for starting positions; this alone can take six hours, and at a time when most drivers would just as soon get a good night's sleep.

Any musher could easily fill up a couple of good-sized boxes just with paperwork by banquet time. Most, however, take it all in stride, although not without some inevitable grouching about bureaucrats and paper-pushers. But there's a reason for killing all the trees: having worked the support side, I know the Iditarod is really a large and complex undertaking more akin to a major military operation than a sporting event. While some of the paperwork may arguably be administrative overkill, most of it—and the draconian measures such as $100 fines used to enforce its timely submission—has evolved out of necessity over the years. The number of potentially show-stopping loose ends in an enterprise of this magnitude is mind-boggling. It's a wonder more race personnel don't get ulcers and suffer screaming nervous breakdowns.

This year's race manager and chief candidate for stress-induced gastric upset is Jack Niggemyer, whom I've known for a number of years. He's held this position for much of the past decade, with a couple of breaks for such diversions as climbing Mount Kilimanjaro and being the Iditarod color commentator for ABC Wide World of Sports. Jack is a musher, of course, but he's never gotten around to running the Iditarod because of injuries and other problems. In fact, many of Bert Hanson's dogs—comprising most of my team—were in Jack's kennel before we moved them up to Montana Creek, and Jack ran them on some of the shorter races like the Knik 200 and the Copper Basin 300. So, Jack knows more than I do about many of my dogs, and he's offered me lots of on-the-side advice and encouragement.

The race manager position is one of the few full-time paid positions in the Iditarod organization; many people who know what the job entails will say whatever the pay is, it's not enough. The race manager must make arrangements for just about everything from Anchorage to Nome, including the actual building of the trail, which is nothing less than a yearly highway construction project. Setting up the two dozen or so checkpoints involves intricate agreements and sometimes protracted negotiations with village governments, lodge owners, and government agencies. Dog lots must be set up, logistics must be arranged, and lodging and work space found for race volunteers and mushers. And all of this must be done within what is often a miserly budget that seemingly can never be stretched far enough.

And once the race is underway, the race manager is the on-scene boss of everything. He must be everywhere all the time and if anything slips through the crack he's the first to be blamed. In 1994, Martin Buser sneaked out of Kaltag ahead of his competitors for the 90-mile run to Unalakleet. Jack was in Unalakleet frantically trying to get last-minute arrangements made, all the while trying to juggle the media and make sure everything was in shape on down the line toward Nome. When Martin made record time and a chance snowmachiner's report revealed him only a few miles out of town, hours ahead of schedule, reliable sources swear Jack actually materialized in at least five different places at once getting things sorted out.

The race manager is hired for a year at a time, and some years the incumbent adamantly (even violently) refuses to be considered for a follow-on term. Jack is one of the few repeat race managers who has managed to keep his sanity (and even several of his friends). Having watched him in the heat of battle on the trail for a few years, I'm just glad I'm not in his position. In more than a few cases, he's had to make decisions where there was no easy way out, which can be very hard on one's social life when erstwhile friends and acquaintances are involved.

The fact is simply the Iditarod is like no other sporting event on earth. It's by far the world's biggest, longest, richest, and most famous sled dog race, and a major part of its mystique is its remote route. This creates a set of problems rivaling even those faced by the Olympics, only without the infrastructure of roads, railroads, and other niceties of normal urban and suburban civilization. On top of everything, the race receives an inordinate share of media attention, not to mention potshots from animal rights activists and other detractors and cynics.

Putting on this incredibly complex affair year after year requires an incredible amount of effort by the Iditarod staff as well as several thousand volunteers. I guess I can't really argue about a few reams of paperwork. Pushing a pencil to fill out a few forms so I can drive my dogs to Nome is infinitely preferable to the headaches and hoop-jumping endured by the folks behind the scenes.

Iditarod Air Force planes wait on the runway at Rohn. The Rohn checkpoint is completely isolated and is often the most difficult to establish and supply.

93

February 3, 1995
Montana Creek, Alaska

Having finished the Copper Basin, we are mainly concerned with keeping our teams peaked up for the Iditarod and working on specific problem areas we've noticed. My dogs can use some work on hills, as much to build their strength as to bolster their confidence. I don't need any more balks at the bottoms of steep mountains, especially if I'm not in a position (or condition) to lead the train up the hill myself.

Fortunately, we have some of the best hill training trails in the state right in our back yard. Our usual 20-mile run includes some serious 100-and 200-foot climbs and is a good workout in its own right, but the ultimate ascent starts right where we would normally turn back for the dog lot.

At the high point of the regular trail, we veer onto another trail continuing on up the flank of the Talkeetna Mountains. Normally used by snowmachiners for access to the wide-open tundra areas above timberline, it's well known by dog drivers as a super training run. After skirting for several miles along the rim of the 200-foot-deep canyon of the South Fork of Montana Creek, steadily climbing all the while, the trail winds for a couple of miles through open spruce forest before breaking out onto the open tundra.

This up-the-mountain trail is about 10 miles long; the last four or five miles climb about 1,500 feet, topping out around 2,500 feet above sea level, which is well above the tree line up here at 62 degrees north latitude. Of course, once onto the treeless upper expanses, the sky's the limit. Given the reasonably firm snow of late winter, there's no real reason an intrepid driver couldn't take a team on up into the heart of the Talkeetnas, whose 10,000 square miles and peaks ranging up to 9,000 feet constitute one of Alaska's lesser known—but no less magnificent—wilderness areas.

I haven't been up this trail before for any number of reasons, but chiefly because it's been repeatedly trashed by the resident moose population. Pothole-like moose tracks in a dog trail can be deadly, dislocating canine shoulders and even breaking legs. No sane musher would willingly run a team over such a trail without a very good reason, no matter how good the training would ordinarily be.

Now, however, new snow and several weeks of heavy use by snowmachiners have yielded a near-perfect trail, smooth and hard. The moose seem to have headed down the mountain in search of more amenable tree-munching areas, leaving the upper slopes to us, although now we have just that many more of the ornery critters to worry about around our dog lot.

I decide to take 10 of the dogs I ran in the Copper Basin 300 and go up the mountain before something else happens to ruin the trail. The dogs are sluggish for the first 10 miles, undoubtedly bored out of their minds by hitting the same old trail again for the umpteenth time. But at the usual turnaround point, when I gee them onto the new trail, it's like I flip the overdrive switch. They instantly sense a new adventure at hand and pull up the first big slope like a space shuttle heading for orbit.

I went a few miles up this trail yesterday but had to turn around before I made it all the way up. Today I think I'll have time to get to the top before it gets too dark to appreciate whatever treasures I might find up there. We're gaining several minutes of daylight a day and it's plenty light until well after six.

Shortly past our previous turnaround point the trail leaves the birch forest and pushes into the open spruce woods. Periodically we cross broad snow-covered meadows that are bogs in the summertime, climbing steadily. Ahead are sweeping vistas of the high peaks of the Talkeetnas painted gold by the late afternoon sunlight. Over my shoulder I can catch tantalizing views of the entire Susitna Valley spread out below. I realize I'm at a much higher altitude with my dog team than I normally fly with my airplane.

The dogs pull resolutely up the interminable slope. Unlike the monster mountain on the Copper Basin 300, though, we're up here exploring on our own volition and it's a mutual enterprise. They want to see what's up here as much as I do and are fully alert and intent, peering off to the side of the trail or up at the peaks. I think they really do appreciate the view; I know from driving Silvertip in my car and flying him in my plane that he thoroughly enjoys seeing the countryside. Other mushers have told me good long-distance sled dogs must be intelligent and curious enough to want to see what's around the next bend. Otherwise they'd never be able to handle the hours on the trail in the bigger races without going sour and refusing to pull.

This climb easily rivals our Copper Basin nemesis. Today, however, there is no hesitation, which is the underlying reason I brought the team up here. If I can get them to take every hill as if there's something new and exciting at the top, they'll be much less prone to balk even if they're tired. And I know there are so many hills on the Iditarod the total climb would probably add up to several trips to the top of Denali.

Mental preparation of this sort is just as important for the dogs as for the drivers. Indeed, top-flight drivers like Martin Buser send a second team of younger dogs on the Iditarod every year. These canine rookies aren't pushed: the goal is to give them an easy trip to Nome so they will come to see the trail as a fun place to be. (And judging from the success of Martin and others using this strategy, it certainly seems to work.)

Finally all I can see ahead is a thin stand of stunted trees and brush. As we pull past them, it's like we've broken out onto the top of the world. The unbroken slope continues up perhaps another quarter mile to a lone snow-frosted boulder atop a knoll. The dogs can sense this is our goal and redouble their efforts, practically loping up the 15-percent grade.

Abeam the great stone, I stop the team. We're on a rise overlooking a vast expanse of tundra leading up to the rugged peaks. The snowmachine trail we've followed up from the lowlands splits into many tracks, each leading to its own mysterious destination behind a ridge or up a side couloir. We're certainly not pioneers up here, since this is a popular weekend destination for motorized explorers, but I know we're the first dog team to make it up here in some weeks. From our perspective it's a whole new world.

Behind us, the sun has just set and the clouds are aglow with vivid reds and golds over the Alaska Range far to the west. Far below, in the valley whence we've come, the lights along the Parks Highway are twinkling on as the late-winter darkness creeps in. There are so few lights they barely disturb the immensity of the silent forests and swamps and rivers. I know there are more than 5,000 people living in the Maryland-sized Susitna Valley, but their impact seems minimal from this lofty viewpoint.

It's taken us less than two hours to get up here from our dog lot, but we might as well have traveled to another world. As much as I'd like to push on to explore the high country, night is falling quickly and I have to get back to feed the other dogs. I hate to leave, but I know I'll be back. Besides, the dogs are already screaming to go; the climb hasn't even fazed them.

I turn the team around and we start back down the trail. The dogs have apparently been anticipating the downhill run and immediately break into a lope. We barrel back down the trail and into the tree line like the Twentieth Century Limited. I ride the brake but there's no way I can stop the dogs quickly when they've got the bit in their teeth like this. I suppose Captain Hazelwood had a similar feeling when he tried to stop the Exxon Valdez. The problem, I suddenly realize, is the hills. Several steep sections we trudged up earlier now become twisting carnival rides as I struggle to keep the sled upright and me on it. And there's worse to come.

I've come to classify really serious downhills in two categories: "yee-hahs" and "omigods." The former is the kind of whistling descent with enough elements of fun and adventure and sufficient pumping adrenaline to overshadow the likelihood of imminent disaster. There is a reasonable chance of survival or at least a smiling demise. My mental behavior model for transiting these declivities is the late, lamented Slim Pickens in *Doctor Strangelove* astride his trusty H-bomb, wildly waving his Stetson on his drop to glory.

The other flavor of hill is the kind that, on a ski slope, you take one look at, break your own leg, and crawl away from on your hands and knees begging for mercy and a hot buttered rum, heavy on the rum. These plunges have no redeeming social value and seemingly offer a direct descent into the underworld. On a dog sled, however, there is no turning back, and in any case you're already committed to the free fall sans parachute before you can do anything about it. After the shock of the initial surprise, as the enormity of the situation takes hold, the chief emotion is a strange type of Eastern fatalism, perhaps accompanied by a fleeting glimpse of the major events of your life and a passing regret at not updating your will.

Of course, nothing bothers the dogs, who would probably enjoy hurtling off a sheer cliff face to see how thoroughly they can trash the sled and driver. This is the mode my team is in as we careen down the mountain in the gathering gloom. My feeble headlamp is virtually no help because I can only see the leaders about half the time as the blind turns come faster and faster.

Shortly the inevitable happens as the dogs whip through a nasty triple switchback on a near-vertical drop between towering spruce sentinels. I overcompensate on the first 120-degree turn and both the sled and I depart the trail in grand style on the second, clearing most of the third while still airborne. In about three nanoseconds I find myself wrapped around a tree, face down in the snow, with my boot jammed through the brake framework on the overturned sled. Maybe Martin Buser could have gotten through this maniac luge run unscathed, but I've got a long way to go before I approach his sled-driving skills.

I enjoy a snack of snow and spruce bark while I contemplate my shortcomings. The dogs, of course, are barking wildly (or perhaps they're laughing?) to go on. I take inventory and find the sled is in one piece and I'm only mildly damaged. As I start to disengage my boot from the brake, the dogs take it as a signal to move on and drag me another 20 feet down the hill. I need 10 minutes to finally extract my impossibly large boot from the incredibly small aperture through which it's been inserted, a process which isn't abetted by the team's impatient yanks on the gangline.

This was a classic "omigod" hill, complete with the belated realization of complete and utter disaster. But this time no harm is done and I have to chalk it up as just part of the game. Back on the trail, we scream down several more yee-hahs and another omigod or two, making it to the

The lowly doghouse is the sled dog's castle. Most are little more than sturdy two-foot-square plywood boxes with holes cut in one side and straw stuffed inside. Anything fancier is wasted effort since the houses suffer many indignities from their occupants, including being chewed to pieces. Sled dogs love to spend an inordinate amount of time on top of their houses, and often prefer to sleep on them rather than in them.

bottom of the mountain fully half an hour faster than we went up it. The dogs have enjoyed the downhill breather so much they keep running even after we hit the lowland sections.

As we roar into the dog lot I marvel at their speed and endurance: we've gone at least 40 miles—including the long climb and several stops—in a little more than four hours. If they can do this on the Iditarod, we're not going to have many problems. For now, though, it's back up the mountain tomorrow with the other 10 dogs. Maybe I'll wear my old baseball catcher's shin guards and face mask for that one....

February 10, 1995
Montana Creek, Alaska

Ron has had to drop out of the race. For a week or more he's been hinting something might be coming up. Apparently a planned April trip to Minnesota to resolve a family matter must now be made during the race. I know he's unhappy about not getting to go to Nome again, and it changes things rather substantially for me as well. I'd hoped to run with him until I could get my sea legs and a good feel for the trail. Now he won't be there and I'll have to do the best I can. I hope I've learned enough to get me through the rough spots.

Anyway, Ron still wants to help me get my stuff accumulated, and says he will sew booties and work with me to get my food drop together, which must be ready to go next week. Ron does say he wants to run in 1997, the 25th anniversary of the race. A number of the mushers who ran the first Iditarod are thinking about doing the '97 race together, with their own old-timers' pot of prize money for their race-within-a-race.

The fact Ron will be 70 years old then—and some of the other drivers will be even older—doesn't faze him a bit. I guess mushing is a lot like golf (and maybe another well-known pastime), in that you can apparently do it no matter how old you are. Joe Redington, Sr., commonly regarded as the father of the Iditarod, actually led the race into Cripple in 1988, when he was 71; Joe finished fifth, a remarkable accomplishment for anyone, much less a septagenarian.

But Ron won't be going this year, and I feel the race as a whole will be the worse off for it. I know his withdrawal has taken some of the wind out of my sails; I'd always assumed he'd be there with me on the trail, but now I'll have to revise my plans a bit. Maybe in '97....

February 12, 1995
Montana Creek, Alaska

There are days when it doesn't pay to get out of bed. Today is definitely one of them, and then some. In fact, if somebody had a video camera, we could sell the footage to the media.

I'm walking in a perfectly ordinary manner from the dog lot into Ron's cabin after feeding the dogs when I slip on the ice and do a classic movie pratfall. Unfortunately, I collapse backward like a toppling spruce onto a two-by-four sticking up out of the ice.

It catches me squarely in the upper right side of my back and the pain is beyond almost anything I've ever experienced. The only thing I can do is roll around on the ice for 10 minutes in tears while Ron and Barrie look on in disbelief. After a while the pain diminishes sufficiently for me to get up and stagger inside, but I know something has been badly damaged. I can't believe I've put myself in the position of possibly not running the Iditarod because of a fool accident like slipping on the ice.

I decide I can drive my car and tell Ron I intend to head for the emergency room at Elmendorf ASAP. Ron says he'll accompany me if I need help, but I think I can probably make it, if for no other reason than the pain will keep me awake all the way.

The 100-mile drive to town is memorable, if only because I have to pull over several times to let particularly bad spasms pass. At the emergency room, the doctor looks at the x-rays and says I've probably cracked a rib, and I almost certainly have torn some muscles and other good stuff inside my rib cage. He gives me some heavy-duty painkillers and advises me to get home somehow before I start taking them.

I manage to get back to Montana Creek, but I know I'm in trouble.

I can barely breathe, and coughing is like getting kicked by a mule. I have to sneeze once and nearly pass out. I realize there's no way I can run my dogs for at least a couple of weeks; I hope they can keep their edge until Kim starts running them in preparation for the Junior Iditarod.

I'm really worried I won't be back in working order before the Iditarod itself, not even three weeks away. I know rib injuries and deep tissue damage can take months to heal, and I will have to be very careful not to re-injure myself and set back the healing process over the next week or two. Is somebody up there trying to tell me something? Or maybe I'm just so inept I can't maintain my own health during a critical period.

Regardless, I'll still be at the starting line on March 4th, even if I have to carry enough serious painkillers to require an escort from the Drug Enforcement Agency. At least I can take some comfort in knowing I won't be the first musher to try the race with a busted something or other. I guess the worst part is I can't blame my disability on something honorable, like a spectacular sled wreck. To have to 'fess up to slipping on the ice like some dumb cheechako is almost as painful as the cracked rib. And of course it hurts worst when I laugh.

February 17, 1995
Montana Creek and Anchorage, Alaska

The one part of getting ready for the Iditarod which is guaranteed to drive the drivers to distraction is the food drop. Planning and executing it is like organizing a Himalayan expedition from scratch. A new musher like me can easily spend weeks putting everything together, not to mention a couple thousand dollars. Even veterans tend to pull their hair out as food drop approaches; sleepless nights and irritable dispositions are the norm while the process is underway.

The rules are disarmingly brief, merely requiring every musher to ship a minimum amount of food out to each of the major checkpoints: this means at least five pounds of food for each dog at 14 locations, in addition to personal goodies and other gear. But it's not as simple as it sounds.

Lots of factors must be considered in assembling a ton or so of food and equipment for a trip of almost 1,200 miles. For instance, dogs get tired and cranky after several days on the trail and can become picky eaters, so a variety of food is required to tempt their palates. This means mushers must anticipate what their dogs might like and try to cover the waterfront with a selection of entrees like lamb, beef, chicken, turkey, liver, beaver, seal, fish, and a breathtaking array of off-the-wall homemade concoctions—all in addition to a basic fare of commercial dry dog food.

Then there's race strategy to be considered. Some drivers like to "rabbit" and go as far and as fast as they can before stopping to take their mandatory 24-hour layover, while some like to get it out of the way early on. Regardless, extra food for dogs and driver must be allocated for one or more likely stopping points.

Many mushers like to ship replacement sleds ahead (the race allows no more than two). Sleds break with alarming frequency, and sometimes they can't be fixed well enough to hold up for the long haul to Nome. Many mushers count on changing sleds after crossing the Alaska Range, and some will switch to a lighter, faster sled out on the coast when they're likely to have fewer dogs.

All drivers also ship out several replacement sets of plastic runner bottoms; the dogs have a tough enough time of it without having to pull a sled with chewed-up bottoms. Booties for the dogs are another

Bags of dog food and supplies sent ahead by mushers await the teams at the Ophir checkpoint. Each musher pays the race organization to ship about a ton of food and other gear to more than 15 checkpoints.

major item—most mushers send out more than 1,000 of them, along with dozens of various lines and snaps. The problem, of course, is deciding just where to ship these key items.

Every musher has to ship out personal food and consumables. For instance, headlamps go through four D-cell alkaline batteries every four to six hours of use, and the bulbs don't last forever, either. Air-activated disposable charcoal hand warmers are another high-consumption item—some drivers use many dozens of them on the race. And there are other small necessities like dry socks and underwear and spare batteries for the inevitable Walkman, all of which have to be laid out ahead of time.

Musher food is no small matter: Every driver must ensure he or she has enough calories and variety to sustain a grueling pace that can demand 5,000 calories a day. "People food" on the race runs the gamut from peanut-butter-and-jelly sandwiches with candy bars on the side to precooked multi-course gourmet dinners, vacuum-sealed and frozen for quick reheating. Even with the most appetizing bill of fare, however, most mushers lose weight on the race, usually because they simply forget to eat the delicacies they've so thoughtfully provided for themselves.

Much of the food going into the bags for the dogs and for me is dependent on the so-called "cooker" I will carry in the sled all the way to Nome. This is actually an enclosed alcohol stove with a metal pot for heating water or melting snow; it isn't actually used to cook. Of course, as the water heats, it's perfect for thawing packages of frozen "people food" like burritos or even entire dinners, so in a sense it actually is a cooker. On early Iditarods, mushers built wood fires to make and heat water; later, charcoal stoves were used, but alcohol cookers proved to be most efficient and are now the standard for mushers everywhere.

The entire complicated inventory has to be sorted and packed into special pre-marked, color-coded bags for each checkpoint by two weeks before the race. Most mushers end up packing 40 or 50 bags totaling 2,000 pounds. The race organization collects and ships all the bags and charges the mushers a flat rate of about 25 cents a pound.

Some drivers claim this is the hardest part of the race. Most will readily say actually running the dogs is anticlimactic and many consider the travails of the trail a positively pleasant counterpoint to the logistical nightmare of the food drop.

As for me, I waited as long as I could because a lot of the meat I'm going to ship out comes frozen in 50-pound blocks and has to be sawed into dog-sized chunks. We've been in the throes of a midwinter thaw, with temperatures in Anchorage as high as 50 degrees. Since I have no frozen storage capability, the meat could have gone bad if I'd bought it and cut it too soon. If I had waited too long, I might not have gotten it cut in time, or I might not have found what I needed because of the dozens of other mushers with similar plans.

Luckily, I timed it right, although it was closer than I liked. The weather cooled off over the past few days and we are almost below zero. I managed to get everything I wanted: 600 pounds of super-premium dry dog food, 300 pounds of lamb, 200 pounds of beef, 200 of horsemeat, 200 of chicken, 100 of turkey skins, and 200 of herring. It wasn't cheap or easy, but the dogs will eat like kings.

My personal commissary is a junk food junkie's delight. Almost everything is precooked and ready to heat and eat, or even to choke down frozen if needed. At worst, a few items only need some hot water, which I'll make at every checkpoint anyway. The menu includes half a dozen pizzas (the slices are individually vacuum-sealed and frozen), several dozen burritos, packages of instant oatmeal, and cups of noodles for every checkpoint. For munching along the trail, I've tossed in 10 pounds or so of trail mix, frozen orange slices, lots of beef jerky, boxes of cheese-and-peanut-butter crackers, and enough chocolate to keep me on a permanent buzz.

What I'll probably enjoy most, though, is my own canned smoked salmon, which I put up this past summer to use on the race. I've been catching, smoking, canning, and, of course, eating my own salmon for almost 20 years, and I never get tired of it. I'm shipping at least a couple of eight-ounce cans to every checkpoint. And there's also a side benefit: it drives the dogs wild. If I ever get into a situation where I need that one special treat to tempt a tardy eater, all I'll have to do is pop a can and step out of the way. I wonder what the critics of the race would say if they knew the dogs were being fed premium smoked salmon that would go for 10 bucks a pound at their local deli? I suppose I ought to ship some decent wine and a sommelier's chain as well; I'm sure the dogs will expect nothing less.

Today is the deadline to get everything turned in for shipment; it's five a.m. and I'm frantically working to finish up. I finally got all the raw materials assembled in my driveway yesterday about noon and I've been working ever since. It's taken several pots of coffee and lots of painkillers to quiet my cracked rib, but as false dawn creeps over the Talkeetna Mountains I toss the last package of booties into its allotted bag.

When I blearily step back and survey my handiwork, I see 45 colorful rice bags, each emblazoned with the name of its designated checkpoint, lined up like signposts across a miniature Alaska: Skwentna, Rainy Pass, Rohn, Nikolai, McGrath, Takotna, Iditarod, Shageluk, Grayling, Kaltag, Unalakleet, Shaktoolik, Koyuk, Elim, White Mountain, Safety, and Nome. Each one is bulging with all the necessities for taking 16 dogs—and me—across 1,200 miles of the Last Frontier.

Now I just have to get them all into the collection point in Anchorage before the end of the day. Fortunately a friend with a big van has graciously offered to run most of my bags into town for me on his regular supply trip for his grocery store (coincidentally named Gee-Haw Supply). I cram the rest of the bags into my long-suffering minivan and forge my way into the city, fortified with double-strength coffee, a handful of Tylenol, and the sure and certain knowledge that things can only get better.

At the food drop collection point, located this year as usual in the receiving warehouse for one of the biggest air freight operations in Anchorage, I am once again staggered at the scope of the logistics required to put on the race. A volunteer force of almost 50 people is rapidly digesting each new load in a most workmanlike manner; many of them are friends with whom I worked while volunteering on past races.

The entire floor of the huge warehouse is taken up by pallets full of Iditarod food drop bags. Each checkpoint is represented by several pallets; as the pile of sacks on each pallet rises as high as a person's head it is wrapped in plastic sheeting and hauled off by a forklift. Most checkpoints have five or six pallets, and some have 10 or more.

If my shipment is any indication, the total for all mushers and all locations will be about 120,000 pounds in perhaps 2,500 separate bags. Most of this will be mailed, taking advantage of Alaska's unique bypass mail system which allows direct air freight shipments to practically any Bush location with a zip code. The balance will be airlifted to remote checkpoints by the Iditarod Air Force.

Of course, it isn't free. Mushers must pay for their shipment, although the rate of 25 cents per pound is very reasonable, all things considered. After my bags are checked in and weighed, my total comes to 1,999 pounds. I give the nice lady at the cashier's desk five new 100-dollar bills and get a quarter back. Still, I feel it's a cheap price to pay to get the drudgery of the food drop behind me.

The next milestone is race day on Fourth Avenue. I just hope I can wake up in time to get to the starting line because right now I'm going to stagger back up the highway to my cabin, take as many painkillers for my aching body as I legally can, and sleep like a hibernating grizzly.

February 26, 1995
Wasilla, Alaska

Kim Hanson is just finishing the Junior Iditarod in ninth place—not bad considering the dogs stopped on her in a ground blizzard on the Yentna River. The Junior is for mushers 14 to 17 years old, and teams are limited to 10 dogs. It's only 160 miles out to Yentna Station and back but it can be a tough little race, like today with the winds blowing on the river.

Kim's parents and I spent most of the day in the race operations room keeping track of her progress. For the longest time we couldn't figure out why she wasn't moving; she admits she fell asleep on the sled when the dogs didn't want to go any farther. However, once she started moving again she set the fastest time for the last 40 miles, which I take as a good sign.

The dogs come in strongly, trotting at a good 10-mile-an-hour pace across the finish line, smartly lined out. I like to think I've trained them right for them to look so good. The only possible sour note is three of the females, including leaders Slipper and Bea, are unexpectedly in heat, which can be very disruptive under some conditions. Still, the team seems to be running smoothly enough.

We take the dogs back to Montana Creek so I can make a last couple of tuning-up runs before the big race next Saturday. My rib is in good enough shape (or rather, is hurting at a low enough level) to convince me I can get back on the sled. If nothing else, I've got to figure out how to handle the team without using some of my still-sundered muscles. But I've got faith in the team; we've come too far together to turn back now.

March 3, 1995
Anchorage, Alaska

It's the day before the race and I'm still not ready to go. I have a list of errands as long as my arm which absolutely must get done today, or else. I cannot understand how I've gotten this far if I've still got this much to do—much less how I'm going to hit the trail tomorrow.

I brought the dogs into town this morning; we'll stay at Bert's tonight and tomorrow night after the run to Eagle River so we don't have to make the long drive down from Montana Creek each day. I've been running around Anchorage all day trying to get last-minute things taken care of—new harnesses, extra booties, a spare-parts kit for the sled, nail clippers for the dogs, more charcoal hand warmers, a new thermos, half a dozen pairs of socks, candy—all of the little things I forgot during the hectic activity of the last few days.

The booties are especially important. I came up short of the 1,200 I'll need and had to wait until our in-house assembly line could get into gear. Of course, all of the booties and other stuff I'm picking up won't fit in the sled, so I'll have to put everything into bags and mail them to the various checkpoints. It's not a big deal—almost every musher does it every year. All I have to do is put a label on the bag addressed to me, in care of the Iditarod Checker at, say, Kaltag. The bag will be waiting for me along with the other stuff I've already shipped out.

This week has been consumed with meetings and last-minute preparations. I had good runs with all of the dogs on Monday and Tuesday, although Kona—one of my secondary leaders—seems to have an injured shoulder, probably from the Junior Iditarod, where Kim had to drop her. However, I've already arranged with Steve

Adkins to borrow three of his dogs as fill-ins for just such an eventuality. The 25-mile jaunt Tuesday night was the settling-in run for these newcomers—Blackie, Ben, and May—and they performed perfectly.

Tuesday was also the rookie meeting. This took most of the day at Iditarod Headquarters in Wasilla; we picked up some useful information, but most of us could have used the extra time to rest and get our gear in order. Of course, we had already watched the same stuff on a four-hour videotape a couple of months earlier and we didn't exactly feel like standing up to cheer. At least they had lots of coffee to keep our eyelids jammed open.

On Wednesday I had to take all the dogs down to Wasilla for the vet exam. Unfortunately, Batman (a big, fast male I was counting on) didn't pass because of potentially serious foot problems. This left me with 17 dogs from which to choose the final 16 on race day—not perfect, but still ahead of the power curve.

Yesterday (Thursday) was the main mushers' meeting at the Regal Alaskan Hotel in Anchorage. This took almost all day but was spiced up by the inevitable wrangling over the interpretation of the rules. This is something that happens every year because of the annual modification of the regulations. For this race, Martin Buser's trademark sled sail was ruled out, as were a couple of other innovative aids for the well-equipped musher.

Of potential interest to me and some of the other rookies was the so-called "competitive-

Mushers draw for starting positions at the Iditarod Mushers Banquet, always held the Thursday night before the race. Here the author draws the number 23 position for the 1995 race.

ness" rule, designed to prevent mushers from dawdling too long behind the main pack. Basically, all mushers must make it to McGrath within three days of the leader, and must likewise reach Unalakleet on the coast within five days of the first driver.

Nobody really knows how the rule will affect things this year. Last year, it would have resulted in only one musher being withdrawn from the race. (The formal term is "withdrawn," which is supposed to imply no fault on the part of the musher, as opposed to "disqualified," which is theoretically reserved for serious transgressions such as cheating and abusing dogs.)

Last night was the big mushers' banquet at the Sullivan Arena in downtown Anchorage. This is always a major community event and probably 4,000 people showed up at the 40-dollar-a-plate gala. Some of the entertainment was provided by the fourth graders from Mount Spurr Elementary; they all recognized me from my student teaching. They did fine, bringing the crowd to its feet with an enthusiastic rendition of Hobo Jim's "Iditarod Trail" (which is practically Alaska's alternate state song) complete with the rousing chorus ending in "I did, I did, I did the Iditarod Trail!"

Then came the formal drawing for position. Each of the 58 mushers got time at the microphone to thank sponsors and say anything that came into his or her mind. Some didn't say much at all, some said way too much; I drew number 23, right behind Martin Buser, and probably said too much. The final musher didn't draw until almost 10:30; Barrie drew toward the end of the evening and pulled number 57, which means she will leave the chute next to last.

Today is theoretically free of meetings and other distractions, but I'm like a headless chicken looking for the last few items on my checklist. I should have had most of this stuff weeks ago, but something always came up to make me put it off. Now I'm paying the price in frazzled nerves and lack of sleep.

I haven't had more than three hours' sleep a night since sometime last week. I'm already reacting like someone on the verge of sleep deprivation, which isn't a good sign so close to the race. But then, I may as well get used to it—as the veterans have told me, the one thing you can't ship out to the checkpoints is sleep.

March 4, 1995
The Iditarod
Ceremonial Start in Anchorage to Eagle River (20 miles)

Race day. The Big One. The end of training and the beginning of reality. Ready or not, I'm on Fourth Avenue amid a surging crowd of thousands of spectators with my team and a handful of volunteer handlers. If I wasn't a zombie from lack of sleep, I'd certainly be wondering if I wasn't finally in over my head.

Actually, the 20-mile run from Fourth Avenue in downtown Anchorage out to the VFW post in Eagle River is only ceremonial this year. The times won't count and the real race will start tomorrow at Wasilla. I'm not even using my regular sled, which I don't want to risk on the potentially rough trails over downtown streets.

I'll also be towing a second sled; this adds drag to keep the dogs from running too fast while they're still wildly enthusiastic. Ron has graciously agreed to ride my caboose today and also tomorrow from Wasilla to Knik; I can at least tap his experience for the first part of the race.

Moreover, I have a passenger in my front sled for the first eight miles today. The race organization decided to raise money this year by selling rides to the highest bidders. It was quite successful and all 58 mushers have a paying passenger. In all, the fares have raised more than $35,000 for the race.

My rider is a businessman from New York who is up here with three of his friends. They paid $500 each for what will certainly be a unique adventure, and I'll do my part not to disappoint them. My game plan is to let the dogs get over their initial excitement and then let my guest swap with Ron and ride the runners on the back sled for awhile.

Bert and the rest of my handling crew are on Fourth Avenue at eight in the morning; my actual start time isn't until about 10:45, which gives us plenty of time to get the dogs ready. The city has trucked in tons of snow to cover a mile of streets to get the teams onto the extensive municipal system of ski trails. I can't imagine what it must have cost.

My spot is directly across the street from Martin Buser, and there is a steady stream of admirers brushing by my team on their way to see him. The scene is absolute pandemonium, especially when the teams start moving up; they are parked so the first teams are farthest away and must pass all the others enroute to the starting line.

As usual, I've only gotten a couple hours' sleep and I'm running on black coffee and nerves. I hope my handlers will keep things in order because I'm not really all here. A few people lean over the temporary fence separating my dogs from the sidewalk and ask for autographs; I think I sign my own name but I'm not sure, and I'm even less certain why they'd want my signature when all the Big Names are close by.

Soon I see Martin getting ready across the street. The race officials tell me I've got 15 minutes to be ready to move. We've already got most of the dogs harnessed up; we've held off on Rocky and Rosie because they chew things when they're nervous, and if they're not nervous now, they'll never be.

Almost in a blur the handlers get the dogs hooked up; all I do is point where I want which ones. I decide to start with Pullman and Bea in lead. Bea isn't really a leader at all, but her brother Nuka is Diana Moroney's world-class lead dog and she comes from a long line of front-end dogs. She serves as an accelerator for other leaders, and may eventually learn the ropes on her own. Pullman is the real leader, but she's barely three years old and has never started off in a major crowd situation. She went to Nome with Vern Halter's team last year, but not in front.

The real reason they're leading is because they're the two who led me most of the way through the Knik 200 and the Copper Basin 300, and who have guided the team for most of the training over the past several months. I've still got Socks and old Slipper in reserve back in the team if I need them, as well as a couple of others who can run up front on the trail in a pinch. Anyway, all we've got to do is get a few blocks down Fourth Avenue and make the sharp right turn onto Cordova Street, where we'll be out of the main crowd area. I figure Pullman and Bea shouldn't have any trouble handling that.

Before I realize it, it's my turn. A race volunteer comes back to help guide us the two blocks to the starting line, which is marked by a huge banner and grandstands on either side, not to mention enough media vehicles to rival Camp O.J.. With a dozen handlers restraining the team, we join the procession to glory—or whatever. As we pass the other teams, I see people I've run with in the qualifying races and others I know only from reputation. Finally we pass Barrie, whose 57th position puts her almost in the starting chute.

Most of the pomp and ceremony and excitement goes right over my head. There is a huge to-do about Martin, directly in front of me. Part of this may be because his passenger for the first part of the run to Eagle River is the new Governor of Alaska, Tony Knowles. The Guv plays the crowd like the pro he is, as does Martin, who is no less the experienced showman, although I'm reasonably certain he'd rather be out on the trail away from the hoopla.

I watch in a trance as the starter gives Martin the traditional five-four-three-two-one-GO! countdown and his team explodes out of the chute and down the alley of snow in the middle of Fourth Av-

The author and handlers take a photo break on Fourth Avenue before the race start.

enue. I feel like a footnote to history as my team is finally led into the starting position. I vaguely hear my name called and catch a snatch of my brief biography, which the announcer gets wrong.

After we're in position with the snow hook set I quickly run up and talk to every dog, telling Pullman and Bea this is the real thing and not to do anything rash. I hear the starter give the one-minute warning and I walk back to the sled. Now the starter's countdown is for me, and before I know it we're off. Pullman is running well and all seems in order: the crowd is cheering, my passenger is smiling, and I even catch myself waving. So far, so good.

Then about two blocks down the street Pullman suddenly veers over the snow berm on the left and into the crowd, scattering bystanders like tenpins. She's apparently spooked by the mass of people and the general turmoil. I jam on the brake and ask Ron to keep the second sled anchored while I go up and get things reoriented. There's a minor tangle, which I get undone in maybe 30 seconds, and then I lead Pullman quickly back over the snow berm to the race course. I rush back to the sled and tell her to go and she immediately heads back toward the curb like she wants to put a nickel in the parking meter.

This time there's a tangle which takes me several minutes to straighten out, and two teams pass us. Luckily the crowd has moved back so I don't have to worry about shooing a lot of people out of the way. In fact, a couple of bystanders help me by lining out the dogs as I untangle them, which is perfectly legal under race rules. (Anyone can help control an unmanageable team, under which category mine definitely falls at the moment.)

After we're pointed the right way again, I unhook Pullman and switch her with Slipper, who has done all this before. I lead Slipper back onto the snow and head back for the sled. I don't even have to say anything and the old veteran leaps off down the street with the team in perfect order behind her to the cheers of the crowd, who no doubt have recorded everything on video. I'm not sure I want to see their footage.

Now we're moving out, swinging around the 90-degree corner onto Cordova Street, making good time as we pass clumps of spectators, all of whom wish us well. I'm starting to feel a lot better and even Ron is wearing a smile on the second sled behind me. Although the sun is shining brightly and the temperature is an unseasonably warm 25 degrees, the dogs don't even seem to notice they're pulling two sleds and three people. Luckily, I'm not carrying any gear in the front sled because of my passenger; gear could add another 100 pounds or more.

I'm still amazed at the power of the dogs, pulling their 600-pound-plus load with graceful ease. This is the first time I've run a team of 16—I only ran 14 in the Knik 200, and the Copper Basin only allowed 12—but it seems completely natural and I'm not worried about keeping them under control on the trail. I am glad, however, we're not starting with 20 dogs as in previous years; that would be just too much.

After a southbound run of 10 or 12 blocks we come to the hill at the end of Cordova Street leading down to the 200-mile city bike path network, which in the winter doubles as a maze of cross-country ski trails—and is occasionally used as a dog track. We pound down the hill and onto the perfectly groomed trail as if we actually knew what we're doing. The bike path runs along the extensive city greenbelt system and there are fewer people down here; the dogs relax and so do I. We're on our way at last.

After another half mile or so I figure the team has settled down enough to let my passenger from the Big Apple get a taste of the real thing. We've already talked this over, and as soon as I stop he and Ron swap places. We're off again in less than 15 seconds, with my passenger-turned-instant-musher hanging on for dear life on the second sled. He quickly seems to get the knack of it and keeps things in reasonable order as we roar around a couple of sharp turns. I look back now and again and I think he's smiling, but I'm not sure.

I certainly hope he's enjoying it, because not many mushers are letting their guests ride the runners today. If he can go home and tell everyone back east how much the dogs enjoy this, maybe we can overcome some of the bad press the animal rights crazies have heaped on the race in the past few years. Besides, the race can always use new supporters to offset our horrendous loss of major sponsors over the past year or two, most of whom have been scared off by groups like Friends of Animals and the Humane Society of the United States and their single-issue cohorts, who are apparently more interested in raising money for themselves than in trying to understand what it's like to run dogs.

We all know the Iditarod is a vulnerable target for these people, who would have every dog be nothing more than a "companion animal" to lie around and get fat and lazy and probably die early from boredom and too many table leftovers. To my dogs, such enforced inactivity would be a fate worse than death. Running is as natural to them as flying is to birds. They're smart, inquisitive animals and they live for the trail. They even get bored when we run the same training trail too often.

Some mushers have suggested the "animaniacs" establish their credibility by going after heavyweights like greyhound or horse racing. Both of these are high-stakes, money-oriented industries which have little room for mediocrity in their animals and even less patience for meddling do-gooders. If the animal-rights folks did poke their noses into their neighborhood horse tracks or greyhound emporia, they'd probably receive intimidating visits from menacing squads of corporate lawyers in expensive suits with shiny black briefcases and no sense of humor, urging them to direct their well-meaning attentions elsewhere, or else. The Iditarod doesn't operate that way, although it's certainly a thought to bear in mind. In the meantime, we far-from-affluent mushers can only head on down the trail and try to circle our sleds when the heat gets too intense.

Soon we reach the dropoff point for my passenger, who seems mildly dazed by the whole experience, but is apparently happy. Ron hops back on the second sled and we roar off toward Eagle River. After a few more miles we slowly pull up on Wayne Curtis and his purebred Siberians. My guys are a little faster than his, and just like in the Knik 200 and the Copper

Basin 300 he lets me by. His leaders immediately start chasing my team and we run together for five or six miles, until his team gets distracted at a congested road crossing and takes a wrong turn.

Ron and I basically have the trail to ourselves for the rest of the way into Eagle River. The weather couldn't be more beautiful (if on the warm side) and the dogs have never run better. If the rest of the race is anything like this, I'll be kicking myself for not doing it sooner. As we cruise across the snow-covered Moose Run golf course on the Fort Richardson Army post I remark to Ron I've always wanted to run a dog team from Anchorage to Eagle River (where I lived for six years), but I never figured it would be in the Iditarod.

The leg from Anchorage to Eagle River is a favorite for spectators. Teams are pulling two sleds for this stretch. Here the author and neighbor Ron Aldrich (on second sled) pass a group of well-wishers.

After a tricky section leading down to the crossing of the town's namesake stream, we haul up the long hill to the Eagle River VFW post, which has been the traditional first checkpoint for the Iditarod since the race's inception. Like the other 20-odd teams ahead of us—and the 30 or so behind us—we receive a rousing reception. The first 20 miles of the race are under our belt. Even if it's just been ceremonial and the times aren't officially recorded, we're still on our way.

Bert and Reb and Kim and Mike and Julie and all the rest of my endlessly patient handlers/sponsors are out here to put the dogs back in the truck. I'm inexplicably tired, probably from lack of sleep as well as the heat. I didn't realize it on the way out but I got extremely warm in my heavy-duty arctic gear, which will keep me toasty down to 40 below or worse. The entire ensemble is constructed to wick away moisture in order to keep the layers next to the skin as dry as possible, so I've never noticed how much I've been sweating.

I've been warned about this loss of moisture and the risk of dehydration, but I never fully realized how insidiously it can manifest itself. And if it affects me this way, how must the dogs feel in their permanent cold-weather outfits? I wander into the refreshment area and down a half-gallon of Tang without even thinking about it. If this happens out on the trail, away from ready sources of water, I can see how I could be in real trouble. Samuel Taylor Coleridge could never have imagined how true his ancient mariner's complaint would ring here in the frozen north country: "Water, water everywhere, but not a drop to drink." At least I'll have my trusty Thermos, and there's always my alcohol cooker, which can melt three gallons of water from snow in 15 minutes.

But today is done and I can continue my last-minute errands. Unlike previous years, when the teams were loaded up at Eagle River and trucked immediately out to Wasilla for the restart only four hours later, we have a respite until tomorrow morning. This development resulted from a dearth of snow in Anchorage and Wasilla just before last year's race. The start in Anchorage was limited to six dogs running a mere 16 blocks or so, down to the bottom of the Cordova Street hill. The restart was moved all the way out to Willow, 20 miles northwest of Wasilla, the closest place with enough snow to permit a link to the Iditarod "main line" west of the Susitna River. Because it would have been impractical to move the dogs and thousands of spectators the 60-plus miles from Anchorage to Willow over a congested, mostly two-lane highway, the restart was postponed a full day.

Sleds make good places to catch naps. Tired mushers sleep in, on, and beside their sleds on the trail to Nome. Here the author rests after the run to Eagle River.

The 24-hour delay before the restart proved to be a smashing success, and the format was formalized this year with Wasilla resuming its normal role as the restart location. For the mushers and the dogs, it's a godsend, allowing an easy shake-out run from Anchorage to Eagle River, followed by a full night's sleep for the drivers and some quality rest for the dogs before heading out on the real trail.

For me, the extra day is a necessity so I can find the last items I need to complete my mail-out packages as well as my gear for the sled. By design, I didn't use my real sled this morning; for that matter, neither did most of the mushers. My good Willis sled (actually it belongs to Bert and has been to Nome twice already) has been completely overhauled and is waiting at Bert's for the ride out to tomorrow's restart.

Like all rookies, I wanted to take so much gear it would never fit into the sled and would likely break the dogs' backs if it did. Bert and Kim helped me weed out the unnecessary stuff, which fills a couple of good-sized boxes, but I've still got a steamer trunk full of odds and ends of dubious utility, but which I feel I'll really need somewhere out there.

Bert assures me I'll have a truckload of stuff to dump by the time I get to Skwentna. He insists I take a bag for just that purpose, ready to be stuffed full of previously essential gear and mailed back to town from the Skwentna checkpoint, which also happens to be the post office. I've seen it happen every year while I've been flying for the race, so I don't know why I'm shocked I might have grossly overestimated my own equipment requirements. But this is different—this is me doing it now and I just can't see how anyone could ever survive on the trail without all of these things. Bert just smiles at my rookie foibles; as he says, he's been there, done that, and there's not much he can do except let me find out for myself.

I finally get to sleep at four a.m. after sorting everything from batteries to booties into bags to be mailed out to the remote checkpoints. I'll only get a few hours' sleep, but at least I got everything done. Now I'm ready to head out on the trail. No more false starts—the next countdown will be the real one.

March 5, 1995—The Iditarod: Wasilla to Knik (14 miles)
Knik to Yentna Station (50 miles)

Yesterday was the rehearsal; today it's show time. When I leave the starting chute in Wasilla in a few hours I'll be well and truly on my way to Nome. By nightfall I'll certainly find out if the months of training have paid off. In any case, there's no turning back now.

I only get three hours of sleep; I'm still groggy when I meet Bert and Kim at a local donut shop for a quick cup of coffee and a sugar fix before we head out to Wasilla. We go over our checklists to make sure we've remembered everything; there have been instances where harried, hurried mushers have shown up at races without things like harnesses, ganglines, and even sleds.

On the 30-mile drive to Wasilla I pass the dog trucks of a dozen mushers, most of whom I recognize. At the old airstrip in Wasilla where the restart will happen, I find a much more informal arrangement than on Fourth Avenue yesterday. The crowds are downrange near the starting chute and along the 14-mile trail to Knik, which parallels a main road for most of its route. The marshaling area is pretty much left to the mushers, which is a blessing because everyone has a lot of packing and serious last-minute preparations to complete.

Almost immediately we realize we have forgotten the bag containing the dog blankets, which I will almost certainly need for some of the thinner-coated dogs. Bert whips out his cellular phone and calls wife Reb, who is standing by for just such a contingency. She says she'll be out well before I move into the starting chute, along with some frozen herring for me to feed the dogs enroute to Skwentna—something else we forgot about.

In the meantime, we go through another sled packing drill, during which Kim tosses out another 20 pounds or so of my hitherto absolutely essential gear as Bert looks on in amusement. I don't dispute her judgment

A stream of mushers passes an impromptu fly-in trail party on the Yentna River. Hundreds of people make their way out along the first hundred miles of the Iditarod in skiplanes, on snowmachines, or even behind their own dog teams to watch the race.

since I'm only running on a couple of cylinders at the moment. Looking at the still-bulging sled bag after she's done, I'm sure I'll still have more than enough to get me through whatever the trail has to offer.

The blankets and herring arrive as advertised, and before I realize it I see Martin's nattily attired and professional-looking handlers hooking up his team for the run down to the starting chute. Like yesterday, he's surrounded by a crush of well-wishers and a cloud of media people. I'm glad they're pestering him and not me; I doubt I could provide them two coherent words.

Now we're in the chute like yesterday, deja vu all over again except Slipper and Bea are up front; I don't want any sudden dives into the crowd today. Ron is on the second sled, but this time there's no passenger up front. We'll drop the back sled at Knik and I plan to move on from there as quickly as is decently possible.

"Five-four-three-two-one-GO!" and we're off. Slipper and Bea rocket down the starting chute—for about 50 feet. Then they stop while Slipper relieves herself in a ladylike manner right in front of about 1,000 spectators. Ron and I just look at each other; there's not a lot to be done when Nature calls, especially when the called party is one of your lead dogs.

Having tended to business, Slipper responds smartly when I yell "Okay!" and we're off again, the amused good wishes of the crowd ringing in our ears. Just like yesterday, I'm sure somebody caught everything on video; I hope Slipper's answer to the call of the wild doesn't wind up on "America's Funniest Home Videos," or if it does, that my name isn't mentioned.

Once we're out of the starting area we cross the busy Parks Highway as the crossing guards frantically shovel snow onto the road for the sleds even while they hold back 20 or 30 cars. Then we roll out onto frozen Lake Lucille, where the Junior Iditarod started and finished a week ago. Clumps of people are scattered all along the trail, some on snowmachines, some with their cars, some on skis, and some even with their own dog teams. They all wish us a good trip, and I sincerely hope their wishes come true.

The run down to Knik goes remarkably smoothly. We're only passed by a couple of teams, which I take as a good omen. Once again I overtake Wayne Curtis and his Siberians and we trade good-natured jibes about the relative merits of our teams. I'm sure I'll be seeing more of Wayne out on the trail because our teams are quite closely matched in most respects.

As we pull onto the lake in front of the bar at Knik, I think to myself how far things have come in the two months since I blasted out of here on the Knik 200. The next 100 miles of trail will be more than familiar, an advantage I can certainly use to help me get everything sorted out for the trail beyond.

Bert and Kim grab the leaders as soon as I check in and lead the team off to the side so we can drop the second sled as well as a bulky bag of booties I've decided I won't need because of the spring-like temperatures and excellent trail conditions. Within five minutes I pull the hook and Slipper and Bea are leading us across the lake and around the old Knik museum, out onto the original Iditarod.

At last we're embarked on the real journey to Nome, leaving the road system behind. The trail is superb and we make excellent time. We're passed by a couple more teams, but not nearly as many as I'd feared. The dogs are cruising marvelously and I can honestly say I'm enjoying the ride. If we can hold this pace, we'll be in Skwentna by midnight, a respectable first day's run.

About seven miles out of Knik I make a quick stop (on Seven Mile Lake, naturally) to throw some herring to the dogs for a snack. Fish is an excellent hot-weather snack because it's got lots of moisture and protein, just what the dogs need to counteract their own dehydration.

While I'm stopped, I cinch up the pistol and cartridge belt I've borrowed from Bert. We've been warned about heavy moose concentrations on the trail and every musher is armed. In my case, I'm packing a

Even wide-open trails on major rivers can conceal dangers. The crossed trail stakes here warn of open water just off the trail up the Yentna River to Skwentna.

.357 magnum around my waist like an Old West gunfighter. I hope I don't have to use it, because it'll mean I've got bigger problems than just figuring out how to get it unlimbered and pointed in the right direction.

After the fish break, we're off again; Nine-Mile Hill is the next landmark, and the dogs take it at a lope. Coming down the other side, though, I notice that the cartridge belt feels a little light on my hips. I check quickly and find that the pistol and its holster aren't there any more. The only thing I can figure is that the holster simply broke loose from the belt somewhere back down the trail.

I briefly consider turning around to go find it, but realize I'd probably cause more trouble running into outbound teams. Besides, it's almost a certainty that a musher behind me will find it and bring it on to the next checkpoint at Yentna Station, and the race organization can return it to me up the trail somewhere. In any case, I sincerely doubt I'll really need it;

Ron has run seven Iditarods without a firearm, and I've never needed one on any of my races so far.

So, I press on into the wilderness unarmed. Actually, I figure the dogs will appreciate not having to tote the extra few pounds. They certainly seem to run a little better as we roll on across the Little Susitna River and past the "Nome 1049 Miles" sign I remember from the Knik 200—this time, of course, it's for real.

As we approach Flathorn Lake, about 35 miles out from Knik, I'm passed by several of the top-20 fast movers, including my neighbor John Barron; the dog he gave me, little Maybelline, is running like a champ even though she's barely 20 months old. I'm impressed at the speed and power of their teams, which have a several-mile-an-hour advantage over my second-stringers. As in the Copper Basin 300, I'm definitely drifting to the back of the pack, but at least there will be lots of room back there.

Just past Flathorn Lake, where the trail enters a belt of trees before crossing a two-mile-long swamp, I hear enough barking ahead for what must be two dozen teams. Apparently everyone has had the same idea: give the dogs a break here before heading out onto the Susitna River for the run up to Skwentna. I figure my guys can use a break from the scorching temperatures and pull into an inviting side trail when we reach the tree line. I unhook the dogs' tuglines and let them cool off in the deep snow while I dig out some more herring for them to munch on.

While I'm there Wayne pulls into the next turnoff. We chat awhile and agree to try to run together on up the trail after everything stabilizes, and then he pulls out. I follow 15 minutes later and we head out onto the wide-open swamp, which has been packed into a boulevard maybe 300 feet wide by the myriad of dog teams and snowmachines that have stopped there over the past couple of months.

About halfway across the expanse, Slipper begins to drift over to the right side of the packed area, apparently following her nose to one of the places where other teams have stopped and snacked. When I try to call her back over to the main trail, she swings completely around to the right and heads back the way we've just come. I notice I'm not the only driver with this problem: one of the Japanese mushers is trying to get his team pointed westward as well.

I stop the team and run up and line everyone out in the proper direction. However, when I give the "Okay!" Slipper comes around to the right again and I have to repeat the procedure. We do this a few more times until I finally just let her keep coming around in a full circle. We cut a couple more doughnuts on the wide-open dance floor before I finally get her headed off the swamp to the west. I hope this isn't a harbinger of things to come; just in case, I decide to put Pullman in the lead at Skwentna, now that we're away from the crowds.

Things go more smoothly out on the river. The trail is wide and well marked and Slipper keeps up a good pace. As night falls I pull out my headlamp and use it to spot the trail markers, four-foot pieces of wooden lath with bands of reflective yellow tape. In the headlamp's beam, the markers are visible for a mile ahead, making it almost impossible to get lost in the dark.

I know Slipper is getting on in years (she's 10) and her night vision is failing. However, Bea has always acted as a sort of seeing-eye partner for her and we've never had any problems at night. Now, though, Slipper keeps wandering to the right, off the beaten path and onto the less-packed snowmachine trails paralleling the mainline. Still, there's no real problem because all of the trails are going to the same place and rejoin each other every few hundred yards. Nevertheless, I think putting Pullman back up front for tomorrow's run makes good sense.

Almost before I realize it, we're at Yentna Station, the first checkpoint on the river. This is one of the checkpoints to which we couldn't ship anything this year, but there's still a full staff of checkers and vets, as well as straw to bed down the dogs if we want to rest. There are a dozen teams still there when we arrive. When I pull in I tell the checkers to keep the team out of the straw because I intend to go out fairly quickly, and I don't want the dogs to get settled in.

I also ask about the pistol I lost back down the trail; they say it was picked up and returned to race headquarters, and the race judges will probably decide to get it back to me at Rainy Pass or Rohn. I'm relieved, not so much at having the pistol to defend against moose, but because it belongs to Bert and I'd have felt bad about losing it. I quickly set up the alcohol cooker and heat some water to mix with the dry dog food; the dogs will certainly need the water after their hot trip this afternoon.

While the dogs are eating and resting I wander into the lodge where the checkpoint is located. The race judge here is Bernie Willis, who built the sled I'm running and whom I know. He says the race is moving very quickly and there haven't been any problems so far. I go back out to check on the dogs just as Barrie pulls in; she says she's going to move straight on to Skwentna, and I wish her luck and tell her I'll see her there.

Back in the checkpoint I talk with Bernie while I wolf down a plate of spaghetti and a quart of Tang. Then I stretch out for a quick nap to rest my cracked rib, which is bothering me again. I also ache all

over and feel as if I'm coming down with a bad cold. But I've made
it to the first remote checkpoint in good order, and I figure I've
earned a little respite. Before I realize it, I fall fast asleep curled up
against the wall behind the stove.

March 6, 1995—The Iditarod: Yentna Station to Skwentna (35 miles)
Skwentna to Finger Lake (45 miles)

When I finally wake up I discover I've overslept and finally pull out of
Yentna Station just after midnight, about four hours after I arrived. I know
this was probably too long a stay, but rationalize the dogs can always use
the rest. The run to Skwentna should only take another four hours, which
I figure we easily can do nonstop. We still won't be very far behind my
schedule, and should be able to move on to Finger Lake and Rainy Pass
by noon.

One of the assistant checkers leads the team out of the checkpoint and
we accelerate onto the outbound trail. The crescent moon has set and my
headlight provides almost the only illumination on the half-mile-wide
river ahead. We have the broad trail entirely to ourselves and we make
excellent time.

Five miles later Slipper starts veering to the right again, and this time
she gets us almost to the river bank on an obscure track leading up to
somebody's cabin before I realize where she's going. When I turn the
team around, the males in the back of the team suddenly pull the snow
hook and surge up into the females. A massive tangle ensues in the waist-
deep snow, and it's so complex I can't readily get into it to start sorting
it out.

While I'm working to get a handle on things a spat breaks out among
half a dozen of the females. To my surprise, they've all ganged up on
Pullman; by the time I can get her out of it she is terrified, although not
really hurt. This bothers me because she may be too spooked now to lead
effectively for awhile. But I don't have time to worry about Pullman
because while I've been breaking up the fight Yankee has gotten rather
intimately involved with Blues, who is apparently a lot more in heat than
I realized.

This is not good, but I'm able to get the team straightened out while the
two lovebirds are consummating their shotgun marriage. On the bright
side, I was going to breed Blues anyway, and Yankee was a leading suitor.
I just wish he could have waited until Skwentna.

Once we're back on the trail things are reasonably orderly for another
four or five miles, when Slipper again veers onto a side trail. This time I

decide enough is enough and put Pullman up front with Blackie, one of the males I borrowed from Steve Adkins. Pullman seems reluctant, but Blackie is eager and starts the team. Once we're underway, Pullman seems to be doing okay and we cruise for perhaps another 15 miles.

Then for no apparent reason Pullman simply slows down, pulls off to the left side of the trail, and lies down. I try to coax her into going on but she doesn't want to move. She's not tired, and all I can think of is she's just scared of the females behind her in the team who apparently have it in for her.

I start to swap leaders around, but discover nothing works. Even Slipper and Bea won't go; they are both in heat and just turn around to try to get to the males. The males have become completely crazy trying to get to the females, and every time I pull the snow hook to try to get the team

A dozen teams are already resting at the Yentna Station checkpoint, 20 miles up the Yentna River and the first checkpoint off the road system. Most will spend less than an hour here before moving on to Skwentna, 35 miles upriver.

to go, they surge up into the females and I have to jump to keep a major tangle—and more Iditapups—from happening. I even try to put old Socks up front with Blackie, but the two amorous males immediately turn around and head for the females behind them.

I continue to swap leaders and use every trick I know to get the team started. I try to pull the leaders by hand to get them going, but the hormone-driven males in the rear of the team always pull the sled up into the females before I can run even a few steps. I sort out a dozen tangles—with a couple of attendant snapping matches—resulting from my efforts to get going. However, nobody is hurt and I've still got plenty of time; I reason a cooling-off period won't hurt so I just sit down on the sled and wait.

While I'm biding my time, a couple of other teams come by. Fellow rookie Kjell Risung says he's also having leader problems, but at least he's moving. I hope my dogs will follow one of the passing teams and get us on into Skwentna, but they don't. Pretty soon I'm all alone on the river; I know I'm fairly close to Skwentna, but if I can't get the team to move I might as well be on Mars.

After awhile I stretch out on the sled and nap. In a few hours I wake up as the first hint of dawn tints the sky behind me. I rouse the dogs and start switching leaders again. On about the tenth try I pair up Weasel and Maybelline; neither is really a start-up leader but Weasel is spayed and Maybelline isn't in heat, and I've tried everyone else.

Sure enough, little Maybelline, who never ceases to amaze me, jumps off on her own as soon as we're ready and Weasel joins in. We're on our way—several hours behind schedule and with leaders who aren't leaders—but at least we're moving. With Maybelline bouncing and playing up front, we roar the last five miles into Skwentna, arriving in grand style about 7:30. The checkers ask where I've been, and I just tell them I've had a little problem with some dogs in heat. They shake their heads knowingly and lead the team to a vacant line of straw.

I get the dogs settled down and locate my food drop bags. I heat some water and start the dogs off with a quart of so of soup to combat dehydration. They all drink and eat ravenously and I feed them as much as they can stand, to the approval of the hovering vets, who are watching carefully for tired dogs after yesterday's hot afternoon run.

Talking with Ben Jacobson, another pilot and rookie musher from the Eagle River area, I decide not to leave until after the heat of the afternoon. I have to think the previous two days of hot weather have worn the dogs out more than I realize, and Ben is of the same opinion about his team. We decide to let the dogs rest in the sun during the day and plan to pull the hooks about four p.m. for the run up to Finger Lake and Rainy Pass. Ben and I feel it will be best if we run together for awhile; after all, two heads are better than one, especially when neither head is thinking quite correctly from fatigue and dehydration.

While I'm feeding the dogs, my friends Rich and Jeanette Keida find me. They were on the handler team at Wasilla and flew out last night in their Cessna, expecting to meet me here about midnight. When I didn't show up, they waited the night in the New Skwentna Roadhouse and came out to see if I'd arrive this morning. I explain to them about my leader problems and apologize for not keeping to my advertised schedule. They can't help me with the dogs (no outside assistance is allowed to mushers) but the moral support is most welcome.

I wander up to the checkpoint, located this year as always in the spacious cabin of Joe and Norma Delia. Joe is Skwentna's permanent postmaster and has played genial host to just about everyone in this end of the valley at one time or another. He's been the checker here since the first Iditarod, and is as much a fixture of the race as the traditional start on Fourth Avenue and the burled arch on Front Street in Nome. I've met him

As many as 50 teams can be bedded down on the Skwentna River in front of Joe and Norma Delia's cabin. The Skwentna checkpoint is a popular viewing spot for race fans flying out from Anchorage, who often clog the small nearby airport with up to a hundred light planes.

many times in the past, usually while flying for the race. He doesn't immediately recognize me because of my post-retirement beard, but then he recalls me from my Iditarod Air Force days.

Inside Joe's comfortable house, some of the local ladies are providing breakfast to mushers and race volunteers, and I gratefully wolf down a stack of pancakes and some excellent sausage, along with enough water and Tang to float a battleship. Then I pull off my outer parka and bib, which are soaked with moisture—mostly my own sweat wicked away from the inner layers—and stretch out on the floor for a long nap.

When I wake up there are only three teams left on the river: mine, Ben Jacobson's, and Tim Triumph's; Tim pulled in shortly after I did but I didn't really notice him because I was so focused on my own dogs. I find Ben and we get ready to move out at four o'clock; Tim says he's going to try to get out ahead of us and we wish him well.

We're ready to go at four. Ben gets his team out of the checkpoint without any problems, but Slipper and Bea, now back in lead, balk and turn into the nearest pile of leftovers. I need some help from the checker to get us pointed out of town, and by the time I'm on the outbound trail Ben is a couple of miles ahead. I don't expect him to wait; I figure I'll catch him at Finger Lake, after which we can run together to Rainy Pass and points beyond, like we'd planned.

A couple of miles out I meet Tim; he's headed back inbound with a sick dog he wants to drop. I tell him I'll see him up the trail and not to worry about us getting too far ahead of him. We all need to hang together back here in the caboose.

Slipper and Bea and the rest of the team are running like the solid unit they should be. The nightmare of the previous evening fades and I put it out of my mind. I decide it will be a good idea to drop Blues and Rosie, the two females most obviously in heat, at Rainy Pass, but they're pulling well for the time being and I see no need to cut my power if I don't need to.

We cruise smoothly across the Skwentna River and toward the Shell Hills, making excellent time toward the Finger Lake checkpoint, 45 miles from Skwentna. After three hours I stop the team at dusk and give them chunks of chicken, which they polish off quickly. After a 30-minute breather we're off again, heading west into the twilight.

About half an hour later, just after dark, Slipper stops for no reason at all. All my fears from the previous night flood back. I begin the process of switching leaders, but nothing works, not even Weasel and Maybelline. The males and females are completely infatuated with each other and nothing I can do seems to distract them. After four solid hours of manipulating and swapping and coaxing all I have to show for my efforts are several major tangles, another girls-only squabble with Pullman the target, and two more litters of pups on the way, this time from Slipper (courtesy of Rocky) and Bea (from master Socks).

Toward midnight the moon sets and I'm at my wit's end. Just then Tim Triumph pulls up behind me. He says he's having leader problems, but I don't think he's having anything approaching what I've got on my hands. I help him get his team around me in the hopes my dogs will follow his. When he pulls out, mine actually take off after him for maybe 200 yards, but then stop again. I yell to Tim to keep going and to tell the checker at Finger Lake I'll camp out here tonight if I can't get the team going again.

After another hour or so of fruitless motivation attempts, I give up for the night and make the dogs some soup. I sit on the sled bag for awhile watching the dogs curl up to sleep and think for the first time about how far back I'm dropping in relation to the rest of the pack. I'm in dead last and am stopped cold again for who knows how long.

I slowly admit to myself the problem with the females in heat—I now have six of them—is much more serious than I'd first believed. The female leaders are all affected and aren't reliable; I can't put my male leaders up front because they just turn around and go back for the females. What's worse, the heat cycle lasts for 21 days, and is only likely to get worse. If I can't get the team to start, much less keep them moving reliably, there's no way I can continue the race. On this depressing thought I crawl onto the sled bag in my arctic gear and collapse; I sleep soundly until the sun comes up five hours later. My dreams are not pleasant.

March 7, 1995—The Iditarod: Finger Lake to Rainy Pass (30 miles)

The bright dawn wakes me about 7:30, beautifully illuminating the Alaska Range to the west in the rich, low-angle morning light. To me, the mountains now represent the impossible dream; I don't see how I'll ever get there, much less through them and into the vast interior of Alaska beyond. Just behind me, I can see we passed Shell Hills last night, which means we were making excellent time before the wheels came off.

I fire up the alcohol cooker and melt more snow for water, as much for me as for the dogs. I inadvertently left my Thermos back at Skwentna, loaded with half a gallon of precious drinking water, and I'm plenty thirsty. I improvise a makeshift water container with a soft cooler normally intended to carry a six-pack of beer. I've brought several of the collapsible containers because they can be kept warm by tossing in a couple of charcoal hand warmer packets and I use them for medicines, film, and batteries I don't want to freeze.

As the snow melts in the cooker pot, I dip a couple of quarts of still-cold water into a gallon-size freezer storage bag, press it shut, and put it in the soft cooler. Then I fire up a few charcoal hand warmers, of which I brought dozens because they're so useful, and put them inside. I don't think the manufacturers of the cooler or the heaters ever quite intended them for this kind of application, but it works. I figure I'll buy another real Thermos at McGrath if I ever get there.

After I mix up warm food for the dogs and get the sled repacked I start the endless round of find-the-leader again. Slipper is cranky after her night in the snow and snaps at any other dog who gets close. Bea is more personable, but she won't start the team by herself. About 10 a.m. I finally put Pullman back up front, even though I don't think she's going to go.

When I hook up Pullman, Slipper is right behind her in the swing position. Slipper seems to have a grudge against Pullman and promptly tries to bite her in the tail, which causes Pullman to start forward with a jerk. With Slipper and the other females growling behind her, Pullman takes off, apparently running for her life. Unbelievably, we're moving again, although not in the manner I'd quite intended.

After a few miles, though, Pullman settles into her normal leading routine and Slipper and the rest of the female heat (or hit?) squad quiet down. It looks like we're back on the trail, and I'm overjoyed because we'll cruise into Finger Lake and on to Rainy Pass in no time at this clip. I'm back in the race and we're making up time.

Now I can relax and look at the scenery and appreciate where we are. I suddenly realize we're within five miles of my 40 acres of wilderness land on Red Creek, where I hope to finish a cabin one of these years. I staked it out with a couple of friends 12 years ago, picking out the land I wanted and then brushing out the boundary lines with a machete and a hand compass. I fly out here frequently during the summer in my little float plane to visit my neighbors' working homestead and to just sit on my 200-foot bluff above the creek looking at the storybook view of Denali to the north.

I wish I had time to detour over to the property. We'd planned to make a trip out there with the dogs before the race, but we were overtaken by events, primarily my cracked rib. Now I wish we'd found some way to make the four-day out-and-back from Montana Creek; the experience of being out on the trail would have been good for the dogs and for me as well, and I might have learned how to anticipate some of the problems I've run into the past couple of days.

But now I have to refocus on the task at hand—keep the dogs running until I get to Rainy Pass, where I'll obviously have to drop several of them. Fortunately, this part of the trail is in remarkably good condition and we're really cruising. For the most part, it's a snow-packed highway maybe six or eight feet wide, running up long snow-covered meadows and cutting through the occasional stand of birch and spruce.

The dogs are thoroughly enjoying themselves and have apparently forgotten about the sex bomb which seems to detonate every time we stop. For now, I have almost nothing to do except stand on the runners in the glorious sunshine and silently thank whoever is listening up there for getting me back in the race.

A little after noon we drop down onto Finger Lake and steam into the checkpoint. The checkers are there to meet me, again wondering where I've been. Tim Triumph is still there and he's glad I made it; he was concerned after my guys wouldn't follow him last night but he had to try to keep his own team moving. I explain about the unexpected slumber party back at Shell Hills and say I want to move on to Rainy Pass as soon as I can. The dogs can't be tired—after all, they've done a lot more resting than running since we left Wasilla.

Some remote Iditarod checkpoints are little more than tents thrown up next to a frozen river or lake where skiplanes can land.

It's barely 30 miles to Rainy Pass Lodge, the next checkpoint. The dogs are moving well and I've got time to make up. I think about dropping Blues and Rosie and maybe even Bea and Slipper, the main actors in the ongoing sex scandal, but decide to wait until Rainy Pass since they're pulling strongly for now and I may need them on the long ascent I know is coming. I tell the checker I'm just going to snack the team and keep moving without dropping any dogs, but I'll need more Heet for my alcohol cooker.

While the assistant checker is getting the Heet, I chat for a minute with one of the chief pilots for the Iditarod Air Force, for which I flew last year. He wishes me well and I tell him I hope to be flying next year after I get this trip completed. We're ready to go barely 20 minutes later. The checker takes the leaders' tuglines and runs the dogs out of the holding area, past the inviting straw and distracting bits of food left by previous teams. Pullman and Bea hesitate, but pick up after maybe 50 yards of pacing by the checker, who is quickly out of breath. I thank him profusely for his help as we head off the lake and into the woods.

We quickly leave the checkpoint behind. The team is running as if nothing untoward ever happened, keeping up a solid 10-mile-an-hour pace. This is the team I've trained all year and I finally start to believe we're back on track.

The trail meanders through the woods and down onto two-mile-long Red Lake, then up a long draw onto a wooded plateau leading to the infamous Happy River. The dogs show no sign of flagging despite the bright sun and temperatures nearing the thirties. Fortunately, enough of the trail is in cool shadow to keep the sun from heating the dogs' dark fur coats.

We periodically break out of the woods onto easy open swales where I can see we are making significant progress into the mountains. Then we plunge back into the forest for another mile or two of twisting excitement as I try to dodge trees and ruts, not always successfully. The dogs seem to be enjoying the run as well, looking off to the sides of the trail. Every tugline is tight and we are covering ground quickly.

After 10 miles or so the trail begins to dip into gullies as it approaches the main declivity to Happy River. The Happy River steps are a series of several precipitous sidehill cuts by which the trail descends a couple of hundred feet to the Happy River at its junction with the Skwentna River. Every year numerous mushers crash and burn here; the spot is notorious enough for cameramen to go to great lengths to make the trip out on snowmachines and helicopters for action shots of mushers in various states of disarray. I've seen some of the clips from previous years and I wish I hadn't: sleds and mushers hurtling through thin air, wrapped around trees, rolling end over end down the impossibly steep slope beside the narrow trail.

There won't be any media vultures here today, though—they're all up the trail with the leaders. I'll have to do this without an appreciative audience. Of course, I have no idea what condition the steps are in, especially after they have been battered and gouged by almost 60 other teams and who knows how many snowmachines. I've become completely fatalistic about it all. The only thing I can do is slow the team down as much as I can and hope I can keep the sled slick side down between the curbs.

I'm anticipating the steps, which are still a mile or so ahead, when the team shoots down a draw into a 50-foot-deep gully. As I stomp on the brake I catch a glimpse of an overhanging tree on the right side of the trail. The dogs swing abruptly into a right turn at the bottom of the ravine and cut the sled straight for the snag.

I have about half a second to avoid disaster. I try to throw the sled over onto its side but miss by a hairsbreadth. The handlebar catches on a protruding knob and the sled comes to a instant stop, suspended about an inch off the trail. The dogs are still pulling, keeping the gangline quiveringly taut. Several fingers of my right hand are jammed between the handlebar and the tree and even through my glove I can feel the beginnings of pain.

With some difficulty I lever my fingers loose; I'll worry about them later—at least they don't feel broken. This is a very interesting situation, especially considering dog teams don't go backward—not easily, anyway—which is what I will need to back the handlebar off the snag on which it's hung up. I'm not even to Happy River and I've already got a mess on my hands.

Looking at the tree, one solution pops into my mind. I can get my ax out of the sled bag and hack the four-inch protrusion off. Before I start swinging with a sharp blade in a confined space at a branch under immense tension, though, I figure it's worth a try to see if I can yank the dogs back momentarily even an inch or so. I go around and grab the wheel dogs' tuglines and yell "Back!" Surprisingly, they yield an inch or two. The handlebar slips down a little on its obstruction and I go back to see if I can work it off.

As I take hold of the handlebar to try to work it free, the team figures it's time to go and gives a tremendous lurch forward. The rotten wood of the snag suddenly splinters and the sled shoots off with my previously damaged fingers wrapped around the handlebar, ensuring they receive yet another blow from the vengeful tree as we careen off toward Happy River.

In another 10 minutes we finally come to the dreaded Happy River steps, marked by a handmade sign inscribed "Hill Ahead" and illustrated with a stair-step line. I stop the team to make last-minute mental preparations and to make peace with whomever seems appropriate. Then I tell the dogs to go, with the brake applied as hard as I can stomp it into the yielding snow.

The first step is a sharp downgrade with a very deep rut, which we negotiate surprisingly easily. The passage of the teams ahead of me has actually helped, because my sled settles into the foot-deep trench in the middle of the trail as if it were on railroad tracks. The second step is a 100-foot sidehill carved diagonally down a 70-degree bluff; again, everything stays stable and upright thanks to the brake-gouged ditch which confines us. The third and fourth steps are equally anticlimactic and before I realize it we're out on the ice of Happy River headed downstream. It's a shame the photographers weren't here—I would have loved to see their looks of disappointment at my relatively dignified passage. I've either been lucky or good, but at least I'm still in one piece.

After another half mile we come to the flip side of the steps: the Happy River hill. This is a quarter-mile upgrade leading from the riverbed up a narrow draw at about a 45-degree grade. The sides of the trail at the bottom of the hill have been wiped out and the sled slides off despite my best efforts. I manage to get it upright, but now I've got another problem: the team won't pull up the grade. I figure it's mostly the heat—it's almost 40 degrees and the entire hill is in full sunlight—so I have to dismount and walk the leaders up the slope.

As soon as I start the ascent, the males in the rear pull the sled up into the females and I have another major tangle on my hands. Fifteen minutes later I manage to get the team lined out on a part of the hill steep enough so the males can't catch up easily. Painfully slowly, I walk the team up the killing slope. I'm so hot I strip off my coat and hat and unzip my fleece liner. And if I'm this warm, the dogs must be miserable.

After half an hour of stop-and-go plodding we crest the hill and I quickly find a place to rest the dogs in the shade. I undo their tuglines and let them lie in the cool snow while I unlimber the alcohol cooker to make water, as much for me as for them. I make a quick soup for them, which they appreciate; I figure this is just what they need to get moving again.

After 45 minutes of quality rest, I hook them back up and try to go, but my nemesis has returned. Pullman won't go; instead, she goes right back over to the side of the trail and lies down. Bea won't start on her own and just looks back at me. I put Slipper back up front with Bea but she won't move either. The only thing my efforts produce is yet another tangle. The males are screaming to get at the females and the females just don't want to go.

It's happened again. I try every combination of leaders and non-leaders I can think of: Bea and Weasel, Pullman and Weasel, Pullman and Slipper, Wild Thing and Bea, Wild Thing and Slipper, even little Maybelline and all of the others. Nothing works. I think to myself we're stopped cold because of the heat, but somehow it doesn't seem very humorous.

After what seems like an hour of frustration, I hear several big snowmachines coming up behind me. These are the trail sweeps, whose job is to police up the trail behind the race. They also help tail-end mushers within the limits of the rules and generally keep the rear of the race moving. I ask them if they can help me get my dogs started by running the leaders for 50 feet or so on foot, like leaving a checkpoint. I'm reasonably sure this will get the dogs moving so they will switch back out of the "sex" mode and into the "run" configuration.

However, the sweeps say they aren't sure they can do that, even though I tell them I don't think it constitutes outside assistance. They say they'll have to go on up to Rainy Pass Lodge and see what the officials say. Half an hour later I hear another team coming up behind me. This can only be Tim Triumph, who I know is the last musher on the trail. He pulls to a stop and I tell him my problem. We agree my dogs might follow his so he pulls around and stops. After several false starts I put Bea and little Maybelline up front and we finally start and keep going.

We immediately come to yet another hill, not as bad as the one we've just ascended, and Tim leads us up and around a sharp left turn at the top. As we round the turn, my gangline catches on a tree at the side of the trail; the team hesitates for a minute and then lurches ahead. The sled pulls free of the grabbing tree but something is not right; indeed, it quickly becomes apparent everything is terribly wrong.

Once around the bend I can see the team lined out ahead. Yankee is stretched out prone and seems to be choking. I set the snow hook and run up to him, where I see to my horror the impossible has happened: the cable gangline has broken, right next to Yankee and Silvertip. Yankee is caught in the middle with his tugline attached to the sled and his neckline attached to the forward section of gangline. Silvertip would be in the same situation except he has slipped his collar.

Yankee's neckline is the only link holding the still-straining front 12 dogs to the sled. He is being brutally clothes-lined and I frantically try to find a way to free him before he strangles. Unfortunately I can't just cut his neckline because the dozen dogs in front of him would bolt down the trail. Without the restraint of the sled they could easily wrap themselves around a tree or tangle up even worse than they are now, with possibly fatal results.

Luckily, Tim has quickly stopped his team ahead of me and is running back to help. He yells to me I have another dog down; I scream at him to cut it loose while I work on Yankee. Tim quickly frees the front dog (Blackie) who is only tangled in a line but is also in danger of choking. Then he rushes back to help me secure the remains of the gangline so the front part of the team won't run off while we cut Yankee loose.

Yankee and Blackie regain their equilibrium within a couple of minutes and are apparently uninjured, but I am shaken almost to the point I cannot stand up. The whole episode, from stopping the sled to finally freeing Yankee, took less than 60 seconds but it seems like a year. Without Tim's help I could have had a major disaster and very possibly a dead or seriously hurt dog, not to mention a runaway team.

I sit down heavily in the snow and try to think. This isn't supposed to happen. Cable ganglines just don't break. It's so rare I don't even have a spare section in the sled. After a few minutes of searching for the best solution, I decide to use the heavy line from one of my snow hooks. It's not as strong as the cable sections so I'll have to put it up front where it'll only have to handle the leaders.

Tim stays around while I tie off dogs to trees and pull the broken section of gangline; after 30 minutes or so I finally get the new section in place and get everything hooked up again. The repaired gangline seems to be in good working order and I figure we can try to get moving again. Before we start off, Tim brings back a bag with 20 pounds of dog food and offers it to me in case I get stalled again. Having already spent an unexpected night on the trail I'm short of food and gratefully accept.

Tim pulls his hook and Maybelline and Bea fairly leap after his sled. This isn't the same team that wouldn't start back at the top of the hill. In fact, they're running so well we repeatedly overrun Tim, forcing me to use the brake to keep a decent interval. Once again I start to feel like we're really going to make it. We're less than 15 miles from the checkpoint at Rainy Pass, where I can drop my problem dogs and sort everything out.

After another five miles we drop onto Long Lake, a mile of wind-polished snow and ice sunk between brooding forested hills. Tim stops in the middle of the lake to make some adjustments, as do I. But when he pulls out, Maybelline and Bea don't follow. I yell to Tim to wait a minute, but he's already out of earshot. I frantically try to get the team moving, but nothing works. The bomb has gone off again.

It's only an hour until sunset and I know it's going to get very cold out here in the middle of the lake. I do everything I can think of to get the team moving again, or at least to get the dogs to move the half-mile or so up to the trees at the end of the lake, where we can have some decent shelter and I can make a real fire.

The only result of my efforts to get moving is the worst tangle I've had so far as the males practically leap into the middle of the females, who obligingly turn around and come back to join in the fun. All 16 dogs are involved in a massive knot I can't make a dent in. In the middle of it, Blues is getting bred again, this time by Blackie. I don't even want to think about the population explosion that will swamp my place this summer.

Worse, the big males are fighting and before I can get them separated, Silvertip has cut Yankee's eye and normally docile Socks has gotten Rocky's muzzle so badly the indestructible Rock is snorting blood. I quickly determine both dogs will be all right, but I'll have to have them checked by a vet when—or if—I make it to Rainy Pass.

While I'm tending to Rocky, Silvertip hooks up with Blues. I miss getting them apart by a couple of seconds as the orgy continues. It takes me an hour to get the tangle undone and the team lined out again, during which time Blues enjoys yet a third roll in the snow, this time with Yankee, whose eye is obviously not bothering him as much as I thought. I kick myself again for not dropping Blues and the others at Finger Lake.

By now it's dark and the dogs simply won't move no matter what I try. I even try to pull them ahead to the shelter of the shoreline but nothing works. Finally I give up in despair and start to hack holes in the thickly crusted snow for them to lie in to escape the rising wind and plunging temperatures. I put dog coats on the ones who need the most protection and then break out the cooker to make them some hot food.

I discover I only have five bottles of Heet and about 30 pounds of food left. This won't last very long. In fact, I'll be in a real survival situation by midday tomorrow because the dogs absolutely must have food and water. I figure in a pinch I can take the dogs one by one over to an abandoned cabin on the far shoreline, but there's probably no food there, and the best I could hope for would be better shelter until somebody comes back for me.

It takes the ax to chop enough polished and hardened snow for the cooker, and two of my precious bottles of Heet only yield a few gallons of cold water. I mix up some of Tim's food and give the dogs enough to get them through the night. I save some water and refill my makeshift Thermos; my thirst is reaching unquenchable proportions and I realize I'm badly dehydrated from my efforts, despite my attempts to drink water wherever possible.

But my main concern is keeping warm during the upcoming night. My thermometer already says it's below zero and the wind is gusting to 10 or 15 miles an hour. I empty the sled and unstuff my arctic sleeping bag inside it. After making sure the dogs are resting as comfortably as can be expected, I take off my boots and crawl inside the sleeping bag still in my heavy overalls. I zip the bag shut and pull the flaps of the sled bag in over me.

I find I stay warm and cozy despite the wind moaning around the

*sled. Mentally, however, I'm a wreck. I can't see any way to continue
the race even if I can get the dogs into Rainy Pass. I'm so far behind
there's no way I can catch up, especially after I drop what will
amount to at least a third of my team. I drift off into a troubled sleep
about midnight as the crescent moon dips below the mountains to
the west. I think to myself it's a cold moon indeed.*

March 8, 1995—The Iditarod: Rainy Pass Checkpoint

The wind howls fitfully across the lake all night, but I'm warm in my
cocoon. I peek out once or twice; the dogs are sleeping soundly, their dark
shapes dimly silhouetted against the lake's frozen white surface. Their
apparent good condition gives me some comfort.

The sun rises about seven and I slowly muster the courage to face the
coming day. Up on the ridgeline above the lake, I can see big spruces
whipping wildly in the wind blowing down from Rainy Pass. Here in the
deep depression enfolding the lake, only an occasional gust penetrates
and the temperature stays down around 10 below zero.

I quickly fire up the cooker with my last three bottles of Heet. I manage
to get the water moderately hot, which I know the dogs will appreciate
after their cold night on the ice. I mix the warm water in with the last of
the dog food and give the dogs their breakfast. They all eat hungrily,
which is a good sign in itself.

When they are finished I collect the bowls and begin the normal getting-
ready-to-go routine, which I hope will get them focused on moving. After
I pack the sled and finish hooking up, the team actually starts, although they
stop after maybe 50 yards. Trying not to lose momentum, I keep switching
leaders, but nothing seems to work and gradually the dogs start to lose
interest and lie down in the rapidly warming sun.

I'm beyond hope. I have to assume this is the absolute, bitter end of my
year of work; I can't think of anything more I can do. I just sit down on
the sled and wait for somebody to come back from the checkpoint to see
why I'm not there yet. I even consider stomping out a message in the snow
in case one of the Iditarod Air Force planes comes over.

About noon I finally hear the whine of snowmachines coming
down the trail from Rainy Pass. It's two of the trail sweeps who passed
me yesterday. One says Jack Niggemyer, the race manager, has told
them to get back down the trail and find out what happened to me. I
figure if Jack has had to personally order my rescue I'm already
counted out of the race. At least I can make a good show about getting
into the Rainy Pass checkpoint to scratch.

The trail sweeps offer any assistance I need and I repeat my request of 24 hours ago—grab the leaders and lead them on foot while I drag the brake to hold back the males. I put Slipper and Bea up front; they are still my best bet despite their being wildly in heat and thus the ringleaders of the conspiracy that has defeated my best efforts. I figure they can have one last chance for glory as we make our final run into Rainy Pass Lodge.

One of the sweeps begins to trot with the leaders and they seem to respond. After a couple of tries and 100 yards my new assistant is completely winded but the team is moving. The other sweep pulls ahead of the team and Slipper and Bea accelerate off the lake and up the trail behind his snowmachine. He maintains position ahead of me

A hunting lodge on Puntilla Lake serves as the Rainy Pass checkpoint. This is the last checkpoint before mushers push on to Rainy Pass itself and down into Dalzell Gorge.

for maybe a mile and when I am sure the dogs are moving on their own I wave him on. Unfortunately, I'm almost positive his actions constitute mechanized assistance, or at least pacing, and I'm reasonably certain his help will cement my disqualification if I don't scratch when I reach Rainy Pass.

Nevertheless, it's a grand ride and the team is once more running like the finely tuned machine I trained over the past nine months. But it's all bittersweet because I don't see any way I can go on after Rainy Pass. In the bright sunshine we sweep onto Puntilla Lake and roll into the checkpoint. The checkers and the vets are waiting for me and give me a warm welcome.

But there are three Iditarod Air Force airplanes on the lake waiting to go with their engines warm, and everyone is obviously ready to close down the checkpoint and move on. This only reinforces my belief I've been declared surplus and without giving the matter any further thought I tell the checker I want to scratch.

The vet immediately gives my dogs a thorough examination and tells me I should drop three of them: Weasel has broken a tooth and has very sore feet, Yankee's eye looks a mess although it really isn't serious, and Rocky's nose has stopped bleeding but he still looks like an old boxer who's gone too many rounds with the new champ. If I also drop the four most troublesome females— Slipper, Bea, Blues, and Rosie—I'll be down to 10 dogs at best, even if I'm not disqualified and I can talk the vet into letting me keep Yankee or Rocky.

When the checker brings me the official scratch form a little later, I sign it quickly, wanting to get this depressing business behind me. I've met the checker on previous races and we talk for a minute before he moves on to load the planes. He says he would have liked to see me go on, and I tell him I thought I would have been disqualified. He doubts that would have been the case, but thinks my decision may turn out to be a good one anyway because the wind is coming up in the pass and it could be a nasty turn in the mountains tonight.

We part and the planes are quickly loaded—Yankee and Weasel get free rides back to town since they were dropped before I officially scratched—and the checkpoint staff disappears toward their new posts on up the trail. I bed down the remaining dogs and trudge into the lodge to make a call on the radiophone to charter a plane to pick up me and the dogs and the sled. I also call Bert, but he's not back from work yet and I have to tell Kim I've scratched because of six dogs in heat. (This is the official reason given to the media as well; I'm sure I'll hear about my doggie bordello for months to come from people I don't even know.)

I grab a sandwich in the lodge and guzzle about a gallon of Tang while I try to put everything into perspective. In the fullness of time—actually only a few hours—I come to realize I may have made a serious mistake in scratching. Now that I've come to my senses, I can see things from a broader perspective. True, I would have had to drop at least five and possibly seven key dogs, and I would have been hard pressed to keep up the necessary pace with the remaining ones. Indeed, I would in all likelihood have been forced to withdraw at McGrath for being more than 72 hours behind the leaders (who are blazing a record-shattering pace on the near-perfect trail).

But I might have regained the use of my male leaders, which would have given me at least a couple of good dogs up front. I could probably have made it over Rainy Pass and tested myself on the Dalzell Gorge and the Farewell Burn. I might even have discovered less really is more, without the unending disruptions of the previous days. After all, plenty of mushers have completed the race from this far back with fewer dogs than I would have had.

Now I'll never know, at least not until next year, and that's rapidly becoming one of the hardest pills I've ever had to swallow. I wish I could roll back the clock a few hours and reconsider my hasty decision. But what's done is done, and I've made myself a very thorny bed to lie in for the next 12 months. About the only thing I know for certain is I absolutely, positively have to go again next year.

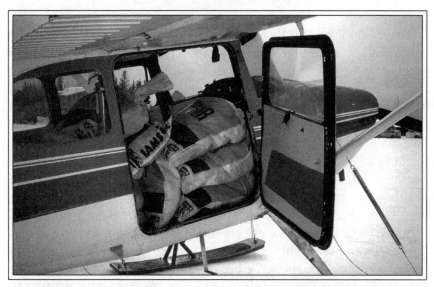

The Iditarod Air Force hauls everything from dog food to passengers along the trail. This skiplane holds 600 pounds of dog food for an isolated checkpoint.

March 9, 1995
Rainy Pass and Montana Creek, Alaska

I spend the night tossing and turning in the recently vacated checker's cabin, alternately imagining myself out on the trail to Rohn and points west and trying to figure out how I can do it next year and what I'll do differently. After one of the worst nights I can remember, I'm up at dawn and out with the dogs. The wind that whipped up three-foot drifts overnight has abated and the temperature is still warm, in the twenties. I am tempted almost beyond resistance to hook up and head for the outbound trail, prominently marked a few yards from my sled.

Even as I look wistfully toward the ramparts of Rainy Pass, only 10 miles distant, the lodge manager rumbles by on his snowmachine picking up the lath trail markers. As I watch him dismantling the trail itself, I realize it is all now really, finally over. I try to busy myself breaking down the sled and getting my gear ready for pickup, but every few minutes I catch myself gazing westward and wondering if I've done the right thing.

Early in the afternoon the plane I've chartered arrives and we load the dogs and some of my gear. The sled and the rest of the equipment will have to wait a few days. As we head back to civilization we roughly parallel the trail, which I now see in a completely new light.

Long Lake glitters like cut crystal in the sunlight, looking just as cold as the endless night we spent in its icy embrace. The hill up from Happy River and the site of the broken gangline look even worse from the air. At the foot of the hill, though, are several teams waiting to ascend it—Joe Redington's "tour to Nome" with half a dozen paying customers-cum-mushers. Last year rumor has it he charged $15,000 a head for what amounted to a mushing dude ranch with all the trimmings, running a few days behind the race all the way to Nome. He sold out the trip, and did the same this year. They seem to be having a slow time of it up the hill, and I can understand why. I wish them well as we speed eastward overhead.

I'd forgotten how marvelously a plane can compress the trail. In a few minutes we pass Finger Lake; the checkpoint shows no sign of activity now. My impromptu campsite near Shell Lake hoves into view shortly. I really was a lot farther along toward Finger Lake than I believed—much more than halfway—but it might as well have been a hundred miles as long as the dogs wouldn't go. The trail still looks good; I hope it's as inviting next year.

Overhead Skwentna I can see life has returned to normal at Joe Delia's. Most of the straw has been cleaned up from the river and even the mountain of Idita-trash has been airlifted out by the Iditarod Air Force. My first night's unwilling stopping place on the Yentna River is just around the bend from the checkpoint; again, even if I'd known how close I was, I couldn't have done anything about it.

On down the Yentna we soar, speeding over miles of river I've flown hundreds of times in my own plane. Now I know it intimately in a way few people can. It will never be the same for me now that I've run it with dogs. In fact, I don't think I can ever fly anywhere any more without unconsciously wondering how it would be on the ground with a smoothly running team. All too quickly we glide to a stop at Kashwitna Lake on the Parks Highway. Boyd Gochanour, an old friend who runs the air service, meets me and listens to my tale in the office over coffee. Again, I've been here many, many times, but everything seems different now. Boyd ran dogs many years ago and understands; the sympathy is more than welcome.

March 10-22, 1995
Montana Creek, Talkeetna, and
Anchorage, Alaska

Within a few days I'm trying to get back to civilian life but it's not easy. I've got a lot of things to think about and it's tough to put everything back together.

Among other things, I busy myself getting on the substitute teaching roster and working on my full-time teaching application for next fall. In talking to other teachers, I do make the happy discovery that most principals in the Mat-Su School District (the home of the Iditarod, after all) are more than willing to let their teachers run the Iditarod, although it involves a week or two of unpaid leave.

I make a quick stop in Anchorage to thank the kids and teachers at Mount Spurr for their support. Before I'm three steps inside the front door, the principal collars me to offer his condolences, but he also says everyone was proud of me for even making it to the starting line. I don't know what to say; apparently what has been a calamitous disappointment for me has been seen quite differently by others.

Then my former host teacher walks in and adds the touch that brings me back to the world of the living. He says the day after I scratched at Rainy Pass, the kids ran frantically into the classroom carrying the sports section of the *Daily News*, in which my scratch was listed along with the reason. They couldn't wait to tell him how "Mr. Bowers' dogs overheated and had puppies!" Leave it to the kids to put it all back in perspective.

I also get a real boost when Hudson Air Service in Talkeetna hires me on for the season as a regular pilot. Cliff Hudson is one of the most respected of the old-time bush pilots, having helped pioneer the thriving Mt. McKinley aviation business almost 50 years ago. Cliff's son, Jay, the chief pilot, tells me I'll be flying climbers to the glaciers within a month, as well as taking tourists from all over the world on sight-seeing flights around The Mountain.

Working as a "Denali Flyer" is something else I've always wanted to do, almost as much as running the Iditarod, and flying for Cliff is the best of all possible worlds. Even better, Cliff also agrees to lease my idle and increasingly unaffordable Cessna 206, which I'd been trying to sell. It seems things are actually working out for me; maybe my travails weren't in vain.

To prove to myself I really mean to go again next year, I call John Allison, a well regarded local musher who hasn't run the Iditarod but who has an excellent line of dogs, and tell him I'm interested in two lead dogs he tried back in February to get me to take on the race. Since Bert has said he might want to run the race next year, I can't count on using his dogs, which means I have to try to put together a new team. John and I meet that evening and close the deal and I take the dogs home with me. Buck and Black Ace are older dogs, eight years old, but Buck in particular is a proven leader, and I'm never again going to be without a trustworthy dog up front who will start the team under any conditions.

Any outside observer would probably still think I'm not of sound mind, throwing money and hope at next year's race when the front runners in this year's trek aren't even to the coast. But this is important to me, a sign of commitment I have to make. Besides, now I have another month of decent snow to solidify my new core team, an advantage I wish I'd had last year.

Despite my determination to do the race right in 1996, I still have to live with this year's ongoing coverage. The race roars to a shockingly fast finish. Montana musher Doug Swingley wins all the marbles (and $52,500 plus a new Dodge truck) in an astounding 9 days and 2 hours. While I was dejectedly camped on Long Lake he was rocketing out of Iditarod, more than 300 miles ahead of me, with nobody even close to him. Even Martin Buser can't catch him; Martin knocks several hours off his own record-smashing 1994 run but it's only good enough for a distant second.

Of course, I never planned to run anywhere near the big boys (and girls). Every day I check the newspaper to see how far my friends and fellow rookies—the ones I should still be running with—have progressed. On Saturday I find out Barrie has been forced to scratch at Iditarod. Two of her leaders were hurt going across the Farewell Burn, and her last decent front-end dog pulled a shoulder on the trail between Ophir and Iditarod. Without leaders, she can't get her team started, and once started can't maintain headway for more than an hour or two. By the time she finally limps into Iditarod, she's completely burned out. I can sympathize, because that's exactly the same position I was in, only for a different reason.

A few days later, Diana Moroney, who gave me my first four dogs, is running for a solid top-20 finish when her sled rams a tree in the Blueberry Hills north of Unalakleet. She barely limps into Shaktoolik with painful injuries. She's hurt badly enough to have to scratch.

My friend and fellow rookie Wayne Curtis plods on with his Siberians, slow but sure and holding in the forties; he finishes in just under 15 days in 41st place. I hope his final leg into Nome from Safety was as memorable as our last few miles into Meier's Lake under the northern lights and the full moon in the Copper Basin two months ago.

Rookie Max Hall, a Briton whom I got to know reasonably well before the race, makes it to Nome after braving a horrendous series of storms that bedevil him almost all the way from Unalakleet. He arrives on Front Street chilled to the bone and looking like the abominable snowman, but is cheerful and polite and very, very British to the end. The newspapers hail him as a reincarnation of the gallant explorers and adventurers who built the Empire.

Andy Sterns, a rookie with whom I ran the qualifying races, is running barely an hour behind Max on the last 22-mile leg in from Safety when another terrific storm explodes. Max makes it through, but Andy gets pinned down in a raging ground blizzard with zero visibility. He decides he has no choice but to scratch in order to get help for his dogs. He's barely three miles from the finish line. He's the only person to ever scratch so close to Nome, and my disappointment can't be anything compared to his.

Ben Jacobson is at the back of the pack but determinedly pushes on. He links up with Larry Williams, who has been sponsored by zillionaire heiress Marylou Whitney in a true-to-life Iditarod Cinderella story. They both get caught in the vicious Norton Sound storms after they leave Koyuk and are forced to hole up in a shelter cabin between there and Elim until the tempests abate. Larry makes it in a day ahead of Ben, who eventually pulls into the chute and under the burled arch after 17 days on the trail. Ben earns the Red Lantern, which he didn't really want but which he is more than proud to receive.

Tim Triumph's best leader, Victory, pulls a shoulder in the Farewell Burn and Tim has to carry her almost 80 miles in the sled. He pushes on with Cooper, a ragtag leader who is a refugee from a trapline work team. Tim is dead last all the way to the coast. He finally makes it into Unalakleet, but it's more than five days after Swingley sweeps through and the race officials withdraw him. Tim refuses to quit and forges on, being hailed as the "phantom musher." Cooper turns out to be one of the best storm leaders ever to run the race, dragging the team through whiteouts so bad Tim can barely see his wheel dogs. Tim actually reaches Nome ahead of Ben Jacobson and Larry Williams, whom he helps through the blizzards around Elim.

Still, his finish isn't official, although many people (especially the media, for whom Tim has become a cause celebre) think he deserves the fabled finisher's belt buckle as much as many of the mushers who finished before—and after—him. I have to confess a grudging admiration for Tim, despite our sometimes-significant personal differences off the trail. The more I think about it, the more I believe he did what I should have done: press on no matter what the odds and run my own race. Next year, I'll remember. (Tim's finish is later officially recognized and he is awarded his belt buckle.)

My interest in my erstwhile peers aside, the pervasive media blitz is too much. I can't watch the coverage without pangs of remorse mixed with undercurrents of extreme anticipation. Every shot of a team heading out of some isolated checkpoint sends chills through me.

I should have been there, and I will be there next year if it's the last thing I do. A major part of my life has been left unfinished and must be made complete. I have seen and experienced just enough—and suffered and despaired and exulted just enough—to know that I now have no choice but to keep at it until I succeed.

The trail and the dogs own me, like an insidious drug owns an addict, like blind faith owns a true believer. Part of me is still out there with my team, on the lonely stretches I didn't get to explore, and I won't sleep easily until I've become whole again.

April 15, 1995
Montana Creek, Alaska

Life goes on. The race has been over for nearly a month and I've been trying to put it behind me, but it keeps forcing its way back into my every waking hour. The best therapy I can devise is just to get as involved as I can in the hectic activity of the upcoming summer. Maybe a steady diet of hard work can get my mind off the events on the way to Rainy Pass.

I've been working hard for the past month learning how to fly around—and on—Mount McKinley for Hudson's. Although I've been flying for almost 30 years, this is "pushing the envelope" even for me. Flying for the Iditarod demanded its own special set of skills and knowledge, but working The Mountain is something else altogether. We fly our ski-equipped Cessna right to the limit of their capabilities—and ours—while still leaving enough margin for safety to feel comfortable. It promises to be a long and interesting summer, although it will be a lot of hard work and 12-hour days.

Like driving dogs, being a bush pilot in Alaska in the summer requires a lot of work and patience to get to the payoff. Nonetheless, payoffs there are, and on a scale that (as Teddy Roosevelt once said of a trip in Colorado) bankrupts the English language. The ever-changing views of Denali, the satisfaction of a particularly well-executed landing under tricky conditions, being able to communicate to a visitor from Outside the overriding sense of awe and respect for the North Country felt by any honest Alaskan—these are rewards worth much in their own right, never mind the paychecks.

I'd hoped to be able to continue running the dogs until breakup, but we were hit with a vicious and unseasonable late-March cold snap.

The temperature hovered around 20 below or worse for most of the last half of March, and only warmed up to zero so the winds could blow. Normally, most mushers in this area will try to get in late-season running to try out puppies and train leaders, but all the trails were blown in and the conditions weren't worth the effort to harness up and go anywhere. A lot of people just found someone to feed the dogs for a few weeks and headed for Hawaii.

The horrible conditions continued into April, and then, after one last 25-below morning, warmed up to almost 60 in less than 12 hours and have hardly gone below freezing since. The belated warmth didn't help the trails, though, since everything melted at an astonishing pace. So, late season mushing has been pretty much a fizzle this year.

Not that I haven't been busy with the dogs. Even though I haven't been running them, I've been setting up to bring them over to my place from Ron's, which means starting a kennel operation mainly from scratch. I've already decided on a name: White-Knuckle Kennels. This is actually part of a long-running inside joke based on some of my early flying exploits in Alaska, but seems especially apt to describe my mushing career so far.

I brought one of the dogs over early. Josephine, a marvelous three-year-old female I acquired back in November, was bred in early February as the beginning (and, as it turned out, the end) of my "planned parenthood" program. Her bloodlines are impeccable, going all the way back to a particularly notable line of dogs on the Seward Peninsula. Josephine herself is a littermate of longtime Iditarod contender Joe Garnie's best leaders. The only reason I got Josephine was because Garnie thought she was too small and sold her to another musher, from whom I picked her up.

I didn't run Josephine in the Iditarod because it's not a good idea to stress out dogs in the last part of their pregnancy. As a rookie breeder, I was as nervous as a new father and wanted to make sure everything was just right when the day came. I needn't have worried. Tough dogs from the Bering Sea coast like Josephine have been giving birth and raising pups under abominable conditions for generations, and the best thing I could have done was just leave her alone, which I finally figured out to do.

Her day came—and went. Now, a week later, she looks like a big bouncing basketball with legs, head, and a tail, but she's as lively and friendly and apparently unconcerned as ever. I worry a bit, but my friends tell me to just stay away and wait. Finally, above the rustling of the wind at one o'clock on this cloudy morning I hear the first pup's cry. I can't quite place it, but then I realize my team of the future is at last making its grand entrance. The others follow every hour or so: huge pups, seven of them, four females and three males, all healthy and yelping, all looking remarkably like their mother. I stay up all night but manage to keep my fumbling assistance away from where it isn't needed. Josephine knows exactly what she's doing; I'm excess baggage.

For people brought up on farms, I suppose animals giving birth is nothing new. For me as basically a nonfarm type, this is suddenly very personal. Josephine is having pups because I want her to, and I'm directly responsible for her and her offspring. I feel these are my pups as much as they are hers, and I realize they are not only a responsibility but a future as well. These pups are intended to become the heart of my team in a few years, and from that standpoint they represent my ultimate commitment to mushing.

In short, I'm no longer a "walk-on" dog driver who drops in on a ready-made team for a quick run and then returns to the real world with scarcely a glance back. In more ways than one, Josephine's pups have tied me to mushing more surely than the strongest chains.

Being a successful "Denali Flyer" can be as challenging in its own way as running the Iditarod. Ski landings on the glaciers surrounding North America's tallest peak can never be taken for granted. Small planes are the only way in or out of the main mountaineering base camp at the 7,200-foot level of the Southeast Fork of the Kahiltna Glacier. The sheer north face of 14,570-foot Mount Hunter towers barely two miles away.

May 15, 1995
Montana Creek, Alaska

The puppy parade resumes with the arrival of the Iditapups. One after another, Bea, Blues, and Slipper have their litters the second week in May. Amazingly, none of the other three females in heat on my Iditarod team got pregnant. In a matter of weeks I've become a full-fledged dog breeder, even if I didn't exactly plan it that way.

I've already taken Josephine and her month-old brood into town to stay at Bert's while the next wave hits, and it's a good thing. Bea is first with five: one male and four females, all different and showing a variety of fathers (at least I know who all of them are). A week or so later Blues has seven black pups with white markings; I suspect Yankee and Blackie are behind these. Finally, old Slipper has two; I'd been worried she wouldn't have any who would survive because of her age.

Bert has told me Bea is a good mother, and she seems to do a good job of minding and feeding her pups. Blues likewise is super-protective of her brood. Despite her best efforts, however, Blues accidentally suffocates one of her pups a few days after it is born. I gently remove the lifeless pup to bury it, but Blues becomes distraught when I carry it away. Not knowing anything else to do, I put the tiny inert form back into her house and she quiets down.

Next morning it is gone without a trace; I assume she buried it or, more likely, ate it. Other mushers have told me good mothers will go to great lengths to keep the den area clean, including licking the sightless pups clean of their wastes. The object of this decidedly ancient and wolflike behavior is to prevent predators from scenting and finding the litter. Eating a dead pup is a logical extension of this self-protective mechanism, and Blues is reaching back beyond the human event horizon for her rearing skills. I am still learning about my dogs.

Old Slipper also has a problem. One of her two pups is very small; after a week it is only half the size of its brother. One evening when I get home from flying, the pup is no longer eating and is sinking fast. I decide to make an emergency run into Anchorage to drop Slipper and her offspring at Bert's. Kim has already said she'll take care of the pup; in the past she's raised several little ones requiring feeding from an eyedropper and hours of close attention.

I make the 100-mile drive to Anchorage as fast as is decently possible given the swelling tourist traffic. At Bert's the sickly pup is still alive, but there is not much to do; it dies in my hands half an hour later. The other pup is healthy, however, and Kim says she'll keep it under close supervision. We'd like to see the remaining pup survive; it will be Slipper's last: she's 11 years old and her last couple of litters have been way understrength.

To grieve for lost pups, especially ones so young they never really started living, is probably wasted energy, but I feel a bit emotional nonetheless. After all, I'm still new at this, and besides, I'm basically responsible for the pups being born in any case. Maybe I'll develop a harder shell to protect against this sort of thing later on. On the other hand, maybe I won't: I've seen veteran mushers break down in tears when they've had no choice but to put down a friend and traveling companion of many years who's been badly hurt or has gotten so old and infirm that allowing the suffering to continue would be cruel.

I guess I'm relearning that mushing, like any other genuinely worthwhile human endeavor, requires a complete commitment from the heart, which brings with it the risk of terrible pain. And I really do think the dogs understand it all even better than we poor, sensory-deprived two-legs.

June 10, 1995
Montana Creek, Alaska

Just when I thought the puppy parade was over, Black Ace—one of the lead dogs I picked up from John Allison just after the Iditarod—turned up in a family way about three weeks ago. This wasn't intentional, of course, and I only discovered it after she was already well along the way to her unplanned parenthood.

The proximate cause of the problem seems to have been a stray sled dog we noticed hanging around Ron's lot back in April and May. Ron also apparently has a few surprise litters on the way from this vagabond.

I thought for awhile about putting down the pups as soon as they were born, but then figured it wouldn't hurt to let her keep them until they were old enough to give away. Fortunately, it's not normally too hard to give away sled dog pups. They generally make excellent pets because they're smart and have good dispositions; besides, I figured there might be one or two I'd want to keep.

She started dropping them this morning while I was at work. As I get home, she's still popping them out. I count at least eight, and as I feed the other dogs she drops a couple more, for a total of 10. For a seven-year-old dog, she's remarkably productive.

They all seem healthy, which is a good start. But this makes a total of 29 pups, far more than I ever envisioned in my wildest dreams. My guess is there will be lots of happy new puppy owners in Southcentral Alaska over the next few months. And I'm going to take whatever steps are necessary to ensure I stay out of the breeding business for awhile.

June 24, 1995
Talkeetna, Alaska

Today is the first day to sign up for the 1996 Iditarod. Even though there's a party down at Iditarod Headquarters and many of my friends will be there, I decide not to go because I can't come up with the $1,750 entry fee this early. I feel I'm leaving myself out of something important, but I'd rather not be there if I don't know for sure I'm going to be one of the players.

Part of it may be the embarrassment of not finishing the '95 race; I made such a show of going for it last year at the sign-up I want to stay as low-key as possible this go-around. Part of it may also be because I'm slightly superstitious and think maybe it will be better if I do things differently this time. Of course, there's a practical side: this is a Saturday, and weekends are big tourist days at Talkeetna. I have to fly and pull in a paycheck so I'll even have a chance to eventually put my money where my mouth is.

So, I fly tourists and climbers back and forth to the Mountain all day while the good times roll down at Wasilla. Part of my normal local-color spiel while acting as aerial tour guide is a casual mention I'm a musher and I tried the Iditarod this year. Somehow I let it slide today; I just don't feel up to it.

Last year I didn't have any idea what I was getting into. This year it's different—a lot different. I'm a year older and a lifetime wiser about this lifestyle I've adopted for the foreseeable future. I'm also way behind the financial power curve and this will definitely be a no-frills race for me if I can pull it off at all.

Even more important, I'm much more on my own now. Barrie isn't running the Iditarod and neither is Ron. I can't expect the same level of support from Bert, either. If I make it to the starting line next March, it will be with quite a different outlook on things.

This time I'll have earned my spot. Maybe it'll mean more to me, and I'll be less prone to throw it all away if I have problems. Maybe I'll have a better sense of perspective. In any case, I have until the first of December to come up with the entry fee; one way or another, I'll find the money. I've come way too far to turn back now.

Virtually all mushers use chain tethers as the primary means of restraint in their dog yards. Sled dogs intensely dislike fenced-in enclosures and will often injure themselves trying to get out. Tethers allow mushers to interact with their dogs on a one-on-one basis and promote socialization with humans. Dogs must usually be kept tied up and separated from one another in the dog lot to avoid unwanted pack behavior (and unplanned pups), although most mushers allow a few well-behaved dogs to run loose occasionally.

July 15, 1995
Montana Creek, Alaska

The summer has been frantically busy. I've been working six or seven days a week at Hudson's, usually 10 to 12 hours a day, sometime longer. We're completely at the whim of the weather, the Mountain, and the Great God of Tourists. It's a crazy business, sitting around drinking coffee on rainy days and flying nonstop until midnight on others.

I usually don't get home until late in the evening, and then it's about all I can do to feed the dogs and drop into the sack. My main consolation is I'm at least earning a paycheck doing something I enjoy (most of the time) and most Alaskans are keeping the same skewed hours I am. We're all trying to wring the most out of the magic but short subarctic summer.

On the puppy front, I've been able to give away several. The smallest of Josephine's seven went to one of my former fourth graders at Elmendorf (with her parents' approval, of course) and four of Black Ace's have gone to other folks around the Valley. I may keep one or two of her remaining males, but I'll drop the others off at the Mat-Su Humane Society, which accepts puppies for $20 each and will hold them until they're adopted.

Bea's pups are down at Bert's now, and Josephine's are back here; we felt it would be good to get Bea's brood socialized with Bert's kids—such pups always make better dogs. I've kept Blues' pups here; I'll probably keep all of them (five males and a female) until I can decide which have the best potential.

Blues' lone female pup, the smallest of the lot, is also the perkiest and most inquisitive. She's managed to escape the pen repeatedly and has completely endeared herself to me. Diana Moroney (who developed the line from which Blues is descended) said the small females in the family tend to be the best leaders, and little Skeeter, as I've started calling the peripatetic escape artist, certainly seems to be headed in that direction.

Josephine's pups remain my crown jewels. They have impeccable bloodlines and great attitudes and are developing into truly beautiful animals with all the makings of top-notch sled dogs. Kim has kept one of Josephine's males, Napoleon, for herself; she'll bring him up to start training this winter. The remaining five are on my lot and each is starting to come into its own. Bonnie and Clyde (each with one blue eye and one brown) are feisty and curious. Pretty Boy (as in Floyd) and Kate (for Klondike Kate, a notorious Yukon madam) are bouncy and gregarious. Belle Starr is smaller and quieter, but no less active and affectionate.

It's amazing how fast puppies can metamorphose from anonymous little fuzzballs with legs to individual dogs with real personalities. There is an almost irresistible tendency to treat them as little humans because they change so quickly into identifiable entities. In many ways they are like children, and it's fascinating to watch as they learn about their environment. I know I'm not the first person to fall under this spell, but that doesn't stop me from becoming sort of a kid again myself as the pups drag me into their play.

And surprisingly, I find I've still got time and affection for all of my dogs—pups and adults—though there are now more than 40 of them. I suppose it's good training for being a teacher. In a way, my dogs are not much different from a classroom full of permanent grade-schoolers, all needing lots of attention and learning and discipline, and above all, lots of love.

This custom license plate says it all: Alaska is the world mecca for dog mushing, and dog trucks are a common sight on the roads during the mushing season.

July 19, 1995
Montana Creek, Alaska

Tragedy comes in many forms, but it's cruelest when it strikes the young. Belle Starr, one of my prize pups from Josephine's litter, stopped eating last week and began to go quickly downhill. A couple of days ago I took her to the vet in Wasilla, where she died this morning, from parvo.

I don't know how the disease got into my lot; it's possible the ravens and Canada jays which make the rounds of the local dog lots to steal dog food brought the virus in from somebody's else's yard. It's also just as likely I or a visitor tracked it in; it's virtually unstoppable under most conditions. The hardest part to take is not the disease's high mortality rate, but rather the suffering it causes and the fact it is so devastating to puppies in particular.

I've been careful to give all of the pups their shots, but the vet said something just didn't work with Belle's immune system. She never really had a chance against this terrible scourge that descended on the canine world barely a decade and a half ago. Within a day or two, Belle was obviously in pain with fever and vomiting and bloody stools and there was nothing I could do.

Professional treatment is expensive and not always successful, and many mushers won't try to throw good money after a sick pup (or simply can't afford to). But I felt I owed it to her. I'd gotten to know her a couple of weeks ago when I found her shivering at midnight in a cold rain. I brought her into the house, dried her off, and then put her under the covers of my bed to warm her. By morning, she was perky and nibbling on my ear to wake me up. As any child knows, it's not hard to quickly become attached to a pup, and I'm certainly no exception.

Losing her was a double blow. Mentally I was prepared for the worst, but it still hurts. And now I must worry about all of the other pups catching the fiendishly persistent virus. My only real defense is to keep on the vaccination schedule, and I've already ordered enough vaccine to protect a small army.

But the damage is done and the vaccine apparently isn't always effective; the odds are I'll lose more pups before the summer is over. The serpent has entered the garden. My puppies—and I— will never be innocent again.

July 26, 1995
Montana Creek, Alaska

The past week has been a painful emotional roller coaster. The parvo has spread throughout my lot and I don't know how much more damage it will do. And I don't know if I'm going to be able to handle it emotionally if it gets much worse.

Two days after Belle died, Pretty Boy stopped eating; I took him in to the vet, determined to fight the virus regardless of the cost. Next morning, he was doing better, but Kate was sick. When I dropped her off, the vet said Pretty Boy looked well enough to go home. However, he collapsed next morning and I had to make an emergency run back down to the vet; he died that afternoon. Kate is still hanging on, basically in intensive care, and the vet says to expect the worst.

And last night Little Guy, one of the three-month-old males from Blues' litter, started throwing up. I pulled him out of the puppy pen and isolated him in a portable kennel, although I fear it won't do much good. After the past week I can't afford to send him to the vet and all I can do is try to give him medication to soothe his stomach and try to help him keep down fluids. Based on recent events, I'm afraid he will be gone in another day or two. His littermates are still okay, but then, so were Kate and Pretty Boy.

Bonnie and Clyde, my two remaining pups from Josephine's litter, seem healthy. The vet says every additional day they stay well is a good sign the shots have taken hold and they won't be infected. I almost break down as I watch them play with each other, next to the empty chains and food dishes of their brother and sisters.

I'm sleeping very badly out of worry for my pups and from trying to come to grips with losing what I've come to think of as my own kids.

Little Bonnie seems to know something is wrong and she's started howling late into the night. Often she's joined by Clyde, and the adult dogs pick up their plaintive cry. It's clear they can somehow sense the loss of their own. Their song is mournful and haunting; it echoes through the birch woods in the misty half-light of the midsummer midnight. I lie awake listening and silently join them in their lament.

This is a sad beginning to what I'd hoped would be an enjoyable training season. Moreover, it's a body blow to my future in mushing, because these pups represented my long-term commitment and were going to be the core of my team a couple of years down the road. I'm starting to wonder if it's all been worth it. There's nothing more I can do now except wait and watch—and grieve.

August 1, 1995
Montana Creek, Alaska

They're all gone but four. The parvo has taken almost all of my pups.

First Belle, then Pretty Boy, then Kate, then Little Guy, Beetle and Mac. Then all six of Black Ace's remaining six-week-olds died within 18 hours of each other, the last three only eight hours after I had left them bouncing and eating happily with their mother.

But the most heartbreaking loss of all was little Skeeter, my favorite of all the pups. She had already learned to recognize her name and would come when I called; she was nervous when I wasn't around and would cry when I put her back in the cage with her littermates when I went to work. Then she'd find a way out, no matter how I tried to mend the wire of the cage door, and would be waiting for me in the driveway when I returned at night.

She stopped eating last Friday and became listless the next morning; I knew what was coming but vowed to fight for her against this insidious, faceless evil. I spent three days feeding her electrolytes every hour or two and cleaning up after her when she couldn't keep down any of the liquids. I kept her warm in bed next to me at night and stroked her to let her know somebody was there.

But it wasn't any use. She got steadily weaker and began losing fluids faster than I could get them into her. By Monday night she could barely move and I stayed up all night trying to keep her hydrated. She finally died Tuesday morning after trying to get out of the airline kennel in which I'd had to isolate her. All I accomplished with my efforts was to prolong her agony for a day or so, and the thought makes me unspeakably depressed.

I know it's easy to sound maudlin at times like this, but the pain is very real. When Skeeter finally went, I broke down and cried as I haven't for many years. It is almost beyond my capability to see the spark of young, vibrant life drained away by a seemingly unstoppable and wanton killer that first tortures its victims—and those who care about them.

Somehow I feel I have failed. I was unable to save my puppies, my commitment to the future. I feel it was my fault, that I didn't do something I should have, that I may even have unwittingly been the agent of destruction. As I take a long, slow walk through the murky forest at three in the morning to get away from the dog lot for awhile, I am prosecutor, judge, and jury for my own case, and I find myself guilty. I wanted these pups brought into the world for my own purposes and I am therefore responsible for their lives—and deaths. I'll have to rethink everything over the next few weeks.

August 10, 1995
Montana Creek, Alaska

For what it's worth, the vet says we're having a parvo outbreak throughout the region, and the standard vaccines aren't completely effective. It's wiping out puppies and older dogs in kennels in this part of the state; Ron has lost nearly a dozen pups already. Everyone says there's not much to do but keep vaccinating the survivors and hope the vaccine will give them at least a fighting chance.

I've become an instant expert on immunology and viral infections. Parvo (actually, canine parvovirus) is one of a family of viruses that includes distemper in cats and minks. Apparently the canine strain is a mutation that jumped species perhaps two decades ago, most likely from the mink distemper virus. It's easy to imagine how big commercial mink farms offered a perfect laboratory for such a virus to perfect its transmogrification.

While vaccines are usually effective against parvo, there is a major hitch: puppy immune systems aren't fully developed until they're about 16 weeks old. For this reason they initially receive natural immunity from the mother's milk. These maternal antibodies begin to diminish after six weeks, but may hang on until four months. While they are present, they inhibit vaccines from stimulating the pup's own defenses.

So, even if a pup is being regularly vaccinated, it may fall victim during the vulnerability window while the mother's protection fades away but before the pup develops its own resistance as a result of the shots. Worse, a puppy's immune system may not be able to stop the infection once it has taken hold. This means an infected pup may not survive even with intensive care at a well-equipped veterinary hospital, like my Belle, Pretty Boy, and Kate.

Once the virus is at work, it will continue to replicate itself like a mindless robotized assembly line. As with all viruses, there is no antibiotic-like cure once a dog is infected. The only course is to treat the symptoms until the immune system has a chance to rally itself, just as for a human viral infection like flu or the common cold.

In the case of parvo, the virus attacks fast-dividing cells, and a growing puppy offers many targets. Usually, the critical nourishment-gathering cells lining the intestines are the ultimate victims; the end of an unsuccessful struggle against parvo is marked by bloody diarrhea and extreme dehydration as these cells die and slough off. The virus is present in unthinkable numbers in these discharges, which are the chief route by which other dogs are infected.

Ron explained to me how parvo decimated dog lots in Alaska back in the seventies before the disease was fully understood. He said mushers were thankful if even one or two pups in a litter survived. In an attempt to develop a parvo-resistant strain of dogs, the survivors were bred over and over, with some success. But still, without the development of good vaccines it's unlikely mushing would be where it is today.

By coincidence, last week I picked up a copy of *The Hot Zone*, which details how the Ebola virus and its cousins emerged from the African rain forests to make devastating but luckily localized attacks on humans. The last part of the book covers an outbreak of Ebola in a monkey importing company's holding facilities in Reston, Virginia, in late 1989. My first shock was the realization I was living barely 10 miles from Reston when the incident occurred and actually drove past the building while it was happening.

The second and more sobering jolt was the eerie similarities between exotic viruses like Ebola and the canine parvovirus that devastated my puppies. Indeed, parvo is the Ebola of the canine world. Like Ebola, it jumped species with terrifying results, wreaking widespread carnage before anyone really knew what it was. Parvo spreads much like Ebola, and is even more long-lived outside its hosts. It is just as lethal to puppies as any of the terror viruses are to humans, and kills just as quickly and as terribly.

Human viruses like Ebola are treated by the experts in the same manner as an enemy biological warfare attack, with precautions like those in *Andromeda Strain*. Unfortunately, I don't have a space suit or a Level Four containment facility, so all I can do is load up my garden pump sprayer and dispense bleach by the gallon while I try to keep up the vaccinations on the ones who are left.

Of course, the damage is already done and nothing I do now will make much difference. The four pups still on my lot—Bonnie, Clyde, Shorty, and Big Mac—have already been heavily exposed and have apparently worked through it on their own. I'm really no better off than Ron and his fellow dog drivers 20 years ago, despite the advances of modern veterinary medicine.

August 25, 1995
Montana Creek, Alaska

We're off and running again. I've been anxious to get moving because the daily training routine will keep me from dwelling on the depressing nightmare of the parvo epidemic. Regardless of what has happened, I still have to get ready to run the race next year.

With Ron's help, I finally get the long-disused three-wheeler to start after a couple of hours of wrench-bending and some Anglo-Saxon language practice. About 10 o'clock, when it's good and dark, I hook up the gangline to the handlebars and lay it out in the driveway. I notice the dogs are watching me intently. When I go inside the storage shed and come out with the harnesses, they start barking. When I walk over and put the first harness on Socks, they all go wild.

I pick out five more of the usual suspects and hook them up amid a deafening bedlam. This will be their first real chance to get off the chains and out of the dog lot since last March and they're all at a fever pitch. As I start the engine, the team goes completely bonkers and gives a bulldozer-strength yank in unison, snapping the four heavy bungee cords I'd put in the line to absorb the shock of pulling the three-wheeler.

The next thing I see is the entire team ripping out of the driveway unencumbered by me or the machine. In my haste I can't get the three-wheeler to start so I shove it out of the way and run over to my van. I roar off after the dogs, betting (and hoping) they've turned back toward Ron's instead of down toward the highway. I hope Socks will keep them out of too much trouble. This isn't exactly how I wanted to start the season.

Sure enough, they're milling around in the entrance to Ron's driveway like a bewildered six-tentacled octopus. As I walk over to them I'm laughing so hard I can barely stand up. Socks is sheepishly trying to lead them back to my place and they're all slinking along behind him. I hop back in the van and call to them to follow me as I drive back.

Sensing I've absolved them, they line out and trot behind my van like ducklings following mama to the lake. Back in the driveway I hook them up to the three-wheeler again (this time without the bungees), toss them all a biscuit, and let them rest for a few minutes. Then I hop aboard and we pick up where we left off, streaking down the borough road to our normal start-of-the-season turnaround point (an unused circle driveway) a mile and a half away.

Socks seems to remember this place from last year and swings into the darkened turnaround just like the pro he is. Suddenly I see somebody is camping there. Socks runs right past the smoldering campfire, under a tarp, and has his nose stuck inside the flap of the poor camper's tent before I can get the team stopped. I race up and get Socks turned around and headed back out the driveway before the half-awake and thoroughly befuddled outdoorsman can react.

With a shouted apology for our interruption, we roll back out on the road. As we trundle back down to the dog lot, I laugh at the absurdity of the situation. Then it dawns on me things could have become serious if the surprised camper had decided to start shooting at what he thought might be a wolf or a bear. To have had several dogs inadvertently shot (and maybe even myself) would not have been an auspicious beginning to the season.

But it turns out to be a good run and Socks shows he's still the number one leader. I'm satisfied—and more than a little relieved—that we're finally back in the swing of training. No more summertime distractions: now the real goal of finishing the 1996 Iditarod is snapping back into sharp focus and I can make concrete progress toward it every day. Maybe it will be a good training season after all.

August 30, 1995
Wasilla, Alaska

I've met some interesting people flying for Hudson's this summer, but I think a pair of young Swedes from the Stockholm area ranks right up at the top.

Nicolas and Johan came over in July—fairly late in the climbing season—to climb Mount McKinley. In fact, by the time they returned toward the end of the month after reaching the summit in 11 days, they were almost the only people left on the mountain.

When we flew them back from the long-dismantled Kahiltna Glacier base camp, they announced they were going to spend the rest of the summer in Alaska hiking the Talkeetna Mountains. After we got over our initial surprise—not many people try the trek across the trailless 10,000-square-mile wilderness of the Talkeetnas—we realized they were serious.

We helped them figure out the best route (or at least one they had a chance of finishing before winter) and then flew them up to the old mining strip at Iron Creek. Then they vanished into the back country and we didn't hear anything from them until yesterday, when they ambled into our hangar looking like they'd just walked from pole to pole.

They said they'd had a few adventures, such as falling into raging mountain rivers, nearly starving, and dodging bears, but otherwise they'd had a grand time. After 25 days they'd finally made it down the Chickaloon River to the Glenn Highway and hitched a ride back to Talkeetna.

As we pumped cup after cup of coffee into them, the talk turned inevitably to dogs. They allowed as how they'd always been interested in dogs in Sweden, but they'd never had much of a chance to get more involved. When I mentioned the Iditarod, they immediately asked if they could see my dogs. Since they needed a place to spend the night, I said why not—I could hook up the trailer to the three-wheeler and they could ride along when I ran the dogs, and then they could help me feed and give some shots to the puppies.

Back at my place, hooking up nine dogs, I was struck by the trailer's uncanny resemblance to a tumbrel cart carrying victims to the guillotine. (I wonder if Citizen Robespierre and his henchmen ever envisioned using dog power to haul the *ancien régime* to the butcher block.) I didn't mention this to my visitors, but I figured they'd get the picture soon enough.

The dogs didn't even notice the triple load and surged out of the driveway. Within a mile, they'd managed to flip the trailer on the back trail, spilling my Scandinavian sojourners into the willow bushes. For the rest of the run I used the engine on the three-wheeler to both help and hinder the team as we rocketed down the narrow, bush-lined track.

When we made it back (it was only a three-mile run) the first thing my somewhat-the-worse-for-wear passengers said was "We want to run the Iditarod." Considering they'd just climbed Mount McKinley and hiked across the Talkeetnas, and one of them had previously biked from Stockholm across Europe and Africa, I had the feeling they might actually mean it.

They asked how much it would cost to run the 1997 or 1998 race; I told them $10,000 to $30,000 if they wanted to rent a ready-to-go team from someone like Joe Redington and show up in December to get their qualifying races out of the way. On the other hand, I mentioned they might come over at the beginning of the season to work as handlers for room and board at one of the big kennels that sends one or two training teams down the trail every year. More than a few young mushers have earned their first trip to Nome that way, breaking in a team of yearlings.

They thought the latter concept might work for them because it would allow them to really learn the ropes and get to know the dogs. They were also concerned about looking like "fire-and-forget" mushers who rent a team for one race and never get on the back of a dog sled again. Given a chance, they want to take up mushing seriously in Sweden and maybe return in the future to run the Iditarod with their own teams.

Anyway, they proposed to come over at the end of August next year or perhaps the year after to start work, and I said I'd try to find a musher who might be able to work with them when the time was right. They also said they could probably get sponsors in Sweden and come up with maybe $5,000 each, which would nicely cover the extra expenses necessary for entry fees, dog food, and gear for the qualifying races and the Iditarod itself. I said that would be a big help, since walking in the door with 5,000-buck checks pinned to their shirts would certainly make a few more mushers amenable to working with them for the season.

They need a ride to Anchorage today, and since the weather is going to be lousy anyway I call in to Hudson's and take a day off. We pile into the van and head down the highway. On the way I decide this will be a good time to stop at Iditarod Headquarters and sign up for the 1996 race. My income tax refund should eventually cover most of it and I'll shuffle some bills until it gets here. Besides, if I don't get my money on the table now, I'll just find some equally frivolous way to spend it. And once I'm signed up I'll be a bit more motivated to keep up my training schedule.

Joanne Potts, the race director and a longtime acquaintance, is glad to see me; she wasn't sure I really meant to try it again this year. As I fill out the paperwork she says I'm number 52, which is a lot of people for this early in the year. She thinks it might be one of the biggest races yet if sign-ups continue at the current rate; this is fine with me—the more the merrier, since it means I'll have some company at the back of the pack. If I'm running with somebody I won't be as prone to scratch if my thinking processes get muddled, which I'm sure they will somewhere out on the trail.

As I drop Nicolas and Johan off at a hostel in Anchorage to wait for their plane, we agree to stay in touch. Now that I'm on the Internet, we decide to use it as our main communications link. I almost wish they could stay and try to run next year, but they've got a lot of work to do in Sweden (including assembling a video of their adventures for Swedish television) before they can head back this way.

> *After a stop at Sam's Club for another 500 pounds of dog food, I hit the highway in high spirits. Getting my entry fee in was my major financial (and psychological) hurdle, and I think meeting the young Swedes and sharing a bit of their enthusiasm was good therapy. I'm finally back on track, and this time I'm going at it in a considerably more systematic and methodical manner than last year. I'll have to scrape to get everything else together, but now I'm sure I'll manage. At least I feel like I almost know what I'm doing this time around.*

September 20, 1995
Montana Creek, Alaska

I've been running the dogs the past couple of weeks with my old beat-up three-wheeler, the same one I vowed last year never to use again for anything except perhaps a suicide attempt. The four-wheeler I borrowed from Bert last year isn't available yet, so out of sheer necessity I've been hooking nine dogs up to the tricycle from hell and going up to 10 miles on trails that would challenge Arnold Schwartzenegger and his personal HumVee.

True to form, I've been up close and personal with the shrubbery at least once or twice on every run, thanks to the fact the three-wheeler has about the same stability as a case of 50-year-old dynamite. The dogs have been fully aware of this, of course, and have positively delighted in whipping me around corners and through ruts whenever they've had the chance.

Yesterday I finally picked up the four-wheeler, making the 100-mile odyssey into town in Old Blue, the $700 dog truck Ron and I acquired a couple of weeks ago. Considering Old Blue needs some front-end work (actually, a lot of front-end work), and taking into account I also picked up a ton of lumber and dog food, the drive home was more like a drunken sailor wobbling back to the ship on Saturday night.

Tonight, as I hook up 12 dogs for the first run on the four-wheeler, it's raining. This has been the normal state of affairs this fall. We've broken all of the rainfall records for Southcentral Alaska, and I think it's rained here on 20 of the last 21 days, sometimes quite heavily. Most people are taking it philosophically, reckoning this is payback for the extraordinary summers and falls we've had for the past two years. I firmly believe there's no such thing as normal weather in Alaska—only extremes some anonymous statistician massages to derive a meaningless average.

This fall, most dogs in this part of Alaska have probably been wondering whether they're training for the Iditarod or an English Channel swim. I'm debating whether I should start breeding for dogs with webbed feet. Running down the narrow tracks with their over-hanging branches laden with moisture is like breaking trail in a rain forest. It's great for the dogs because it keeps them cool, but I've been thinking about investing in a diver's dry suit.

In addition, some sections of the trail are so muddy there's no way to stop anything with wheels—with or without brakes—if the dogs don't want to cooperate. On a previous run with the three-wheeler, they dragged it fully 50 yards through the goo after they flipped it and tossed me into a mud puddle the size of Lake Erie. The snow is going to be positively welcome this year, and the sooner the better.

Mud or no, the dogs are getting back into shape quickly. I can already tell the difference, especially on the cooler nights when they aren't as oppressed by the unseasonable warmth. It's clear they are happy to be out on the trail again after being canine couch potatoes all summer. With the exception of a couple of the old veterans like Rocky and Socks, who probably wouldn't get excited if they were turned loose in a dog food factory, they are all frantically eager to run.

I'm methodically working to train 24 of them, and to identify the ones that won't make it for one reason or another. Already I've decided old Slipper, who is 11 years old, won't start. She is, as always, more than willing to run and is still a wonderful leader, but it's time for her to retire. She can help train puppies and go on local runs as long as she can pack her harness, but there's no point in subjecting her to the rigors of the Iditarod or even a serious mid-distance race at her age, especially with the new rules which will automatically disqualify a musher if a dog dies. Besides, her night-blindness seems to be slowly getting worse, and I'm worried she might hurt herself on the long runs in the dark that comprise so much of any distance race in the winter.

In a way, it's a little sad to see the inevitable end of such an illustrious career, but she's more than earned her pension. She'll join Chewy and Josephine and a couple of other not-quite-varsity dogs. They'll still get to run often enough (and Josephine will probably have several more litters of exceptional pups), but they're just not Iditarod material. In any case, I'm not going to get rid of them unless someone wants a pet: after all, they're family now, and they'll always have a home here.

October 4, 1995
Montana Creek, Alaska

I haven't gone two waking hours since March without turning over in my mind what I should and shouldn't have done on the trail to Rainy Pass. I've run every mile countless times and examined everything from more angles than Dostoyevsky. All of the introspectives come down to the same conclusion: I should have kept going. Whatever trials and tribulations I'd have encountered would have been trivial compared to what I've put myself through since then.

I think the major lesson I've learned is very simple, and goes well beyond anything I did or didn't do after the start of the Iditarod. It's something very basic, something I thought I'd certainly absorbed by the time I graduated from high school. In the words of every coach I've ever had, I didn't want to finish the race badly enough. I didn't take it seriously enough and I didn't sacrifice enough. And I paid the price in the end.

Finishing the Iditarod, much less eventually doing well, is a matter of desire and determination, and must extend to every facet of training and even life itself. To read my journal from last year, one would think I understood this, but it took a baptism of fire (or ice) to finally bring it home.

This summer has seen what can best be characterized as a stiffening of my resolve. I've been able to step back and take a more or less objective look at just what I'll need to do to improve my chances to finish. It's clear my preparation last year was riddled with too many inconsistencies and waverings of purpose. Despite the occasional flashes of insight, I was a basically a dilettante.

One of my biggest problems was my consuming involvement in student teaching in Anchorage during the week; I never really built the continuity with the dogs I needed. I missed too many subtle signs from them I should have noticed: stopping on hills, missing commands, becoming unfocused at critical times.

And I definitely didn't work hard enough to bond with my leaders. I truly didn't appreciate the value of a good leader until suddenly I didn't have any when it counted the most. I made a big mistake by using Pullman in lead almost exclusively for the qualifying races and even for training because she was a little faster than Socks. Running back in the team, Socks drifted away and seemed to lose interest—and I missed the signals.

This year I've gone out of my way to make sure Socks and I are best buddies and he gets his fair share of time in front. He could have kept me on the straight and narrow on the way to Rainy Pass and beyond if I'd only realized how good he was—and is.

I've managed to get pretty close to Buck as well; I consider this an accomplishment of sorts, since he was terribly timid when I first got him, and coaxing him out of his shell took months. This is important, because Buck is my secret weapon this year. Like Socks, he's a mature, mellow 'power-steering' leader and is big enough to drag the whole team if he has to; unlike Socks, he sets a good pace. I wish I'd had him during the Iditarod, and in fact I could have: John Allison offered him to me in January but I figured Pullman would be all the leader I'd need. I'll not make that mistake again.

Of course, I won't have any females in heat. I now realize I let the "heat wave" distract me when I should have dropped the offenders and kept moving. It wasn't an insurmountable problem. Steve Adkins has told me how he somehow made it to Nome with most of his team in heat, putting up with all manner of mayhem in every village. Plenty of other mushers have encountered even worse events of this nature and still made it through in good order. In any case, I'll be using more big males this time, and the females will all be "on the pill."

The biggest single change has resulted from the dogs being at my place instead of over at Ron's. Now I know there is no substitute for staying close to the dogs in a physical and emotional sense. I am forced to pay attention to them whenever I'm home, and I've learned worlds about all of them I simply missed when they were out of sight and often out of mind.

There's no such thing as a part-time dog musher. The commitment must be total, both physically and mentally, and the dogs must become a part of daily life. Continuity must be maintained, or critical trends and important nuances will be missed. Only now am I starting to understand what the really serious mushers have gone through to get where they are—and I appreciate their accomplishment even more.

November 4, 1995
Montana Creek, Alaska

Enough autumn, already! Mother Nature has been dealing from the bottom of the deck to Southcentral Alaska this fall. If winter doesn't get here soon, we may be running the Iditarod on four-wheelers, or maybe in boats.

First came weeks of rain, then a few tantalizingly brisk mornings in early October, spreading a crust of ice over enough lakes to scare everyone into taking their airplanes off floats a couple of weeks early. Finally the snow started to fall late on the 10th, dumping six inches around Willow and an inch or two here at Montana Creek. The adult dogs were beside themselves with eagerness, remembering snow meant sleds, which in turn meant lots of interesting runs.

Then came the sucker punch: the temperature slithered back up to hover right at freezing, followed by days of cold rain. It's difficult to imagine a worse situation for training dogs. Enough rain-soaked snow remained on the still-frozen ground to make trails impassable, too slick for four-wheelers and too thin for sleds. And the dogs were thoroughly miserable to boot, shivering in their houses and under their trees in the bone-chilling drizzle.

My running log began to look like it was written in disappearing ink, with week-long gaps. I had no choice but to continue with the four-wheeler whenever I could catch a break in the hideous weather, even though I had virtually no control in many places where a thin layer of mud and lake-sized puddles had formed over the waterproof frozen ground. About all I accomplished was to keep the dogs from completely losing the conditioning I'd so painstakingly put on them in August and September.

By the end of October the rain stopped and we actually had another grudging few inches of snow. The first weekend of November surprised everyone (especially the harried weather prognosticators) by being forecast to be nearly perfect for dog driving, with bright sun, no wind, and temperatures in the teens.

On Thursday night before the weekend, Bert called and casually mentioned daughter Kim would be bringing up six Russian exchange students and their sponsors on Saturday morning for sled rides, maybe 15 people or so. And by the way, he said, Channel Two News from Anchorage would probably be coming along to tape the whole thing.

After I recovered from the shock, I frantically ransacked my untouched-since-March storage shed to find the snow hooks, quick releases, and miscellaneous pieces of rigging necessary to fit out the sleds. I finally got everything together about four o'clock this morning and caught a few hours of sleep.

Now it's show time. Kim arrives about noon with her girlfriends and the exchange students, along with their sponsors and chaperones plus several of their teachers from Anchorage. Mercifully, the television crews can't make it, which is a major relief: the last thing I need is a close-up of my dog lot and typically cluttered premises splashed all over the six-o'clock news.

The unfortunate thing about such publicity is dog lots can be messy places, especially after the weather we've had the past couple of months— and mine is no exception. My dogs all have shelter from the elements and plenty of chain to move around, and they're as healthy as horses. However, some people think dog lots should look like living rooms, which is a difficult mind-set to combat, especially when the cyclopean eye of the idiot box magnifies the smallest detail and takes everything out of context. Somebody, somewhere, would see something he or she didn't like and I'd be weeks trying to set things right.

The potential for bad press is compounded because there have been several notorious cases of neglected and abused dogs in Southcentral Alaska over the past couple of years—none of which involved serious mushers—and dog lots have become a hot-button issue. Worse, the borough Animal Control code is apparently copied from some urban Lower 48 set of ordinances and makes no official distinction between a well-cared-for dog team and a sweatshop puppy factory. Every dog is assumed to be a potentially rabid pit bull and every kennel owner is guilty of neglect until proven otherwise. Most mushers loathe any involvement with Animal Control officers because, like any good bureaucrats, the critter cops can always find some "t" not crossed or "i" not dotted.

I went through a particularly gruesome episode with Animal Control last year after one of my dogs got excited and nipped me on a training run. Even though it was my own dog and was my fault, and I wasn't even hurt, I dutifully reported the incident (against the dire warnings of all my musher friends) when I got a tetanus booster shot. Extricating myself from Animal Control's spider web took me two months, including a 10-day quarantine for the dog, half a dozen letters and phone calls, a 100-dollar fine, and a trip to court to get two additional tickets thrown out. At one point I was seriously worried about being able to continue training for the Iditarod.

Needless to say, I have no intention of ever reporting another dog bite, or even giving Animal Control the time of day if I don't have to do so. It's a sad commentary that the Mat-Su Borough, the dog mushing capital of the world which proudly advertises itself as the Home of the Iditarod, has an animal control code easily capable of shutting down any respectable musher on the strength of a few groundless accusations, while the true animal abusers never seem to get caught.

Anyway, for an entire day there are 20 people buzzing around my tiny cabin and dog lot, a goodly number of whom speak lots of Russian and very little English. I'm continually concerned that if any of Kim's guests gets bitten by a dog or injured on the sleds, I'll probably lose everything I own, not merely the dogs and any hope of running the Iditarod. I finally just stop worrying about it since there's not anything I can do.

Once things get moving, Kim and a friend take the sleds on three-mile runs giving rides to the Russians and their Alaskan sponsors. While the girls are handling the main event with the dogs, I'm able to chat with the Russian chaperones and American teachers. I'm surprised to find out the Russians are from a suburban area near Moscow, not a lot different from, say, one of the bedroom communities near Anchorage. They've never seen a dog lot, and apparently have little experience in rural, near-wilderness settings like the Upper Susitna Valley.

When Bert told me I was going to be invaded, I simply assumed the Russians would be from the Far East or Siberia, areas with close ties to Alaska since the collapse of the Iron Curtain (which was often called the Ice Curtain in this part of the world). These visitors are actually more like the Europeans who flood Talkeetna every summer, with Continental outlooks and experiences. Although Southcentral Alaska's forests and climate make it almost identical to much of northern Russia, including areas near Moscow, the 49th State might as well be on another planet for these folks, judging from the questions they ask.

I studied Russian for several years in college and was reasonably fluent at one time, but I avoid any conversations. To say my command of the language is somewhat rusty would be an understatement: Russian decays very quickly for non-native speakers like me, and I'd be lucky to get from the Moscow airport to a hotel without winding up on a bus to Kazakhstan.

To my visitors' great interest, I point out a couple of my dogs have actually been to Russia. Eddie and Weasel ran on the Hope '92 race from Nome to Anadyr with Diana Moroney; Eddie made it all the way, but Weasel had pups in Provideniya, a couple of which are now mainstays of Diana's team. I've often thought it a strange irony some of my dogs have traveled to places I've never been—such as Russia, a place I've wanted to visit for many years.

The entourage departs about sunset; I'm relieved everything went well. Next time, though, I'd like a bit more warning. I can use the time to brush up on my Russian so I can minimize the chances of inadvertently causing some kind of international incident. I wonder how I'd say, "Sorry about that—maybe the doctor in Anchorage can sew your finger back on...."

Foxes are found all along the Iditarod. They scavenge leftovers from checkpoints and prowl the remote stretches waiting for mushers to stop their teams for a snack. Unfortunately, they also sometimes carry rabies.

November 15, 1995
Montana Creek, Alaska

Every musher is, by definition, an astute observer of wildlife. This sort of goes with the territory because a dog team isn't too far removed from being wildlife itself.

For instance, on the trail it's hard not to take more than a passing interest in moose and other wilderness denizens capable of eliciting hair-raising reactions from an easily excited pack of instinctive predators.

Even in the dog lot there are more animals to consider than just the dogs. A moose can wander into a dog yard, creating instant mayhem as the dogs go ballistic trying to get at it, even though most of them probably wouldn't know what to do with it if they caught it. Bears occasionally figure out that chained dogs aren't a threat and will nonchalantly parade right through the lot looking for munchies while the dogs cower in their houses. (While bears don't eat dogs, it's been rumored they will take puppies if the opportunity presents itself.)

And smaller critters merit attention, too. Canny foxes and coyotes prowl the edges of the lot looking for food, and squirrels and mice and voles can demolish a bag of dog food faster than it can be unloaded from the truck. Even the resident house cat wandering where it shouldn't can cause a commotion, since not all sled dogs are exactly on speaking terms with felines.

But easily the most persistent of God's creatures that bedevil mushers are the ravens. Central to Native mythology for millennia because of their longevity and intelligence and mischievous exploits, ravens can drive a musher to distraction. Indeed, the black beaked bombers sometimes seem to make a game of playing with a frazzled kennel owner, staging hit-and-run raids on food caches and trash dumps with the skill and cunning of a Special Forces A-Team. Edgar Allan Poe had nothing on mushers where ravens are concerned, and many a frustrated kennel owner would love to tell every one of the brazen beady-eyed birds "Nevermore!"

Ravens and dog lots are (to the ravens anyway) a marriage made in heaven. There are always scraps of food and bits and pieces of all kinds of interesting things around the place, and that's enough to mark it as a raven shopping mall, complete with food court. It doesn't matter if the munchies or baubles are in plastic bags or boxes; ravens can outwit even child-proof containers with dismaying ease, usually by simply ripping them apart with their powerful beaks and claws. The dark demolishers can even open commercial trash containers: on the now-closed Adak Naval Station, it was a serious offense to leave a dumpster unlocked. The feathered felons knew how to pry open the swinging side doors, after which they would throw everything inside, outside, where they would sort through it like browsers at a yard sale.

Racing season opens up a whole new world of possibilities for the beady-eyed beasts. Ravens long ago deduced that sled dog races are nothing more than long-distance smorgasbords with lots of good scenery. They seem to know mushers' favorite spots to snack their dogs on the trail and won't even wait for the team to get out of sight before they descend for their feast. When my team sees a group of ravens on the trail ahead they treat it as a chance to get even with the arrogant aviators. The ravens, of course, will wait until the very last second to flutter out of reach of the frantic dogs, which steams up the team even more.

Ravens have discovered checkpoints, naturally. In some places they are even worse than wolves about breaking into mushers' food bags. And the damage isn't limited to rifling food bags. At a particular Iditarod checkpoint which will remain nameless, a local cabin owner unwittingly repainted his airplane the same colors as the color-coded Iditarod food bags. He never could figure out why the resident ravens were so bent on tearing holes in his fabric-covered wings for no apparent reason.

The dusky demons have begun to use my dog lot as a central staging point now that winter is here in earnest. I can almost set my clock in the morning by their raucous cries as two dozen of them strut around the yard just out of reach of the frantic dogs. If I've left anything outside and unprotected, such as a dozen bulging trash bags I'm planning to take to the dump, I've only got a few minutes to get dressed and charge out the door to scare them away or else my driveway will look like a truck bomb detonated in the borough landfill. Of course, they know I have to go to work sooner or later and will set up shop in convenient nearby trees and wait for me to leave. As if that's not bad enough, they will sit on their perches and talk back and forth to each other; they have dozens of different vocalizations and I think I'm finally starting to recognize the ones for "silly human" and "when is he going to leave?"

At my place they've been year-round yard guests from Hell. I've been at my wit's end for months trying to figure out how to chase them off and keep them away. Of course, killing one is out of the question. It's supposed to be the very worst kind of bad luck, and besides, I'm quite sure they're smart enough to take their revenge by turning my place into a real-life replay of Hitchcock's "The Birds" if I waste one of their brethren.

For awhile I had some luck with bottle rockets. However, I couldn't use the most effective ones (with the shrieking three-stage whistle) because they drove the dogs bonkers. So, I contented myself with the simple kind that just pop at the end of their flight, although I had to launch at least three or four just to get one in the general vicinity of my target, and the net effect was to make the dogs think they were under attack by Iraqi Scuds. Unfortunately, the extremely dry conditions this summer forced me to shut down my homemade Patriot battery for fear of burning down the whole valley. By the time the fall rains hit and it was safe to practice backyard rocketry again I forgot where I put my remaining arsenal and the local fireworks stands were shuttered for the season.

I've got an idea that may finally solve the dilemma of the devilish dinosaur descendants. I know where I can get some live traps and I plan to capture a few of the more brazen birds. Then I'm going to make some special harnesses and tuglines and hook them up in front of my leaders. I figure it will add at least five miles an hour to the team's speed and will be an object lesson for the rest of their clan. And if all else fails, I'll just put up a big KFC sign out front; that should scare them all over into the Yukon Territory....

November 21, 1995
Montana Creek, Alaska

What a difference a year makes. Last Thanksgiving Eve we had just been buried under several feet of snow, followed by a 30-below cold snap. The dogs had been idle for a couple of weeks and I was flat on my back in the Elmendorf Hospital emergency room with pneumonia.

This year we have minimal snow, but enough for decent training, and the temperature has been relatively moderate, only hitting 20 below for a few nights. I'm a lot healthier and the dogs are running often and well. Barring any major problems, we've settled into what might develop into a good training season.

Tonight's run is a beginning of sorts. For the first time since the last Iditarod, I've hooked up 10 dogs on the sled (because of marginal trails I've so far limited my training runs to eight). We're headed out for an easy 18-mile run, actually a break-in cruise for a couple of the dogs. In particular, I haven't run Buck for a week or so because of an apparently injured shoulder, which fortunately turned out to be little more than a bruise.

I expect a good run, but when we explode out of the lot and onto the trail I hang on for dear life. Somehow adding the extra two dogs has crossed a magic threshold and the team suddenly comes together as a fully functioning, Iditarod-quality unit. Indeed, I am chiefly worried the team will go too fast during the first mile or so, risking all manner of injuries too horrible to contemplate. I stand on the drag to keep the headlong rush down to something manageable, but the dogs just want to keep running and I finally give up and let them roll.

Normally they will slow down after the excitement wears off. To my amazement, though, Buck keeps up a blistering pace, loping for mile after glorious mile, and the team stays right with him. Everything is as perfect as I've seen it this year. The temperature is a brisk 10 above and the sky crystal clear. To the west the setting sun has erected a palace of reds and yellows and pinks. At every turn is another picture-perfect view of Denali 60 miles to the northwest, its peak aglow with the rich, golden winter light, its rugged flanks steeped in deep blue shadows.

Even when we reach the steepest hill on the trail, the one which has always given the team pause, they charge into it at a dead run, shifting smoothly into low gear to grind their way up the steep 200-foot ascent. As we crest the grade, I glance back over my shoulder at one of the finest views in this part of the state, just as Denali's four-mile-high summit flames a fiery orange with the very last of the sun's rays.

Still the dogs don't let up. At the top of every hill, they accelerate as if they had just left the yard. I try to stop them at the far end of the run to give them a break but they won't have it; little Maybelline screams to go almost immediately and the others respond by roaring off back down the trail. I have to catch the sled as it careens by, but I'm not at all put out. Finally I have a team again, and this one seems to be better than last year's in every measure I can imagine.

With Buck bounding effortlessly on, we roll away the miles on our way back home, toward the fading sunset. In my mind's eye I project myself out past the Alaska Range, cruising for the western horizon with Nome somewhere beneath the brilliant evening star. At first I try to put myself in last year's race, pretending I never scratched at Rainy Pass, imagining this is somehow a way to reclaim what I lost.

Gradually I realize last year is ancient history. There must be no more dwelling on the past, only a focus on the future. This isn't last year's team; this is the team with which I'll share the trail to Nome in barely three months. This finely crafted machine is going to give me a chance to redeem myself, and not just in my imagination.

Now, finally, I've been jolted into the look-forward mode. I'm preparing to run the upcoming race, not trying to relive the last one. As the team tears around the last corner and Buck breaks into a sprint for the last quarter-mile into the yard, I silently thank him for putting everything into perspective. There's a lot of work yet to be done, but now I'm satisfied we're all back on the right trail.

November 26, 1995
Montana Creek, Alaska

We're just sliding into our first serious cold snap of the season and it's already 30 below and dropping. When the clear, still, glacially frigid nights start to dominate our area late in November, and temperatures plunge to levels considered brisk even for the Last Frontier, the dogs must suffer along with us humans. After I feed the dogs I walk through the lot to see how they're coping with the onset of the "real Alaskan winter."

Wolves, of course, have survived for thousands of years in 60 below and worse, but they have always had the advantage of freedom of movement to find shelter. Dogs on chains can only curl up in their houses or on the ground.

Some dogs have coats thick enough to insulate them from cold ground and frigid air; these hardy individuals seem to be impervious to cold. For instance, Silvertip is what I call a "40-below" dog; he's at least three-quarters wolf and his wild heritage has endowed him with a deceptively thick coat which lets him sleep anywhere he wants, no matter how cold it gets. I'm continually amazed to see him sleeping on his house or on the icy ground at 30 below, curled into a compact, heat-conserving ball with his bushy tail covering his muzzle. His coat will be covered in frost, which means he is insulated so well his body heat doesn't even melt the fragile frost crystals. He and a few of his cohorts just can't be coaxed into their houses during the winter, although during warmer seasons they will sometimes deign to use their accommodations when it rains or the sun gets too hot.

Others, especially those whose gene pools include breeds less adapted to cold weather, can run into problems when the weather turns really cold. Martin Buser said an old Native musher once told him the best indication of a dog with insufficient insulation is to look at the size of the hole melted in the snow underneath it in the morning: the bigger the hole, the more heat the dog is losing. It's been estimated a dog can consume as many as 2,000 calories a night shivering on below-zero ground. This is not insignificant when the dog in question is already burning several thousand calories a day, as is common in training.

The net result of any calorie shortage in dogs is the same as in humans: an inevitable drop in weight as fat and muscle must be metabolized just to break even in the daily calorie battle. On an extended race, when the dogs need up to 10,000 calories a day and every calorie is critical, a cold-induced deficit can quickly spell major trouble.

Sometimes on the trail, dogs can simply curl up and let falling or blowing snow cover them up. They sleep very comfortably in their natural snow caves, which serve admirably to insulate them from the outside air. However, there are surprisingly few places on the trail where this kind of refuge is available. All too often the snow is too thin or the wind too strong.

Another partial answer is the use of dog blankets, which cover everything from the neck to the tail and wrap around underneath. The dogs can wear these while running; they're especially useful in windy conditions when even the best-insulated dogs can lose heat at astounding rates and can risk frostbite as well. However, dog blankets have limitations: they're expensive, they can be tight enough to restrict a dog from curling into an energy-efficient ball, and some dogs will simply eat them if given the chance.

The best solution to combat calorie loss when the dogs are at rest is a good old-fashioned bed of straw. Of course, the insulating properties of lowly straw are certainly not a new discovery—humans have been using it for everything from bedding to roofing since prehistory. More recently, it's been conclusively proven that a dog can sleep very comfortably on even a little straw, with or without a dog blanket, at 40 or 50 below zero.

In fact, every big race provides straw at the checkpoints, or allows mushers to ship it out for their teams. The Iditarod ships huge amounts of straw to the checkpoints. Much of it is mailed, but every bale for the remote locations has to be flown in: I personally flew 45 bales into the frighteningly short strip at Rohn Roadhouse for the 1994 race (back before I took leave of my senses and decided to see everything from the ground). But the effort is worth it and it's most gratefully received by dogs and mushers alike; more than a few exhausted mushers have grabbed a quick nap next to their dogs on an inviting pile of straw.

However, there's something more to straw that seems to have a special appeal to dogs. Maybe it's the hint of all the various life forms it has encountered on its journey from the golden fields of autumn to the depths of winter. Perhaps it's the unexpected, explosive scent of summer in the bleak olfactory wasteland of the long subarctic night. Whatever the reason, introducing sled dogs to fresh straw is like turning kids loose in a toy store. They will nose it, sniff it, poke it, turn it, toss it, roll in it, bounce in it. Ultimately they will circle and circle like their wolf ancestors and finally plop down with the canine equivalent of a sigh of contentment.

Tonight I decide it's time for new straw for everyone. The dogs can somehow sense when I intend to straw them before I break open the bale. They become even more excited than at feeding time, regardless of the temperature. As soon as I shake out the first armful into the first doghouse, the clamor becomes earsplitting. They all know what I'm doing and they all want their share immediately.

I stop and watch each dog's reaction to the gift, even though I know I'm keeping the others impatiently waiting. The old veterans are predictable: because they bed down on straw at checkpoints on the long races, they have come to regard it as an omen of respite from the rigors of the trail. Their pleasure is plain to see; they savor the straw almost like a gourmet lingering over a particularly notable meal.

Some of the younger dogs play in the straw in a sort of instant reversion to puppyhood. They drag it completely out of their houses, spread it out, nudge it back into a pile, and jump into it. Whether the straw is in the doghouse seems to be purely secondary, and they are just as likely to sleep on it out in the open.

The puppies—now seven and eight months old—simply go ballistic. They don't yet really know what straw is, but it's obviously something different and fun to play with. Considering some of my pups haven't even figured out what their houses are for and actually seem to enjoy camping out in the cold, I'm not surprised at anything they do.

Their straw ends up scattered to the four winds (which are mercifully absent at the moment), along with their feeding dishes (which they enjoy stealing from each other) and even their houses (which they push around like hockey pucks on icy ground). I make sure some of the straw winds up wherever they seem to be sleeping, usually while they tie me up with their chains and try to lick me to death and chew my boot laces. For the pups, I guess strawing time is really just another excuse for them to play with their most favorite toy of all—me.

A strange game, this mushing business. We learn to take pleasure from the simplest and most unlikely things. Whoever would have thought humble, common straw could lead to such an entertaining and ultimately satisfying experience. I guess it all goes back to the most fundamental rule I've learned so far: if the dogs are happy, I'm happy.

The musher's alcohol cooker is one of the most important items carried on the sled. An outer metal bucket with ventilating holes encloses a special burner and supports a three- to five-gallon pot in which snow or water can be melted and heated. Most mushers fuel their cookers with automotive-variety HEET or equivalent products. Cookers can boil several gallons of water in ten to fifteen minutes under most conditions. The hot water is poured into a plastic bucket containing dry dog food and frozen meat; most mushers normally don't actually cook in their cookers because of the potential for bacterial growth.

December 10, 1995
Montana Creek, Alaska

My place is barely a mile from the Alaska Railroad and I can easily hear and even feel the trains rumbling by. As I feed the dogs tonight, the evening fast freight is thundering north to Fairbanks. Listening to its whistle moaning through the snow-covered forest, I have to think anyone who genuinely likes trains must appreciate dog teams.

I've been a train nut for years; I owe that to my father, who used to take me down to the Frisco yards in my home town in Arkansas to watch the last of the grand old steam engines working out their days on switching duty. When I went to college in Colorado, I spent many weekends exploring ghost towns and the hundreds of miles of abandoned railroads that once linked them. I became intimately familiar with long-gone names like the Rio Grande Southern, the South Park, the Colorado Midland, and the Silverton Northern. And I fell in love with steam engines, spending hours watching them wind through the mountains in one of their last redoubts along the Colorado-New Mexico border on the Denver and Rio Grande Western's Durango narrow-gauge line.

I suppose steam engines have always held a fascination for many people. They are (or were for their time) a culmination of man's inventive genius, harnessing the elemental powers of fire and water and steel in masterpieces of engineering. At the same time, they are completely visible: the great wheels, pistons, driving rods—everything is out in the open, not concealed behind impersonal metal streamlining as in a diesel engine or an airplane or a car. Steam engines impart a sense of purpose and raw power in a way matched by few of man's creations.

And a steam locomotive also has a very human side. The engineer and fireman who serve it are in a kind of symbiosis with their machine, tending

189

its needs as they would a living thing. And the engine seems very much to be alive, breathing smoke and steam, drinking water, eating fuel, and moving in a marvelously complicated rhythmic dance. Add in the deep, lonesome wail of a steam whistle on a dark night, and it's no secret why the steam engine has remained an indelible part of our culture even though it has vanished from the mainline rails.

The links between railroads and steam engines and dog teams may not be obvious at first glance, but any musher can easily see them. Perhaps the most obvious connection is that dog teams and trains are means to travel, and at least in this country saw their heyday in a previous, less complicated era. They are both the stuff of legends and evoke special emotions in many people. Even the narrow dog trail isn't a lot different from a railroad track, and there's an unmistakable resemblance between a dog team pulling a sled and an engine pulling cars.

But the real similarities go much deeper. Like steam engines, dog teams are living, breathing entities requiring special care from their drivers. They must be watered and fed at regular intervals and must have their moving parts frequently checked and sometimes even oiled; all mushers carry various liniments for sore canine feet, wrists, and shoulders, just as steam locomotive crewmen carry oil cans. Checkpoints on the big races could easily pass for water tanks and fueling stops; the dogs can only go so far before they must pause for more fuel for their fireboxes and water for their boilers.

Like the old steam engines, dog teams can be temperamental, requiring patience, tact, and diplomacy, and often as not a firm hand to correct wayward tendencies. Most striking of all, though, is the intense bond between the engineer and his engine, be it mechanical or canine. The old steam engineer came to know every creak and groan and rattle of his steel steed, just as the dog driver knows every signal from his dogs.

And finally, with the old engine crews as with mushers, pulling into the station or the checkpoint isn't always the object of the exercise. The trip is the thing, and the stop at the end of the track—or trail— is nothing more than a temporary layover before the next journey.

December 20-21, 1995
Forks Roadhouse, Alaska
The Forks Roadhouse Christmas Race

This has come to be called the Winter of No Snow. Our small area around Montana Creek has been fortunate in having maybe eight or ten inches total this season, enough to make decent trails. Elsewhere, though, it's been grim. Anchorage is looking at its first snowless Christmas in a decade, and many mushers around Palmer, Wasilla, and Big Lake are still training on dusty trails with four-wheelers.

The newspapers have been full of stories about the lack of snow and how it's affecting winter activities, especially dog mushing. The Copper Basin has only two or three inches, and Fairbanks only five. Organizers of the big early-season races are starting to become worried, since the historical pattern indicates this may be a really dry winter.

Just 10 miles south of us, Sheep Creek Lodge had to cancel its 100-mile race scheduled for last weekend, which would have been the kickoff for the racing season. They have a little snow, but not enough to connect to our good trails just a few miles north. The only other place with decent running is on the other side of the Susitna Valley, out toward the Peters Hills. This area always has snow because of its location and rising terrain, although this year it's a lot less than normal, not really much more than we have here at Montana Creek.

When Sheep Creek Lodge cancelled its race, Forks Roadhouse out on the Petersville Road decided on the spur of the moment to hold one of its own. The format is the same: two 50-mile heats on successive days. They're doing it today and tomorrow (in the middle of the week) to avoid the crush of urban snowmachiners who will infest the place over Christmas weekend.

As soon as I heard about the race, I frantically worked to get our old dog truck over to the local motor surgeons so they could get it running. Once they got inside it they found a list of woes as long as my arm, but they got it sufficiently reassembled for me to put my temporary dog boxes on the back, throw the sled on top, and rumble over to the roadhouse for the race. I sounded like an Alaska Railroad freight train because the muffler system ended somewhere directly under the cab, but here I am at the first race of the season in the entire state, along with 10 other diehards.

Obviously I don't intend to win anything; this is mainly to see how the dogs will do in the company of some serious mushers, such as Jeff King (the 1993 Iditarod champ), who brought two teams, and Roy Wade, a perennial contender in the local mid-distance racing scene. Steve Adkins, a good friend just down the road who shares our training trails, is also here; he has a good, solid team and hopes to take home a little money if he can.

Of course, Ma Nature played a little joke on us by dumping 10 inches of snow out here last night (we only got two or three at Montana Creek) and the trail is like a good deep-dish pizza: soft and extra punchy. At the musher's meeting I draw number 3, just like I did at the Sheep Creek race last year, and at the Copper Basin 300 also. As usual, it means I'll just get passed by everybody else.

After lots of coffee we hook up and hit the trail. This is the shortest day of the year, but it's starting off as a beautiful one, with lots of fresh snow and a gorgeous late-morning sunrise over the Talkeetna Mountains to the southeast. The race course has been shortened to only 33 miles from the original 50, ostensibly because some of the teams don't have enough conditioning. This disappoints Steve, who has been running up to 40 miles already on our good trails and was looking forward to taking advantage of the better training we've been getting.

I have a good start and my 12 dogs quickly work out all their kinks. We're cruising and having a great time on what is essentially a training run over a new trail. Of course, Jeff King immediately shows why he is an Iditarod front-runner as he passes everything in sight. He started number 10 or so, but he motors by me about 15 miles into the race like I'm standing still. Naturally, everybody else passes me by the time I get back, but I still have a very good run and a remarkably good time overall—only two hours and fifty minutes for 33 miles, better than 11 miles an hour. I'm only 35 minutes behind King, who has blasted around the course at more than 15 miles an hour. If my guys can hold a pace like this for the Iditarod, I'll be in super shape.

The next day dawns dreary and we start before the sun is actually up. Several teams have trouble getting out of the gate, and since I'm starting last today my team sees everything. Sure enough, I have to stop half a dozen times for minor mix-ups by the time we're two miles out. Then I try to pass another musher who is stopped and his dogs manage to get mine into a colossal tangle. Silvertip and Yankee start snapping at each other because Wild Thing is in heat and Pullman, my fast leader, stages a sit-down strike, along with Weasel, who can be very temperamental when she wishes.

My first impression is, "Been here, done this, got the T-shirt." This is an eerie recreation of my troubles on the Iditarod, when I let a few dogs in heat precipitate everything into the toilet. The musher with whom we've knotted up gets his dogs straightened out and then says he's going to turn around and scratch. I decide there's no way I'm going back; if I don't work through this I'm no better off than I was eight months ago.

After 20 minutes untangling and swapping around half a dozen dogs, I've got things sorted out. Wild Thing with her feminine wiles is back in wheel where nobody can get at her and old Buck is up front in place of Pullman. Now he has a chance to show his stuff, and show it he does. He starts us off smartly and the remaining 30 miles turn into nothing more eventful than a normal training run. We've sacrificed half an hour, but we don't lose any more. Buck storms across the finish line at a dead run, looking good all the way.

I get the red lantern, but my overall time is a surprisingly fast six hours and 15 minutes for both days, for a very respectable 10 miles an hour. Had we not spent so much time stopped, we'd have had the same time as yesterday. I couldn't be more pleased with my team. They've performed exactly as we've trained and Buck has shown he's just as good as I'd hoped. Moreover, bouncy little Maybelline has been the co-leader all the way on both days. She's a natural up front, setting a terrific pace and generally having more fun than the law allows. I hope John Barron doesn't want her back—she's a keeper and I can guarantee she'll get her share of leading on the races to come.

As I herd the dog truck back down the narrow, snow-covered road in the deepening four-o'clock dusk, I feel tired but relieved; this has been my first red lantern, but I couldn't be happier with it. I may not have a world-class team, but the dogs certainly look solid enough to hold their own. If they don't make it to Nome this time, it won't be their fault.

December 24, 1995
Montana Creek, Alaska

Christmas Eve again, and not a lot going on. The lack of good snow throughout much of Southcentral Alaska seems to be having a depressing effect on everyone, especially mushers. Aside from the Forks Roadhouse race a few days ago, there's nothing on the horizon for weeks except going round and round on our local trails as long as our scant snow cover holds out..

The Knik 200 has been postponed; the race follows the Iditarod Trail out to Skwentna, but the trail is bare dirt for the first 20 miles, from Knik out past the Little Susitna River. Worse, the Yentna River—which is the entire far half of the race—is threatening to become one huge lake of overflow because very thick ice has frozen the mouths of side streams all the way to the bottom in places, forcing them to flow out over the top of the river ice.

This could have major ramifications for the Klondike 300 on January 20th (which I plan to run) and for the Iditarod in March because they use the same trail as far as Skwentna. Ron says he remembers a winter in the late 1960s that froze early and hard with very little snow; the Yentna was completely impassable to dog teams for almost 40 miles because of overflow, and other rivers weren't much better. Odds are we will have enough snow to run the Iditarod, even if the route has to detour overland to avoid the river, but early races may be postponed until February. This will make for a very hectic race season, and some of the rookies who have to qualify may be out on a limb unless the Iditarod relaxes the qualification requirements.

Our local trails are still in reasonably good shape so I decide to hook up 12 dogs and hit the trail about sunset. I feel being out with the team is the best way I can celebrate the occasion, and besides, they need the miles. After a few pauses in the initial mile or two to straighten out some minor rigging problems and to swap Socks for Pullman in lead (she's in heat and is getting moody), we make very creditable time around the 20-mile loop. As we reach the turnoff for the dog lot, I decide everything is going so smoothly we might as well keep going for 30 miles. Socks seems a little surprised when I give him a "haw" instead of a "gee" but as soon as we're steady on the outbound trail everybody speeds up smartly.

After a mile we come to a particularly tricky part of the trail, requiring the team to jump up over a two-foot bank while the musher adroitly levers the sled up behind them. I miss the bank and the sled flips. It's not a big thing, but I'm upset at screwing up and jump off to pull the sled up the bank. The dogs, of course, do their best to help, and as soon as I get it started over the lip they yank it several feet, pinning me under it with my foot twisted in the bridle at the front of the sled. I try to turn the sled on its side but I can't get the correct angle, and the dogs yank again. This time my foot gets caught in the brake at the back of the sled while the rear runners pin me flat on the ground.

I'm worried my ankle is about to be badly sprained and there's nothing I can do about it. As I make one last effort to tip over the sled and get out from under it, Socks starts the team and I pop free. Unfortunately, Socks is heading one way and I'm pointed another, and as I stagger to my feet the team and sled are 20 yards down the road and moving fast. There's no hope of catching them. I've done it again: my Christmas present to myself is to lose the team.

I'm so mad I feel like chewing tree bark. However, I have a secret weapon for just such a development—my cellular phone. I fish it out of my parka pocket and call Ron's place; to my frustration, he's not there, but I leave a message to head the team off if he can. I have to assume Socks will take everybody back to the lot; he knows the way well enough. We're only about five miles from home and my only worry is the sled will spill or overrun the wheel dogs on a hill, or there will be a tangle and a dog will be hurt. But for the meantime, there's not much to do but hoof it.

Last year when I lost the team I was worried about them getting lost or heading out to the highway; this year that doesn't bother me, but my own stupidity does. I knew better than to let go of the quick-release rope, which I wrap around my wrist as a safety line; I've always considered getting dragged behind the sled to be much preferable to losing the team. But I was getting irritated at myself and forgot some fundamental procedures. At the least, I could have set the snow hook, which would probably have prevented the team from pulling away so quickly.

It takes me an hour to walk back. As I near the lot, Ron meets me and says the team was waiting patiently in the driveway with only a minor tangle or two. As usual, Socks has brought everybody home in one piece, except for me. Ron even comments on how orderly the dogs are; just like last year, I have to pat myself on the back for training them well even as I kick myself in the rear for losing them in the first place. Ron just laughs and says any experienced dog driver who hasn't walked home a few times is doing something wrong.

I go inside and stew for awhile, contemplating the possibility of hitching everybody up and going out again. But I know the dogs didn't do anything wrong and I wouldn't be proving a thing to take it out on them. So I decide to give myself a real present and hop in the car and run over to Steve Adkins' place. He's offered me a deal I can't refuse on one of the best leaders in this part of the state.

I've temporarily got a decent bank balance because I've just sold my airplane. Of course, this is the same one I used to fly for the Iditarod and which was the vehicle to get me interested in running the race in the first place; O. Henry would have loved the whole affair, I think. Anyway, I happily write Steve a check for Lucky, whom Steve ran in the 1994 Iditarod; as I sign it I think this is infinitely better than shopping till I drop in one of the malls in Anchorage for stuff I'd just lose or put on a shelf after a few months.

I actually look at this as a blue-chip investment and I don't blink an eye as I watch a grand change hands—proven lead dogs can easily bring $5,000 or more. In Lucky's case, I already know he's a super leader, and Steve has two even better leaders who are sure to put him in the money this year. If Lucky is even partly as good as Hank and Crystal (his other two prodigies) I'm going to be in good shape. After last year, I know I need the extra depth in leaders, and Lucky will be my third first-rate male front-ender. I look at it as stacking the deck in my favor. Besides, he's not even five years old yet, and is just coming into his prime; there's no question he'll be with me for a long time, even after Socks and Buck are comfortably retired.

I stop by Ron's on the way back for a bit of Christmas cheer. In a fitting turn of the wheel, Lucky is directly out of Ron's best line of dogs, the ones with which he helped pioneer the early Iditarods and Yukon Quests. As the evening grows pleasantly late, Ron reminisces about some of the truly legendary dogs he's had in that line and some of the incredible things they've done.

After I get back to my place I can hardly get to sleep; Santa has just stopped by and given me the best gift anyone could have wanted. I can't wait to get up in the morning and put Lucky up front with Buck. I finally drift off to sleep with Iditarod dreams of glory dancing in my head. This will be the year—now I know it for sure.

Sometimes mushers will run together on isolated stretches of trail, both for the company and to help each other if needed.

197

December 30, 1995
Montana Creek, Alaska

Lucky has proven to be everything I expected and more. He and Buck were perfectly matched up front on Christmas Day, roaring around a 30-mile run at speeds up to 20 miles an hour, and averaging 12 or better. The next day I hooked Lucky up with Socks, with virtually the same result on a 40-miler. I was so pleased I could hardly contain myself: the team genuinely looked like Iditarod quality, much more so than last year.

Today I'm taking the dogs out on a 50-mile run. The weather is great and the trails are still good. I'm secretly pitying the poor mushers down south of here who are still rumbling around on four-wheelers in clouds of dust like the old 20-mule teams hauling borax through the Mojave Desert. Lucky and Buck are up front and we storm out of the lot early in the afternoon like we really know what we're doing.

After half an hour I stop to clear up a minor tangle up front. Dangerous Dan, whom I've recently acquired from John Barron, is a greyhound-looking yearling who can go like the wind, but who does so with a great bounding, loping run which tends to enmesh him in the tugline of the dog ahead of him if I don't set the rigging up right. When this happens, he also has a habit of chewing through whatever catches him, which has resulted in several quick tugline replacements in the past few runs. Whenever I see him snarled up I have to stop quickly and fix things to avoid a real mess. We're working through it, but for the time being I'm still learning how he operates, and he's still learning the ropes, so to speak.

As I return to the sled, my new rocket-powered team decides to go. My left foot is partly on the runner—with my full weight on it—and the lower part of my left leg does a violent half-twist as the sled jerks forward. I hear an ominous pop from the general vicinity of my left knee and collapse on the trail as the team roars up the hill and out of sight. As I try to get up to catch the team, I realize my left knee isn't quite what it was a few moments ago. I've never had knee problems in my life, but now I feel like an NFL quarterback who's enjoyed the loving attention of opposing linemen for too many seasons.

And then there's the equally immediate problem of the team, which is merrily bounding up the outbound trail without the benefit of my enlightened guidance. In the adrenaline-driven urgency of the moment, I stand up and start hopping and walking after the team. There isn't much pain, but I know I'll pay later for what I'm about to do. I'm not as worried about the team as I might be because I know where they're going—down a cul-de-sac to a turnaround, and I'll catch them as they come out or find them at the end of it with the sled spilled. On the other hand, it's more than three miles, and I have no choice but to stomp up the trail like Captain Ahab grimly pursuing his white whale.

After half an hour the team doesn't reappear and it becomes obvious they didn't make the turnaround. This probably means a tangle of some kind, plus an extra mile and a half walk back into the cul-de-sac. As I push into the dead-end trail, I hear frantic barking far ahead; this definitely means the team is stopped and snarled. I hope they haven't chased a moose off into the woods, in which case I'll be all night getting things straightened out, provided nobody's hurt.

I finally reach the end of the road but the team isn't there. It takes me a minute to realize what they've done. Leading from the cul-de-sac is a disused tractor trail, which they've somehow found. This trail leads about 100 yards through the trees and then drops off the edge of the world down a nearly sheer 30-foot embankment into a creek bottom. I don't even want to think what might have happened as I stumble up to the edge of the precipice, looming like a vengeful god over the suddenly quiet team spread out below.

Beneath my feet is a scene of canine confusion that is bad, but miraculously not as gruesome as I expected. Buck and Lucky apparently went over the bank and down the 60-degree slope with everybody else in hot pursuit. The sled hung up on a stump about halfway down, preventing it from overrunning the dogs. Only the front few dogs are tangled across a fallen tree at the bottom of the hill, and those not badly. Dangerous Dan has chewed through the leaders' tug lines, but they have stayed put even though they could have kept going, for which I am endlessly grateful.

Somebody once told me dog mushing is really just a never-ending series of problem-solving exercises ranging from trivial to cosmic. This is one of the bigger ones, easily comparable to my little cliff-side derailment on the Copper Basin 300 last season. I can't go forward because the cat trail degenerates into a morass of fallen trees; this leaves only the option of getting the sled turned around and back up the cliff. Hanging onto a tree on the impossibly steep slope, I try to lever it around just to see if I can, but my newly mangled knee quickly informs me this isn't a viable option.

With a sigh I go to Plan B, which means unhooking the sled, tying it off, untangling the dogs, leading them back up the hill, rearranging the sled, and letting the team pull it back to reality. This takes about an hour, punctuated by sudden discourses of colorful language on my part as I discover the limits of my newly reduced mobility. Finally the team pulls the sled over the edge onto the level ground on top. The sled is amazingly undamaged, despite its high-velocity head-on with the stump; I've got to thank the builder (Keith Poppert, a real old-time craftsman down in Wasilla) for putting together a seriously tough piece of equipment. In this case, I can definitely say they still make them like they used to.

After a few more minutes sorting out the remaining tangles and looking for injuries (none I can find, thanks to the sled checking up before it could plow into the team), we're off again. I find I can stand on the runner without much trouble, but anything more strenuous gets my attention instantly. I decide to go ahead and finish the run since the dogs are now rested and raring to go; I also figure this will be good practice for the Iditarod, where I'm certain to bang myself up and have to live with the consequences.

Fifty-plus miles later we pull into the yard at a lope. It's been our longest run of the season, and the dogs have once again proven they are practically bulletproof. The team has averaged a steady 10 to 11 miles an hour for five hours, which is exactly what I want them to do—and what I'll need to get to Nome.

What's more, we've recovered from a near-catastrophe and pushed on in good order. I feel my training program has been vindicated; this team may not be top-20 quality, but it's strong and solid, and unquestionably ready for bigger things. All we need now is enough snow for races like the Knik 200 and the Klondike 300.

In the meantime, I totter inside the house to put some dog liniment on my now-screaming knee—the doctors may not approve of it, but I'll bet it works. If it's good enough for my team, it'll certainly be good enough for me.

January 1, 1996
Montana Creek, Alaska

The New Year is upon us—which means it's less than 60 days until the Iditarod. Last year about this time everything was starting to happen in a rush: I had just spent New Year's Eve at Skwentna on the Knik 200 and was frantically getting ready for the Copper Basin 300. This season the pace is decidedly more measured and I'm still in the same old pre-Christmas routine, thanks to our miserly snowfall which has postponed the mid-distance races. Nonetheless, the dogs are in great shape and I have no doubt I could go run the Iditarod with them tomorrow if I had to (although I'd have to take it easy for a few days until they got their real long-distance legs). Tonight, though, I'm going to harness up some puppy power.

I've been putting off trying out the pups until they were eight or nine months old and I had some spare time. Both of these conditions have now been met and I have no excuse for waiting any longer. I've been anticipating this and dreading it at the same time. In a perfect world, all of the pups would pull the first time I hooked them up and all I'd have to do would be to get them in shape for next year's race. Unfortunately, things never work out so smoothly, and I'll probably be lucky to get two or three naturals out of my eight candidates.

The top mushers raise 30 or 40 or even 100 pups a season and have the luxury of keeping only the very best. Pups that don't pull right away get new homes quickly. People like me who have only a few pups have to try to work with the entire spectrum, which requires a lot more effort to try to bring the less promising ones to their full potential.

Kisser

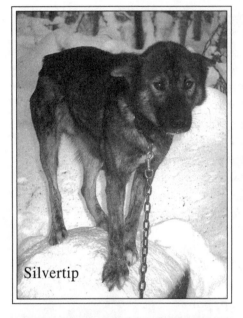

Silvertip

Maybelline

I start off with Big Mac and Shorty, two of the four pups who survived the parvo epidemic. They're now eight months old and are robust, bouncing bundles of energy. First I put Socks, Weasel, and Rocky on the gangline to act as "mentors" for the pups; these three are the most stable

Iditarod sled dogs are often of no specific breed, and can range from 30-pound Maybelline to 65-pound Buck. In between can be anything from Silvertip, who is two-thirds wolf to pure-white Weasel to Lucky to Kisser. The one common attribute of all good Iditarod dogs is a good attitude and the willingness to keep going under even the most abominable conditions.

and reliable adults on the lot as far as training pups is concerned. But when I literally have to haul both of the pups out to the sled, I get a sinking feeling; this is not good.

Sure enough, both of them lie down and drag as soon as we start. I don't even try to go any farther; the pups need more exposure to adult dogs in general and to the process of hooking up and leaving the yard specifically. I rearrange the housing assignments to make room for the reticent youngsters right next to the hookup area; I'll give them a few weeks of watching the adult dogs get harnessed up and generally getting into the let's-go-running frenzy. Sooner or later they'll get the picture and we can pick up where we left off.

Next I try Little Pal, Squeaky, and Bullwinkle, three more Iditapups who were at Bert's house in town during the summer and escaped the virus. Squeaky and Little Pal drag piteously but Bullwinkle looks as if he might be interested in running. I put the first two in the sled and keep going. Slowly but surely Bullwinkle starts to figure it out. He keeps running, trying to drag only when the speed gets too fast. Whenever he does this I step on the brake to keep Socks down to an acceptable pace. We go half a mile and turn around; by the time we get back Bullwinkle seems to be holding his own. He needs more confidence-building work, but he's most of the way there.

Weasel

Lucky

Buck

For the grand finale I hook up Josephine's three remaining pups, now nine months old. Kim has already harness-broken Napoleon—somehow nicknamed Nepo—while she had him in town (where he missed the parvo outbreak), so I'm not too worried about him. I've worked a bit with Bonnie and Clyde, harnessing them up and jogging with them down the borough road for a few hundred yards.

I have no trouble getting them out to the sled, a very good sign. When I pull the hook and we head out of the driveway, Nepo is keeping up with Socks and little Bonnie is bouncing around like a well-hit handball next to Weasel, but she shows no fear of running. Lumbering Clyde is almost as big as Rocky, who resembles a main battle tank. Clyde is a bit timid at first but slowly seems to warm to the idea and starts to move ever faster like a freight locomotive gradually picking up speed.

After half a mile or so things are going so smoothly I decide to try a three-miler. By the time we reach the turnaround, everyone has settled down and we're moving quite well. On the way back we steadily pick up speed until we're cruising at an astonishing 14 or 15 miles an hour. Nepo is pulling so hard he's outrunning the old veteran Socks up front and big Clyde is doing a highly workmanlike job of bringing up the rear.

We steam into the yard as fast as my mainline team. This is beyond my best hopes—these three pups are 24-karat keepers, and I consider the evening's work a major success. After I get everyone put away I go over and spend some quality time with Josephine, their mother. I wish I still had the rest of the litter, the ones who were the first to succumb to parvo back in the bleak days of July.

I think Josephine may have another chance or two to help out my long-range team-building plans. Even though she's not an Iditarod-quality performer herself, she'll make an even bigger contribution over the next year or two by giving me more pups like the three who showed such incredible promise tonight.

January 20-23, 1996
The Klondike 300

The Knik 200 has finally been cancelled: no snow. The Copper Basin 300 started on time last weekend on marginal trails, but was stopped after the teams got 70 miles because of 65-below zero cold. Now it's time for the Klondike 300, the only remaining 300-mile race in Southcentral Alaska. I've planned to run it all along; I don't need it to qualify for the Iditarod, but I want to see how the team (and I) will do in a serious race.

And this promises to be a serious race indeed. The decision has already been made to hold it regardless of conditions. Teams have been limited to 12 dogs instead of the normal 16 because even the veterans don't think they could control a big team on the thin trails. And the trail itself has been drastically rerouted—indeed, it changed almost daily up until a few days before the race.

John Barron, who won the race last year and is on the Board of Directors, warned me the trail might not be so good in places; coming from him, that means it'll be a near-disaster for drivers like me. We're also worried about the cold: it's been 20 to 40 below from Big Lake to Talkeetna for the past several weeks, and everybody is a little gun-shy about staging a repeat of the aborted Copper Basin race.

Saturday—The Klondike 300: Big Lake to Sheep Creek (80 miles)
As usual, I've been up all night getting everything ready after returning from the mushers' meeting. I doubt I'll ever get a good night's sleep within a week of a race. This time, everything is complicated by the minor inconvenience of my dog truck having a cracked engine block; I've borrowed a friend's pickup and lashed my dog boxes to the back. After a restful two hours' sleep, I load up my 12 A-string dogs and bounce 50 miles down the road to Big Lake.

When I pull onto the lake and park the truck it's 30 below zero. If we're lucky it might warm up to 20 below for an hour or two this afternoon. Some of my friends who helped me last year are waiting to act as handlers. Nobody's moving very fast, and—also as usual—I'm starting to have second thoughts about this whole affair.

I check my watch and discover we're behind schedule. The 26 teams are leaving two at a time; I get to go head-to-head with Martin Buser. This is about like matching the Budweiser Clydesdales against a team of Triple Crown thoroughbreds—we might give them a run for a little ways, but the natural order of things will reassert itself pretty quickly after that.

As my start time draws perilously near, we are frantically hooking up the dogs and bootying them. The sled is packed—sort of—and I just hope I've got everything in it I'll need. I'm still trying to get my parka on as we get into the starting gate. I don't even hear the countdown and look up from fiddling with my parka zipper to see Martin's team exploding out of the chute. The starter yells at me to go and everybody backs away from my team, leaving me holding on to the handlebar with one hand and the infernally stubborn zipper with the other. I don't get fully assembled until we're half a mile down the trail, which fortunately runs along the level ice of Big Lake for the first couple of miles.

While I'm putting myself together, my fresh-out-of-the-box team pulls up to Martin's heels; I must step on the drag to hold them back so they won't overrun him. I don't want to pass him because he'll just return the favor in a few hundred yards and we'll run the risk of a high speed tangle. Suddenly he slows and pulls over to the ice road paralleling the trail, where a pickup-load of people seem to want a picture, which he obliges. In the meantime, we zoom past. I've actually passed Martin Buser, even though I know it will be short-lived. Sure enough, he catches me a mile later and shoots by. However, I'm not being passed by too many other teams, and my guys are hanging in there better than I'd hoped. Maybe this will work out okay after all.

After we leave the smooth ice of Big Lake, the trails steadily deteriorate. By the time we reach Little Cow Lake, about 25 miles out, things are looking really grim. As we lurch up off the tiny lake onto the 300-yard portage to Cow Lake, there isn't a trail to speak of—just bare roots and dirt and stumps. I wouldn't drive a four-wheeler over it on a bet, but nobody tells this to the dogs, who merrily bound through the nightmare as if it were just another fun run.

As we crest the small hill the trail turns sharply to the right and downhill around a big birch with an exposed root. The sled catches the root, tips over, and suddenly I'm dragging behind it, attached only by the tie-off rope looped around my left mitten. I try to hang on, but the rope pulls the thick mitten right off my hand and the team roars on down the hill onto the lake. I jump up and shout at a musher 100 yards ahead to stop the team. (The rules of the trail call for any musher to always try to stop a runaway team.) He tries and misses, but then I notice two cross-country skiers on the lake who have deployed themselves like a special forces ambush team to catch my free-wheeling dogs. As I watch, they neatly corral the leaders and bring everything to a smooth stop.

Relieved beyond words, I stomp out to the team. I thank the skiers profusely for saving the team (and my chance to finish the race). Of course, the dogs think it is all a lark and zoom off as soon as I climb back on the runners. They're still rolling when we get to Red Shirt Lake, whose three-mile length we traverse quickly.

Off the far end of Red Shirt the overland trail picks up again, and this time it is simply beyond words. The track winds up a small inlet creek in the middle of a swamp studded with protruding clumps of dirt and grass, all frozen solid. It looks for all the world like a pinball game with a zillion mushroom bumpers, except I'm the ball and the dogs are playing a mean tune on the flippers. The sled spills several times but I hang on for dear life and finally figure out how to ride it low and loose to minimize the impacts.

But the pinball swamp is nothing compared to the ensuing "trail" through the woods. There aren't any trees in the right-of-way, but that's about all that's missing (besides the snow). It's a maze of roots, potholes, fallen logs, loose sticks, rocks, and worst of all, stumps and stobs up to eight inches high that can easily rip the bottom out of the sled if I'm not careful. It is simply not a sled trail, or any kind of a trail, for that matter. Now I know why the trailblazers refused to run their snowmachines over it. Any normal human would have a tough time merely walking this morass, much less trying to guide a bouncing, 100-pound sled over it behind a team of overeager dogs.

Fortunately the worst part only lasts a few miles and then we're on South Rolly Lake, which is part of a race course for sprint mushers. As I pull onto the lake, where our trail shares theirs for a couple of hundred yards, I notice a 16-dog sprint team roaring around the far end of the lake at 20 miles an hour. I wonder if they have any idea of the hideous trail only a stone's throw from their groomed speedway. I'm tempted to just let my team follow the sprinters and call this whole thing off before I destroy the team, the sled, and me.

Somehow I manage to get my leaders to stay on our trail, which leaves the lake, follows a road, and then drops down a hill to North Rolly Lake. We slightly overshoot the entrance to the down-trail to the lake and I have to stop the team and let everyone maneuver over to the two big boulders marking the gateway. In the process the lead and swing dogs get tangled across the rocks and break a couple of necklines, which I stop and fix before proceeding.

Starting down this hill from a dead stop turns out to be maybe the luckiest thing I do on the whole race. After 10 yards, I see to my horror the slope is impossibly steep, narrow, and winding. I jam on the brake and feverishly unhook my big snowmachine-track drag, which I've had up out of the way to keep it from catching on the obstacles in the trails. As soon as the drag hits the icy snow I jump on it with both feet so hard I think I've sprained both ankles. I manage to hold the team to a slow lope down the hill and only kiss three or four trees, barely missing a major crash-and-burn at the bottom where the trail makes a sharp left turn onto the lake around a huge birch. As I regain my composure crossing the lake, I can't imagine why anyone would have chosen such an exercise in madness as part of a major race—it's positively dangerous.

After the hill conditions moderate somewhat as we traverse smooth lakes interspersed with short stretches of horrible trail. I take some wrong turns on a few of the lakes thanks to the sparse markings, but manage to get straightened out without much trouble. We roll onto Long Lake behind the town of Willow about five hours after the start; I know it well, having landed my little float plane on it many times, and my good friends Rich and Jeannette Keida live on its upper reaches. The lake is 40 miles from the start, so we're making very reasonable time. Still, I've not seen any other mushers for almost an hour and I'm certain everyone has passed me. This doesn't bother me too much, since I'm not trying to win this race or even qualify for the Iditarod.

The dogs settle into an easy 10-mile-an-hour pace as we pull onto the section of trail running in the ditch line beside the Parks Highway. It's dark by now and cars and heavy trucks roar by not 20 feet away. The dogs remain blissfully oblivious to everything, trotting steadily on. After awhile we dip down to Little Willow Creek and cross under the highway bridge to work our way back toward the Talkeetna Mountains on a section of trail I haven't seen before.

I know the trail to Sheep Creek (the first checkpoint, only nine miles from home) runs along the Anchorage-Fairbanks Intertie powerline and will be impossible to miss once I'm on it. However, the trails we are following to get to the powerline seem to be wandering around a bit, and I take half a dozen abortive excursions up likely-looking branch trails until I figure out the overall pattern of things.

Eventually I see the 100-foot Intertie towers etched against the starry sky and we follow them northward. Ten miles later we hit a stretch of trail John Barron has warned me about. He had to put it in himself a couple of weeks earlier the old-fashioned way—with his dog team, because no one would run a snowmachine over it; he was worried it would be really rough. As it turns out, it's not as bad as some of what we've already survived, although it's extremely slow going with lots of brush overhanging the trail.

Mount Foraker, the third highest peak in Alaska at 17,400 feet above sea level and southern companion to Mount McKinley, towers 70 miles in the distance beyond the Yentna River.

As we draw nearer to Sheep Creek, I start to recognize familiar landmarks and stretches of trail I ran in the Sheep Creek race in December of 1994. We manage to avoid any more major upheavals and pull strongly into Sheep Creek a little after nine o'clock. To my shock and surprise, I find I'm not last—in fact, I'm the fourteenth musher in, right in the middle of the pack. The checker asks me if I saw anyone else, because half a dozen mushers seem to be lost on the trail, a development I find completely understandable given my own experience.

I just shake my head at my good fortune and tend to the dogs, who are in good shape and excellent spirits after the tough run. The temperature at Sheep Creek is 32 below, which has been normal for our neck of the woods in the evenings for the past month or so. I've dropped off a bale of straw to supplement whatever the race provides, so my guys get enough bedding to hole up for a week. After they're fed and settled down, I head inside the lodge for a bite to eat and to catch up on what else has been happening.

I find out John Barron was the first driver in, just after six o'clock; I can't imagine how he kept his sled upright at that kind of a pace. He's preparing to leave at 11 or so, followed closely by his son Will, Steve Adkins (another of my neighbors), and Martin Buser. Everyone is grumbling about the abysmal trail and the confusing markings. Apparently almost every driver got lost somewhere or other, many more than once; one has called in from Willow, where he returned after wandering around on the trail to Sheep Creek for hours. Several others are still unaccounted for, although no one is worried they will eventually turn up. This kind of pathfinding exercise isn't normally expected in a big race, but it's definitely part of mushing, and there's no substitute for "trail sense" to keep things from getting out of hand.

I also learn the hill down onto North Rolly Lake that scared me so badly wasn't even supposed to be part of the race trail—it's actually a footpath marked by mistake. I hadn't noticed as I screamed down the twisting incline, but there were pieces of sleds all over the hill from several calamitous wrecks by the mushers ahead of me.

The hill directly caused two mushers to scratch. Bob Welch, a rookie trying to qualify for the Iditarod, hit a tree so hard it splintered his sled, split his sternum, and broke a rib so forcefully the jagged end almost pierced his heart. A musher close behind him happened to be an emergency medical technician and immediately determined the injuries were life-threatening. The EMT borrowed a pistol and fired several shots in the air to get the attention of a circling airplane, which landed on the lake and evacuated Welch to the hospital, where he is in satisfactory condition—but definitely out of the Iditarod for this year.

Given the bad, confusing trails and the bitter cold, I think it will be prudent to play things more cautiously for the rest of the race. I decide to drop into a semi-survival mode, running mostly during the day and giving the dogs plenty of rest. After all, I'm not trying to win any money, and the Iditarod this year will likely be a full couple of weeks of what I'm seeing here.

We have to double back over the same trail to Willow before we turn west to the Susitna and Yentna Rivers for the run out to Yentna Station and Skwentna, after which we'll return directly to Big Lake. My new game plan is to leave Sheep Creek just before dawn, so I can hit the worst part of the trail to Willow about first light. I was having trouble seeing things in the trail in my headlight beam on the way in, and I don't want to risk hitting something that might hurt the dogs or wreck the sled. I also want daylight to make sure I don't get lost on the maze of sloughs and channels in the rivers, which have additionally been crisscrossed by thousands of snowmachiners, who use them as highways.

> *Most important, I resolve to drive the dogs all the way out to Skwentna (the farthest point on the race), regardless of how long it takes. Once I'm out there, I can't scratch, since the only way to get the dogs back will be to run them in to Big Lake. After my Iditarod fiasco last year, I intend to finish this race if it's humanly (and caninely) possible. The Klondike has become a critical personal benchmark of my ability to keep myself going; I'm not going to blow it now.*

Sunday—The Klondike 300: Sheep Creek to Yentna Station (70 miles)

After a quick meal and a few hours' nap I'm up to get the dogs ready about five o'clock. It's pushing 40 below, but the dogs aren't bothered. On the other hand, Yankee and Buck had a minor altercation during the evening. They apparently got cranky because they were tired and snapped at each other for a few minutes. This is an occupational hazard when running a team heavy on big males like mine is this year; I try to minimize the opportunities for conflict, but some will flare up regardless.

Buck has a couple of minor bite marks; Yankee is up and ready to go, but he winces when I touch his tail while harnessing him up. Buck must have gotten him there, and it appears painful enough to convince me to drop him because the tugline on the back of the harness will probably bother him as he runs. There's no point in subjecting him to any extra harassment. He's a proven performer and is in good shape; he'll be ready for the Iditarod even if he doesn't finish this race.

Finally we're ready to go. The checkers tell me half a dozen teams have scratched already, and I should watch out for two teams still straggling up the trail from Willow. We roll out of the checkpoint and back out onto the trail in good order. Old Socks is leading; he's not my fastest leader but he's utterly dependable, especially on questionable trails like the one we're on. Besides, I don't want an express-train leader bounding through this stuff, where I have almost no time to react even under the best conditions.

We make good time for an hour or so down the powerline trail, which is just as bad as I remember it coming in. We pass one of the lost teams limping dazed back the way we came; the driver says his sled is busted and his dogs are beat and all he wants to do is get into Sheep Creek and scratch. I feel thankful my team is basically in one piece and resolve to keep it that way for the remaining 200 miles.

We work our way south as the predawn light slowly brightens, exposing a cold, frost-covered landscape—and the grim trail. As we go up a low hill I know has a sharp drop on the far side, Socks takes a wrong turn, following what looks like a recent trail. I know it's not the correct path, but I assume it will quickly loop back to the main trail like these little spurs always do. Two seconds too late I realize the side trail isn't going to rejoin the main one in time.

Even as I'm getting ready to stop the team and bring them around, the sled comes to a wrenching halt in the middle of a thicket of willow shrubs that have grown up where the original forest was cleared from the powerline right-of-way years ago. I almost pitch over the handlebar and into the team, which is in complete disarray with dogs everywhere. Necklines have snapped, tuglines have come loose, and the gangline is wrapped around every dog and tree in sight.

The one- and two-inch-thick trunks of the willows look as if they've grown up through the team and the sled, so completely are we tangled. I have never seen anything so snarled. And if I ever get everything back in order, the way ahead is down a 50-foot slope strewn with fallen logs. The main trail is at the bottom of the hill, but there's no way I'm going to get there from here.

At least nobody is hurt and everything seems to be more or less intact. The problem will be one of somehow extricating team and sled from this boreal jungle. With a sigh I walk up and sit down next to Socks and ponder the situation. The sun is slowly coming up over the Talkeetna Mountains to the southeast and we watch a beautiful sunrise even as I work out a salvage plan.

By the time the pink and blue of dawn have given way to the orange and yellow of the sun as it rises above the jagged ridges, I am well on my way to sorting things out. I have to use my saw and ax to do a bit of unauthorized logging, but eventually I get enough working room to lead the team back up the hill, and then to manhandle the sled around to face the way we came.

After lining out the dogs, replacing the broken snaps and lines, and reconnecting everything, we're off again—directly back up the trail for a few hundred yards until I can find an open area to bring the team around. It's taken the better part of an hour, but we're underway in the proper direction again, none the worse for wear. As we bounce on down the narrow, brush-choked trail, I'm too busy fighting the sled to even think about getting mad or frustrated. It's just been part of the game, yet another problem to be solved in what has been—and promises to continue to be—a long string of problems.

We eventually make it back to the better trails and then under the Little Willow Creek bridge and onto the ditch line along the highway. It's mid-morning on a Sunday but there's still plenty of traffic. In particular, I notice at least half a dozen dog trucks headed north over a space of half an hour, probably on their way for a day of training runs on the relatively good trails in the upper Susitna Valley (or maybe heading up to Sheep Creek to pick up teams which have scratched from this race).

In western Alaska, only the larger rivers have significant greenbelts of trees.

I wave at them and every driver gives me a thumbs up or a flash of the lights in encouragement. I guess word of the tough trail on the Klondike is spreading; it's starting to look like anyone who finishes will have uncontested bragging rights for awhile, and other mushers certainly appreciate this.

Crossing Willow Creek as I continue down the highway, I notice there's a team lined out behind the Pioneer Lodge, apparently one of the ones that scratched. I'm getting thirsty and we'll be heading out onto the river in a few more miles, so I stop, tie off the dogs to a tree in the parking lot, and clump into the bar (which is open—this is Alaska, after all). There are a few people having breakfast and they look at me like I've just landed from Mars.

Then I realize I probably look a sight, bundled up like some kind of polar mummy with icicles hanging from my beard, moustache, and eyebrows. I flash them a winning smile, hastily get a big glass of water, avail myself of the facilities, and head back out to the team, which has welcomed the 15-minute rest. Then we're off down the highway, waving at Sunday-morning travelers and generally having not too bad a time, all things considered.

After threading across Long, Crystal, and Vera Lakes, we debouch onto the swamps stretching to the Susitna River five miles away. The race route jumps from one trail to another and I'm glad I'm doing this part during daylight, because I'd surely have missed at least a couple of the turns. Most of the junctions are marked mainly with fluorescent surveyor's tape, which is fine for daytime but almost invisible at night. There are a few reflective Klondike 300 markers for night use, but not nearly enough. I can only guess how many of the teams ahead of me got lost going through here before dawn this morning.

Finally the trail re-enters the tree line hugging the 100-foot bluff overlooking the mile-wide river bottoms. We meander for a couple of miles on a well-defined but unmarked trail and I start to wonder if we're on the right track. I flag down an oncoming snowmachiner and ask him if this is the proper trail; he says it is, and the hill down to the river is just ahead—and I should be careful to take a left at the bottom.

In short order we plunge down a steep hill onto a frozen slough. The dogs want to go right, which I know heads back upstream, but I straighten them out quickly and we roll out onto the open expanse of the river. From here on we are supposed to follow the main snowmachine trail down the Ohio-sized Susitna to its junction with the equally broad Yentna, then up the Yentna to Yentna Station and ultimately Skwentna before turning around and retracing our steps back to Willow and then Big Lake.

In the middle of its broad cliff-lined flood plain, the Susitna's central channel has frozen up in a 100-yard-wide jumble of ice blocks, some standing several feet high. The trail is a highway packed down by thousands of snowmachines over the past couple of months. There are no roads west of the Susitna and most residents of the area use the frozen rivers for routine transportation as casually as automobile drivers use the freeways.

Where the trail runs along the sandbars and smoother sloughs it is as much as 100 feet wide, with as many interlaced branches as the river under its blanket of snow and ice. Occasionally everything narrows into a yard-wide path snaking bumpily across the wasteland of the main channel to better terrain on the far bank. There is only a thin covering of snow on the ice, maybe a few inches, and where it has been packed it's barely an inch.

There's no way to get a snow hook into the crust securely enough to stop the team. The only way I can inspect booties and straighten out tangles is to gently talk the dogs into stopping, set the hook as best I can, and lay the sled over on its side atop the hook. Then I figure I have a couple of minutes before the dogs get restless and start to go, dragging the overturned sled and the scraping hook, albeit slowly enough to allow me to easily catch them.

Fortunately things are going fairly smoothly. I do have one problem, though: my brand-new, top-quality dog booties are wearing through frighteningly fast on these abrasive trails. Normally the booties should go 60 miles or more, but my bigger dogs are blowing them out in as little as 15. This is disturbing, if for no other reason than the booties cost 70 cents each and I don't have an unlimited supply. Even worse, snow and ice will pack into a bootie with a hole in it, and the net result will be to amplify any damage to the dog's foot. I'm worried I'm doing more harm to feet by inadvertently running holed booties than I would if I didn't bootie at all.

Finally I stop and rip off all the booties on the bigger dogs, except for a handful of sensitive or already-injured feet which must stay wrapped. I figure the dogs won't be any worse off without booties, and besides, we've been training on hard, icy trails at Montana Creek all year and their feet have held up pretty well so far. In any case, I'll give them all a good check at Yentna Station when we get there later this afternoon and decide what to do down the road.

As the day wears on, the dogs start to slow down, to perhaps six or seven miles an hour. This is a normal phenomenon: dogs tend to run more slowly during the day, and especially when they're out in wide-open spaces like rivers and lakes. Nobody seems to know why, other than dogs are mainly nocturnal and just don't like to be exposed to the glare of day. I personally think they just get bored looking at miles and miles of nothing but miles and miles. At least at night their universe has bounds; out here on the broad river in the bright sun, and from their next-to-the-ice viewpoint, it just looks like a lot of white.

Another problem is overheating—even at 20 below. All of the dogs are extremely well insulated, and their coats are especially thick this year because of the bitter cold we've had at Montana Creek. On a windless day like today, with the sun additionally warming the darker-coated dogs, they generate enough heat trotting to stay uncomfortably hot.

Many of them try to "dip," or grab a mouthful of snow from the trail on the fly; sometimes the less-adept ones will lose their footing and flop comically down for a second or two before bounding back to their feet. Once in awhile one of them does a truly Chaplinesque pratfall on a patch of ice and gets tangled; then I have to stop the team and go straighten out the miscreant, who often as not is already up and ready to go by the time I get the sled completely stopped.

I only meet one team on the Susitna; I chat with the other driver for awhile as we run together. He spent the night on the river, apparently not wanting to risk the unfamiliar trail in the dark. Then his team got away from him this morning and he was just recovering them when I came by. He keeps stopping for various reasons and drops slowly behind as my team keeps up a steady if not exactly blistering pace.

For the next five hours we trundle down the Susitna and up the lower Yentna. I've seen the Yentna several times before on the back of a sled, on both the Knik 200 and the Iditarod last year. Of course, I've flown over it so many times I can recite the landmarks in my sleep, which still doesn't make things go any faster. The only breaks in the numbing monotony are dozens of snowmachines roaring up the trail, some of whose drivers courteously stop while my team goes by.

I also get passed by a pickup truck hauling a 500-gallon fuel tank to a lodge on up the river. In fact, the snow is so thin this year a few brave souls have driven vehicles all the way to Skwentna. Even more than in most years, the frozen river has become an all-purpose extension of the state's minuscule highway network.

Finally we round a big horseshoe bend as dusk is falling and see the lights of Yentna Station on the far bank. Half a dozen teams are there, including leaders John Barron and John Schandelmeier, who have already been out to Skwentna and are on their way back to Big Lake. I ask the checkers where everybody else is, and they tell me 12 teams have scratched—almost half of the original starters in the race. Martin Buser and several of the other big names have dropped out, some because they didn't want to risk their teams on the bad trails and some because they got lost or didn't feel they had a chance at the money. Others—like Bob Welch—have broken sleds or broken bones, or both.

This has apparently turned into some kind of iron-man race, and those of us who haven't gotten lost or banged up are hanging in there for better or worse. In fact, aside from a handful of contenders who are after the prize money (which is considerable: $10,000 for first place and $5,000 for second) most of the remaining drivers are rookies who are simply trying to finish in order to qualify for the Iditarod. I don't need to qualify, but I'm determined to finish anyway; hearing only a few of us are left actually makes me feel better about what I'm doing. Besides, there aren't any more pre-Iditarod races I can easily do this year, so this is the only show in town.

As soon as I get the dogs fed and settled down, I decide to drop Buck, who has been packing his harness and little more for the past 30 miles. He has a bite wound near his right front wrist from his Sheep Creek tiff with Yankee, and it's bothering him enough to cause him to favor it. The vet agrees and gives him a shot of antibiotic to prevent any infection; he'll fly out tomorrow and will be waiting for me at Big lake when I get back.

I'd have kept him in the team if I could, because I wanted to put him in lead on the way back to see how he performed on the trail in a long haul. I still have nightmares about the Iditarod last year, when I spent so much time becalmed because I didn't have leaders who would start the team. Buck has been a major part of my plan to combat that scenario and I would've liked to test him.

But I have to think about the rest of this race. We are about halfway done, with 150 miles to go. The next leg is up the river to Skwentna, then return to Yentna Station, maybe 75 miles total. It shouldn't be a hard pull, except the trails along the river aren't marked and several of the front runners have admitted they got lost in a section about halfway to Skwentna where the river braids into dozens of channels. The hordes of snowmachiners have put trails up almost every slough, and they don't all go through. Ramey Smyth, one of the best young mushers in the state, inadvertently got turned around on his way back to Yentna Station in the dark and went up river almost to Skwentna, costing him several hours.

I decide to leave just before dawn so I'll hit the maze during daylight going out and coming back. Although I've been on the river plenty of times before, so has everyone else, and if they're getting lost, I can, too. Besides, the dogs can use a good rest, considering they didn't get as much as they needed at Sheep Creek, what with teams going and coming and Yankee and Buck keeping everyone awake with their quarrel.

As I settle in for the evening in the Yentna Station lodge, the leaders prepare to make the 75-mile dash back to Big Lake and glory—and a paycheck. They can't leave until they finish their mandatory layovers (a total of 16 hours at any combination of checkpoints of the race), which means the front-runners will roll out shortly after midnight. With any luck, they'll be across the finish line by nine or 10 tomorrow morning. I leave them to their race and collapse into one of the overstuffed chairs in the tiny sitting room/bar/dining room.

As I half-doze, the lodge owner, Gary Gabryszak, is playing the guitar for the checkers and a radio reporter. He does "The Wreck of the Edmund Fitzgerald" and several other standards in a highly polished style. When someone asks him he admits he was a professional musician and worked with many well-known groups in the Lower 48 before he came to Alaska with his family some years ago.

It's no more surprising than running into John Denver or Jimmy Buffett in Talkeetna, which happened a few years back. As has often been said about Alaska, it may be a big place, but it's a small world. You never know who you'll meet out here.

Monday—The Klondike 300: Yentna Station to Skwentna to Yentna Station (75 miles)

I finally zonk out in a small bunk room in the lodge loft, oblivious to a host of aches and hurts and a painfully blistered frostbitten fingertip. After a sound sleep the checker wakes me up at five o'clock. I hope the dogs feel better than I do, but it's time to get moving. Already I've spent 10 hours here, far longer than most of the stops I'll make on the Iditarod.

It's only 30 below when I start hooking up at 5:30; first light is still a few hours away. We're headed up river by six, the dogs running well in the moonless predawn dark on the deserted river. It's Monday, and the weekend snowmachiners have long since returned to Anchorage; we'll have the river completely to ourselves.

Despite the lack of moonlight, I have no problem making out the river banks and even the trail itself. Lucky has been up front since we got down onto the Susitna River; having watched him unerringly choose the best trail for hours on end yesterday, I am content to run with my headlight off for the most part and let him lead us as he wishes.

As the light slowly brightens behind us I have to switch dogs around a few times to keep the team lined out and running smoothly. This is part of the ongoing management of any dog team on a long run; sometimes dogs will tire or decide not to pull in a particular position. Conversely, some dogs will run faster than their neighbors—or the dogs in front of them—causing a rash of slack lines. For instance, if the swing dogs are too fast, a front-ender will often as not slow down just like a motorist backing off the gas to force a rude driver to pass.

These anomalies become apparent in the form of drooping tuglines and ganglines and disruptions in the even pace of the team. Fixing them is analogous to a pilot continually fine-tuning an airplane engine, fiddling with the throttle and mixture to suit changing conditions such as temperature and altitude. Sometimes it seems half of the effort of keeping a team going on a long haul is successfully playing an endless head game with the dogs. They are, after all, only flesh and blood, and they get frisky or tired or even bored just like humans. And they can and will simply stop if they don't feel like running any longer.

The musher's job is to stay ahead of this malaise. The best way is to keep the front end moving so the rest will follow. Sometimes this gets tricky and too many leaders can even be a bad thing. In practice, running two good leaders together on some trails doesn't promote peaceful progress. All too often, two strong-minded front-enders won't agree on where to run when faced with several equally good choices, such as on a river with a 100-foot-wide snowmachine highway.

This can result in one leader yanking everyone over to the side he or she prefers, shortly followed by a jerk in the opposite direction as the other retaliates. It doesn't help the team's confidence to weave down the trail

A team takes a break on the Yentna River. Frequent short stops on boring river runs can help keep the dogs interested.

like a seasick snake, so one of the clashing canines has to go back in the team to restore harmony.

One option to get around this problem is to go to a single leader, which is what I did yesterday because I had an odd number of dogs in the team after dropping Yankee. Lucky did quite well up front by himself, keeping his own pace and smoothly selecting the best trail from the maze of snowmachine tracks without having to drag a partner to one side or the other. Of course, there are drawbacks: single lead is a lot of work, and a single leader frequently sets a slower pace and tires more quickly than with a helpmate.

Today, though, single lead isn't an option because I've removed one of the gangline sections after dropping Buck; two blank spots isn't a good idea in most circumstances because it strings everything out too much and makes for more difficult handling on tight trails.

This morning Lucky is going well enough, but co-leader Maybelline seems to have gone a bit sour and isn't her usual perky self. She's slowing Lucky enough to allow the ever-eager swing dogs to overrun, causing even more of a slowdown as she turns to glare at the tailgaters behind her. It's not a matter of a tired team—exactly the opposite. I've got to find the combination which keeps the energy flowing in a smooth and usable form. So, I juggle leaders and swing dogs until I get a lineup that works well.

This is why a good roster of "go-dogs" or trail leaders is necessary. These are dogs who will run up front in lead or swing but aren't always very good on commands. On trails with few distractions or turns they can frequently lead by themselves, but more often they act as accelerators and pacers for the main leaders and perform an important function in keeping up the team's speed.

A good co-leader or swing dog can be just as critical as a super-smart power-steering leader on many stretches of trail. Fortunately, I've got four or five good front-enders in this category and I shuffle through them until I find one who runs well with Lucky. Maybelline is quite content to run in swing, where she pulls hard and now seems to be enjoying the run.

Once we're moving smoothly, I can relax a little and enjoy the trip up the river in the brightening dawn. The trail is impossible to miss in the daylight, even without formal race markers, and whenever there is a choice Lucky makes the proper selection without a word from me. Of course, the team's speed drops off once the sun comes up and we trundle along at our customary seven or eight miles an hour; this isn't going to win any races but it's more than acceptable under the circumstances. It just means an extra hour or so on a 30-or 40-mile run, but at least I won't have to worry about getting lost.

About five miles short of Skwentna, just about where my last year's Iditarod team stalled for several hours on the first night of the race, I notice a team heading toward us. I remark to myself they're moving quite well, and then I see why: there's no driver aboard the sled. I have to try to stop them; it's a primary rule of mushing, not to mention common courtesy and good sense. However, we're closing at almost 20 miles an hour, so I'll only have one shot to grab them. If I miss, there's no one behind me for four or five hours.

I yell for Lucky to whoa up, and the team stops quickly as if they understand what's happening. I manage to get my snow hook into the crust but I know it won't hold long as I leap off my sled and jump into the path of the oncoming team. The fast-moving leaders shy away from me but I manage to clamber aboard the sled.

We go perhaps 50 feet before I can find the snow hook and get the team stopped. Then I find the second hook and set it as well, and finally I tip the sled over on both hooks for good measure. There's no question of trying to get the runaway team back to Skwentna; they'll be fine where they are for the time being. We're only a few miles out of the checkpoint and the hapless musher must be close ahead. In any case, I can certainly find someone with a snowmachine to come back if necessary.

While all this has been going on, my team has been getting excited and is about to yank the hook. I make the fastest 50-foot dash on record back to my sled and swing onto it just as everyone rockets off toward Skwentna. The missing musher is about a mile up the trail; he looks like he's been walking for several miles already and isn't in the happiest of moods. He cheers up significantly when I stop to assure him his team is in good shape and not too far ahead. I know how he feels—I've already been through this back at Cow Lake. There's nothing more frustrating than losing your team, especially when you know they're likely to go 30 miles down the river without you.

We pull into Skwentna a little before noon; I've already decided to keep the stop here as brief as possible so I can get back to Yentna Station. I much prefer to spend the night there to prepare for the final leg back to Big Lake, which will involve the worst sections of trail on the race, and for which I definitely want my wits about me.

In my haste to get food ready for the dogs I make the water too hot for their soup; I pour it into the dry dog food anyway, but they won't touch it. Normally I could cool it off with snow, but there isn't any handy that's clean enough to use. Finally I give up and throw them some frozen beef chunks. By the time we leave I've wasted more than two hours. I should have just checked in, tossed them some meat, and then checked out. I'm still learning.

We've been here so long Lucky has a bad case of checkpoint-itis and won't start the team. It's my fault, and I can't blame him; I know he's probably tired from working in lead for two days and would love to stay here for awhile. I put Pullman up front and we move off under our own power. Once we're away from the checkpoint things settle quickly into the normal trail routine. I'm mad at myself for letting the team down, but I'm glad to see Pullman leading so enthusiastically; she hasn't been up front for a month because she's been in heat. I have to remind myself one reason for running this race is to check out the leaders under realistic trail conditions, and so far it's worked out well in that respect.

About halfway down river to Yentna Station, as we come out of a back

221

slough, Pullman takes a turn I don't remember; she's chosen what appears to be the main trail, but something doesn't feel just right. I let the team go on across the river, and am relieved to see trail markers resembling Klondike 300 stakes. But after another couple of miles I realize we're lost: we're heading back up river and I'm not at all sure where we should be.

I turn the team around and we backtrack. At every side trail we stop and I check for other sled tracks, but none is the trail I'm after. After half an hour of cautious probing in the fading late-afternoon light, we're finally back to the last place where I was positive we were on the right trail. I turn everyone around again, and it becomes obvious what has happened. Coming up river, we turned into the back slough on one side of a big pile of driftwood; on the other side was another, bigger trail which looped back up the river to several lodges on the north bank.

We never saw it on the way up. Not only that, the stakes on the false trail (probably put there by snowmachiners well before the race) looked enough like Klondike markers to fool anyone. Now I know how Ramey Smyth and a lot of others got lost here. One bonafide Klondike marker at the fork would have saved everyone a lot of hassle. I'm just glad I had a bit of daylight left; at night I'm not sure what I'd have done.

As the team senses the shadows deepening, we accelerate to our normal nighttime cruising speed of 10 miles an hour. There's no way to get lost from here on in because the river has only one channel between well-defined banks. As we roll smoothly along, I gaze to the southwest: the glowing first-quarter crescent moon is about to set, with the brilliant evening star close behind it. To the southeast, Orion is rising with his unmistakable belt of glittering diamonds and red Betelgeuse marking his shoulder. In the northern sky, the Big Dipper is beginning its stately swing around Polaris, and the aurora is already glowing a faint green on the far northeast horizon.

It's another moment out of time and space. I truly can't imagine any place I'd rather be than gliding down the Yentna behind my dogs on this perfect evening, with a warm lodge a few miles ahead, in a race I now am confident we'll finish in good order.

In an hour or so the lights of Yentna Station hove into view like a lighthouse welcoming a sailor into harbor from the darkened sea. As we pull up to the checkpoint, I notice there aren't any checkers to meet us. Another driver, Shawn Sidelinger, is just bedding his team down—the runaway team I stopped earlier in the day—and he says the checkers and vets took the last plane out a few hours earlier. We're on our own; the winner, John Schandelmeier, crossed the finish line at Big Lake at nine this morning and all the trail help has headed home, leaving the lodge owner to cover everything.

As I get my team settled down Shawn tells me he only pulled in half an hour ahead of me. I know he left Skwentna at least three hours before I did, so I'm curious what happened. He says he was lost on the river for several hours after making a wrong turn; it took him seven and a half hours to cover the 35 miles back from Skwentna. I ask him which wrong turn; as I expected, it was the one I missed, and we both get a good chuckle at falling into the same trap in broad daylight.

We decide to run together on in to Big Lake because we're not sure how well the trail will be marked; maybe two heads will be better than one. We also decide not to leave until a couple of hours before dawn next morning; we'll use the predawn darkness to make good time on the river, but we want to hit the snowless overland stretch on the far side after sunup.

After we get the dogs fed and they're all sleeping soundly, we head up to the lodge for a sandwich. That's one nice aspect of longer races: the checkpoints invariably offer something in the way of food and lodging, even it's just a bowl of campfire soup and a place to toss a sleeping bag. More than that, they're places to relax for awhile and catch up on what's been happening along the trail.

Even among the leaders on a high-pressure race like the Iditarod, there's a sense of camaraderie not found in many other sporting events. Everyone is on the trail together for days on end, and what affects one affects all. To be sure, the front-runners will play mind-games with each other as the race closes in on the finish, but everyone knows it's all too easy to get caught in a storm or wreck a sled, and the underlying sense of cooperation against the elements is always there.

As we're sitting in the lodge munching a quick burger, the television is on (powered by a chugging generator outside the window) and I catch the end of the 10 o'clock news on Channel Two from Anchorage. The blow-dried sportscaster casually says, "Well, another dog race is over. John Schandelmeier survived the 30-below cold to beat John Barron by 18 minutes to win the Klondike 300..." and that's basically it for his coverage of the Klondike.

Nothing about the cold, no mention of the abysmal trail, no word of the dozen drivers who have scratched or been injured—just a perfunctory 10-second blurb tossed off while trying to suppress a yawn. Then he moves on for a several-minute interview with Doug Swingley (last year's Iditarod winner) down in Minnesota running the Beargrease.

Maybe I'm too close to the subject or perhaps I'm just too tired, but

I'm very disappointed by the brevity of the coverage of the only 300-mile race to be run so far this season in Alaska and by the cavalier assumption the race is "over" just because the winner has crossed the finish line. I'm tempted to get on the lodge's radiophone and call Channel Two to ask them what I should do now that the race is over and I—and half the mushers remaining in the race—are still out here on the trail.

No distance race is ever over until the last musher crosses the finish line. That's why mushing is the only sport with a red lantern, a recognition the last finisher has struggled at least as hard as the winner. Moreover, most long races have several prizes for important aspects such as sportsmanship and best dog care, and sometimes these are awarded to mushers who don't even finish.

Luckily the Frontiersman, the twice-weekly local newspaper for the Mat-Su Valley, will have a good spread. And KMBQ-FM, the Valley radio station, is providing ongoing coverage and has promised to hang in there until the last musher is in. I suppose it's expecting too much of the Anchorage media to treat dog mushing like Alaska's official state sport and not just a seasonal curiosity.

Tuesday—The Klondike 300: Yentna Station to Big Lake (75 miles)

Four o'clock comes early. The lodge owner's wife wakes Shawn and me and we fumble for our boots and heavy parkas. It's minus 35 on the river bank and easily 40 below on the river. We take our time and have our teams ready to go by 5:30. There's no moon and first light is three hours away, but the stark contrast provided by the snow cover lets us make out all the detail we need to keep oriented.

Both our teams move smoothly in the darkness; I'm following and drop back to maybe a quarter-mile spacing. This is a comfortable distance to keep my guys from overrunning. Any team following closely behind another (we call it "chasing") will tend to run faster than normal and will inevitably wind up literally on the lead driver's heels—just like my team did with Martin Buser for the first mile or so out of the starting gate on this race. However, chasing requires too much use of the brake, and I don't think the frequent reminders to slow down help the team's spirit for the long haul.

We settle into an easy 10-mile-an-hour nighttime pace. I leave my headlight on so Shawn can see I'm still back here; we agreed to keep an eye on each other at least until daybreak, and I'm keeping my end of the bargain. Still, my light seems out of place, and my team could easily follow the bobbing pinpoint in front of us with no trouble.

I plan to do a good deal of my Iditarod running at night, especially since we'll have a full moon for the first several days of the race. The dogs love to run under any kind of a bright moon (the old-timers' "running moon", and there is usually more than enough light to allow the driver to keep the headlight off. The net effect is magical, as I've experienced on other races. I feel the full moon will be a good omen for the Iditarod this year, and I intend to use it to help me get a solid start on the long haul to Nome.

This morning, even though there is no moon at all, the trip down to the mouth of the Yentna goes very quickly and we have no difficulty staying on the trail. One checker at Skwentna said the race marshal sent out a special snowmachine team to beef up the markings on the inbound leg from Yentna Station to Big Lake and they appear to have done a good job.

The only potential problem is the temperature, which has been steadily dropping ever since we left Yentna Station. I'm starting to feel a bit too cool even inside my expedition-quality outfit. I check my little zipper thermometer: it's off-scale low, which means it's below minus 50. I don't know how much below, but I think it's all academic once it's this frigid.

This is the coldest I've ever run a dog team, but the soul-numbing temperature doesn't seem to bother the dogs, who cruise obliviously on. I remind myself this isn't nearly as bad as it can get up here: John Barron and Ron Aldrich have both told me how they ran various Yukon Quests with temperatures hovering between 60 and 70 below. I can't really say I'm cold, but there do seem to be some unexpected minor leaks in my layered, heavily insulated armor. I think it's mainly the thought of getting stranded without proper protection in this kind of deep freeze that makes me shiver.

To reassure myself, I extract a few fresh charcoal hand warmer packets from my inside pocket and rip them open; I'll keep one inside my fleece inner jacket and put the other ones in the improvised glove I'm using to replace the mitten I lost back at Cow Lake. These things make a huge difference; the ability to keep my fingers warm seems to do much to bolster my overall resistance to the cold. It's certainly mostly psychological, but it seems to work—and who am I to change something that works, especially when it's 50 below.

We turn into the five-mile slough cutting over to the Susitna River just before dawn. Then, just as the light brightens to a dull gray, the team stops. I'm sure there's nothing physically wrong, and the dogs can't be tired, since we've come barely 25 miles. Moreover, the problem seems to be focused on Batman, the co-leader, who seems not to want to go. Pullman, the main leader, seems ready enough to move but won't go when Batman holds his place.

It could be Batman has gotten a bit cold running up front and is tired of acting as a windbreak for the rest of the team. After all, a 10 mile-an-hour wind at 50 below makes for a chill factor somewhere down near minus 100. It's just as likely he's only bored and wants a breather.

So, as the sun's first rays gild the top of Mount Susitna to the southwest I play the old switcheroo game up in the wheelhouse. After several permutations of the lead and swing dogs which yield a mile of halting progress, I find a combination that clicks: the same pair that stopped in the first place. It seems we just needed to wait for the light to brighten a bit, or for Batman to shake off his chill, or perhaps the extra distraction involved in my swapping dogs around recaptured their interest.

I suppose I could just as well have stood up front and waved my arms and done a dance—anything to break the combination of indistinct light and relentless cold and the monotonous trail down the wide river channels. But most importantly, we don't stay immobilized like we did on the Iditarod last year; this time we're moving—and I intend to obey Newton's laws of motion and stay that way until we get to Big Lake.

In another couple of hours we come to the hill leading up from the river. The dogs charge up the steep 100-foot slope as if they had just started the race, then continue at a good pace along the wooded upland track. Soon enough we come to the land of abominable trails; we're not doing more than four or five miles an hour through the grabbing brush and protruding roots, and that's plenty fast for me. It's all I can do to keep the sled upright and generally pointed in the right direction. As we carom from stump to root to rock, I'm thoroughly convinced I made the right decision to do this during daylight.

As we come off North Rolly Lake and start up the infamous hill that claimed so many sleds and bodies on the first day, I have time to examine it more closely. It is even steeper and narrower than I remember, and so tightly hemmed in by unyielding trees I don't see how anyone made it down. The uphill sides of several of the trunks look as if they've been skinned by chain saws; I can only imagine the carnage here and be glad I was lucky enough to have dodged this particular bullet. I think it's a reasonable assumption there won't be any more dog races down this monster for the foreseeable future.

After another unspeakable stretch of trail including the pinball slough, which is just as bad from this direction, we come out onto Red Shirt Lake. By now the sun is well up and is glaring directly in the dogs' faces. The three-mile-long lake looks even more like a river than the Yentna, and the endless expanse of white starts to work on the dogs as soon as we move away from the shore. They go slower and slower until finally one just sits down, followed by the whole team. I know exactly what the problem is: they think they're back on the river and what's more, they're starting to overheat from the sun beating on their dark fur.

This is precisely what happened on the Iditarod last year after we steamed up the Happy River hill in bright sun and 40-degree temperatures. However, this time none of the females are in heat and I can use my ace in the hole: Socks. I quickly put Old Reliable up front and stick the ringleader of the sit-down strike in the sled bag to let her cool off. Then with a quick "Okay" we march off across the snow desert of the lake.

As usual with Socks, we're not going very fast, but we are most assuredly moving and show every indication of continuing. If so many of the ladies hadn't been so seductive on the Iditarod last year, turning Socks into a slobbering basket case like all the other males on the team, I could have simply put him up front and kept moving when the female leaders faded out. I'd certainly have been into Rainy Pass a day or two earlier. Oh, well—I'll have another chance a month and half from now to make good.

With Mister Automatic up front we move steadily across the chain of lakes down to Cow Lake, where I lost the team on the outbound leg. The hill coming down onto the lake looks just as bad as it did when I got flipped off the sled, with absolutely no snow. I take a quick look for my missing mitten but it's not to be found; I'd hoped to pick it up if I could because it'll cost 70 or 80 bucks to replace it.

After Cow Lake the inbound race trail takes a shortcut back to Big Lake we didn't use coming out. Like many other trails in Alaska, the cutoff follows a seismic survey line. Cleared of trees years ago by petroleum survey crews, such avenues through the forest become de facto winter highways once the uneven ground has been covered with snow—only there hasn't been enough snow to cover up the stuff that's supposed to be covered up.

What I thought was going to be a reasonably easy 12 miles to the finish suddenly turns into the worst stretch of trail I've seen so far. Entire trees are down across the trail, which is also strewn liberally with stumps, rocks, and all manner of brush and other obstructions. Still, I can see where other sleds have made it through, so I swallow another handful of Tums and hold on tightly.

For the next five miles I do more serious sled handling than I've done in my short but (by now) very eventful mushing career. The swath through the trees—I can't dignify it by calling it a trail—runs like a Roman road straight through the forest, directly up and down whatever happens to be in its path. There have been no attempts to find easier ways down through gullies or up over the short, sharp hills. I think the Roman engineers would've laughed themselves silly looking at this barbarian imitation of their work.

Luckily, the worst hazards have been marked with crossed trail markers. One of them is a ravine perhaps 50 feet deep and twice that across, with impossibly steep sides. At the very bottom, just when the dogs are moving fastest despite my attempts to keep them slowed down, the trail makes a sudden swerve to cross the channel of the stream responsible for this monstrosity. As the team jogs right and then back to the left, I'm left gaping at the open creek bed, which looks like a tank trap about three feet wide and as many deep.

An old wooden pallet has been wedged into the banks as a sort of bridge, and someone has thoughtfully tossed a bale of straw next to it; the straw has obviously been smashed by more than a few drivers who missed the crossing. I manage to keep one runner on the alleged bridge while planting one foot on the bale to keep the sled upright. I stumble in the straw and get dragged behind the sled as the team inexorably pulls it on up the opposite near-cliff. As I finally regain my precarious perch on the runners, I can at least congratulate myself for not wrecking the sled, although I may have wrecked my shoulder and certain other parts of my person.

Now I know why Martin Buser, who trains on these trails, suggested the race not use this segment for the outbound leg. He was worried fresh teams would have been impossible to control on this stretch with the minimal snow cover, and especially in the ravine. Having now seen it firsthand, I heartily applaud his foresight; the ravine would have made the hill down to North Rolly Lake look like kindergarten. Besides, I don't think the borough would have had enough emergency vehicles to pick up all the pieces of sleds, dogs, and drivers.

By the time we get to the Little Susitna River I'm not surprised at anything any more. This Zen-like state of equanimity is a blessing because it keeps me from running screaming into the woods when the trail quite literally drops down to the river ice over a sheer five-foot bank. The dogs have to jump down onto the river ice while I keep the sled from tumbling on top of them. When I finally shove the sled over the edge it is vertical, and almost goes over on its back until the dogs pull the front end forward. All I can do is hang on to the handlebar for the knee-popping drop, which I manage to survive without breaking anything. The other bank of the 40-foot wide river is the same thing in reverse: the dogs somehow scramble up (I don't know exactly how) and then I have to lever the sled up and hold on while they pull everything up and over the lip.

Fortunately the Little Su marks the end of the obstacle course and the trail becomes merely awful once we're up the bank. A couple of miles later we swing onto an open slough where a pair of snowmachiners is waiting. I stop to ask them what the trail is like ahead; they say it's okay. I tell them it's been a horror story behind me, but they allow as how they wouldn't know about that because nobody's been crazy enough to drive a snowmachine over it.

I inquire how far it is to Big Lake; it's only a couple of miles, for which I am profoundly thankful. Then one of them says, "By the way, you're ninth." I almost fall off the sled in surprise. There's no way I can be so far up in the standings unless everyone else has scratched, gotten lost, or been abducted by aliens. I know almost half the original 26 starters have dropped out, but that still doesn't put me into the top 10. All I can do is shake my head and push on; this race is getting weirder by the mile.

As we push on across the open swamps interspersed by stands of spruce and birch, the dogs seem to be flagging a bit in the bright sun when we cross the exposed areas. I try to remedy the situation by singing to them; the only song I can think of off the top of my head is Hobo Jim's Iditarod song, whose refrain of "Give me a team and a good lead dog and a sled that's built so fine" seems marvelously appropriate for what we've come through.

My serenade actually appears to work; I can see the dogs' ears prick up and one or two will occasionally peek around to see what's making the terrible noise. I feel like an overdressed arctic cowboy crooning to the herd, but there's nobody out here to critique me, and the dogs seem to enjoy it. They keep pulling steadily and soon enough we bounce onto the ice of Big Lake; the finish line is only a few miles ahead and I think the dogs want to get there as badly as I do. Our collective fun-meter is pegged by now, and all I can think of is a steak dinner and the dogs no doubt are daydreaming about their cozy boxes full of straw.

As we proceed at a civilized pace across the lake I wonder if anyone is watching from the houses and lodges lining the shoreline. If this were a weekend, there would be thousands of people out here, since this is one of Anchorage's major getaway destinations. Even if we don't have an audience, I've got to feel a little proud that we've made it this far and are still looking good, no matter if the winner did pass this way more than a day earlier.

At three o'clock we round the last bend and I see the finish line in front of the Klondike Inn and its icebound boat docks. There's not a soul in sight. As we close on the banner strung across the ice, I'm trying to decide whether to run the dogs over to the truck, which is still parked out on the lake, or drive them up to the lodge. Then a solitary figure darts out of the bar and beats us to the chute by 50 feet. He tells me he's the checker as he welcomes us in.

Nobody expected us this soon—we've actually made pretty good time considering the bad trail, a bit more than nine hours. Shawn, who left Yentna Station with me, arrived almost an hour ago, just about the time difference I'd expected because of my leader problems at sunrise back on the river. Before I drive the team over to the truck, the checker says I really did finish in ninth place—in the money, no less. All I can do is shake my head. The world is truly turned upside down when my team can pull off a single-digit finish in a major sled dog race.

Of course there are only 12 mushers left out of the original 26. I don't know if this speaks to my good luck, my determination, or my questionable judgment. On the other hand, I do know if I'd scratched without a really good reason—like death or dismemberment—I couldn't have lived with myself and I would have had severe doubts about my ability to try the Iditarod again. In any case, we're finally done and we who stayed the course will definitely have something to talk about. After all, we finished when Martin Buser and several other big names didn't, and we kept ourselves and our dogs in reasonably good shape in the process.

After I get the dogs fed and bedded down in the truck, I head inside the lodge for a quick bite to eat. As a pleasant surprise, I discover I'm going to get my lost mitten back. The same cross-country skiers who caught my team on Cow Lake were kind enough to pick up my glove and leave a note at the Klondike Inn saying they had it.

A couple of earlier finishers are still in the lodge when I come in from the cold. They are among the rookies who refused to scratch because they needed to qualify for the Iditarod; they had a sensible reason to stick it out. When they find out I'm already qualified and don't need this race at all, they look at me like I'm several sandwiches short of a picnic. One of them asks why I did it when I really didn't need to. All I can say is it's a long story, longer than he probably wants to hear right now. Maybe I'll tell it to him in Nome.

February 14, 1996
Montana Creek, Alaska

Be careful what you ask for, it might come true—Part II. Our record-setting snow drought in Southcentral Alaska is finally over. Boy, is it over. After a pleasant four or five inches last week for appetizers, the main course arrived Friday and kept coming until this morning. By Saturday noon we had almost 18 inches of new snow, and it was still falling at the rate of two inches an hour.

My trusty snowblower, which I'd never even started this winter because of the dearth of snow, was in near-constant operation as I tried to keep ahead of the fluffy deluge. Finally the skies cleared Tuesday morning, revealing more than three feet of freshly fallen Alaska sunshine at my place, and more near the mountains. Somebody living out on our normal 20-mile loop measured 51 inches.

I've never seen this much snow fall in one storm, at least not in the Upper Susitna Valley, which tends to be much drier than locations nearer the coast or the mountains. Anchorage caught more than 30 inches, bringing the entire city to a slipping and sliding stop.

The late-season snow derby winner is the town of Valdez, over on Prince William Sound. It's normally one of the snowiest inhabited locations on the planet, with more than 30 feet of annual snowfall, but until this storm rolled in they had barely an inch on the ground. Now they have about 10 feet, and residents there are actually breathing a sigh of relief because their late-season ski festivals (including a national extreme skiing championship) are safe.

In our area, though, it's a case of way too much of a good thing. Our trails are buried much too deeply to try to break them open with the dogs, and the snow is so light snowshoes don't work. Worst of all, snowmachines don't ride up and over it to pack it down—they just plow into it and bury themselves.

At the beginning of the season, Ron and Steve Adkins and I chipped in to overhaul one of Ron's old dual-track Alpines—arguably among the best go-anywhere snow vehicles ever built—especially for setting trails. Like my snowblower, it sat idle for months, waiting for a chance to prove itself, but now it just bogs to a sputtering stop in this stuff.

Even the hordes of recreational snowmachiners from Anchorage who normally descend on us after every good snow are crying in their beers at the local lodges. Anchorage prohibits snowmachine use in the city, and under normal conditions these expatriates are so determined to use their machines they will run under conditions too abominable even for a dog team—but not now. It will take another few days for the snow to settle enough to be usable by the iron dogs. Then our problem won't be too much snow, it will be trying to avoid being run down by motor mushers working off a season's worth of frustration in our back yards.

But at least there will be enough snow for the Iditarod. We'd all been worrying about trail conditions after the Klondike 300 torture test, but it's been snowing all the way to McGrath and things are starting to look at least passable. This year has been a perfect example of my long-held belief there is no average weather in Alaska—only extremes from which meaningless averages are derived by statisticians. And you know what Mark Twain is alleged to have said on that subject: There are liars and damn liars, and then there are statisticians. And as I repeatedly shoveled one of my shed roofs to keep it from collapsing, I could think the number crunchers must be having a field day about now.

But I'm not worrying about driving dogs for the moment: it's Iditarod food drop time again. I tried to get ahead of the power curve this year by getting my meat cut and bagged early, but the snow derailed my schedule. After I finally got my driveway blown out for the last time and then excavated the dog food and other items buried under their protective tarps, I worked from noon yesterday until seven this morning to organize all of the little things I'll need on the trail.

I have 54 Iditarod food bags lined up in my driveway, each bulging with everything from dog food to batteries to paper towels. This year I'm shipping out more than 1,800 pounds of munchies for the dogs, which in total is far more than I can ever use, but which might be just right for a particular checkpoint if I get stuck for several days.

In a change from last year, I've shipped out 20 bags of dry dog food from (gasp!) Sam's and Wal-Mart. I've been catching flak from other

other mushers for using it instead of the high-priced spreads whose emblems are prominently displayed on the sleds and parkas of the Big Names. Actually, I've been feeding Sam's professional-grade stuff since last spring and—for my dogs at least—it's turned out to be as good as the elite fare at half the price.

Anyway, the dogs sure like it and it got them through the Klondike 300 in grand style. There's nothing wrong with the fancy-name kibbles, but they're a bit spendy for somebody like me who doesn't have a big sponsor (and especially a sponsor who happens to be a deluxe dog food company). This is just another of the tricks I'm learning this time around to keep the cost down without sacrificing quality.

The Iditarod food drop is a massive undertaking. Here the author's venerable dog truck (minus the dog boxes) is loaded with 54 bulging bags totaling more than a ton, ready for the 100-mile trip into Anchorage. The race will ship out more than 100,000 pounds of musher bags, plus another 50,000 pounds of race equipment and supplies to two dozen checkpoints scattered between Anchorage to Nome.

I've gone over my checklist at least three times to make sure I've packed everything I intended, and I'm finally to the point of closing the bags and loading them on my old dog truck for the 100-mile ride to Anchorage. After I tighten up the nylon tie wrap on the last bag, I go sit down on the porch steps and survey what I've wrought.

My first thought is of last year, when I had such high hopes and saw the multicolored bags as a map of my trek across Alaska. This year it's a bit different. The bags still outline my itinerary, but I don't see them as magic stepping stones on a carefree camping trip. This time they represent tough goals to be won by hard work, one at a time, with patience and determination. I fully intend to open every one of them myself this year, culminating with the ones in Nome.

The next two weeks will go all too quickly and there are still many things to do before the race starts. Day by day, I'm getting closer to finishing what I started two years ago. But for the moment, I've reached a major milestone for this year's race, and I might actually enjoy the normally tiring drive into town.

And when I've finished the food drop, I can go pick up my new Bernie Willis sled, finished just a couple of days ago. One of the more valuable lessons I've learned is a good sled is worth everything you pay for it. It has to be rugged enough to withstand the incredible abuse it will receive even on a short race (witness last year's Copper Basin 300 and the Klondike 300 just past) but easy to fix when it finally meets the inevitable immovable object.

Bernie is a pilot and an aeronautical engineer (and an Iditarod veteran) who appreciates simplicity and ease of maintenance. In the best Alaskan tradition, he has applied modern technology to an old concept. His sleds ride like Cadillacs but can be fixed with duct tape, hose clamps, and bungee cords. After last year I vowed never to be caught on a race trail without a Willis sled and the first thing I did when I sold the Cessna was give Bernie a call. The sled will be an interesting replacement for my airplane.

I do know one thing: running the sled will probably cost me more every year than the plane ever did, what with care and feeding of the dogs and all the expenses connected with races. And that, in turn, means I'll have to work longer hours at Hudson's to earn the money to pay for everything. There's a twist I hadn't thought about: I sold my plane, so I'll have to fly more. Only in Alaska....

February 24, 1996
Wasilla, Alaska

It's Kim's turn in the spotlight as she takes most of my team on the Junior Iditarod. This year the race has turned ugly, with lots of fresh snow out on the river and strong winds to drift it into a hard-crusted obstacle course, all combined with subzero temperatures. Bert and Reb and I have been waiting all afternoon as the delays grow longer and the reports from the trail grow worse.

By the time the first couple of teams have crossed the finish line on Lake Lucille, conditions have become so bad most of the trailing teams are delayed well into the evening. The race marshal finally decides to move the finish line back up the trail almost six miles. Everyone moves out in a convoy of dog trucks to intercept the inbound teams.

After an hour of waiting, the teams start to straggle in, somewhat the worse for wear. Kim gets the red lantern, but she has held the team together in the face of the elements over a difficult-to-follow trail and everyone looks to be in good shape. As I expected, the dogs didn't set any new land speed records. But they continued to work for her even when things got tough, and that's what counts.

I'm proud of her and of the dogs. Like the Klondike last month, just finishing in good order has been an accomplishment. And now it's almost time for the big show on Fourth Avenue. Kim will be riding my second sled out of the starting chute this year. After tonight, no one can say she hasn't earned it.

February 29, 1996
Anchorage, Alaska

I-Day is approaching with terrifying speed. I know how the citizens of south Florida must have felt as they watched Hurricane Andrew grind inexorably toward them, or the inhabitants of Pompeii as the ash cloud from Vesuvius began to descend from the heavens. Or perhaps more appropriately, one of my friends said I'm starting to have the "deer in the headlights" look.

The week has been almost completely consumed with meetings and banquets and all the other events leading up to the moment of truth on Fourth Avenue. Of course, there have also been the last-minute shopping trips for all of the zillion things I think I'll need to take with me on the trail: my checklist actually has more than 150 items on it, all of which I'll try to stuff into the sled, many of which I'll probably discard even before I leave the starting gate.

I'm riding back to Montana Creek with Ron and Steve Adkins after the mushers' banquet in Anchorage (I've drawn number 50). I didn't want to drive my car back because I'm already so tired I was worried about falling asleep and running off the road. As I half-doze in the passenger seat, the realization sinks in that my date with destiny on Fourth Avenue is barely 24 hours away.

Granted, I'll get a brief reprieve after Saturday's 20-mile run to Eagle River, but it's time to put on my game face. Once I leave the restart in Wasilla Sunday morning, I will be living on the back of the sled for two weeks, with only occasional stops at checkpoints to remind me civilization still exists.

I've been having serious cases of the butterflies all week and I haven't gotten enough sleep despite my best intentions, but now I'm shifting into the go-to-Nome mode anyway. I'm mentally beginning the adjustment to the race routine, to the checkpoint-to-checkpoint rhythm that will govern everything for almost 1,200 miles.

Last year I didn't have the faintest idea what I was walking into; I might as well have been a fifteenth-century sailor pushing off toward the new continent claimed by all the legends to lie just beyond the horizon. This year I know only too well the new continent is a lot farther than the horizon, and there are plenty of places along the way where I can fall off the edge of the earth if I'm not careful.

I'll sleep as late as I dare in the morning and then load the dogs and my gear and the sled onto the dog truck for the trip back into town. Ron has graciously agreed to feed my remaining dogs while I'm away, and to house-sit my cabin to make sure the generator works and the pipes don't freeze. I've already paid as many bills as I can; at least my most ravening creditors will remain at bay until after I return. I'll have enough things to occupy me on the trail without worrying if the bank will be trying to repossess my car.

And I've got to make certain I have enough left on my credit card for an airline ticket back from Nome. The $700 or so for drivers to ship themselves and their dogs back to Anchorage has become a hardship for shoestring mushers; more than a few have had to sell dogs and equipment in Nome to get cash for a ticket. Until a couple of years ago the fare was half what it is now, but new airline management stopped the good deal. To its credit, the airline contributes to the race, but this still doesn't ease the way home for mushers who finish out of the money.

Partly to attenuate return expenses, the race started paying every finisher $1,000 in 1990, but dwindling budgets killed the stipend within a couple of years. The net result since then has been to hang some mushers out to dry after they've struggled to Nome. It's an often-cited example of how the Iditarod has become so expensive many mushers are simply unable to afford it any more. This cost inflation has especially affected Native drivers from cash-short Bush communities who must fly their teams to the start of the race and home from the finish.

Hopefully the long-awaited Iditarod lottery should be running for the 1997 race. It been officially authorized by the state, but as usual, the devil is in the details. Once it's up and running it may ease the race's fortunes somewhat and might provide more than enough income to give finishers and teams a free ride home.

The Idita-Rider program is still going strong. At the musher meeting this afternoon I met my passenger, Nancy Bee from San Mateo, California. (I keep thinking she's from Sacramento because of the newspaper there with the same name, which is part of the chain which owns the *Anchorage Daily News*.) Last year the Idita-Riders generated $35,000; this year has been equally successful and the mushers think it's a pretty good idea.

One of the program's goals was to help drivers and their dogs get back from Nome, but this year the money will go to the race general fund. We've chalked it up to hard times for the Iditarod, which has already had to lower the '96 purse from $350,000 to $300,000 (not that I'll ever see any of it). But everyone agrees: before too much longer we need to make sure everybody who gets to Nome can get home without having to mortgage the dog lot.

Another topic which surfaced in the mushers' meeting was the infamous Rule 18, better known as the Expired Dog Rule. Adopted last year, it says simply if a dog dies on the race by any cause other than external force over which the musher has no control, such as a moose or snowmachine, the musher will be automatically withdrawn from the race, or disqualified if there is evidence of negligence or abuse. The discussion was supposed to be strictly behind closed doors among the mushers and the race officials, but it leaked quickly to the press and was common conversation at the banquet this evening.

The rule may have been a well-intentioned attempt to reduce dog deaths on the race, but most mushers feel it was instituted as a knee-jerk response to placate supposedly jittery sponsors. In theory it might look good, but in practice, drivers feel it is a gross overreaction and will be unworkable because it leaves no room for good judgment and common sense. The bottom line is Rule 18 considers a musher guilty until proven innocent if a dog dies.

And unfortunately, dogs sometimes die on long races. Just like human marathon runners in perfect shape who drop dead in the middle of a run, apparently healthy dogs can expire of causes that are unknown—or more importantly, unforeseen and unpreventable. For example, a dog might be seriously injured or killed by, say, a branch sticking out into the trail. While everyone strongly agreed negligence and abuse should be swiftly and harshly punished, mushers argued long and forcefully they should not be expelled from the race for what effectively is an act of God.

The issue wasn't really resolved. Mushers were unhappy because Rule 18 turns the race into a crap shoot: no matter how well we take care of our dogs and watch the trail, we're history if a dog dies. And given nearly 1,000 dogs running to Nome over a two-week period, the odds are one or more won't make it.

But as bad as this sounds, it's still an extraordinary track record. For comparison, someone did a statistical study to show the rate of death would be far higher among the same number of ordinary "civilian" dogs over a two-week period, and no one would stigmatize the owners of the deceased dogs or fine them the tremendous investment a musher forfeits if he or she is pulled from the race. We'll see how it works out, but the stage has been set for a really bad situation on the trail this year.

The other main issue in the meeting was the usual one: trail conditions. Snow cover is still far less than normal. This means brush and shrubs and even rocks will be showing through on some stretches of trail where they haven't been seen for years, and the trailblazers will have a lot less leeway in where they put the actual trail. This will mean sharper curves, steeper slopes, rougher trails, and less direct routes in many areas.

What most worries everyone is the stretch from Ophir through Cripple to Ruby. There's been a massive, unseasonable thaw in the area and trails are flooded or have refrozen into glare ice. The rivers are mostly open and no one is certain how the trail will cross them. Worst of all, planes have not been able to land anywhere near Cripple, a vital rest stop 55 miles into the wilderness, because of abominable overflow conditions and soft snow. More than likely, the food and equipment we've carefully planned for Cripple will be dropped back up the trail at Ophir, the nearest place with a serviceable runway.

This will leave us a 170-mile run over atrocious trail, and we must be completely self-sufficient for all of it. Even for the top mushers, the run will take almost 24 hours, including at least five or six hours of rest along the way. Extra dog food, extra booties, extra people food, extra Heet for the alcohol cookers—all must be carried from Ophir. There will probably be a checkpoint of sorts at Cripple, although no one is quite sure where it will be. Since it will probably have to be run in on snowmachines it will offer little besides a couple of tents, a checker, a veterinarian, and hot coffee. No one is looking forward to this torture test. Some mushers are already looking for tiedown straps to fasten extra bags of dog food atop their sleds. For this stretch, at least, we may well get a taste of the travails of the old-time freight drivers as they fought their unwieldy sleds over abysmal trails. It promises to be the ultimate camping trip for back-of-the-packers like me. I fully expect it will take me 30 or 40 hours to get to Ruby, maybe longer. That's a long time between checkpoints in a race, especially for the Iditarod.

But there's not much to do about it now. I file the airfare problem and Rule 18 and the Ophir-to-Ruby marathon in the back of my mind along with everything else and try to sort out what's going to be critical for the next 24 hours. I've just dropped off to sleep when we pull up to my place. I thank Ron for the ride home, stumble into the cabin, and fall into bed still in my clothes. For me the race has already begun.

Sled dogs are the subject of many veterinary studies every year. Weighing selected dogs before and after the race is part of many such projects.

March 2, 1996
The Iditarod
Anchorage to Eagle River (20 miles)

Ten o'clock on a bright Saturday morning: we're on Fourth Avenue in Anchorage for the ceremonial start. The proverbial journey of a thousand miles is about to start with a single step, or rather, a whole bunch of steps by my frantically eager dogs. I'm as ready as I'll ever be, and the dogs certainly look to be up to the journey ahead. In any case, there's no turning back now—it's redemption time for me.

The bedlam is at its customary earsplitting level with almost 1,000 dogs in a frenzy to go to Nome. The temperature will be up around freezing for the 20-mile run out to Eagle River, which is great for the crowds but lousy for the dogs. Also, we're only running 12 dogs for this leg as a result of a new rule designed to keep teams under better control when they're frisky and full of energy at the start of the race.

We'll still be pulling two people and two sleds plus carrying our Idita-Riders, for a total load of as much as 700 pounds. Most of the mushers think this may be a bit much for just 12 dogs, but then, this leg doesn't count for time so we can take it easy. Like last year, everyone is worried about the heat affecting the dogs, especially those like mine and Steve Adkins' and some of the ones from the Interior which have been training in subzero temperatures all season.

Since I drew number 50 out of 61 this year, I'll start 49th. This is because there are only 60 teams—the number one bib in the race, and the first starting position, is honorary. The parking spots are arranged in reverse order so the trucks of teams already started can drive off without interfering with teams waiting to go. This means my spot is near the front and every team before me passes by on its way to the start a block away.

It's quite a fashion show. I'm still amazed by the money some of the frontline kennels put into their teams, with color-coordinated harnesses and sled bags and musher outfits. Some of the handler crews are uniformed like Olympic squads, especially those sponsored by outdoor-gear companies. And the sleds are technological wonders, some with fancy seats and special handlebars and more gadgets than James Bond's trusty Aston-Martin (or is it a Beamer he's driving now?).

For low-budget drivers like me and Steve Adkins and John Barron, things are a lot simpler, and I'm not so sure I don't like it that way. My harnesses are off the rack at the local musher supply store, my handlers are friends in jeans, and my sled is a standard Bernie Willis model, solid quality but far from the dream machines gliding by. My sled bag matches my slightly-the-worse-for-wear cold-weather gear, mainly because

The author at the start of the Iditarod with Silvertip, his former personal pet and accidental sled dog who is mostly wolf. Wolves have long been out of favor as sled dogs and Silvertip is a throwback to the early days of the century when mushers sometimes ran wolf hybrids or even full-blooded wolves in their teams.

Bernie's wife found a matching piece of fabric when she made it.

Soon enough the bib numbers passing by creep into the 40s and we get the dogs out of the boxes and harnessed up. The teams are starting at two-minute intervals, with every fifth team waiting three minutes to allow a television commercial break. Hooking up goes smoothly and before I realize it we're in the grand parade up to the banner marking the starting chute. People I haven't seen for years shout encouragement from the crowd, to which I weakly wave back and put on my best smile.

Now it's my turn. The team is lined out smartly with old veteran Socks up front; I'm not taking any chances about going over the berm and into the crowd this year. I dimly register the one-minute warning, then suddenly it's 15 seconds, then the final five-second countdown. The starter shouts "Go!" I yell "Okay!" and the team leaps away from the starting line with as much energy as any of the Big Names.

No dives over the berm, no hesitations—we're well and truly off and running like we know what we're doing. I take it as a good omen.

With Kim on the second sled and Idita-Rider Nancy Bee in mine (I keep thinking she's from Sacramento), we

A full 16-dog team Iditarod team is an incredibly powerful pulling machine. In some cases, each dog has its own holder for the stop-and-go procession to the starting line.

make steady progress out of downtown Anchorage and onto the network of bike trails which become ski and dog trails in the winter. The only hitch is a new stretch of trail about five miles out, where the downhill curbs have been obliterated by the dozens of teams in front of me. I see the sled is going to slide off the trail as we cut across a corner. I warn Nancy to hang on but we dump despite my best efforts to keep everything upright; sleds just don't maneuver well with people in them. We crunch against a tree and she takes some of the impact. She says she hurts a bit, but all I can do is try to joke with her and point out mushing is sometimes a contact sport as we pull back onto the trail and push on.

A few miles later, after a storybook run through the snow-covered birch forest, we stop to let Nancy out at the pickup station; she's forgotten her bruises and has apparently enjoyed the trip. She says she'd love to go on to Eagle River, but I'm worried the extra load in the afternoon heat would prove too much for only 12 dogs. Besides, I know there are some bad stretches ahead and I'm worried another crash might sink the entire Idita-Rider program.

Kim and I press on. She wants to run the Iditarod in 1998, as soon as she's eligible, and probably with some of these same dogs. This is a preview for her and I tell her by the time we unhook the second sled in Knik tomorrow she'll already have run a good chunk of the race.

After a couple of hours of sun-slowed running and the usual spots of awful trail and another sled spill or two, we pull up the final hill into the Eagle River VFW post that has been the first checkpoint since the race's inception. The dogs are in superb shape and this has actually been a good warm-up run for them.

After we get them all cooled off and fed and into the boxes I wander inside for the traditional bowl of moose stew and cornbread. As I eat I'm tired and still filled with uncertainty. Nome is more than 1,100 miles away and this hasn't been any kind of an indicator of what things will be like out on the trail a week or 10 days from now.

For a moment I consider packing it all in and letting go of the Iditarod. I wouldn't be the first person to do so. Then I realize that's not an option. I have to do this race if I want to live with myself. Finishing it is probably the most important thing I'll ever do. It has become a Holy Grail for me, a pilgrimage I can no longer explain to anyone, and maybe not even to myself. With a sigh I finish a last cup of Tang and head out to the truck. I'll need all the sleep I can get before the restart tomorrow—the real beginning of my long-delayed trip to Nome.

March 3, 1996—The Iditarod: Wasilla to Knik (15 miles); Knik to Yentna Station (50 miles)

We're in the procession of teams creeping toward the restart on the old Wasilla airport with steady old Socks in lead. The day is already hot and clear, just what I didn't need. I wish we could have some 30-below Klondike 300 weather so the dogs can feel comfortable.

My back-in-the-pack start means it's almost noon, with the heat of the day soon to come. The first teams are already 25 miles down the trail; they'll run until mid-afternoon or so and then pull over and rest in the shade. I'll still be plugging along, making slow time on the wiped-out trail. This is a disadvantage of a late draw, compounded by my slow team. The best I can expect is an average eight miles an hour, as opposed to the 10 or 12 of the better teams.

We start in the same order and at the same times as yesterday in Anchorage. The starting time differential will be evened up on the 24-hour layover, but in the meantime I'm starting out behind the power curve. Unfortunately, my dogs have trained in cold weather and have heavy coats. This means I just can't run them as fast or as long as I'd like in balmy weather like this.

The author's team erupts from the starting chute at the Wasilla restart of the 1996 Iditarod. Socks and Maybelline are leading. The next stop is Knik, 14 miles away, where the second sled (ridden by Kim Hanson) will be dropped.

Some mushers have begun breeding for dogs with thinner coats, on the theory you can always put a coat on a cold dog, but you don't have many options to cool off a thick-coated canine. I can already see I'll have to go to a night-running schedule quickly, but today I have no choice but to slug it out as best I can.

All too soon we're in the starting gate. Kim is on the second sled again, which we'll disconnect at Knik, 15 miles away. Today we have all 16 dogs hooked up so the weight penalty won't be as severe. The announcer gives me a special mention; we met at Yentna Station while he was covering the Klondike 300 for KMBQ-FM. He's becoming hooked on dogs himself and I wouldn't be surprised to see him running the race one of these years.

"Five, four, three, two, one, GO!" We roar out of the gate just like yesterday, but 100 yards down the chute Socks decides to relieve himself before the day's business gets too hectic. This is his trademark: when he wants to do his thing, he just stops, no matter if he's in lead and we're rocketing out of the starting chute of the Iditarod itself. It's a frustrating habit, but one we've never been able to train him out of. So, we stop in front of 500 cheering fans while Socks unconcernedly decorates the snow.

Then we're off again as if nothing has happened. I turn to Kim and we shrug at each other. The crowd seems to love it. I suppose it's Socks' way of reminding us who's actually driving this train. Actually, I'm more than willing to put up with his foibles in return for his solid leading. Unlike last year, I'm not really worried about getting the team to go with him up front, and the occasional unexpected pause that refreshes is more than worth the minor distraction it causes.

If he has a serious flaw, it's his speed: he'll get you where you want to go, but you go at the "speed of Socks," which is about eight or nine miles an hour tops—unless he's excited about something, such as a sprightly young female running next to him. This is why he's not pulling up front for one of the Big Names any more.

On balance, though, he's really quite an extraordinary dog. I'll be the fourth musher he's guided along the Iditarod. He took Vern Halter there first; Bert bought him for the 1993 race and then loaned him to Bruce Moroney for the 1994 trek. Last year I should have just let him take me to Nome if I'd had any common sense, but I didn't really realize what an asset he was—and is. This year I'm fully convinced if I can just stand on the runners long enough, Socks will eventually get me to the City of the Golden Beaches.

Just in case, I've got four other leaders behind him in the bullpen. Pullman went to Nome with Vern Halter in 1994 just before Bert bought her; I ran her last year and I know she can add extra speed under many conditions, but she's not as strong and consistent as Socks. Old Buck may be as steady as Socks, but he's never been on the Iditarod, and I'm a little uncertain about his performance out on the coast, where the wind and endless stretches of sea ice have caused many a good team to founder.

I'm hoping Lucky will add an all-around boost to the team; he's got speed and is a good command leader as well. Finally, a couple of weeks ago I borrowed Will Barron's leader, Diablo. He's fast, but I haven't had much chance to run him with the team; if I can get him to go consistently up front we'll have real speed, but he's a big question mark.

I've got several co-leaders who can run up front to help the leaders. Little Maybelline is up front now with Socks; she's irrepressible as always and can often tease him into tacking a couple of miles an hour onto his normally stodgy pace. I sometimes think Socks (who is eight years old) speeds up when she's around in order to impress her. Batman is also good up front, and I know he runs well with Pullman. Bea is usually a good front-ender, as is Steel, another dog I borrowed from the Barrons' lot at the last minute. Wild Thing is also a known quantity in the wheelhouse, but she can be notoriously moody.

Back in the engine room, I've got Bear, Yankee, Rocky, and Kisser, all big, powerful Iditarod veterans and rock-solid under every condition I've ever seen. I've also decided to take Panda (Socks' daughter), a promising two-year old; she's done well all year and can run up front if she feels like it. I'd really like to get her to Nome, or at least as far as I can, so she'll have the experience for next year's race.

Convoys of teams are not unusual, particularly early in the race, or when difficult trail or bad weather is expected. These five teams on the Yentna are quite content to play follow-the-leader for awhile, occasionally chatting back and forth and checking out each other's teams.

Finally there is Silvertip, my three-quarter wolf and erstwhile personal companion who has become quite a good sled dog, if a somewhat improbable one.

Putting together this lineup involved some painful trade-offs. I left behind Weasel—one of my favorites—and Rhythm, two good co-leaders and Iditarod veterans, in favor of the Barron dogs; I don't know if I'll regret that decision, but what's done is done. Anyway, I've stacked the deck as much as I can, and all I can do now is play my hand as the circumstances permit. Besides, I know every musher on the trail has gone through the same quandary I have: leaving good friends behind on the journey of a lifetime is one of the hardest things anyone can ever do.

I review all of the players as we trundle down the trail to Knik. As I expect, we get passed by several teams—including Rick Swenson's superbly conditioned powerhouse—which means I'm drifting back to the tail end already. I expected this, though, and my plan is to just keep pushing this first day to get back up into the middle somewhere. If last year was any indication, I need to make sure I get to Skwentna before we take a long rest. I can see what things look like down the trail once I'm there.

We make good if not spectacular time to Knik, passing hundreds of spectators lining the route. Since the trail parallels a main road there is a constant flow of cars and trucks with horns blowing and well-wishers waving and shouting. Many of them stop to take pictures and I eventually give up trying to wave back at everyone. None of it seems to be bothering the dogs, but like me, I'm sure they will be glad to get out on the trail, away from the hubbub.

Bert and my handlers are waiting at Knik. We disconnect the second sled and I spend a few minutes checking booties and making minor adjustments to the gangline. It's already hot, above freezing, and the bright sun promises a miserable next few hours for the dogs. Nevertheless, we have to press on to stay on schedule. I'm not too worried about overheating because we'll be going very slowly. It will just be a long, slow slog over soft trails; like the rest of the trip, it's something we must do one step at a time, until we eventually get to Nome.

The trail leaves the road system at Knik, but roads are a relative concept in Alaska in the winter. This end of the Iditarod Trail is a thoroughfare for droves of snowmachines, and the race itself provides a grand excuse for a series of parties stretching for 100 miles.

Accordingly, hundreds of motor mushers share the trail with us, most of whom are fortunately considerate of the dogs. There are the odd few, however, who roar by the teams without realizing how unnerving and potentially dangerous they can be. I try to be patient as we plod on; nightfall will chase most of the snowmachiners back to town and should bring cold temperatures to firm the trails.

As we pound on through the afternoon we play leapfrog with a dozen other teams. Most of the fast movers have pulled ahead and we back-of-the-packers have pretty well sorted ourselves out. Some are veterans running young teams to Nome for seasoning, a few are semi-veterans like me, and the rest are rank rookies like I was last year.

We know we'll be seeing a lot of each other over the next couple of weeks and keep up a genial banter as we pass each other and occasionally run together. It's a little too early to organize convoys; these will coalesce naturally down the trail as conditions require. For the time being we're all feeling out our teams and getting mentally prepared for the long haul.

By six o'clock we're approaching Flathorn Lake, 40 miles from Wasilla. Almost everyone else has stopped and rested for couple of hours by now. My team has continued to look strong and I've kept going, albeit very slowly, sometimes no more than a few miles an hour along the soft, punchy trail. I'm starting to pass some of the front runners who have camped out during the heat of the day. They'll be up and running shortly.

When they blow by me after their siestas it will probably be the last time I'll see any of them until Nome.

I can already see this trip will be a hare-and-tortoise exercise, with my plodders playing the turtle. I wish I had some more speed so I could spend less time on the trail and more time in the checkpoints, but it's just not going to happen. I guess I'll have to content myself with looking at the scenery from the back of the sled for hours on end. Sooner or later we'll get to Nome.

The shadows finally start to lengthen after Flathorn Lake. We pick up a little speed as we tumble (literally) down onto the broad frozen expanse

Two dozen snowmachiners are having a trail party near the mouth of the Yentna River. Such parties are common sights for mushers until well past Skwentna. At night their bonfires form a line of beacons strung out for miles up the river.

of the Susitna River. I'd been warned about the short, steep grade down onto the river, but nobody told me about the reverse curve in it; I manage to hang on to the sled as it bounces on its side onto the river ice. Nothing is hurt, and I'm sure this will be only the first of many spills.

There are half a dozen parties out on the ice, each with a bonfire and an attendant cluster of snowmachines. The fires twinkle in the deepening dusk, a series of beacons marking the way up the river. As we pass each one Socks wants to go see what's going on; once or twice I have to stop the team and go up to lead him past the temptation of free hot dogs and other goodies.

We quickly move the next 15 miles up to Yentna Station under a brilliant full moon. I leave my headlamp off most of the time; I can actually see more without it. In any case, this is all familiar territory; the dogs have been out here at least half a dozen times in the past couple of months and they seem somewhat bored with it all.

We pull into Yentna Station just before nine. I'm actually ahead of many of the fast teams who are only now moving up the river after their afternoon rests. However, I stop longer than I'd planned to give my guys a breather, and a number of teams I passed roar through with only a brief pause on their way up to Skwentna and Finger Lake. I doubt I'll see any of them again.

March 4, 1996—The Iditarod: Yentna Station to Skwentna (35 miles); Skwentna to Finger Lake (45 miles)

While I'm feeding the dogs at Yentna Station the checker comes over to warn me about a particularly bad overflow condition up ahead. Apparently water from Moose Creek, a tributary of the Yentna, is flowing out on top of the river ice and has blocked the main trail with cold slushy water as much as two feet deep. He says a trail has been marked around the inundated area, but even as he talks to me someone comes over and says six teams are reported to be caught in the mess.

I decide to wait and go with another musher after we've got some more information. Overflow can mean nothing more than wet toes for the dogs, or it can entail a serious swim through chest-deep water. I'd prefer not to get in any deeper than I have to, and I'd rather have someone there if anything untoward happens.

Just before midnight a trio of snowmachiners pulls in from up river with word of a good trail around the overflow. Steve Adkins and I decide to move out and get past it before it gets worse. We run up the river for a few miles and then hit a wall of fog, actually steam from the open water of the overflow condensing in the cold night air. The bright full moon helps, but there are still stretches where we can't even see our lead dogs. As we're probing our way through the fog, I feel like we're sneaking past some malevolent dragon lurking in the mists.

Steve has pulled 100 yards ahead of me when I hear a shouted "Whoa!" Through a fleeting rift in the fog I see Steve wading out to pull his leaders back to a dry stretch of trail. I barely get stopped before Socks goes in, too. The overflow is almost impossible to avoid; I was lucky Steve was ahead of me or I'd have been in it. As Steve maneuvers onto the bypass trail, which we missed in the fog, I try to turn my team around. The effort results in a huge tangle costing me half an hour.

While I'm straightening things out, three more teams materialize from the mist. Two manage to find the dry trail, but one plows through the overflow—which has deceptively grown a thin shell of camouflaging ice thanks to the now-subzero temperatures—before I can yell at him to stop. He immediately breaks through well over his knees and his dogs are in up to their necks, but he manages to get through the 30-yard-wide lake and moves on; I never find out who he is.

After I get my bunch of pound rejects lined out and around the overflow, we resume our stately pace up the river. The moon reflecting off the snow is so bright I can see every detail of the trees along the banks.

Getting the dogs fed and bedded down in the checkpoints is always the musher's first priority. Once the dogs are resting, the musher will often stay away from the team for as long as possible to avoid disturbing them.

There is absolutely no need for headlamps, and drivers aren't even turning them on unless they are coming up on another team and want to pass. My dogs have accelerated to perhaps 10 miles an hour, but I'm starting to have too many interruptions when one or another dog gets tangled or tries to stop for whatever reason.

At this stage of the race I'm still sorting out who runs well with whom, and in what positions. I'm experimenting with different arrangements while I have the luxury of a good trail; however, the research costs me an extra hour or two because of the repeated stops. When we're moving, we're moving well; when we're stopped, I'm working hard shuffling dogs to find the best all-around combination. As the race goes on I'll be looking to eliminate disruptions; I can see now I'll need a smooth-running team that can make up in steady progress what it will certainly lack in speed.

As we move upstream in the moonlight I link up with another driver; my team follows his and we make our way toward Skwentna. We pass all of the spots where my last year's effort started to come unraveled. Several are etched in my memory because of the sheer frustration I was experiencing in just trying to get the team to go. This year things are vastly different and we sail serenely on. Slowly but surely I'm starting to leave my ghosts behind.

We finally round the last river bend into Skwentna at six in the morning, just as first light tinges the eastern horizon. I'm only a couple of hours ahead of last year's pace, but I'm not worried about the team now. My plan is to rest here for several hours and then start working up to Finger Lake. I briefly consider pushing on immediately but the team seems tired, which isn't surprising considering we've been on the trail more than 18 hours with only a couple hours' rest at Yentna.

Most of the teams that arrived at Skwentna during the night have already headed up the trail. There will be 30 or more of them at Finger Lake by midday, all waiting out the afternoon heat before challenging the infamous Happy River Steps and the 20 miles of bad road on up to the Rainy Pass checkpoint. I'd have liked to push on with them but our slow speed didn't get us here soon enough. We took six hours to cover 35 miles from Yentna Station; most teams needed only four. I can't keep up with the speed merchants; I'll have to run my own timetable and let the chips fall where they may.

Now, however, I have to take care of the team. The first task is to get the dogs settled in, look them over, and get some food and water into them. I start at the front of the team and work back, giving each dog a biscuit, then I reverse and work forward unsnapping tuglines; this is a signal we'll stay here for awhile—and it also prevents them from inadvertently bolting with the sled while they're still in the "go" mode. Then I work back to the sled again, pulling off booties and giving each dog a hands-on thank you which doubles as a quick once-over for any obvious problems.

When the dogs are comfortable I take my plastic bucket over to a much-used hole in the river ice for water, which I drag back to the sled and pour into the alcohol cooker. Getting the cooker going is a critically important step; it must be done quickly after arriving to make sure the dogs get food (and the soaked-up water) while they are still in a mood to eat; tired dogs sometimes will simply curl up and go to sleep, ignoring even the most appetizing meal. Because of the intense calorie and hydration demands during the race, the dogs absolutely must eat and drink on a regular schedule; even one missed meal can spell trouble.

Once the water is heating I pull my food bags over and open them; as I half-expected, some of the meat looks like it has melted and refrozen, so I decide not to feed it. The last thing I need is sick dogs from eating spoiled meat; it's happened before and has knocked entire teams out of the race. I included alternative meats less vulnerable to thawing, so I should be okay. From my "people bag" I extract the booties and necklines and snaps and batteries and gloves and other equipment I'll need for the next couple of legs and put the rest in my return bag. I'm thankful we can salvage our used and excess gear by shipping it back—none of us wants to waste any more than we must.

Most checkpoints are outfitted with sturdy quonset-type tents dubbed "Dodge Lodges." They provide places for vets to work on sick or injured dogs or for tired mushers and volunteers to grab a quick nap. This one is at Finger Lake.

After 15 minutes over the hot blue alcohol flames, the water is steaming and I pour it into the buckets, in which I've assembled a mixture of dry dog food, frozen meat, and anything else I think will tempt the dogs to eat. While the food soaks, I help the vet check the dogs and work on any problems we find. Usually these focus on feet, wrists, and sometimes shoulders; many small irritations and cuts and aches can be treated on the spot. Diarrhea is another constant threat, and the vets have an extensive arsenal of medications to combat it.

As I expected, my guys are in great shape except for some irritated feet from 100 miles of stomping through soft snow. As I kneel next to each dog I massage each afflicted paw with ointment; Martin Buser calls it "praying to the dogs" and I don't think he's too far wrong. The dogs are our central concern out here, and our efforts to keep them happy and in good health on the way to Nome may be closer to a prayer than most people realize.

When the dog food is ready, less than 45 minutes after we arrived, I feed it to the dogs, who devour it like I've starved them for a week.

The sound of 16 dogs slurping water and food is probably the sweetest music any distance musher can hear: it means the dogs are healthy, eating, and well-hydrated.

Only after all this is done and the dogs have settled down in the warm morning sun can I worry about myself. This is all part of the routine I'll repeat two dozen times between here and Nome. It will become so automatic I'll be able to do it in my sleep in a few days, and I may well have to. The professional racers have this checkpoint routine down to a fine art. Minutes are precious in their end of the business, and the faster they get the dogs fed and bedded down, the more time they have for a nap and the sooner they can be on their way.

By now barely half a dozen teams remain here; last night more than 40 crowded every square foot of the river. It's quiet now and at least my guys will get some quality rest. I climb the steep river bank to the checkpoint, located as always in Joe and Norma Delia's spacious cabin overlooking the river. Breakfast is waiting inside, courtesy of the Skwentna Sweeties. As I shamelessly stuff myself with bacon, eggs, and sourdough pancakes I catch up on the race grapevine.

The most shocking news is that one of Rick Swenson's dogs died in the overflow back at Moose Creek. This is especially confounding given Rick's spotless history: he has never had a casualty in 20 years of running the race. No one knows whether the dog, Ariel, drowned or died of shock or something less obvious, but now the musher with the most impeccable record of dog care in the history of the race stands to be thrown out by virtue of the nefarious Rule 18.

I sympathize with Race Marshal Bobby Lee, who must be under incredible pressure right now as a member of the three-person committee deciding Rick's fate. An Iditarod veteran himself, he was the only member of the Rules Committee to oppose the expired dog rule, and now he is in the impossible position of probably having to eject one of the top contenders from the race because of it. If he lets Rick go on, there will inevitably be cries of favoritism; after all, what if it had been me or another unknown musher? Any of us lesser lights would have been dumped without so much as a thank you. If he pulls Rick, he'll become the lightning rod for criticism from all quarters, or worse, he will be accused of carrying out some kind of imagined vendetta against Swenson.

It's a no-win situation, but I've known Bobby for some time and I'm certain he will make an honorable and fair decision based on the rule as it is written, even though he makes no secret of his dislike for it. In the meantime, the race judges have allowed Rick to continue to Rainy Pass, where they will let him know their ruling. I can't imagine how he must feel. Many of us agree he has the best team in the race and we know how much time and effort he's put into it. To risk losing everything on what is basically a roll of the dice, an act of God over which he had no control, is not fair—but that's the way the rule reads. It's unfortunate, but maybe it will take withdrawing someone as illustrious as Swenson from the race to get the rule changed.

After I catch a few winks while my perspiration-soaked parka and heavy bib dry out, it's mid-afternoon and time to go. I know the first couple of hours on the trail will be warmer than I'd like, but I have to get on to Finger Lake, 45 miles up the trail. I should get there late this evening and then I can wait a few hours so I can have some daylight for the always-harrowing run down to the un-aptly named Happy River.

I clean up around the sled, pack everything in (still too much), and start to bootie up the dogs. The temperature is so warm I don't need to bootie everyone, only the ones with existing foot problems or historically vulnerable feet. Some mushers bootie every dog every step of the way but most are like me, only bootying as necessary. The process still takes half an hour, but I consider it time well spent because it keeps me close to the dogs on a one-on-one basis.

Once the booties are on, I stand up the dogs, hook up their tuglines, and line them out away from the straw. This is usually the point where the mind games begin. The dogs can be somewhat reluctant to leave their comfortable beds, but the veterans all know moving off the straw is the signal to get back to work. Most of my dogs have run the Iditarod more than once and they shake off the sleep and stretch themselves in preparation for moving out. Some of the younger ones take a few minutes and a bit of coaxing to get adjusted.

Just in case, I have one of the checkers guide my leaders through the maze of straw piles from departed teams; left to their own devices, the dogs would poke around in every interesting spot. Fifty yards later we have a clear shot at the outbound trail and I give Socks the "Okay!" to get moving. He doesn't even hesitate as he pulls everyone forward; I'm only beginning to appreciate his capabilities. It's too early to think about getting to Nome, but I start feeling better after coming through the first real checkpoint experience of the trip in good order.

The trail out of Skwentna is different from the one we took last year. It stays in the open as it crosses a vast snow-covered swamp, exposing the dogs to the hot sun more than I'd like. They slow down, but keep going. After a couple of hours we finally plod into the tree line about the same time as the afternoon wanes and the temperatures begin to cool.

Now we begin to climb into the Shell Hills. The dearth of snow has turned the trail into a twisting thread which snakes its way up sharp slopes and hairpins itself around huge trees and rocks. The dogs are having a difficult time maneuvering through the maze. They want to run but I can't let them speed up for fear they'll injure themselves. At one point the team is strung out across three near 90-degree corners around immovable objects; this is worse than difficult—it's dangerous.

Despite my best efforts, the sled repeatedly bangs off trees and more than once jerks to a wrenching stop as protruding stumps snag the brake bar. Low-hanging branches wipe me off the sled a couple of times and once I narrowly miss being skewered by a stout branch jutting from the side of the trail like a punji stake. It's an ugly trail and I wonder how the fast teams kept up their speed as they rolled through here this morning.

After two hours of work we finally pull onto five-mile-long Shell Lake. I've spilled the sled several times but everything seems still to be intact. However, Lucky is limping. I stop to check him out but can't find anything. I leave him in the team, hoping it's just a sore muscle and he'll work it out. I'd hate to lose one of my key leaders before the race even gets going.

We move quickly past Shell Lake Lodge and onto the series of swamps leading up to Finger Lake. The trail is better here, consisting mostly of open snow meadows punctuated by short traverses through the trees to the next straightaway. Moreover, the cool of the early evening is beginning to firm up the trail, allowing us to accelerate by several miles an hour.

A couple of miles past Shell Lake, as we enter the area near my 40 wilderness acres on Red Creek, I meet a convoy of snowmachines growling down the trail. They courteously pull over and stop. As I draw abeam them I see it's several friends from Montana Creek who have homesteaded next to my property at what we now call Red Bluff. They've been out to Finger Lake and are just returning.

Last year they waited for me out here for hours, but of course I never showed and they went home wondering what happened. We chat for a few minutes and I assure them things are off to rather a good start this year. We part company on a positive note: they back to Shell Lake and Montana Creek, I and my now-rested team to whatever lies around the next bend.

Shortly we pass the place where I had to camp last year after Slipper quit. I remember the trees, the trail, the view of the mountains—everything is the same, except we're charging on by without even a second glance. I can now see we're only a few miles from my land at Red

Bluff. I never fully realized one of my major debacles last year actually occurred almost within sight of my own property. Silently I check off another demon on my list as we glide on.

We hardly notice the sun has gone down because the moon is so bright. I only turn on my headlamp when we plunge into the trees, and even then it's not really necessary. We make fairly good time to the checkpoint, slipping down onto Finger Lake just before midnight.

I had hoped to be able to warm up for a little while and dry out some of my gear, but the checker advises us we cannot go into the lodge and must stay outside. Moreover, we must melt snow for water; apparently, water was available from the lodge during the day, but their well has gone dry. There are six or seven other drivers here and no one is happy about being left out in the cold with no water. Granted, the temperature has been in the 20s all day, but it's now well below zero under the clear skies.

The worst news is Lucky: the vets look at him and pronounce his shoulder to be injured. At almost any other checkpoint I'd take several hours to work on him and see if he could recover enough to go on, as he has during training runs. Then I'd consider carrying him in the sled until he was well enough to go back on the gangline.

> *However, there's no way I can keep him in the basket for the upcoming run to Rainy Pass; this promises to be some of the worst trail on the race and I'd be worried about injuring him further if I kept him in the sled. In any case, conditions here are so austere I don't think I can take enough time to work on him properly. So I reluctantly drop him; I have a feeling I'll wish I had him later on.*

March 5, 1996—The Iditarod: Finger Lake to Rainy Pass (30 miles); Rainy Pass to Rohn Roadhouse (32 miles)

Those of us stopped at Finger Lake tend to our dogs as best we can and try to grab quick naps on top of our sled bags. Finally we all wake up about two o'clock, miserable and shivering. Without even talking to each other, we collectively decide to leave this decidedly inhospitable place as quickly as possible. Our stay here has been so unpleasant we'd rather face the treacherous Happy River Steps in the middle of the night.

I quickly throw the dogs some frozen beef, bootie up, hook up, and leave. I immediately feel better about being on the trail, even though I know I'm headed for a hazardous section without benefit of daylight. At least the moon is still up and we won't be completely in the dark.

After eight or nine miles of relatively easy going the trail starts to drop down a series of heavily forested benches to the final "steps" into the gorge. The last couple of miles leading to the steps are simply beyond belief. The lack of snow has worked its evil here and the trail is a duplicate of the one coming up to Shell Lake, only worse because of the sharp, twisting downhills.

In one place, the trail swings suddenly 20 feet up the right side of a ravine in which we've been traveling and then drops just as suddenly down again. I can see in the headlamp the entire stretch is a sidehill pitch worn smooth by 50 teams in front of us. There is no way the sled will stay upright all the way through this roller-coaster. The team pulls up and onto the slope smoothly enough, but the sled starts to slide sideways even before we reach the apex. I wrench the handlebar to try to lay it over on the uphill side to keep it from plunging down into the brush below, but I lose my footing. With no further ado the sled flips inverted and shoots down the hill, with me hanging on for dear life and shouting "Whoa!" at the top of my lungs. I zoom past the wheel dogs who look over at me and the sled in what I assume is surprise. All I can do is hang on and try to spit out mouthfuls of snow so I can keep shouting for the team to stop.

The sled eventually comes to rest upside-down, wedged against a clump of willow shrubs at the base of the hill. It has almost completely swapped ends and its path is marked by a string of uprooted dogs still attached to the gangline. I'm only slightly banged up and the dogs don't seem to be in any trouble, so I set about straightening everything out. Twenty minutes later we're ready to go, this time with my foot planted firmly on the brake.

Half a mile further the trail plunges unexpectedly down a 50-foot ravine, with a sharp right turn before the bottom. My brake is totally ineffective and the dogs flip the sled almost instantly. Once again I'm yelling "Whoa!" at the top of what's left of my voice while bouncing behind the supine sled. To make matters worse, Socks misses the turn and goes on to the floor of the ravine, following a trail blazed by an equally unfortunate driver just ahead of me.

As I right the sled at the bottom and assess the situation, the loud silence is rent by a cry just ahead of me: "Whoa! Whoa!" And then from behind: "For crying out loud, WHOA!" A couple of minutes later comes an answering shout from back up the hill: "Whoa! STOP, DAMMIT!"

Indeed, as I work to get the team unsnarled and back on the trail, I notice we Finger Lake exiles all seem to have hit this stretch of misery about the same time. Judging from the periodic cries echoing through the moonlit darkness, we're all having about the same luck negotiating the impossible trail. It seems the trademark cry-in-the-night of the tail-enders at Happy River this year is a plaintive "Whoa! (Insert expletive here)!"

Knowing others are out here sharing this wholesome outdoor adventure doesn't make the trail any easier, but it does relieve some of the tension. A few minutes later I catch up to a couple of my cohorts who have been encountering about the same fortunes as I have. We take a break in the moonlight and commiserate about the horrific trail and shake our heads at the insanity of it all. We ask ourselves if we're having fun yet and decide to hold our decision until about July.

We stagger on in a loose convoy to the Happy River steps. This year they're narrow, icy ramps glued to the side of a near-perpendicular slope. Jack Niggemyer said it took several days to build them from scratch and they should be almost as good as last year. This somehow isn't as comforting as it should be to those of us staring at them up close and personal on this fine moon-washed morning, especially after 50 or so teams before us—and who knows how many snowmachines—have pounded them into near-rubble.

There is one change this year, however. The steps are announced by a special sign the Iditarod has made up: a reflective black-and-yellow diamond-shaped hazard sign like you'd see on a highway, with a logo of a dog team and the warning "Watch Your Ass!" I've heard about the sign, but I still have to laugh out loud; I suppose gallows humor in a situation like this is better than no humor at all.

As I see the team ahead of me go over the lip and down the first step, I lean on the brake to bring my guys to a complete halt and wait for a couple of minutes. When I don't hear anything resembling splintering wood, cries of agony, or Anglo-Saxon invective, I assume the way is clear one way or another and gently urge Socks over the brink.

Socks, of course, considers this all great fun and needs no urging. It's all I can do to keep the brake jammed into the rut worn by previous teams, and this only restrains the team to a fast trot down the steep ramp. At the bottom the trail levels out and switchbacks sharply to the right. I lose my balance in the turn and spill the sled; this provides me with a scary look down a 50-foot cliff lurking just off the trail, but I get everything upright in time for the next downhill pitch.

We ease down the second step with no problem. The last ramp down to the floor of the gorge is the narrowest, with a 30-foot sheer drop on the left. It cannot be more than two feet wide and is plainly the worse for wear; I ride the brake and tell the dogs "Easy, easy!" as gently as I can. I also find myself involuntarily leaning as far as I can into the comforting cliff on my right.

About 10 feet from the bottom the sled starts to slip off the left side. I lean hard to the right and balance up on the right runner until we hit level ground. Then we're down one last short drop and out onto the open river. I shout in triumph: we've come down the infamous Happy River hill in the middle of the night without a catastrophe.

The driver ahead of me, Ralph Ray, has stopped; we rest for a few minutes and celebrate our small victory with half-thawed packets of juice. Shortly another team comes shooting off the bottom of the hill. I congratulate the driver as he goes by, but he just shakes his head and makes a nervous comment about the steps not being as bad as he'd expected. Considering he probably expected to be wrapped around a tree somewhere back up the slope, I have to interpret "not as bad as expected" in a relative way.

Anyway, we're still in one piece. Although I know the trail isn't much nicer from here on to the Rainy Pass checkpoint, we're just that many miles closer to Nome. I remind myself I couldn't scratch here if I wanted to: no mortal could go back up the trail we've just come down. And there's no way to airlift the team and sled out of here, so I have no choice but to go on. I have a feeling I'll be using this rationale often as I push on toward Nome.

After a decent interval we forge on up the long steep hill climbing out of the river valley back onto the plateau. At the top of the hill we pass the kink in the trail where my gangline snapped last year and almost cost me a dog; Yankee, the canine in question, doesn't seem to notice as we power quickly by.

Eventually Ralph stops and I pull ahead. We cross Long Lake, scene of my final debacle last year; its profile is forever ingrained in my mind. I am able to pinpoint the exact place I spent the longest, most depressing night of my life.

This year we cruise purposefully on in the moonlight as dawn streaks the sky behind us. I strike an especially evil creature from last year's bestiary, one which destroyed my very will to go on. I feel like St. George on his horse doing his thing with the dragons, except my trusty steed has four paws and a big wet tongue and is named Socks.

Past Long Lake the trail goes through a number of particularly bad stretches, usually involving (but not limited to) side hills on steep slopes, glaciered patches with no footing, abrupt descents terminated by right-angled turns, and of course the customary menagerie of stumps, sticks, stones, clods, ruts, and various other impedimenta.

But we work our way through it and finally pull onto the disused, snow-covered runway at Rainy Pass Lodge at mid-morning. I am acutely aware of the last time I was here: I was about to terminate my first Iditarod for what eventually turned out to be no real reason at all. We roll down onto the ice of Puntilla Lake and into the checkpoint. A couple of the people waiting at the checkpoint were here last year; they understand what this means to me and I am grateful for their congratulations. I assure them I'm in this one for the duration, and mean every word.

"Watch Your Ass!" shouts one of the race's special warning signs advising of hazardous trail ahead. These signs always get mushers' immediate and undivided attention.

Nome is still 1,000 miles away, but I've effectively exorcised my biggest demon and I feel upbeat. I don't know what Socks and the team think about all of this, but I'd like to think they're ready to tackle the outbound trail later this afternoon. Of course, I think they'll be a little more ready after I get some food into them and let them have a quality siesta.

I get the checkpoint routine done within an hour and let the dogs rest; they look particularly contented in the warm midday sun. The back-of-the-pack crowd is all here or due to arrive shortly; other drivers have stretched out on their sleds in the warmth or even sprawled in the straw next to their dogs.

We're all planning to leave around mid-afternoon for the 32-mile run over Rainy Pass to Rohn. Sketchy reports from up ahead indicate the infamous Dalzell Gorge is actually in reasonably good shape this year and no one seems to have had any real trouble. I'm looking forward to the run, even though I'll have to do the Gorge itself after dark.

Before I rest, I stop into the lodge for a proper lunch; I did this last year after I'd scratched, but I think the food tastes a lot better this time around. As I eat I catch up on the race scuttlebutt: as everyone feared, Rick Swenson has been withdrawn from the race. In fact, he's here at Rainy Pass and the ski-equipped Beaver to pick up his dogs and sled is already enroute.

When I meander down to my team Rick is standing nearby. I go over and offer my condolences and we talk for a few minutes. I assure him we're all behind him and hope this can be worked out somehow. He's understandably depressed and says he won't be back next year. He's already posted a sign in the lodge advertising his team for sale.

He says he doubts many of the other Big Names will return next year if the rule stands. He argues that not many people will invest up to $50,000 to build a world-class team which might be tossed out of the Iditarod on what amounts to an random act of chance. There are other races, he points out, and if the Iditarod doesn't get its act straight it will be eclipsed sooner rather than later.

I sympathize with him. I left the race here last year myself, but for decidedly less controversial reasons. As someone has said, he is now a bonafide martyr to the cause, for all the good that does him at the moment. I go back to my team hoping he'll reconsider and return next year. He has become a central symbol of the Iditarod, a role model for hundreds of mushers like me who will likely never even place in the top 20, much less win the race five times. I lie down for a nap with some misgivings about the future of the Iditarod if it can't heal the grievous rift it has opened with Rick and all of us who support him.

After a most refreshing doze in the sun we're all up and getting ready by three or so. On one side is Linda Joy, a 42-year-old grandmother who runs the dog tours at a bed and breakfast just down the road from me at Montana Creek. She's been carefully planning and preparing to run the race for three years and seems to be enjoying things so far—with the exception of a close encounter of the worst kind with a tree back around Happy River. The right side of her face looks like she lost a fight with a berserk cement mixer, complete with a black eye the size of a dessert plate. Nonetheless, she's cheerful and doesn't wince too much when we hang her new nickname on her: Dances With Trees.

On the other side is Lisa Moore from Fairbanks, who lived many years in Nome and went to school there. She scratched in Koyuk in 1994 and, like me, has a demon of her own to exorcise. She was the last-place musher struggling down the Yukon whom I watched at Galena that year as the northern lights danced over the Brooks Range. Her mother ran the Iditarod in 1980. When Lisa finishes (she emphatically points out it's 'when,' not 'if') they'll be the first mother and daughter to have raced.

Andy Sterns from Fairbanks is also running back with us. He scratched literally at the gates of Nome last year when a terrific storm pinned him down. Race Marshal Bobby Lee drove out to find Andy after Max Hall, who was traveling just ahead of him, barely made it into town. By the time Bobby found Andy, two of his dogs were becoming hypothermic and Andy didn't see any way to save them except by putting them into Bobby's truck, which meant scratching.

Three teams work their way up onto the windswept tundra after leaving the Rainy Pass checkpoint on Puntilla Lake. The summit of Rainy Pass itself is 20 miles ahead and almost 2,000 feet higher.

Andy's was by far the closest scratch to the finish line, barely three miles from Front Street. He has a crackerjack team this year and can afford to wait in the checkpoints and make fast dashes up the trail. His team is several miles an hour faster than mine, and he could probably run in the top 20 if he pushed the issue. He, too, is chasing a ghost, except he'll have to wait 1,000 miles to finally put his to rest.

So far we're not traveling together, but we seem to keep running into each other at checkpoints and are generally keeping to similar schedules. I'm out before most of the others at 4:30; they'll probably pass my slowpokes before we reach the summit of Rainy Pass, a 20-mile, 1,500-foot climb, all on a windswept trail well above timberline.

As Socks leads us out of the checkpoint and onto the outbound trail, I quietly put a stake through the heart of my last demon. Last year I watched these same trail markers being pulled up as my hasty decision to scratch began its corrosive yearlong attack on my resolve and self-confidence. I silently thank Socks for getting me past my own failings in a more than symbolic way.

Now we're on fresh ground and I can run the race for its own sake. The trail will be far from easy, and I'm sure I'll have low points I can't even imagine, but I'm running on my terms now, and those terms are very simple: don't quit, no matter what. I know now I've got a solid team; we may not go fast, but we go, and I've promised myself I'll stand on the runners forever if that's what it takes to get to Nome.

This commitment has become very real to me; I remind myself of it whenever I start to feel we're going too slowly, or whenever a faster team passes me. I'm continually fighting a mental battle to make sure I'm not the team's limiting factor. I'm finally starting to have complete faith in my team, the team I've trained all winter and which I'm becoming more and more certain will get me to Nome.

The first part of our climb into what is for me a truly new world is a gradual pull up the eastern approaches of two-mile-wide Ptarmigan Pass. It is substantially lower than Rainy but makes a great 70-mile loop to the south before reaching Rohn. Rainy Pass is actually a subsidiary but more direct pass cutting across the loop of Ptarmigan. The race has been run through Ptarmigan once or twice in the past when the Dalzell Gorge was too dangerous.

This year, in fact, the annual Iron Dog snowmachine race from Big Lake to Nome and back (two weeks before the Iditarod) used Ptarmigan on the way out. The motor mushers ran into overflow on the South Fork of the Kuskokwim River bad enough to completely engulf a couple of their machines. The surviving teams returned from Nome via Rainy Pass but had an extremely difficult time powering up through the Gorge. However, they broke a good trail for the Iditarod in the process, and our trailbreakers have apparently improved it even more.

Within a mile after leaving Puntilla we are crawling steadily upward across the bleak, interminable rolling tundra. Because the wind has swept away most traces of the trail, as it always does up here, the track is permanently marked every few hundred yards with crude six-foot-high wooden tripods. Anything less substantial would never withstand the ever-present wind, and would not be visible when the gale whips up ground blizzards thick enough to obscure the team in front of the sled even while leaving perfect visibility at eye level.

Today the scenery is magnificent in the rich afternoon light as we work our way toward the branch canyon leading to Rainy Pass. We're in the heart of the Alaska Range; ridges on both sides tower to 6,000 feet or more. Fifteen miles to the north, and visible up every side valley, are the breathtaking granite pinnacles of the Cathedral Spires, their sheer rock walls rising as much as a mile above the glaciers at their feet. Mount McKinley—Denali—is more than 80 miles northeast, but its skyscraping 20,000-foot height lets us catch a glimpse or two of it and its 17,000-foot neighbor Mount Foraker despite the intervening terrain.

I've flown this route more times than I can count, at all altitudes and in all flavors of weather. I recognize the landmarks and know exactly where I am from a purely geographical standpoint, but being here on the ground is a totally different reality. There is something much more three-dimensional about surface travel, looking up at the mountains which lose much of their impact from the cockpit of an airplane. And the trail is far from the direct route afforded by a plane, varying from mile to mile and even step to step in a way the pilot can never experience.

The barren, often windswept summit of Rainy Pass in the Alaska Range is more than 3,000 feet above sea level, the highest point on the race.

As the shadows of the ridges creep over the valley through which we are running, the dogs pull steadily up into the pass. After we leave the open tundra, we follow a stream bed for a few miles, and then skirt a small lake. Parts of the trail are over open rocks the size of bowling balls; there may have been snow covering them for earlier mushers, but there's nothing now but raw stone.

Finally we shoot straight up a forbidding slope. After 15 steep minutes, most of which sees me walking beside the sled or even pushing it, we crest the pass. I can't help but be reminded of our crowning climb in the Copper

Basin last year. Now as then, I stop the team for a brief rest and a survey of our hard-won domain.

It's just past sunset. To the west, the series of rugged ridges descending to the broad Kuskokwim Valley is suffused with luminous golden backlight from the just-vanished sun. The mountaintops on either side and behind me are a radiant violet in the alpenglow. The full moon is already up in the east, a robust globe of weathered ivory hovering over the snow-mantled peaks.

There is no wind, and the absolute silence is broken only by the quiet breathing of the dogs. We are the only living creatures in this elemental universe of light and sky and snow and rock and shadow. In a journey laden with too many hours of work, pain, anxiety, and discouragement, this is one of the treasured rewards, one of the jewels beyond price which makes distance mushing in general, and the Iditarod in particular, worth all the sweat and worry.

However, it's all downhill from here, and that means my Light Brigade must now charge into the Valley of Death, culminating in the Dalzell Gorge. With some trepidation I give Socks the okay and we plummet down the open snowfield toward the Pass Fork valley, which will join Dalzell Creek in a couple of miles. After that, it's only a few miles through the Gorge, then five easy miles to the haven of the checkpoint cabin at Rohn.

Enough light remains for me to get the lay of the land as we careen into the narrowing valley and cross the timberline (in this case, more properly the brush line). This proves fortuitous because the steeply descending trail down Pass Fork turns out to be a nasty piece of work.

There isn't enough snow for my brake to be really effective and all I can do is dig it in hard when we're crossing a patch of crusty snow or even bare dirt. The trail twists and turns through narrow rocky ravines and across half-collapsed ice bridges over Pass Fork itself, mercifully only a few inches deep in most places. At one point an avalanche has partially blocked the canyon; the trail plows directly up and across the jumble of hardened snow and rocks.

In the deepening dusk I'm worried I'll miss something and wreck. The dogs are full of energy and charge on as I brake and swerve and lean behind them. Despite the cool temperatures and downhill run I'm soaked in sweat from manhandling the sled. We bang more than a few rocks and sideswipe more trailside willow bushes than I can count.

Eventually the trail begins to level out as we merge with the main valley of Dalzell Creek. The gorge is still a few miles ahead and we've got some fairly straight and level running between here and there. At one point the marked trail makes an abrupt detour for no apparent reason. By the time we bounce up and over a bank and through the hinterland and rejoin the beaten path, I'm convinced the trailbreakers were imbibing something stronger than coffee.

Not too much farther on, the trail makes another excursion 100 feet or more directly up the south wall of the valley. We then run along a wooded, ever-narrowing bench hung on the side of the mountain for a half-mile until I see another of the now-infamous yellow warning signs: "Dangerous Trail Conditions Ahead." This is the Dalzell Gorge.

The Dalzell Gorge is one of the most infamous stretches on the entire Iditarod. The original trail high on the slope above the canyon is unusable, and the race now runs through the very bottom of the gorge. There is always open water and treacherous ice and more than a few mushers come to grief here every year.

Based on advice from race veterans, I stop the team at the top of the precipice and disconnect four tuglines in the rear of the team. I don't want too much power for the maze we're about to enter. After all, it's mostly downhill and excess energy can only be dissipated in unhealthy ways, of which the Gorge provides more than enough.

With a deep breath and a transfusion of Tums, I give Socks an "Easy,

267

easy, easy!" which he interprets as a green light for the Indianapolis 500. Thankful I've disabled at least four cylinders of my supercharged motor, I hang on for dear life as we surge into the abyss.

The grand entrance to the Gorge is a plummeting descent of 200 feet that seems like 1,000. It takes every bit of my strength to keep the brake stomped into the churned-up trail. Even so the dogs reach a dangerous velocity before the bottom and it's all I can do to keep the sled upright. Suddenly the trail flattens out and we're moving along an eerily quiet, shadowy, forested tunnel.

I can sense we're in a deep cleft in the mountains. The moonlight doesn't reach this far down so I can only probe upward occasionally with my headlight to glimpse the rock walls looming overhead in the darkness. The narrow valley floor is a maze of huge spruce trees, seemingly far too large for this part of Alaska. As we work our way deeper into the canyon, it seems ominously like a page lifted directly from J.R.R. Tolkien's *Lord of the Rings*, one of his dank mountain chasms inhabited by goblins and orcs and other things I don't want to think about.

Shortly I can also hear water rushing very close by—too much water for my peace of mind. I know Dalzell Creek is open in many places but the trail is allegedly dry, provided I can stay on it. It's small comfort, given everything I've heard about this place.

Soon enough the trail begins to jump back and forth across the stream on ice bridges not much wider than the sled. The creek bed is marked by collapsed ice ledges and holes which must go down six or eight feet, with flowing water at the bottom. I've been told the water isn't more than a foot or so deep, but I don't think anyone could easily recover from a plunge into one of the icy pits yawning a few feet beyond the shoulder of the trail.

In some places we squeeze between giant spruce sentinels and the caved-in ice of the creek, while in others rock walls brush my shoulders. Fortunately the trail is in excellent shape. If anything, it's too good and the dogs want to go too fast. As we veer through the darkness I feel even better about disconnecting four of my horses.

Quickly I develop a rhythm for swinging around the tight curves and lining up the sled for the right-angled swerves across the ice bridges. I ride the brake almost continuously and learn to play it like a well-tuned piano. After awhile I seem to merge with the sled, intuitively leaning and braking and accelerating. I'm thankful for the flexibility of the Willis sled, which gives me a welcome extra measure of control and confidence.

It's a nonstop exercise in sled handling which doesn't allow a second's lapse in attention. I don't have time to cast more than a glance up at the huge cliffs which in places crowd the creek through gaps no more than 30 or 40 feet wide. I see enough, though, to form the subconscious opinion this place might be a surpassingly beautiful getaway in the summer, if there were any way to get here.

I know the Gorge is only a couple of miles long, but it seems like all night before we debouch suddenly onto the frozen moonlit expanse of the Tatina River. Rohn is only five miles away over a speedway trail down the river ice. I stop the sled and stand there for a full five minutes shaking with relief. Nothing in my training or any of the mid-distance races I've run could have prepared me for what I've just been through. It's simply something I had to experience for myself.

The five-mile run down the Tatina River from the Dalzell Gorge to Rohn Roadhouse is one of the most beautiful of the race.

The Gorge has actually been very benevolent, but still I feel as if I've skirted disaster by the narrowest of margins. Without question it's been the most precise and professional—and ultimately satisfying—job of sled driving I've ever done, and as I calm down I start to feel moderately pleased with myself and the team.

Socks in particular has been rock-steady up front all the way through, never going too fast but always keeping up enough speed to give me steering way. Self-congratulations aside, I'm not in any mood to go back and try it again. Right now all I want to do is get on into Rohn and take a well-deserved rest.

We arrive at Rohn half an hour later in high spirits. As we pull down the tree-lined runway to the checkpoint I remember the last time I was here, in 1994 with my big Cessna. In six trips I flew in 45 bales of straw for the race, using wheels to land on the icy, sloping 1,200-foot-long runway because there wasn't quite enough snow to use skis. Every landing was an adventure of its own, although not quite on a par with what I've just come through.

Teams must run alongside the narrow, snow-covered ski runway at Rohn before pulling into the checkpoint. Winds often make this runway treacherous for Iditarod Air Force pilots.

Quickly we stop in front of the old trapper's cabin nestled deep in the spruce forest which has served as the checkpoint since the first Iditarod. I find to my pleasure the checker is my friend Jasper Bond, whom I flew from one end of the race to the other in 1992 on his first visit to Alaska. A self-employed potter from Minnesota who unabashedly describes himself as a mushing groupie, he seems to have found his ultimate calling in the Iditarod.

He's rapidly become a checker, a responsibility normally reserved for veteran Iditarod mushers. Moreover, he's become one of the best in the business; his checkpoints are well organized and as musher-friendly as often-austere conditions permit, just what tired drivers need after something like Rainy Pass and the Dalzell.

Once I get the dogs fed and bedded down among the sheltering spruce trees I head over to the crowded cabin to dry out and catch a nap. The first thing I find out over a bowl of steaming soup is that the trail's apparently random excursion back above the Gorge was to bypass a bull moose which stomped through Sven Engholm's team earlier in the day, injuring three dogs. Barely five hours before I went through, the same monster roadblocked several other mushers for an hour until a passing snowmachiner put in the bypass.

After the harrowing trip through the Alaska Range, the Rohn checkpoint is a most welcome sight. Checker Jasper Bond has been the gracious host at the vintage trapper's cabin for the past few races.

For all anyone knows, Bullwinkle is still there, obstinately defending his little piece of paradise. We must have blissfully zipped right around him in the dark. It's just as well I didn't know about him; I had my hands full with the sled and I doubt I'd have done anything with my old .44 magnum except spook the dogs.

As usual I spend too much time visiting with Jasper despite his repeated urging to get some rest. In addition to catching up on the last year or two, I know he and his crew have some good stories to tell about their two-week stint setting up the checkpoint here and guarding mushers' food bags from the valley's wolf population. At least two wolf packs roam this area and they long ago deduced this time of year means food at Rohn.

They'll get all they can eat when Jasper's bunch pulls out in a couple of days and leaves hundreds of pounds of leftover dog food for them. If nothing else, Iditarod means a respite for the local prey animals because the predators are stuffed on lamb, beef, chicken, and kibbles.

I guess it's just the presence of a friendly face here in the middle of this incredibly beautiful nowhere, but I feel right at home and wish

Nestled in the forest under the jagged peaks of the Alaska Range, the old cabin at Rohn is used by the Iditarod for a few weeks during late February and early March. This is easily one of the most picturesque locations on the entire trail.

I could stay here for a couple of days. Eventually I stretch out on the plank floor underneath the table while my heavy gear dries out over the well-stoked wood stove. It's a most pleasant rest, made all the better by the good company and spectacular surroundings. For the first time on the race, I drift off to sleep with carefully guarded optimism: I might actually make it to Nome this year.

March 6, 1996—The Iditarod: Rohn to Nikolai (94 miles)

I oversleep at Rohn and don't hit the road until late morning. This will be the second longest stretch between checkpoints and I estimate it will take my slow freight train at least 12 hours to work across the Farewell Burn to Nikolai.

I'd hoped to be moving at dawn to have the cool of the morning for the 30-mile run down the South Fork of the Kuskokwim to Farewell Lakes and then up onto the Burn itself. It promises to be another hot day and I'd have preferred to shut down out in the Burn for awhile to spare the dogs another unwelcome day on the beach.

While everyone says there's nothing ahead to match what we've come through, I've heard there's tricky trail before we get to Farewell Lakes. The area where the Post River flows in from the south is reputed to have a lot of glare ice, and the so-called buffalo chutes are supposed to be at their usual worst.

The old trapper's cabin at Rohn is a relic of the early days of the century when the Iditarod Trail was still in daily use during the winter. Now maintained by the Bureau of Land Management, the cabin has served as a checkpoint for every Iditarod.

The chutes include stretches where the trail crosses open tundra with little snow cover and then plunges into narrow paths through the scrub forest. Periodically the trail crosses small clearings where buffalo (yes, buffalo) congregate to browse. The buffalo were native to Alaska after the end of the last Ice Age but vanished, possibly from hunting by early humans arriving from Asia.

In the 1920s a number of bison from the Lower 48 were brought to the University of Alaska, and a dozen were eventually transplanted to the

Farewell area. The now-wild herd now numbers in the hundreds and supports a limited annual hunt.

The shaggy herbivores have supposedly never bothered dog teams, but based on my experiences with moose, I'm a bit wary in the presence of unpredictable animals weighing a ton or more that can run like the wind. And I'm not sure what the 15 instinctive predators harnessed in front of my sled would contribute to an encounter with the normally placid creatures. All told, today promises to be interesting, at least in the sense of the old Chinese curse: "May you live in interesting times."

The first few miles out of Rohn thread across the wind-scoured ice and rock-studded sandbars of the braided South Fork. Soon we duck into the trees on the south bank and begin to climb up onto a wooded plateau paralleling the river. The trail is in excellent shape and we're making good time, at least for my plodders.

After a few minutes I notice the dogs looking around and then I hear snowmachines; two of them shortly pull up behind us. I stop to let them by and chat with the riders. They're from the *Anchorage Daily News*: outdoors editor Craig Medred and photographer Jim Jager. They say they're going all the way through to Nikolai.

I tell them I think the trail is supposed to be pretty good on across the Burn. They look at each other before allowing as how that's generally true but there might be a few bad stretches. They tell me to watch for their snowmachines up ahead. While I try to figure out this last cryptic remark they roar off up the hill and out of sight.

Half an hour later the team comes off a steep hill onto a 100-yard stretch of glare ice. The sled yaws wildly as we hit the slippery surface and by the time I get it stabilized, riding the brake to keep the gangline taut, I see the snowmachines parked up ahead. The newsies are snapping pictures as we draw abeam. I nod and they wave back. Before we reach the next tree line they've zipped ahead of us again.

A couple of miles on we skitter onto another particularly treacherous patch of ice. As I work overtime to keep the sled pointed up the trail, once more I see the snowmachines off to the side, their occupants documenting my unsteady passage. Once again they zoom ahead. Now I'm starting to get the picture, so to speak. When I crest another ridge a mile up the trail and see them waiting on the other side of the intervening ravine, I wonder "What now!?" and stomp on the brake.

This time it's a real winner: the Post River glacier. It's not really a glacier, just a slanting sheet of ice where countless repeated overflows have created the skating rink from Hell (which must finally have frozen over). The snowmachines are a quarter-mile farther on where a tributary stream has created its own steeply sloping mini-glacier, up which we must find a way after somehow surviving the wicked 200-yard stretch just ahead.

After we careen down the hill and start gingerly across the void I notice a lone tree trunk sticking out maybe 20 feet downstream of the trail. Halfway across, the sled starts to slip slowly down the gently inclined ice.

Many mushers say the twenty miles of trail between Rohn and Farewell Lakes is the most difficult of the entire race. This is the South Fork of the Kuskokwim just west of Rohn; the trail runs for several miles across the bare gravel bars and shallow braided channels.

With the sudden insight of one about to undergo a calamity, I see what's coming and there's not a thing I can do: the sled is going to hit the four-inch-thick snag, and hard. I dare not get off the runners because I can't even stand up on the water-greased dance floor. I don't want to try to slow the dogs, who are barely finding enough traction to keep moving, or I'll have a tangled, and potentially dangerous, mess sliding across the ice, and probably wrapped around the snag as a bonus.

Like a truck in a slow-motion freeway crash, the sled slips inexorably toward the snag, which looms like a concrete bridge abutment. My brake is completely useless on the case-hardened ice. I have only one real choice: I can try to turn the sled over and take the impact on the runners, or I can leave it upright and let the superstructure absorb the shock.

I instantly decide I can't risk breaking the runners; I could be immobilized out here in the middle of the wilderness. So I leave the sled upright and simply hang on and ride it out. I know intimately how the captain of the *Titanic* must have felt as his doomed ship bore down on the waiting iceberg.

Ten feet, five feet, two feet, CRUNCH! I know immediately I've broken something, but the sled still seems to be mainly intact. It literally bounces off the snag and the dogs pull it on to the edge of the ice, where I stop to survey the damage. The whole episode has taken less than a minute, but the mind's remarkable time-slowing ability has stretched it into about two days.

Miraculously the runners are unbroken, but the good news ends there. The heavy-duty carbon-composite brush bow that could fend off a whole forest of trees is broken at its right-hand anchor; it was never designed for broadside impacts and its severed end now juts a foot out from the side of the sled. The front right stanchion is splintered and both of the rear stanchions supporting the handlebar are cracked at the bottom where the crosspieces are joined.

However, the sled is still runnable; absent any more catastrophes I should be able to nurse it into Nikolai for repairs. In the meantime I slap a couple of hose clamps on the front stanchion to keep it from shattering further. I cinch another hose clamp on one of the two rear stanchions and wrap the other one as best I can in duct tape. Finally I stretch a bungee cord around the protruding brush bow to bring it back into a semblance of alignment.

Captain Kirk of the starship *Enterprise* would understand my tactical situation: we've got hull damage and the front shields are down. We can't take another phaser hit, but we can make it to Starbase Nikolai if we can stay away from the Klingons. I signal the engine room for full impulse power and we edge out of the sled-eating nebula—right into its evil twin.

In the urgency of the moment I've forgotten about the ice ramp stretching up the floor of the ravine in front of us. I feel like Robert Falcon Scott staring at the icefall blocking the way to the South Pole: What in all that makes any sense in this world am I doing here? Even as I ponder, the dogs are already scrabbling up the slope and I can see they're going to cut close around a rock outcropping on the right bank. The sled will be dragged into the rock wall in a replay of the episode with the snag a few moments ago.

Once again I have the option to leave the sled upright and bash the upper works, or lay it over and absorb the impact on the runners. We're going more slowly for this encounter, so I opt for the runners. I fall down a couple of times trying to get leverage on the slick ice but I get the sled flipped a few feet before the crunch point. With me dragging prone on the ice as a human sea anchor, the slick plastic runner bottoms kiss the stone and glance off with no damage; thank heavens for small favors.

Around the outcropping I see yet another disaster looming. The ice field ends in about 50 yards and the trail resumes over a bed of jagged grapefruit-sized rocks with absolutely no snow cover. The dogs are just reaching better footing and are starting to accelerate. If I can't get the sled upright or the dogs stopped before the end of the ice, the rocks will probably rip every stanchion out of the still-undamaged left side.

The runway at Rohn is in the foreground and valley of the South Fork of the Kuskokwim River stretches away to the west toward the Farewell Burn.

I frantically scream at Socks to stop, which he does, reluctantly, barely 10 feet from the beginning of the rock garden. Face down on the ice, I hold on to the now-stopped sled and gather my wits. When I look up, I see the Daily Newspersons snapping away. I must have presented quite a sight coming up the ravine, hanging on for dear life and shouting for the team to cease and desist.

With as much dignity as I can muster I politely ask if there is any more of this. I can't stand another photo session like this one. Trying not to grin, Medred admits this is the end of the bad stretch. I hope he's right. Bernie

Willis builds good sleds, but nothing short of the battleship *New Jersey* can take more pounding like this without disintegrating.

The news crew stays behind to gather up their gear and I press ahead. There are some bad spots, and the buffalo chutes are nothing but bare tundra and ice in places, but we don't encounter anything more of the magnitude of the Post River icefall. Rather, as we work our way up behind Egypt Mountain on our way to Farewell Lakes and the Burn, our main adversaries become the glaring sun and increasing heat.

I'd hoped to rest during the afternoon, but we're behind schedule and I need to keep the dogs going, even if slowly. I make frequent short stops and give them snacks of frozen fish and meat; this seems to keep them from melting down and we chug inexorably on across the Farewell Lakes and up toward the Burn.

About the only distractions are great piles of buffalo droppings in some of the open meadows which the dogs simply must investigate before we can proceed. We don't see any of the shaggy beasts, but I know they're all around us, probably demonstrating their superior intelligence by sheltering from the sun among the trees.

At one point we pass a group of long-abandoned log cabins which obviously date back to the early part of the century. This must be the old Pioneer Roadhouse I've heard about. It was one of the stops on the original Iditarod trail, just like the old roadhouses at Skwentna and Rohn. I give the dogs a brief rest while I look quickly around. One of the caved-in cabins would have been the old dog barn, another the bunkhouse where exhausted mushers rested or waited out storms.

This must have been a bustling place back in the trail's heyday, from about 1910 through the 1920s. From November through March, teams would have been arriving every day carrying supplies and mail to isolated mining camps with names like Ophir, Flat, Iditarod, Poorman, Long, Council, Solomon, and of course, Nome. Some of the returning sleds would have been carrying out the season's cleanup of gold; one series of teams in 1916 brought more than a ton and a half of the precious metal back to tidewater at Knik.

It's a strange feeling to know I'm really following in the footsteps of the old mail and freight drivers who were Alaska's unsung heroes. Probably only a handful of people outside of Iditarod mushers have seen these cabins since the wilderness and hard winters began to reclaim them more than three quarters of a century ago. I get the dogs up and moving with a renewed sense of perspective; we're only the latest in a long and honored procession of teams to struggle over this trail.

By now the warmth is at its peak but the dogs seem willing to keep going. Unlike some of the high-powered teams, I'm not worried about overheating because we just don't go fast enough for the dogs to work that hard, and I make lots of short stops just in case. This seems to be the way I'll run the rest of the race: keep chugging on while everybody else is resting. It's the only way I can compensate for having what is apparently one of the slowest teams in the field.

By mid-afternoon we start up an endless series of rolling hills to the Farewell Burn. As we crest one last ridge we're suddenly swallowed up in the Burn itself. The biggest forest fire in Alaska history roared through here in the summer of 1978, burning more than a million acres. The smoke was so thick it darkened skies in Anchorage enough to cause street lights to turn on in some parts of town.

The trail across the Burn to Nikolai can drift in within hours when winds come up. Sometimes the trail is all but obliterated and the driver and dogs must fight their way through on instinct and luck.

I was flying C-130s at Elmendorf at the time and we were pressed into service to fly fuel and supplies out to the fire fighting crews. We made a number of trips to McGrath and the old Federal Aviation Administration strip at Farewell Station, about 10 miles south of Farewell Lakes.

At the time I never dreamed I'd be running dogs through this blighted expanse of charred snags. From the trail it is so all-encompassing it leaves no room in the mind for even a memory of living forests. The only words to describe it are bleak and desolate, on an apocalyptic scale. Even though the fire was almost two decades ago, there is little second growth, at least in this part of the affected area.

Still, from flying over this part of the Burn I know it is a veritable Serengeti with hundreds of moose, caribou, buffalo and even Dall sheep sharing the frozen range. They take advantage of the usually light snow cover in this area to forage on the abundant grass which took the place of the forest. Roaming between the open areas of the Burn and the lush tree line of the Farewell Lakes, they mingle in numbers I've not seen elsewhere in Alaska. The thriving population of grazing animals also supports several wolf packs, which I've seen in the past from the air. We see none of the residents, although their tracks are everywhere.

The dogs trot unconcernedly on, gazing around at their surroundings and apparently enjoying the trip through a new environment. With no standing trees, our visibility at the crest of every ridge is excellent. However, the Burn is so vast the only vistas are of devastation and of the clean white line of the trail piercing the jumbled wasteland. Atop one ridge I can see at least 20 miles of the trail, arrowing toward the distant hills forming the western horizon beyond the Kuskokwim River.

In a way the Burn has a stark beauty of its own, representing a kind of renewal-in-progress. Fires are part of the natural cycle of regeneration; a century from now this will be a healthy mix of forest and rangeland. It's difficult for humans to grasp the time scale on which this grand plan plays out, but here and there I can see the signs of new growth which prove Nature is proceeding at her normal pace despite our worries.

The trail is in excellent shape and as the afternoon heat wanes we pick up a bit of speed. I pass two other mushers who left Rohn before me and who have been resting their teams during the day. I come on Lisa Moore in a sheltered hollow and we decide to run together into Nikolai. Our teams are well matched and we run almost nose-to-tail, making good time as we whittle away the 40 miles remaining to Nikolai.

Soon the sun sinks below the horizon in a glorious explosion of crimson, orange and blue. Out here on the Burn the sky is so huge the effect is overwhelming. Just after dusk, as we cruise across the flats on a hard, fast trail, I see a dark shape dart onto the trail ahead and then, seeing us, flee back to a safe distance.

It is a very healthy fox which has been scavenging for scraps where mushers have been feeding their teams along the trail. It stays perhaps a hundred yards off the trail and parallels us for almost a mile, hoping for a handout. When we continue, it stops and looks wistfully after us before returning to its vigil for the next team.

In the gathering dusk the team speeds up to 10 miles an hour, a breakneck pace for my Clydesdales. Lisa and I swap the lead every five miles or so as we reel off the miles to Nikolai. Except for a stretch of semi-frozen overflow and a small open creek or two, the trail stays good and the evening is ideal for running.

I vividly recall a particular training run at Montana Creek where I imagined cruising on the far side of the Alaska Range. Tonight is the perfect fulfillment of that vision: the brilliant evening star ahead, the moon rising over the Alaska Range behind me, the twin colossi of Denali and Foraker glowing softly in the last of the alpenglow over my shoulder—and Nome somewhere under the western horizon, much closer than it's ever been for me before.

The Farewell Burn was the scene of Alaska's largest forest fire in the summer of 1978. Almost 20 years later much of it is still desolate wasteland. This can be a very treacherous stretch of trail when the wind blows and snow begins to drift. Here Lisa Moore pauses her team ahead of the author's.

Eventually I drop behind to realign some dogs and arrive in Nikolai not long after midnight. We've been on the trail more than 14 hours straight but we've pulled through in relatively good shape. Still, the team deserves a rest and the sled needs repairs. I've sent out plenty of food and I decide to take my 24-hour layover here instead of in McGrath as I'd planned.

I've got plenty of company: eight or ten teams are here finishing up their layovers. Nikolai has become a popular place to rest over the past few years because of its friendly atmosphere and relative quiet compared to the usual media circus in McGrath, 50 miles further on.

After I take care of the dogs I amble down to the checkpoint to see how the race is going. The computer printouts faxed from race headquarters show the leaders are already more than 100 miles ahead, pushing from Ophir to Ruby over what is apparently a horrible trail. Moreover, they've all taken their 24-hour layovers, so we back-of-the-packers are really much farther behind than the mileage would indicate. But this isn't a problem: the leaders are racing for a paycheck; all we want to do is finish, hopefully in decent time. After all, getting there is supposed to be half the fun.

While I make a sandwich in the checkpoint cabin I marvel at the race communications network provided by GCI, one of Alaska's competing long-distance companies. Every checkpoint has a fax and phone, replacing the ham radio nets of early races. At villages like Nikolai, modern satellite-based phone service has been available for a decade or more, so faxes are nothing new.

At remote checkpoints satellite dishes were flown in along with generators and enough communications gear to make the Pentagon proud. Cripple, which is nothing more than a couple of tents somewhere along the Innoko River at the halfway point of the race, even sports a video phone link back to the race headquarters in Anchorage; of course, it probably will be dismantled by the time we rear-enders get there in a few days.

One nice spin-off for ordinary drivers is people can call from anywhere in the world to race central and have a message faxed to mushers along the trail. Here in Nikolai I find half a dozen messages of encouragement from my family and friends; they're a real boost and remind me someone is watching no matter how lonely it gets. I'm especially surprised by a message from my sister Ann in New Mexico; it seems I have quite a cult following there and I'm responsible for a significant jump in Internet usage as they hit the Iditarod home page.

Finally I stagger over to the village public works building about five a.m. and hang my parka, overalls, and boots next to the boiler to dry out. Then it's up to the storage room on the second floor where zonked-out mushers are sprawled everywhere, scattered among boxes, parts bins, and discarded furniture. I find a comfy-looking piece of foam padding and collapse for my first real sleep since several days before the race began, about a million years ago.

March 7. 1996—The Iditarod: 24-hour layover at Nikolai

After a solid rest, I'm up at mid-morning to see to the dogs. Hot water is available in the village washateria located in one end of the municipal office building; this makes feeding the dogs much easier and means we don't have to fire up our alcohol cookers to heat the water.

While the dog food soaks next to the thumping washing machines I head upstairs to the village community center on the second floor. A tiny restaurant occupies a large serving window with three or four stools at one end of the large room; it hasn't been open long and the owners are trying to eke out some extra income.

Checkpoints, like Nikolai, offer a chance for teams and drivers to rest and recover. Dogs quickly learn to appreciate the straw and respite from rigors of the trail.

Nikolai is an Athabaskan Indian village of barely 200 people. As in most remote Alaskan Native settlements cash is a scarce commodity, especially in the winter. The Iditarod represents a major boost to the local subsistence-based economy. I'm more than happy to contribute my share for a plate of sausage, eggs, and pancakes.

While I'm eating I get into a discussion with the city administrator, who is white and lives most of the time in Anchorage. He tells me this isn't an unusual situation for Bush villages. Part of his job is also to secure grants and other financial aid for the village, and this requires experience and connections not readily available from local sources.

For his part, the administrator is as staunch a partisan of the village as any of the locals, and he genuinely seems to understand their unique needs and issues. It seems like a typically practical Alaskan solution to an otherwise intractable problem. As I head out to feed the dogs a camera crew asks if they can do an interview. They're from Channel 13 in Anchorage, which is teaming up with the cable-based Outdoor Channel for what should be exceptionally good coverage of the race. They have made a promise to cover the tail-enders in addition to the front-runners, a decision I find very refreshing. I'm just surprised to find myself the tail-ender in front of the camera.

For the better part of an hour they follow me around as I feed the dogs, work on the sled, and muse about the Iditarod and life in general. For me it's quite the bully pulpit, even though I know they'll probably throw out 90% of the tape.

Lisa Moore comes over and together we explain exactly why we're doing this: to finish, period. I'm not sure the reporter has encountered this approach to the race—no money, no glory, just the chance for a run down Front Street and the official finisher's belt buckle.

Lisa probably puts it best: our race is a series of obstacles. We get past the obstacle at hand and then go to work on the next one, which may be only 20 yards down the trail. We run the race one problem at a time, and sooner or later we'll get past the last one and finish in Nome. We may ultimately get beaten by forces beyond our control, but we'll never give up without a hell of a fight. This is the paramount lesson we've all learned in our various paths to this year's race.

> *I hope the message translates in the instant-gratification, winner-take-all frenzy pervading the media these days. I'm afraid we back-of-the-packers are hopelessly old-fashioned. Maybe we'd have made good nineteenth-century pioneers, battling our way West with our covered wagons to the promised land beyond the horizon. In any case, I doubt Nike or any of the other big sports advertisers will be beating down our doors to be their spokespersons.*

March 8, 1996—The Iditarod: Nikolai to McGrath (48 miles);
McGrath to Takotna (23 miles); Takotna to Ophir (38 miles)

The remainder of my stay in Nikolai is blessedly uneventful, divided between feeding dogs and sleeping. My official layover is completed about one a.m.; the dogs are ready to go after their rest and we're on the trail to McGrath within minutes.

We make good time, at least by our modest standards, but the run to McGrath is downright boring. The endless oxbows in the broad

Kuskokwim River blend into one another and I repeatedly nod off on the back of the sled. Again, I've flown this area many times but down here on the river I might as well be on another planet as I watch bend after bend slowly unfold in front of me.

As the sun comes up I know we're at least in the general vicinity of McGrath because I recognize a couple of distinctive hills. However, it's three more long hours before we finally pull around the last tree line to see the town sprawled out along the high river bank.

As soon as we're into the checkpoint and the dogs are taken care of, I drop Bea. She hasn't been pulling since the beginning of the race and I have finally given up hope she will toughen up on the trail. I evidently made a mistake bringing her; she had foot problems all winter and ran far fewer miles than the other dogs. With 20-20 hindsight, I wish I'd brought one of my other seasoned veterans, but there's not much I can do now.

A team leaves McGrath, whose main street is the airport parking ramp. The town is a major staging point for the Iditarod logistics effort. Everything for the remote checkpoints at Rohn, Ophir, Cripple, and Iditarod is flown from here by the Iditarod Air Force. Many mushers take their 24-hour layovers at McGrath because of its good facilities.

I spend only a few hours in McGrath, just long enough to feed the dogs and make a quick trip to the local hardware store for more hose clamps to finish fixing the sled. In previous years when I was flying for the race McGrath was one of our major bases and I know the town well.

Founded in 1907 as a steamboat landing to serve the Ophir gold district, it assumed its current identity when the Army built an air base here just before World War II. Even today main street for the town's 500 people is the airport parking ramp. Among other things McGrath has the only bar for 200 miles in any direction—McGuire's, right next to the airplanes along with two grocery stores, hardware store, roadhouse/restaurant, airline terminal, flight service station, and local public radio station, KSKO-AM. The radio station is the only one for about the same radius as the bar and is a favorite information source for mushers on the trail.

As much as I'd like to grab a quick brew at McGuire's ($3.00 per can and you have to put up with the bartender's atrocious jokes), I have to get moving. I hope to be in Ophir tonight, almost 60 miles up the trail. We roll out of the checkpoint and across the Kuskokwim and are on the 20-mile trail to Takotna a little past noon. I'm running during the heat of the day again, but I don't have much choice.

I soon discover this relatively short haul involves a nonstop climb up a long ridge before it drops abruptly down to Takotna. It takes forever for the dogs to pull up the endless slope over a million moguls created by fast-moving snowmachines. There is nothing more frustrating for a dog team than an uphill trail with two- and three-foot moguls. The dogs can't get up enough speed to pull cleanly over the tops of the bumps, resulting in a nauseating pull-drop-slam-stop rhythm which causes the team to work twice as hard as on a smooth trail.

Even the expansive view as we creep along the top of the ridge can't make up for the drudgery. The dogs are much relieved when we finally roar down the 500-foot hill to the river for the last couple of miles up to the town. By the time we pull to a stop in front of the tiny town's combination community center and school it's taken us almost four hours; most other teams have done it in three or less. I'm going to have to get used to spending a lot more time on the runners than everyone else, but as long as the dogs keep moving, so will I.

My plan is to change my runner plastic here, snack the dogs, and move on to Ophir. Changing the plastic normally takes 10 minutes, but as I rip off the scarred bottoms that have withstood everything since Fourth Avenue I find a hidden legacy of the Post River collision: the heads have popped off four of the retaining screws on the metal guides which hold the plastic. I can't get the new plastic back on without re-anchoring the metal to the wooden runner.

This is well beyond the capability of my minimal trail tool kit. Fortunately the checker finds a power drill and we string an extension cord from the community center to the sled, across the village's main street. I carefully countersink new holes and reattach the metal with drywall screws which have magically materialized from someone's garage. It takes two hours to do everything properly. I'm glad I didn't wait to change the plastic at Ophir, a true ghost town where I'd be strictly out of luck.

I'm finally ready to move out just after sunset on the 38-mile run to

Ophir, which the checker assures me is actually closer to 30. Just before I pull the hook, Rich Bosela, who finished the race a few years ago, comes back into town with apparently ill dogs.

They could have eaten spoiled meat; the recent warm weather has partly thawed some of the meat in the food bags and I've heard several

The one-lane gravel road from Takotna to Ophir was built in the 1920s to connect the mines in the rich Innoko mining district to a steamboat landing on the Kuskokwim River. Although isolated from the state's highway network, it is still maintained for vehicles during the summer—at least as far as this "State Maintenance Ends" sign, a mile or so short of the Ophir checkpoint.

reports of sick dogs. I've carefully avoided feeding my team anything that even appears to have melted and so far haven't had any problems. I hope Rich can get everything squared away and get moving again; he's a charter member of the back-of-the-pack group and has been good company.

The trail to Ophir follows an old road built back in the 1920s to connect the mining district to a steamboat landing on the Kuskokwim River. Barges have replaced the steamboats and several of the mines are still active, so the state maintains the road. It's not connected to the rest of the state road system and isn't plowed over to Ophir in the winter, but it's just fine for dog teams and snowmachines.

The first thing we encounter on leaving Takotna is a brutal eight-mile grade up to the pass leading to the Innoko River and Ophir. The climb is all on the road but that doesn't make the 1,000-foot ascent any less difficult. The dogs pull steadily up the slope as light snow starts to fall. I'm thankful my team includes more big dogs than most; they may be slow, but they provide solid pulling power for hills like this.

Once at the top we start down Independence Creek and into the heart of the old mining district. I've heard the view is spectacular during the day, but with the darkness and the snow my horizon is no farther than my headlight can shine. We make reasonably good time down the long grade to the upper Innoko River valley. The snow continues to fall, not heavily but enough to obstruct vision and force me to put on my ski goggles.

At the bottom of the hill the road crosses Independence Creek on a bridge. The bridge is fine but the approaches are wiped out by overflow. This is the first serious overflow the dogs have had to actually negotiate and Pullman, who is spelling Socks for awhile, does her best to tiptoe around it, to no avail. It's only an inch or two deep but it's 50 feet across and looks ugly; finally I urge her through it and across the bridge.

I have a sinking feeling we'll see a lot more of this and I'm soon proved correct. Every bridge for the next 15 miles (and there are more than a few) is preceded or followed by stretches of overflow of varying severity, usually less than an inch of water over slick ice. Pullman gradually learns to find her way through these situations, which I'm glad to see.

Fortunately none of what we're encountering approaches the heavy-duty flooding we were able to bypass back on the Yentna. On the other hand, we don't have much choice but to splash through this stuff, which the dogs most assuredly do not like. Regardless, we have to adapt as best we can because the trail from Ophir to Cripple and up to Ruby is supposed to have more water on it than the Everglades. It may well be sink or swim if we want to get to the Yukon.

We finally pull into Ophir just before midnight. We've taken a little more than four hours to come the 30 or so miles from Takotna; everyone else has done it in two or three. It's been almost 24 hours since we left Nikolai, slightly more than 100 miles ago. We've spent 18 hours actually on the trail, considerably more than anyone else for this stretch.

It's another measure of just how slow my guys are. I wonder what it must be like for the leaders to cruise between checkpoints at 12 miles an hour or better. But then, we're still moving, and that in itself is a major improvement over last year.

The powdery snow continues to fall while I work with the dogs in the checkpoint. The white stuff will be a help on the trail later because it's only a thin coating and will cushion the rock-hard ice underneath for the dogs. Hard, fast trails are nice, but they can take a toll on the delicate bones and ligaments in the dogs' wrists.

This 1930s miner's cabin on the summer-only road from Takotna to Ophir is now used only seasonally. Venerable cabins, buildings, and mine works from Alaska's pre-airplane days can be found along many of the state's trails and old mining roads.

We usually remedy these carpal aches and pains with neoprene wrap-around sweats during rest periods, but sometimes inflammation persists and the dog must be dropped. So far only Socks has had problems of this nature but I've carefully put on his leg sweats at every stop and he's doing fine. He acts his age whenever we get ready to leave a checkpoint but is always trotting happily within a mile or so. Like my other Iditarod veterans, he's a trouper and would rather push on up the trail than get left behind.

In the meantime the snow is merely a nuisance as it sifts into everything including the sled bag despite my best efforts to keep it out. I finally get the dogs settled and drag over to the classic 1930-vintage miner's cabin which has been the checkpoint here for decades. It's hard to believe there were more than 1,000 people living here during the boom days of 1907; now Dick and Audra Forsgren's cabin is one of only a couple of buildings left standing.

The cabin has always been one of my favorite places on the race, at least when I was flying. Now it's full of people and I have to go find a place to sleep in the "Dodge Lodge" out back, a quonset-type tent with an oil heater and straw on the floor which is being used for extra bunk space. I wake up in half an hour shivering uncontrollably and stumble back into the cabin, where I stretch out on bare floor next to the wood stove. I don't sleep well thinking about the ugly trail we must face when it gets light.

March 9-10, 1996—The Iditarod: Ophir to Cripple (about 45 miles); Cripple to Ruby (about 125 miles)

Because of a widespread midwinter thaw, the entire Innoko River valley, which the trail traverses, has become a semiliquid morass. Skiplanes have not been able to land at any of the spots along the Innoko River where the Cripple checkpoint is usually set up. A skeleton checkpoint called Cripple was finally established, but no one is exactly certain of its location, other than it's not quite as far down the trail as Cripple normally is.

As a result of the access problems, the race manager decided to have all the food we intended for Cripple shipped to Ophir instead. Every musher planned a major replenishment of food supplies at Cripple, the jump off point for the longest and arguably most difficult leg of the race. Now we must haul all of our food from Ophir for both the leg to Cripple and the continuation to Ruby, more than 170 miles in all.

Even for the fastest teams this will result in more than 24 hours total time between food drops, which means at least three meals plus snacks for the dogs. Considering the dogs will eat a pound or two of food at every feeding, and snacks will add another couple of pounds, the front-runners must provision themselves with an extra 50 pounds of food or so.

For slow teams like mine, the on-our-own time may be more than 36 hours, and accordingly I manage to stuff almost 80 pounds of food into, on, and around my sled. To accomplish this feat of legerdemain

I toss out all of the junk I should have left at home in the first place; I surprise myself at how much room can be made in a sled bag when the need arises.

I also decide to drop Batman. He's had an open sore on one of his front foot pads since before the race and even with booties and lots of ointment, it's not improving. He's game to go on but I'd just as soon not expose him to what I fear is coming between here and Ruby.

He's a big guy and I don't want to carry him in the basket. Besides, he's done his part to get us this far and deserves a rest and a trip home. This leaves me with 13 dogs, more than enough to get me to Nome. After all, Ron Aldrich said he actually started the race with 12 dogs one year and had no trouble making it all the way.

The old miner's cabin at Ophir, owned by Dick and Audra Forsgren, dates to the 1930s. One of the two surviving buildings in Ophir, it has been the checkpoint here since the first Iditarod.

As I get ready to leave, the checker says the trailbreakers had to build 17 bridges across open streams on this portion of the trail, and there are many dozen more places where the trail traverses overflow. Apparently the piece de resistance of this wilderness construction effort is a crossing of the Innoko River 10 miles before Cripple. The checker warns me to be very careful not to get off the narrow built-up path on this makeshift bridge or risk going swimming in flowing water at least two feet deep.

The only good news is it's been cold at night and some of the overflow has frozen up, although other spots have reportedly opened. Any way I look at it, it's going to be a hellaciously bad trail, hard ice where the recent thaw and freeze has glazed the snow, punctuated by stretches of slush or open water.

I've heard the trail has been especially hard on some of the front-runners and they've had to drop more dogs than expected at both Cripple and Ruby. DeeDee Jonrowe supposedly had to carry a dog in the basket for 100 miles; this can't have helped her chances for a top finish. This convinces me to keep my dogs well under control, since I'm hoping to keep as many as I can all the way to Nome.

I urge the team out onto the trail with no small amount of trepidation. As we leave the comforting security of the checkpoint behind I wonder what shape we'll be in when we finally reach Ruby, which for the moment seems impossibly far away. For the first 15 miles the trail is deceptively good. We make excellent time in the cool morning air and I begin to think this has all been much overrated.

Then we start to hit the overflow. Every sidehill and stream crossing offers its own little version of misery. The dogs can tiptoe around the edges of some of them, although the sled still plunges through the middle like a water ride at Disney World. In other places the team resembles *Miss Budweiser* leaving a rooster tail of spray as 50-odd paws splash through the slush.

Even where the overflow is frozen it is often fractured into shards of ice like a department store window after a street riot. The dogs somehow pick their way through the debris with the aplomb of fakirs crossing beds of hot coals. I stop the team after the worst mine fields, expecting to see shredded booties and blood on the ice, but instead am constantly amazed at what Will Barron calls the dogs' "craftiness" in avoiding injury. I finally yield to the dogs' better judgment and let them do their own thing. They'll get us through if I just trust them and keep them headed down the right trail.

We pound on through the morning and into the afternoon. The few drivers who trailed me out of Ophir pass me; one of them says Rich Bosela scratched at Takotna, which means I have officially become the last racer on the trail. I've finally drifted all the way to the back of the pack.

About noon I notice what I first take to be a team on the trail ahead of us. As we draw slowly closer I see it's someone pedaling a trail bike with ATV-sized tires. I think I might be hallucinating but a sharp slap from an overhanging spruce branch convinces me I'm fully awake.

I haven't the faintest idea what the intrepid cyclist is doing out here in the middle of God's own nowhere, although he wouldn't be the first adventurer to try the Iditarod via something other than dog sled or snowmachine. Flying for the race I've seen cross-country skiers and even hikers on showshoes trailing the dogs, but a bicycle this far out in the wilderness is something new.

This only seems to fit the increasingly weird atmosphere which seems to permeate this stretch of trail. The worst part is the biker is actually going as fast as my dogs much of the time. He finally stops; I try to make conversation with our improbable fellow traveler but discover he's apparently from some Germanic-speaking country and doesn't seem to understand English. My attempts at fractured Spanish and Russian don't get anywhere either so we end up waving at each other in primitive sign language. Finally I figure out he wants to follow me. The dogs don't know what to make of this apparition and I have to lead them around it. I swing back onto the runners with a wave and we push off down

Past Ophir, on both the northern and southern route, the trail traverses a huge expanse of rolling hills and forested river valleys before reaching the Yukon. The terrain includes vast stretches of taiga such as this. (Taiga is Russian for "land of little sticks.")

the trail at what I consider a good pace. I turn to look back and see he's easily keeping up with us, maybe 50 yards behind. I suppose Martin or Doug or DeeDee might be able to outrun this contraption, but my pack mules insist on walking to Nome and I resign myself to having company all the way to Cripple.

Shortly after I take the lead in this convoy we reach a well-marked turn off of the main trail. After 100 yards on this detour we break out of a tree line onto the Innoko River bottoms. Dead ahead is the infamous temporary bridge, and it looks even worse than the checker described it.

It is actually no more than several spruce logs laid across the open part of the river, anchored on what's left of the ice attached to either bank. Spruce boughs have been laid on top of the logs and then covered with snow to form a semblance of a walkway. By now, of course, there's not much snow left and the whole affair more resembles an elongated brush pile than a major engineering work. The approach is across river ice awash in six inches of flowing water, as is the 50 feet from the bridge to the far bank.

I've got Pullman up front and after a moment's hesitation she charges through the overflow and onto the span. She's over it and into the equally bad stuff on the other side before the sled is actually on the logs. I have my hands full trying to keep the sled lined up on the bridge, which seems to get narrower as I get closer. The water off either edge is deeper than I care to contemplate; all I want is for Pullman to keep going to the opposite shore and get the sled back onto terra firma.

Suddenly Pullman decides to look for a better way around the far-side overflow, but when she leaves the trail she breaks through the ice up to her collar. She flounders in the freezing water while I yell for her to go on. The sled is stalled in the middle of the bridge and I have no room to step around it to help her out of the water without taking a plunge myself. Luckily she clambers onto thicker ice in a few seconds and makes a beeline for the far shore, followed by the rest of the team and finally the sled and me.

I stop everyone on the far side and straighten out a few minor tangles. Pullman has been nearly fully immersed but the sun is warm and the temperature is almost above freezing; I decide the best medicine is to push on and let her dry out in the open air. Besides, she's shaken herself nearly dry and obviously wants to go on.

As we pull off toward Cripple, now only a few miles distant, I glance back and see the continental cyclist sitting on the far shore pondering his options. He's watched the whole frantic episode and I'd give a penny for his thoughts about dog mushing right now.

Once across the river the great god of overflow calls a truce for several miles, apparently having had enough fun with us for the time being. We're slowed down to a crawl because of the heat and the bright sun and it's another two hours before I finally see a banner emblazoned "Cripple" stretched across the trail on the far side of a 100-yard patch of inch-deep water. With a sigh I urge Pullman across the moat into the dubious refuge of the ephemeral Cripple checkpoint.

We splash under the banner to the applause of the checkers and the vet, all of whom I know. It's three p.m. and I'm the last musher into the checkpoint. One of the checkers says he won a bet by the mere fact of my making it this far, which reassures me no end.

Half a dozen teams are still here waiting out the afternoon heat and I join them. There's no water for our cookers, but the snow is so heavy and crusted because of the recent thaw it easily yields plenty of liquid. The dogs gratefully accept the moist food and curl up in the snow for a rest in the sun. They don't realize it but they've lessened their load for the next stretch by 15 pounds or so.

I chat with the checkers and the other mushers, who of course are all dues-paying members of the unofficial tail-enders club. Everyone has had similar experiences with the overflow and the ice. No one is looking forward to the next 125 miles to Ruby, which promises to take 24 hours or more. We've gotten a not-exactly-reassuring message back from one of the teams to go through earlier: it says simply the trail is hazardous and in bad shape until we get to Sulatna Crossing, 75 miles farther on where the trail picks up another old mining road for the last 50 miles into Ruby.

The Cripple checkpoint is nothing more than a wide spot on the trail next a suitable skiplane landing area on the frozen Innoko River. Tents, straw, dog food, and other equipment are flown in (and out) by the Iditarod Air Force. Teams are bedded down on lines of straw wherever a place can be found among the straggling black spruce trees.

The only bright spot is a much-rumored "hospitality tent" at Sulatna Crossing. The official checkpoint at Sulatna was discontinued several years ago because it was difficult to supply by air. The new incarnation is a private operation but has the race's blessing, and is supposed to have food and a place to rest. Everyone is looking forward to it as a badly needed break in what is rapidly becoming a torture test.

While I'm trying to rest, the mystery cyclist finally comes in. After more gesturing, we determine he is from Austria, and he has pulled a muscle and needs to rest. The checkpoint crew will be here until tomorrow so they offer him a place to crash for awhile. As near as I can make out, he's actually trying to get to Nome on his bike. Unless I can get my guys to speed up from their turtle's pace, he may well beat me there.

By six o'clock the assault of sunlight has subsided. The general mood is this is not going to be a walk in the park, but it's something we'll just have to get through. Ruby is the shining light at the end of the dark tunnel; everyone will be much relieved to be on the Yukon for a couple hundred miles of relatively easy running.

Knowing I'll eventually be passed by everyone else, I leave before several of the others. The trail isn't too bad for the first 20 miles or so as we run down the east side of the Innoko River to the site of the old Cripple Landing, now completely vanished. In its heyday just after the turn of the century it was a steamboat stop serving the mines in the gold belt which stretched south from Ruby all the way to Ophir and McGrath and down to Iditarod.

This part of the modern race trail wasn't part of the original Iditarod, which actually ran southwest from Takotna to its namesake town. However, there's plenty of history on the northern route. The Serum Run of 1925 went down the Yukon along the Yukon Mail Trail, passing through Ruby, Galena, and Nulato enroute to Kaltag and the coast, just as we will do in a day or two. And the Ruby mining district has been producing gold for 90 years; its ghost towns of Poorman and Long are every bit as intriguing as their southern counterparts of Flat and Iditarod.

However, we're not seeing a lot of history as we punch along the trail in the fading light. Lisa Moore has caught up with me and we've been running more or less together for a couple of hours. The trail passes the site of old Cripple Landing and strikes out cross-country, northeast toward Poorman, about 40 miles distant. Soon we're both passed by the rest of the teams that waited longer at Cripple before leaving.

Once again I'm bringing up rear of the race, but I'm confident my team is solid and not about to quit on me. And I feel better knowing I'm still moving with others of similar station. In short, I'm not alone this year; it's a comforting feeling. I'm still very much a part of this race, even if I'm not about to keep the leaders looking over their shoulder for me.

The trail climbs steadily away from the river, following the base of a low ridge. Of course, such a sidehill trail is prone to overflow this year and we are quickly back in the messy business. We labor over an endless succession of low rises and drop down into anonymous gullies, each with its own little soggy surprise at the bottom. We pass one particular section I distinctly remember flying over a couple of years ago looking for Ron; unfortunately I have no idea how far it was from anywhere, so the information only serves to confuse me further.

As the sun sets, the deepening twilight begins to collapse our universe. The moon is rising later each evening and when night falls the darkness is complete, costing us what little orientation we've had from looking at the terrain around us. We feel as if we've been swallowed by a great featureless void through which we seem to make no progress.

Later in the evening we come to another detour off the main trail. After a half mile or so we enter a forest paved with semi-frozen overflow. Without warning we're running along the glare ice of a 40-foot-wide river. I look down and in the beam of my headlight I clearly see bubbles moving in the current beneath the not-so-thick ice. I suddenly have an overwhelming urge to be anywhere else.

We follow the channel for a few hundred feet and Lisa yells to stop; the erratically marked trail has jumped off the river to the left and she's just barely caught a glimpse of a reflective marker off in the trees. After I wrestle the team to a stop I notice the spruce boughs originally used to block the channel and divert teams off the ice have been swept aside. Someone must have roared on down the thinly frozen slough to who knows where.

As I'm scrambling on the ice to lead Socks back onto what looks to be the correct trail, I see another team coming back up the river. Mark Black, another of the back-of-the-pack rookies who passed us a couple of hours ago, pulls to a shaky stop. He says he went right through the flattened barrier and down (or up?) the slough for several miles.

When he didn't see any more trail markers he got suspicious, and when the river ice started to crack ominously underneath him he got downright scared. At 250 pounds and six-foot-something, Mark is no lightweight and he had no illusions about trying to float like a feather across thin ice. He is quite relieved to be back here, although none of us is really sure where "here" actually is.

Lisa gets her team pointed toward the nearest trail marker gleaming dully through the trees and gets underway. She has to stop several times to negotiate tight turns but is eventually out of sight on the other side of the tree line. When the trail appears clear I get Socks aimed in approximately the right direction and gently urge him into the trees.

While Socks is a superb leader, he has a habit (which I actually encourage) of going directly from marker to marker at night; Pullman is actually better at following faint trails, but she's not up front at the moment. Socks charges off toward the marker and promptly tangles us around at least two trees. I walk out in front of him to see what's ahead and discover every team ahead of us has apparently picked its own way through the closely packed birch and spruce trunks. I can't see how to negotiate this obstacle course with anything less maneuverable than a four-wheel-drive ATV with a working reverse gear.

Mark comes up to help me get untangled. We can't believe anyone would try to put a trail through something like this and don't even want to speculate on what horrific hazard existed on the main trail to force such a drastic rerouting. By the time we creep out of the Maze, as we've come to call it, we've lost at least an hour. I'm soaked with sweat, which is not good because I've got no easy way to dry my heavy outer gear. And as far as I know it's still 50 miles or more to the hospitality tent at Sulatna Crossing. This is going to be a very long night.

In a mile or so we're back on the main trail and moving steadily again. I start to pass other mushers who have pulled off the trail for brief rests. So far my guys are doing okay and I keep going. As near as I can figure, eight or ten of us are out here banging along this part of the trail. Without doubt we're the only humans within 50 miles. As we pass each other we feel like the last inhabitants of a lost world, slowly working our way to some distant and rumored remnant of civilization.

The moon finally rises after midnight but sheds no illumination on the endless country through which we are traveling. If anything, the moonlight distorts reality and further frustrates our efforts to orient ourselves. The trail is a faint line cutting through trees and across tundra, ever arrowing toward the northeast. At least the Big Dipper and the North Star are constant above me; everything else seems to be a strange, dimly lit dream.

At one point I crest a hill and see a string of faint lights strung out over the ridges ahead like ancient Druidic hilltop beacons. They are campfires and headlights of mushers who have stopped to rest for a few hours before resuming the trek. These few nights of the race are the only time this particular constellation will shine all year—actually two years, because the northern route is only used in even-numbered years.

Again the Tolkienesque images of mysterious fairy lights and murky wilderness and epic journeys flood my increasingly fatigued mind. I usually dust off *Lord of the Rings* every few years, but from now on it will always remind me of this voyage through a half-imagined landscape far removed from reality as I previously thought it existed.

Finally I stop the team and climb on to the sled bag for a nap. The temperature is surprisingly moderate but still I wake up shivering in an hour. This seems to be a practical natural alarm clock and many mushers use it. I rouse the dogs and we slowly pull on up the trail as the first hint of dawn outlines the low mountains to the east.

An hour or two later we cross a major stream I assume is the North

Fork of the Innoko, which means we're making measurable progress. I'm reasonably certain we're within 20 miles of Sulatna Crossing and the Holy Grail of the hospitality tent and I decide to keep pushing until we get there.

After another uphill slog and a haul across upland woods and meadows, including a stretch where the trail perilously skirts the edge of a 50-foot cliff, we enter the old mining district. The main signs of human activity are huge piles of tailings from placer mining.

At one point we climb up to a snow-covered runway lined with shuttered buildings. I've seen this from the air; it dates to pre-World-War-II days but is still used occasionally in the summer. For now it's completely deserted, with doors hanging forlornly open and abandoned 1940s-vintage trucks buried under snowdrifts.

Leaving the runway we climb up a ridge toward what's left of Poorman. In the glory days of the Ruby mining district 80 years ago Poorman was a boom-town; this trail was a bustling thoroughfare for thousands of miners year-round. Now, a few old cabins lie half-hidden in the trees, all abandoned. No one has lived here for many years and my sleep-deprived mind can easily imagine the ghosts of departed miners lurking in the shadows.

We cross a number of old ditches used to drain diggings and channel water to the hydraulic nozzles which could wash a whole cliff into the sluices in a few days. Some gullies are 10 or 15 feet deep with near-vertical sides. To cross them the trail makes abrupt dives and climbs with little warning. In my less-than-alert state I spill the sled more than once.

The dogs are starting to show signs of fatigue but I don't want to stop them until we get to the tent and can have a good, long rest. Eventually we start down the long grade to the Sulatna River and the decrepit steel bridge at Sulatna Crossing. Just before the bridge we pick up the 1920s-era mining road leading 50 miles north to Ruby and the Yukon River. Like the road to Ophir, part of it is state-maintained but only a few miles around Ruby are plowed in the winter.

We trundle up to the bridge and I see the old plank decking has long since rotted away; in its place is a four-foot-wide pathway of modern plywood laid across the rusted girders with a 20-foot drop to the river yawning below. More than a few teams would balk at this kind of obstacle, but Socks casually leads us on across without hesitation; he never ceases to amaze me.

On the other side of the river I start to look for the tent. I don't see it in the immediate vicinity of the bridge, so I assume it's a couple of miles further on where the old checkpoint used to be located. By this time I can't wait to get the dogs fed and bedded down and have a good rest myself in the tent. I'm surprised when I don't see anything at the old checkpoint site, but assume it's got to be close.

We press on for another mile or two and then I see half a dozen teams parked along the trail ahead, obviously intending to camp out for the remainder of the day. Linda Joy walks over and says this is the hospitality tent, whether the tent is here or not. No one else knows where it is and nobody wants to go any farther up the road chasing what now seems to be a mirage. It's getting hot and everyone has had a rugged trip up from Cripple. I can either stop here or thread my way past the bivouacked teams and continue what seems to be a wild goose chase for the elusive tent.

With a sigh I stop the team and prepare for a camp out. It's late morning and the temperature must be pushing 40 in the warm sun. There's no way I'm going to drive the dogs through the afternoon in this heat after what we've just survived. I chat with Lisa Moore and Linda Joy while I'm melting snow for the dogs' lunch. We declare this an official meeting of the back-of-the-pack club and compare notes on the trail. We all admit to getting derailed in the Maze and have seen so much overflow we're worried the dogs will grow webbed feet.

And we all agree we're beat, mushers and teams alike; this has been a far tougher run up from Ophir and Cripple than we ever imagined. It's been almost 30 hours since we left Ophir yesterday morning and the brief rest at Cripple didn't do much good, nor did the quick naps along the trail.

Everyone plans to spend at least six hours here before pushing the last stretch to Ruby. It's only 50 miles and it's all on the old mining road, but it includes a lot of heavy-duty climbing as the right-of-way skips from valley to valley over 1,000-foot ridges. It will definitely be better this evening when the dogs can keep cool.

I busy myself feeding the dogs and checking feet, which are in surprisingly good shape considering the glacier's worth of ice on the trail. After a lazy nap in the sun I wake up to find most of the other teams gone. It's about four o'clock and the shadows are starting to lengthen. I get the dogs up and off the snow at the side of the trail where they've made their nests.

In the process Silvertip and Bear, who have run happily together for several hundred miles, get into a snapping match. I pull Silvertip away and Bear decides to get in his licks while he can. Unfortunately he misses and chomps my left hand, with which I'm trying to extract Silvertip.

I react instinctively by flailing my right arm for support, but I hit something very hard with an unintended full-force karate chop. I don't know if I've smashed a nearby six-inch birch trunk or the sled, but I instantly know I've done something bad to my hand. Even Bear and Silvertip suddenly quiet down as they realize I'm no longer in a very playful mood.

Within minutes the area around my fifth metacarpal between the little finger and the wrist is starting to swell and turn an ugly yellow and brown. If it's not broken, it's a good imitation. I try to flex it and find I have no strength left for many movements I normally take for granted.

I stare at it and can't believe I've done something this stupid: I've disabled my hand in the middle of a two-week ordeal in which I already don't have enough hands. Worse, it's my right hand, and I'm right-handed. And just for good measure the back of my left hand shows a perfect impression of the arc of Bear's front teeth; there are several puncture wounds and more than a little blood but I can still move all my fingers so I don't think he's hit any tendons.

I don't have much choice but to press on as best I can and have everything looked at in Ruby, if and when I get there. Just to be safe I open my medicine kit and take a couple of amoxycillin pills normally intended for the dogs; at least I can try to ward off any infection. I know everything will start to hurt sooner or later but I don't want to take any of the heavy-duty emergency painkillers I've brought along for fear of impairing my judgment, already at a low ebb because of fatigue and lack of sleep.

Bootying the dogs takes twice as long as normal and I can't pull the Velcro tabs as tight as I'd like, and I have to work the snaps on the tuglines with my left hand, but we're ready to go in half an hour. I can still hold on to the handlebar with my left hand and a couple of fingers on my right, so I give Socks the okay and we move off up the road.

Immediately we begin to climb, but the dogs are rested and pull steadily. After an hour we creep around an uphill bend and see a mirage floating at the side of the road: the long-lost hospitality tent. It was really here all the time, just eight or nine miles farther than any of us imagined.

As we get closer I can see it's the real thing, an old 12-man Army tent, the kind with the pointy top and the inevitable stovepipe poking out. As we pull up a man and woman come out and wave; they're the first non-mushers I've seen for 24 hours. I set the snow hook and go inside the tent.

It is indeed the haven I'd hoped it would be, except I don't really need it after spending most of the day camped out back down the road. However, the hosts—one from a communications company in Anchorage and one from Sam's Club—insist I have something to eat and rest for at least a little while. This is an offer I can't refuse; I decide on a couple of bacon cheeseburgers.

While the hostess fires up the grill, I go back out to the sled and toss the dogs some dry food and frozen beef: if I'm going to eat, so should they. In another of the small coincidences I'm getting used to on the race, the kibbles the dogs are happily gobbling are one of Sam's house brands, albeit their top of the line. To my knowledge I'm the only musher using it on the race. It's been a big hit with the dogs out here on the trail and I haven't had even a hint of the diarrhea plaguing other mushers.

Then I'm back inside relaxing and asking questions. Apparently the tent is 12 miles past the Sulatna bridge because a mining airstrip just up the ridge is the only place the Beaver on skis could land with the equipment and supplies. Most mushers have stopped here over the past several days, some for extended periods, and everyone has pronounced it a Really Good Deal.

When the host says he's a med-tech in Anchorage, I remember to pull the thick mitten off my right hand so he can look at it. I'm shocked at the extent of the swelling and so is he. Half the hand looks like it's on its way to becoming hamburger. He says it's broken and I'm not in a position to argue.

Then he says they have something which might help: Sam's is giving away sample packets of naproxen, a new anti-inflammatory drug supposedly better than ibuprofen, and they've got a good supply. It won't make me drowsy or silly so I decide it might be worth a shot. He grabs a handful and I pop several on the spot and stuff the others in my pocket. I chase the pills with the best burger I've had in a century.

After an hour I have to get moving; Ruby is only 38 miles away, but at the breakneck speed my team is traveling I could be staring at an all-nighter. Back on the road—literally—I notice we have the luxury of mileposts marking the distance to Ruby and the end of this little exercise in madness. As expected, the road climbs repeatedly over ridges and dips down into valleys. What I didn't expect was for all the culverts and bridges to turn into nightmares of overflow which make the road to Ophir look like a pregame warm-up.

As an example, not far past the tent the road makes a sweeping horseshoe curve set into the side of the mountain; at least 100 yards of the roadway are encased in ice up to five feet thick sloping down toward the inside of the bend. I have to stop the team to try to scope a way through the mess. There's no way to stay on the road itself, and the infield is a morass of ugly brown snow and willows. I urge Pullman onto a narrow band of snow in what would be the downhill ditch; it's laced with water-slicked ice patches but she gets us through and I manage to keep from spilling the sled.

The road has one of these winter wonderlands every mile or two, some much worse than others. On a couple of them both the dogs and I get our feet wet despite our best intentions. I can't wait to try this after dark, which will be in an hour or two. I give up all hope of making decent time; this may turn into a tougher test than Happy River.

Just at dusk we pull into the semi-ghost town of Long, center of a major gold rush in 1911. It's strictly a summer place now, and many of the dozens of old buildings and cottages have evidently been kept in repair over the years. But the relatively good shape of the place, combined with the eerie

The village of Ruby perches on the south bank of the mile-wide Yukon. It was a major boom town in 1911.

snow-covered stillness, gives the entire town a strange post-apocalyptic feeling, as if it has been abruptly abandoned and suspended in time. As I glide silently through the streets on what is obviously a modern road complete with highway signs, I wonder where all the people have gone. I feel like the only human left on earth after some global cataclysm.

As night gathers around the hills the road becomes increasingly spooky, with half-concealed old cabins and buildings and mining works scattered along its unplowed route. My acute lack of sleep, aggravated by the increasing pain in my hands despite the naproxen, isn't helping matters and I'm starting to hallucinate. At least once I stop the team and try to pull them onto the shoulder to let an imaginary truck by. Another time I find myself carrying on a conversation with someone walking alongside the sled; the dogs slow and stop, wondering what strange commands I'm giving them.

As we work up onto a pass well above timberline (for some reason I remember this on a map as The Hub Hill) the northern lights launch themselves across the sky in ever-intensifying waves of writhing incandescence. Staring at them as the dogs float ahead of me I know I am losing my grip on reality but there is absolutely nothing I can do.

My sleep-starved mind goes into a sort of free fall, a truly strange but somehow not frightening state in which images and ideas and words and sounds all float together in a primordial mental stew. Hurtling from this free-association zone come combinations which could never have been formed without a breakdown of normal mental barriers. Some are bizarre, some are beautiful, some are surprisingly logical, some are simply improbable. They all sail past my helpless consciousness as I try to grab even one or two to hold on to.

Through all of this I have intervals of lucidity, apparently frequently enough to ensure the team continues to run smoothly on the road. And the hallucinations continue to pop in and out of focus as well, aided by the powerful stimulus of the undulating aurora overhead. At one point I go for several miles down the road wondering why I haven't gone under what is unquestionably an illuminated overpass ahead; finally I realize it is the arch of the northern lights.

I am jarred back to full awareness about 15 miles from Ruby. We've just come down a long grade and the road is crossing a valley, but it has completely vanished under overflow for as far as my headlight can probe. It is as if a cascade of ice has oozed from the nearby hillside and engulfed everything in its path. There are no trail markers and no road signs. I try to guess where the right-of-way goes by following the fall line of the ice where the freezing water has flowed over the shoulder and created an icy wall as much as three or four feet high.

By now Socks and Pullman are both in lead, but they balk at the expanse of ice. I finally find a relatively negotiable strip of snow at the foot of the ice cascade and lead them down onto it; they promptly try to climb back onto the ice, which is completely impassable. After 15 minutes of repeated urging they slowly feel their way across to a stand of trees.

Beyond the trees is yet another sea of water-glazed ice where the road should be, with a trail marker in the middle of it. Socks heads for the marker but I see it isn't going to work and yell for him to stop. As I flounder up to lead him back to a bypass trail someone has made, I break through the crust of snow into overflow above my knees. I begin to wonder whether Ruby really exists, or whether we've wandered into some alternate dimension especially reserved for tormented mushers.

After at least an hour of work we finally reach the end of the glacier where a recognizable roadway emerges from under the ice. According to the mileposts we haven't even come a mile since this exercise in futility began. Now the road starts a steep incline back up to timberline. I remember flying over this particular stretch a couple of years ago, but again I can't put this pearl of knowledge into any useful perspective as we climb toward the still-bright northern lights.

I am now incredibly tired and drift back into my on-again, off-again dance with reality. The next 12 miles or so are a confused jumble of images. At one point I'm flying for the race and watching myself down below. Then I'm driving a car along the wide, smooth road and am surprised when I turn the steering wheel and nothing happens. Overhead the northern lights provide a flickering celestial illumination for this journey into the surreal.

Finally I catch a glimpse of what I recognize for dead certain as an airport beacon. We're within a couple of miles of Ruby and the end of this nightmare. The road comes to an intersection I know is only a mile from town, and almost immediately I can see the reassuring yellow and silver of street lights across the valley.

But there is one last surprise. The road, scraped down to the ice on this stretch for use by village traffic, plunges down a steep slope toward the Yukon. It's mostly sidehill with an icy two-foot berm on the downhill side. The dogs know there's a checkpoint ahead and are accelerating. I have the brake jammed into the diamond-hard ice but the sled still drifts down into the berm, banging into it again and again.

Halfway down the slope is a final hummock of glaciered overflow, sort of a parting insult from the trail to me. The sled hits it and I lose my footing; we flip and I am dragged down the icy road for 50 feet before I can get it and myself back upright and continue to the bottom. We limp past outlying houses and then climb a quarter-mile up the opposite hill to the checkpoint.

I am, as is becoming my custom, the last musher into town. As I check in, I reflect on my current state of affairs. I'm running last in the race. I'm soaked up to my pants pockets in overflow. I'm bruised and hurting in a dozen places from assaults by trees and icy trails. I haven't had any meaningful sleep in two days. I've just come through the weirdest visit to never land I've ever experienced. And as I pull off my mittens both of my hands are so outrageously swollen and discolored the checker and the vet immediately send someone to roust out the village public health aide.

Someone asks me what I think of the trail up from Ophir and Cripple. The only line I can dredge from my half-functioning brain is another question: "Other than that, Mrs. Lincoln, how did you enjoy the play?"

I'm so tired and in so much pain I'm not sure I can continue. The thought of scratching is slowly working its way forward from the nethermost recesses of my mind. As I fight off overwhelming waves of fatigue laced with deepening depression I mechanically start to work on getting the dogs fed and settled in. Shortly I become aware of someone standing beside me and look up to see Emmitt Peters, who won the race in 1975. He lives in Ruby and is an old friend of Ron's and an acquaintance of mine.

Emmitt says his wife, the village health aide, is on her way to check on my hands as soon as I finish my checkpoint routine. Then he says I'm

really doing just fine and he's glad to see me here in one piece with the team in good shape. Coming from him, it's the highest compliment and strongest support I can receive. I'm deeply grateful for his confidence. I realize that if he thinks

Emmitt Peters of Ruby, the "Yukon Fox," won the Iditarod in 1975, the second Native musher to win the race. His record pace of 14 days and 14 hours was more than five days faster than the previous best; it stood for five years.

I'm okay, things can't be nearly as bad as I think, and I don't have any real reason not to go on.

About then the checker hesitantly asks me if I'm going to scratch; I laugh so hard he must think I've lost whatever remains of my sanity: Not only no, but hell no. There's nothing wrong with the dogs some good rest won't cure. The sled is still more or less intact, and I can hang on to the handlebar as long as it takes to get to Nome, with or without hands. Emmitt has helped me chase my ghost of Rainy Pass back to its lair and I don't intend to let it out again.

I do decide to take my mandatory eight-hour Yukon-River layover here, like virtually everyone else in the race has already done after their jaunts up from Ophir. I'm sure if I've made it this far I can probably survive just about anything. As the old saying goes, anything that doesn't kill me can only make me stronger.

As I work on the dogs the northern lights burst overhead in a

renewed frenzy. Now they're no longer the vaguely threatening backdrop for my journey through fantasy land and I can sit back and enjoy their ethereal beauty. As they play across the sky in intricate swirls and shimmering cascades I reflect that the great white expanse I see at the foot of the hill below the checkpoint is really the Yukon. We've actually made it more than halfway through the race. In more ways than one, I have to believe it's downhill from here.

March 11, 1996—The Iditarod: Ruby to Galena (52 miles)

Inside the checkpoint Emmitt's wife looks over my hands. There's not much she can do except clean up the bite wounds and give me some antibiotics to combat any infection which might infiltrate the swelling. She agrees with the vet my right hand is broken. It's grotesque: released from the confines of the mitten it resembles an eggplant with fingers. No broken bones are apparent, but a hairline fracture would do the same thing. She suggests I get it x-rayed at the regional clinic in Galena when I get there. She also remarks Emmitt ran to Nome one year with a broken hand; I feel a little better—at least I'm in distinguished company.

In the meantime I need to get dry, find something to eat, and then get some sleep. For the first count, I hang my dripping gear on racks thoughtfully placed around the roaring wood stove. For the second, the checkpoint has been lavishly provisioned by the townspeople and I graze contentedly for half an hour while I read a handful of faxed messages waiting for me on the bulletin board. All things considered, the messages of encouragement are especially welcome.

I'm warmed by the reception from the people of Ruby. People come and go all evening and everyone has a good word and a pat on the back for the mushers. The town was founded in 1911 as part of the gold rush to this area and the local Athabaskans gradually moved in. Now the almost 200 people live from fishing and hunting and a limited number of jobs, but their hospitality is unlimited, and it's most gratifying.

But the thing I need most—sleep—will not come so easily. When I lie down on my sleeping bag, the pain in my right hand becomes excruciating, so intense I cannot even think about sleeping. I suppose somehow the swelling is affected by body position. I've already taken more of the naproxen but it's only marginally effective. And I still refuse to use any of the high-powered stuff I'm carrying because it would put me out of the picture even more effectively than the hallucinations which so warped reality for the trip over from Sulatna.

All I can do is toss and turn and try to find a position which allows some relief. By sitting up I can doze off for maybe five minutes at a time. These catnaps are apparently all I'm going to get, which means I'm not going to make much of a dent in my steadily growing sleep deficit. At least the dogs are resting well outside, and they're the ones who are going to do the hard work. But I think I'm going to make a lot of use of the fold-down seat on the sled in the next few days.

I finally give up trying to snatch fragments of sleep and decide to leave at mid-morning. My right hand is even worse than last night; the swelling is so bad I can't even make a fist. However, I can still use enough fingers to bootie up the dogs and get ready to go. As I'm working down the line I decide to drop Panda, my two-year-old female. The trip from Ophir has frazzled her more than the other dogs and I don't want to push her to the point she doesn't like the trail. I'm happy just to have gotten her this far; she'll be a first-line dog next year.

There are still a couple of teams left when I check out. Lisa Moore and Andy Sterns will both pass me down the river somewhere and I'll be the last one into Galena, keeping my tail-end record intact. But I remind myself we're still moving; that's more than some teams can say, including one of the early leaders who scratched here because his dogs quit on the river ice.

As we head out onto the mile-wide Yukon I'm awed by its sheer size. It is undoubtedly the least-known major river in the country, even for Alaskans, most of whom have never seen it in person. It's easily a match for the Mississippi and even had a large fleet of Mississippi-style steamboats working its muddy waters for the better part of a century. The last of the Canadian boats retired in Whitehorse in the 1960s; today the opulent *Nenana*, the last big American stern-wheeler to work the Yukon, is on display in Fairbanks.

I wish I had a steamboat as my guys plod down the river in the bright morning light. We're definitely the slowest team in the race, at least partly because I keep running during the daytime. If I were doing this properly, I'd be traveling on the Yukon mostly at night and giving the dogs quality rest during the day, but I'm out of sync thanks to the Ophir-to-Ruby demolition derby. This is another consequence of being at the back of the pack: I don't have much leeway to adjust my running schedule to take advantage of darkness or weather because of the constant worry about being left behind.

Additionally, there's the rule which says we must be into Unalakleet within five days of the leader or risk being withdrawn. Lisa and Andy and I and all the other tail-enders are trying to stay well ahead of that deadline, and so far we're succeeding: we've got until Friday morning to cover the 250 miles and it's only Monday. In fact, we're a day and a half faster than last year's caboose.

The trail down the broad Yukon is good but b-o-r-i-n-g. The modern snowmachine highway is out on the snow-covered river ice; the old mail trail kept mainly to the wooded shoreline because of the vagaries of the Yukon's yearly freeze-up and the lack of snowmachines and airplanes to easily find a safe trail. The overland route also provided more shelter from the wind and the sun and wasn't as subject to the drifting that often demolishes unprotected trails.

I'd much rather be in the shade of the spruce trees on the bank as the dogs slow down in the midday sunshine. By two p.m. we're making only two or three miles an hour; this is no faster than I can walk beside the sled, which I do occasionally to stay awake. Lisa and Andy pass me several hours out. Pullman accelerates to chase

Most mushers will only run their dogs for two or three hours without a break and a snack. On the vast expanse of the Yukon, and especially during the heat of the day, frequent stops are very important to relieve the boredom and keep the dogs (and the musher) focused.

them for a few miles but we quickly drop back to all ahead slow as the faster teams pull away.

Finally the cool of the late afternoon perks everyone up again and we're turning a respectable seven or eight miles an hour. As the sun sets we come through a slough I know is within 10 miles or so of Galena. I've flown into this place so many times over the last 20 years I know almost every hill and tree by memory, and for once being on the ground isn't much different from being airborne—only slower.

The town was founded in 1919 as a steamboat landing for a lead mine whose ore was lead sulfide, or galena. Athabaskan Indians in the region gravitated to the town over the years, but its major feature—the airport—was built as an Army base in 1941 during the massive pre-World-War-II buildup in Alaska. The airfield became a major stop for thousands of Lend-Lease planes heading to Russia, and later evolved into a frontline Cold War fighter-interceptor base.

That's where I came in, flying C-130s out here for many years to bring in everything necessary to keep a modern 500-man military base operating at peak efficiency. The base was put on caretaker status in 1993 but the town still has almost 600 people and is one of the biggest settlements on the Yukon River in Alaska.

As we come in sight of the familiar lights of Galena it's just dark. I turn my headlight on for the final miles into town. Overhead, in a reprise of last night's standing-ovation performance, the aurora is already gearing up for another evening of celestial fireworks.

Suddenly I realize this is deja vu: For a moment it's the 1994 race and I'm standing on the river bank at Galena watching the headlamp of the last-place musher work slowly down the Yukon toward the checkpoint as the northern lights flare over the Brooks Range. Fast-forward to 1996: Now it's ME bringing up the rear of the race, MY light out on the river.

Galena hugs the shore of the Mississippi-size Yukon River. The regional airport and a small inactive Air Force base lie behind it, sheltered by high levees to protect against the spring floods.

The musher out on the ice I thought could just as easily have been me IS me. And in a deliciously ironic twist, Lisa Moore—the tail-ender whose light I watched two years ago in this very same place—is already at Galena watching me.

It's all too much to take and I can't restrain myself from laughing out loud. As if sensing my feelings, the dogs accelerate across the river and up the bank into town. We steam into the checkpoint in good order, in last place but definitely still in the race. This has been a particularly satisfying arrival, another milestone on what I'm guardedly starting to believe is going to be a successful trip to Nome.

But first things first. Taking care of the dogs consumes an hour and a half, after which I head into the checkpoint to see the M.D. who's volunteering as the communications person. He takes a look at my right hand and pronounces it fractured, and then arranges for an x-ray at the local clinic. Surprisingly, keeping the hand jammed into the heavy cold-weather mitten has acted as a whole-hand splint and has kept the swelling down. It still puffs back up once the mitten is off, but at least I can get some use out of it on the trail.

The x-ray is inconclusive; nothing is obviously broken, but that doesn't rule out a hairline fracture, which still seems the most likely diagnosis. The doc says to keep taking the anti-inflammatory pills and check the hand at subsequent checkpoints. He sends out a fax advising vets down the trail to examine my hand the same way they would check one of my dogs' feet. I wonder if they might decide to drop me from the team if it starts to look too bad.

March 12. 1996—The Iditarod: Galena to Nulato (52 miles);
Nulato to Kaltag (42 miles)

Mileposts are virtually unknown on the Iditarod, but the people of Kaltag are kind enough to provide a marker on the seemingly endless, featureless run along the Yukon River.

By the time we've gotten the x-ray done and I'm back at the checkpoint, we've killed four hours and it's well past midnight. I grab some food and then try to get some sleep. No luck—same as last night in Ruby. The best I can do is nap sitting up, even though I really, really need some serious shut-eye.

By four a.m. I decide I've spent too much time here trying to chase sleep that's not going to come. I groggily bootie up, hook up, and head out. Again, I'm not the last one out but certainly will be bringing up the rear at Nulato, 50 miles away. The lights of Galena take forever to slide from view even though the dogs are actually doing fairly well in the predawn cold. And it is finally cold, maybe 20 below, enough to help keep me alert. I have to stop to pull on some more layers of insulation but it feels good to be back in temperatures resembling what we've trained in all winter.

We motor on down the river as the day slowly fills the sky behind us. We pass all the landmarks I remember from two decades of flying: Pilot Mountain, Bishop Rock, the village of Koyukuk. Andy and his greyhounds pass me at Koyukuk—once again putting me in the race caboose since Lisa left ahead of both of us—but we're still making reasonable time. Almost before I realize it we're running past a long riverside ridge which leads to Nulato, another Athabaskan village on the west bank of the river.

The village was already ancient when the Russians founded a trading post here in 1838. In 1851 Athabaskans from up river raided the town and massacred 53 people, mostly local Natives but also the Russian manager and an English naval lieutenant who was looking for information on a lost polar explorer (and who may have unwittingly precipitated the attack). Today Nulato is one of the larger villages on the river with more than 300 people, but the local economy is still largely based on subsistence.

The trail makes a last grand swing across the Yukon to Nulato and we clamber up the bank to the checkpoint. I'm the last one in, of course, but my timing is back on track and I can let the dogs rest a few hours during the heat of the afternoon. I don't intend to spend very long here; Kaltag is less than 40 miles away, after which we make the big jump out to the coast at Unalakleet. Besides, the weather forecast is for snow to move up from the Aleutians overnight, and I'm not big on getting caught out on the river in it.

While I'm feeding the dogs, Lisa decides to move out for Kaltag. She arrived here a couple of hours ahead of me on the run over from Galena and, like me, wants to keep moving. I wave to her as the checker leads her team to the outbound trail and her dogs start down the steep bank to the river below. She gets about 100 yards out onto the white expanse when her dogs decide to quit.

I watch as she tries to motivate them to go again, but they will have nothing to do with the forbidding void of the Yukon. After 10 minutes of cajoling she throws up her arms in resignation and simply drops anchor in place. She marches back up the hill to the checkpoint, muttering she'll wait the dogs out no matter how long it takes. I know she's intensely frustrated and a little worried: this is what happened to her on the 1994 race. By the time she reached Koyuk, less than 200 miles from Nome, the dogs just wouldn't go at all and she had to scratch.

After my dogs are squared away I head into the checkpoint and offer Lisa some reassurance. If nothing else, her dogs will certainly follow Socks when I leave; she's far from stuck. But she says in no uncertain terms her team will leave under its own power, or else; I understand exactly what she means and appreciate her determination. She wants to conquer this problem on her own, just as I did back at Rainy Pass.

The Koyukon Athabaskan village of Kaltag on its high bank marks the end of the 150-mile journey down (or up) the mighty Yukon.

While our teams rest outside—mine in the dog lot and hers on the river—we munch on brownies as we watch the live satellite telecast of Jeff King's triumphant procession down Front Street and under the arch in Nome. He simply walked away from Martin Buser and the rest of the field after Kaltag. He didn't set a record, but he's only a couple of hours slower than Doug Swingley's nine-day cannonball run of last year.

I reflect on the vast gulf between the professionals like Jeff and the back-of-the-packers like me. Their teams routinely cruise at 12 or 14 miles an hour and they have their checkpoint routines down to precise sciences. Unlike my lovable but eclectic collection of veteran hand-me-downs and untried youngsters, their dogs are all reasonably alike in breeding and running habits and form coherent teams.

They don't have the disruptions and irregularities which plague me in trying to mold a unit from a menagerie ranging from 35-pound Maybelline to 75-pound Yankee. The thought occurs to me that with their well-oiled pulling machines they might actually be having fun out here, or at least more than I am.

Finally we get ready to leave. Socks dutifully lines out the team on the outbound trail, where I hold everyone while Lisa strides purposefully down the river bank to her recalcitrant crew. She doesn't even need to get them up: they're ready to go and move off smartly as soon as she steps on the runners. I'm happy for her and hope this has been her turning point.

Andy has his team ready to go behind mine and we all leave Nulato together. Five miles down river, Andy and I keep straight at a fork in the trail while Lisa heads left on an unmarked track. The teams run almost parallel, we up against the right bank and Lisa out in mid-river. These big-river trails always rejoin at some point and we think nothing of it as we cruise quietly on for a couple of miles.

Then Andy brakes to a sudden stop and Socks almost plows into him. Our trail is swamped with major overflow, a situation which has obviously developed very recently. We search for a way around it and finally spy a tenuous trail to the left; this morass has surprised at least one other team before us. I gingerly urge Socks onto the bypass, which is little more than a single sled track through uncompacted waist-deep snow. But it gets us around the overflow after several hundred yards and probably 20 minutes of lost time.

Once back on the trail we rejoin the branch on which Lisa has been running, although she is by now at least a couple of miles ahead. Andy and I have no idea why Lisa took the left hand fork and missed the overflow, especially since we were on the main, marked trail. Feminine intuition, we finally surmise, or else her leader has a better nose than ours.

A few miles later Andy passes me and moves off into the gathering dusk. Soon it begins to snow, part of the storm which is apparently moving faster than expected. So far no one on the race has had any weather problems to speak of, but it seems we might get caught.

This often seems to happen on the Iditarod: storms hold off long enough for the leaders to blaze to Nome and then sock the middle of the pack or the tail-enders. Simple probability would suggest the fast-movers get hit on an equal-opportunity basis, but it never seems to work out that way except in a few really notable years, such as in 1991 when Rick Swenson led his team through a screaming blizzard for 50 miles over Topkok to Safety and a dramatic victory over Martin Buser and Susan Butcher.

Soon the snow begins to accumulate more quickly than I'd like. By the time I see the reassuring flash of the Kaltag airport beacon against the clouds 15 miles later, it's a couple of inches deep and beginning to drift. Socks plows through it unconcernedly and I am doubly glad he's probably one of the best wind and snow leaders ever to hit the trail. This is the kind of situation in which his marker-to-marker skills are most useful. As my headlamp illuminates each reflective strip he moves methodically toward it, feeling out the trail as he goes. All I have to do is keep finding the markers and Socks will do the rest.

We finally leave the Yukon and pull into Kaltag about midnight. People have been living here since the earliest Natives began using the 90-

Teams run for several blocks up the main street of Kaltag to the checkpoint. At the end of the 90-mile Kaltag portage, an ancient Native trade route to the Bering Sea coast, Kaltag has been inhabited for many centuries.

mile portage to the coast. Its 200 or so residents are asleep as we check in. I've spent some time here while flying for the race so I'm reasonably familiar with the town.

All things considered, it's actually been a fairly pleasant and blessedly uneventful run down the legendary river. Because of the snow, I plan to wait until after dawn to start over the Kaltag portage to Unalakleet on the Bering Sea coast. I'm not interested in trying to find an unfamiliar trail in a snowstorm without at least the help of daylight. I've already got plenty of problems to deal with and I certainly don't need to lengthen my odds— after all, it's still more than 350 notoriously tough miles to Nome.

After taking care of the dogs in a somnambulant daze I stumble up to the checkpoint in the village community center. It is deserted except for half a dozen mushers sprawled out on the benches along the walls. The checker and the vet have retreated to their bunks elsewhere in town after exhorting us to leave as soon as we can.

Lisa and Andy and I aren't pleased at the implied kick in the pants; we're fully a day and a half ahead of last year's rear-enders and will reach Unalakleet two days ahead of the Friday deadline, even with an average run. Indeed, we have every intention of making it to Nome in time for the awards banquet on Sunday afternoon. We need no urging to try to finish the race in a timely manner, and we don't appreciate being all but tossed out of town just because we're the last people in the race.

All of the other mushers save Lisa and Andy and I plan to leave in the wee hours of the morning; they constitute the rest of the now well-defined

The Kaltag checkpoint has been located for many years in the log-cabin community center.

back-of-the-pack crowd. The three of us plan to stay no more than six to 12 hours behind them all the way to Nome, but for now we (and I in particular) need a few more hours' rest. We're making great time and shouldn't have any trouble reaching Nome for the big party.

In my years as a volunteer pilot for the race, I made a point of working the back of the pack because I figured those were the people who deserved the most help and support. Many days I was the airborne trail sweep checking on the progress of a driver who was a little overdue or who might have been having problems with his or her team. There was never a shortage of volunteers willing to wait and work with the tail-enders. As long as the mushers were still making an effort to get to Nome, we were going to keep the race open until they got there.

They were chasing their dreams; the last thing we wanted to do was to push someone who looked to be lagging but might really just need some solid support and a friendly face to keep the dream from turning into a nightmare. And after last year, I can honestly say I've been there, done that.

March 13-14, 1996—The Iditarod: Kaltag to Unalakleet (90 miles)

By daylight the snow has mostly stopped and the sun is shining much of the time. This is a pleasant surprise, as is the relatively light dusting we've received, barely two or three inches. The first item on my agenda is to find the vet so I can drop Diablo. There's nothing really wrong with

Training the dogs to rest at every opportunity is an important part of preparing for the Iditarod. Veterans of the trail to Nome waste little time in making themselves comfortable in checkpoints.

him except he's started to stage occasional sit-down strikes when he doesn't like something.

This is partly my fault since I borrowed him only a few weeks before the race and didn't really have a chance to work him into the team or get to know him. In any case, he's not mine and I'm not going to try to discipline him as I might one of my own dogs. The last thing I want to do is ruin him for Will Barron, who was gracious enough to loan him to me at the last minute.

Dropping Diablo has focused me even more closely on the remaining 11 dogs. We're almost a week and a half into the race now, and I'm finally learning how much they love to play games with me. Some of them are getting very good at driving me to distraction as the trip stretches on. The veterans especially know how to keep me wondering what's really happening.

Getting out of a checkpoint is a perfect example. Unlike the Big Name teams which can usually be seen bounding and barking to go even at stops far down the trail, moving my mixed bag of lovable mutts often requires a series of mental fencing matches.

For instance, even though they all know we're getting ready to go when I move along the line to bootie up, most of them won't even move when I kneel next to them to work on their feet. Some even resist when I start pulling paws into the cold air—just like humans who don't want to come out from under the covers when the alarm clock goes off.

After I get the booties on, I hook up the tuglines and stand everyone up. Often as not I must physically move a dog off the straw, like turning over a sleepyhead's bed and dumping him (or her) onto the floor. Regardless, once I get to the back of the team and hook up the wheel dogs and climb on the runners they all know it's time to go, and that's when the real fun begins.

Rocky, a classic Malemute-looking 70-pounder with the most laid-back attitude on the team, is one of the best wheel dogs in the state. However, he's on his sixth Iditarod and knows every trick in the book. Among other things, he eats his harness whenever I don't get it off in time at a checkpoint; he's on his third one, which I've already had to tie together in two places with parachute cord.

He's also figured how to get every last second of rest wherever we stop. Until I give the actual command to go he is an inert mass of fur curled on the straw or the snow. Only when I give the "okay" does he bound to his feet and pull as hard as a bulldozer, all within about half a second. I still get questioning looks from bystanders who wonder if I'm just going to start the team and drag him to the next checkpoint.

Bear, another of my big horses, tries the Rocky routine but with his own variation: he actually won't get up when the team starts. I have to stop even before we get moving and haul him upright by his harness. Then he will go maybe 50 yards and fall down, allowing himself to be dragged like a sack of rice until I stop the team again.

As I walk up to him I can see him watching me out of one eye, pretending to be completely exhausted. Once again I grab his harness and lever him onto his feet, admonishing him about his responsibilities to the team. Then it's like he's been reborn. He's positively jumping to go and pulls for all he's worth as we move out again. It's his little game and he gets me to play it every time we leave a checkpoint. I can't imagine what onlookers must think.

Then there are the "blondes;" every musher has a couple of these. These are the ones who, if they were human, would get stuck on an escalator for two hours if the power went out. They manage to cause more tangles and general mayhem than the rest of the team put together. They like to go visit other dogs in the team and even to go visit other teams if any are handy, regardless of the confusion they cause.

The old and the new rub shoulders in Alaska's bush villages. Here the modern snowmachines of the trail sweeps are parked next to the old log-built Kaltag town hall, practically in the shadow of the village satellite earth station.

Lisa Moore has at least one of these; her ditzy dog is named Buckethead. Mine are Wild Thing and Maybelline. And not only the ladies qualify for the "blonde" label: Kisser, one of my males, fits the criteria perfectly even though he thinks he's God's gift to every female on the trail.

Even when the team is ready to go I can often find the blondes turned around gawking or casually sitting chewing on their toenails. Sometimes it seems I have to send them an engraved invitation to get their attention. When Lisa or I have to stop out on the trail all we have to say to fully explain the situation when the other pulls up is, "Blonde trouble again."

Lisa says being a blonde is a state of mind; I think it might be a result of having no mind. Indeed, there are times I'm sure if I look in one of Maybelline's ears I'll see daylight out the other side. Sometimes I wonder what I'd do with them if they weren't fast runners—and if they didn't follow Socks anywhere like schoolgirls with a crush on their teacher.

On the other side of the coin is Silvertip, my wolf and onetime personal pet. He likes to run in the back of the team where he can be near me and if I put him up front he spends most of his time looking back to see if I'm still there. When we're preparing to move out he's not only up and ready, he's jumping up and down and jerking the sled and howling to go. He pops his tugline so hard I'm worried it might break.

He's so big and strong he sometimes pulls the hook all by himself. When I stop out on the trail I have to be careful to securely anchor the sled because he'll yank the hook when I least want him to. I only wish he would keep pulling with such enthusiasm after we're 20 or 30 miles down the trail, when he starts to goof off and I have to stay on his case to remind him he's working for a living these days.

And then there's Socks. He's the consummate leader who has pulled out of so many checkpoints over half a dozen Iditarods and Lord knows how many shorter races I think by now he does it in his sleep. Like Rocky, he's basically an inanimate object until it's time to stand up.

But he's got a built-in "go" switch that automatically activates whenever I step on the runners. It doesn't matter whether the rest of the team is ready or not, or who's playing games or looking the other way: Socks goes. And he's big enough (a healthy 60 pounds and strong as an ox) to drag the whole team if he has to, which is sometimes the case. But with Socks up front we always move out, even if we have a few fits and starts as things get worked out.

Of course, Socks has to make his one, defining gesture to remind me he's actually running this show: he will always wait until we're a half-mile out on the trail and will then simply stop and unconcernedly relieve himself. I think he likes it even more if I'm shouting at him at the top of my lungs for stopping in the middle of the trail or coming down a hill. When he's quite finished, he'll look back at me as if to say, "This is how we do things in MY team—any questions?" And then we'll be off for a steady run of 50 or 100 miles.

I think any musher will admit sometimes you're not sure exactly who's running the team. But when you've got a foreman like Socks you're more than willing to put up with a few quirks, especially if he keeps order in the rest of mobile zoo in front of the sled.

This morning as I get ready to pull out, the checker and some of the local kids are cleaning up the straw piles from a week's worth of teams and the janitor is sweeping out the community center where we were sleeping only a few hours ago. There's little doubt the race is a closed book here and I'm starting to feel like a footnote.

Andy departs a half-hour ahead of Lisa and me, and Lisa passes me within a mile after we leave town. I'm also overtaken by the trail sweeps on their high-powered snowmachines pulling heavy sleds, who will certainly play a more prominent role in the race for us if the weather turns bad on the coast.

Slim and his crew are old pros at shepherding tail-enders up the trail and it's good to know they'll be around if anything really serious blows up. Of course, they still can't offer any assistance to mushers which is prohibited in the rules, but they can certainly help in other ways no less important or effective. More than a few back-of-the-packers over the years owe the trail sweeps a debt of gratitude.

One of the benefits of running behind the trail sweeps is their big machines and sleds act as first-rate groomers, especially when there's enough fresh snow to resurface the chewed-up trail. I can't complain about the trail condition today as my guys pull steadily through the thick forest and occasional open meadows up the 15-mile incline to the 800-foot summit of the Kaltag Portage. The only problem is the bright sun, which heats up the dogs' dark coats and necessitates frequent brief cooling stops.

When we reach the summit a few hours later we take a break. The panorama down the long, straight valley stretching away to the southwest is impressive. I'm far from the first dog driver to see this view. This portage has been used for thousands of years as a route linking the great interior highway of the Yukon River and the coast, with its rich bounty of marine resources.

Dog teams have probably been traveling through here for a millennium or more; non-Native mushers—and the Iditarod Trail— are very late arrivals in this part of the world. Indeed, our goal of Unalakleet at the western end of the portage has been continuously inhabited for at least 2,000 years, as have several of the coastal villages through which the race runs.

My immediate goal is the Tripod Flats shelter cabin, 35 miles from Kaltag. It and another cabin at Old Woman, 50 miles out, are commonly used by mushers, snowmachiners, and hunters. They are useful progress checks on this third longest leg of the race, and if the snow flurries I see drifting in over the mountains from the south get much heavier the cabins may be welcome refuges.

As we move slowly down the valley the snow is occasionally heavy but the showers are moving quickly and the sun still dominates the scene. However, I don't like the idea of a south wind in this area because it often portends a storm. The weather out here is notoriously—and all too often fatally—fickle. No one takes it for granted.

Flying for the race I've been caught numerous times by fast-moving fronts in this area. In 1991 I flew over Kazuo Kojima barely 10 miles east of Unalakleet as he was making good time across the tundra in the warm afternoon sunshine. Within an hour a major storm roared in from the southwest and Kazuo didn't stagger into the checkpoint for six uncertain hours, having been all but trapped by high winds and heavy drifting snow virtually within sight of town.

And during that hour's lull before the storm I flew up to Shaktoolik to pick up some dropped dogs and very nearly flipped my airplane in unexpected winds gusting to 70 knots. The storm lasted for three days and temporarily shut down the race. In short, I—and a lot of other people—don't trust the weather out here any farther than we can see it, and even then we're not always sure.

That's why there are shelter cabins scattered along most of the winter trails in this part of the state. Some are like the one at Tripod Flats: a snug log cabin set in a wooded swale, built and maintained by the town of Kaltag and the Bureau of Land Management, with a good stove and bunks and stocked with firewood. Others are plywood shacks belonging to local fishermen or hunters standing austerely on bleak shorelines or expanses of tundra. But they all provide refuge to whomever needs it in this land where an hour's jaunt on a snowmachine or dog team can turn into a week-long survival exercise.

When I finally pull up to the Tripod Flats cabin Lisa's team is stopped in front of it. As much as we'd like to stay here a few hours we decide it's best to push on before dark to the Old Woman cabin, 15 miles ahead. Then we'll be only 40 miles from Unalakleet and in a better position to check out any changes in the weather.

The snow flurries continue to come and go. I still don't see anything serious—but then, I didn't see anything coming back in 1991, either. We move smoothly down to Old Woman, marked by its namesake flat-topped hill jutting immediately behind it. Andy is there when we pull in just after sunset; he says he's been there for a couple of hours, which just shows how fast his speed merchants are. He decides to wait a while and then move on with us just in case the weather turns bad.

Like almost all shelter cabins this one has a wood stove. While our cookers are steaming next to the sleds making hot water for dog food we decide to get a fire going in the stove to warm up the cabin. Lisa rummages around in her sled bag and produces three artificial fire logs; she says she's shipped them out to most checkpoints and carries them in case she needs to camp out. I can't argue with her logic as the logs start instantly and make a cheerful fire. Besides, I learned years ago to carry a 20-pound bag of easy-lighting charcoal in my plane for exactly the same purpose.

We tend to the dogs for awhile as their food soaks. After a few minutes we become aware of a strange glow dancing in the treetops, much like firelight. Since we're done with the cookers, I look around for the source. To my chagrin I see bright orange flames shooting two feet out of the chimney of the cabin. Waves of heat are radiating from the cabin's roof and sides. We run inside and find the stove starting to glow cherry red.

Old Woman cabin is just in front of its distinctive flat-topped namesake mountain. The hill is a prominent landmark on the long run from Kaltag to Unalakleet.

The fire logs are burning hotter than a meltdown in a nuclear plant and my overriding thought is we're going to be responsible for torching the Old Woman cabin. We don't have any water to throw on the logs so all we can do is shut the damper and hope for the best. As we wait anxiously for the inferno to simmer down I look at the discarded label from one of the logs. One warning says never to use more than one at a time, another says don't stack any wood on top of the one on fire, and a third cautions never to use these in a wood stove. We've managed to flaunt all three simultaneously and the result has been spectacular. The folks at Underwriters' Lab will use us as their poster kids for the next decade.

After several minutes the blast furnace returns to merely volcanic levels and we retreat outside to escape the sauna we've created. I'm certain there's an inch less snow out here than before we lit the stove, and the dogs seem to be panting like they've just run all day in the sun. I hope it's just my imagination as I start to feed.

Working down the line with the dog food, I remember an experience Aaron Burmeister told me he had here in 1994 on his rookie run. He had eight dogs in Kaltag but dropped one before moving on to Unalakleet. At Old Woman, he stopped to feed, and put out eight bowls of food without thinking. When he looked around, he saw eight dogs eating. The eighth dog was a wolf. It finished its food and vanished instantly into the trees, leaving Aaron to wonder exactly what was going on.

I have a wolf eating with my team as well, but Silvertip has been with us since we left Fourth Avenue and is doing quite well for an accidental sled dog. I wonder what he thinks about our trip so far, and whether he can sense his cousins lurking in the shadows.

The new Bureau of Land Management shelter cabin at Old Woman, 50 miles west of Kaltag on the trail to Unalakleet, replaces an older plywood shack a mile away. It is one of two similar BLM cabins on the 90-mile Kaltag Portage. Like many such refuges along Alaska's trails, it offers a secure haven to any traveler who needs it.

Some of the old-timers ran wolves and wolf hybrids, raising them from puppies or breeding them with huskies. In 1932 and 1933 Slim Williams ran a team of wolf hybrids from Alaska to Chicago for the World's Fair to promote what would ultimately become the Alaska Highway. It was quite a sensation at the time, but wolves haven't been much in vogue as sled dogs since then.

We nap for an hour or so in the almost charred cabin. Before we depart we are careful to leave some food for ghost of the old woman, as is the tradition; she is said to watch over those who remember her. We make sure we set her a proper feast: we almost incinerated her house tonight and we certainly don't need her mad at us—it's still a long way to Nome. We've already chased enough ghosts and we don't need any chasing us at this point.

As usual Andy pulls out a half hour ahead of Lisa and me. It's snowing as we follow the trail up onto the open tundra paralleling the south side of the river. Despite the stereotypical scenes of treeless ice and barren tundra most people associate with the Bering Sea coast, there are actually quite a few trees out here. Most of the larger rivers have substantial green belts and the Unalakleet River which flows down the western part of the Kaltag Portage is no exception.

Some of the checkpoints on the Iditarod can be almost 100 miles apart. At some point on these marathons, mushers must "camp out" for several hours to feed and rest the dogs. In a few instances, conveniently located shelter cabins are popular camping locations, such as the Old Woman Cabin.

The trail from Old Woman to Unalakleet stays mostly just up out of the tree line, on the tundra a few miles south of the river. While this is a more direct route, it is much more exposed and is especially vulnerable to any snowfall and accompanying drifting. Over the years hundreds of permanent reflectors have been put up to mark the trail through this section, nailed to any convenient bush or tree. Where there are no trees there are crude wooden tripods.

However, the permanent markers only give a general idea of where the trail runs at any given point. They outline a corridor up to 100 yards broad, while the actual hard-packed trail is only six or so feet wide. The uncompacted snow off the trail can be a couple of feet deep and can be very difficult going for a dog team.

The exact track is marked by Iditarod-standard four-foot-high wooden lath stakes with reflective tape. When the hard trail becomes obscured by snow, the trail stakes are the only effective way to accurately trace it across wide-open stretches of tundra. Tonight we notice there are already a couple of inches of snow from earlier showers covering everything.

Fortunately Andy seems to have had little trouble following the trail and Lisa is following his sled tracks. I am also reassured when I can see the reflection of the rhythmic flash from the powerful beacon at the Unalakleet airport almost 30 air miles away. As long as I can see the beacon flash I know there is no snow falling between us and our destination.

So, while Lisa's leader (aptly named Brains) does a good job of following Andy's increasingly faint tracks I scan the western horizon for the comforting strobe from the beacon. After half an hour of good progress, however, I start to lose the beacon; shortly thereafter it begins to snow fairly heavily. Since the snow is moving up the valley toward us, Andy's tracks grow steadily harder to pick out, even though we know he can't be far ahead.

Brains keeps moving but the snow squalls continue to increase in frequency and intensity. Finally the tracks from Andy's sled all but disappear under as much as six inches of new, wet snow. Brains slows to a crawl as she works to find the trail. Lisa and I discuss whether we should stop and wait out the snow or push on.

Finally we creep over a rise and see Andy and his team waiting at the bottom of a ravine. He says the new snow became too deep for his leaders to find their way and he decided to wait for us. We have a quick council of war. We know the trail drops back down onto the Unalakleet River about eight miles prior to Unalakleet, and by our best guess we are within 25 miles of the town. Our main concern is to get off the open tundra before we get trapped out here by heavier snow or—my real fear—winds which will instantly create impassable drifts.

We decide to see if Socks can take us marker-to-marker. Lisa says if Socks can get us out of this she'll buy him a steak. I don't add that I already feel I owe him a week's worth of T-bones for what he's already done for me. I move my team to the front and shine my headlight on the next trail stake.

Socks picks up the cue immediately and sets off for the bright reflector. Soon we have a pattern worked out: I spot the marker and Socks takes us to it. Once in awhile when we have to rely on the imprecise permanent markers he wanders off the narrow packed trail and we flounder until we can locate it again. Still, we make slow but steady progress.

After a couple of hours a lull in the snow gives us hope; I can even see the reflection of the Unalakleet beacon again. But the respite is short-lived and the next squall strikes with renewed intensity. In a few minutes it's so thick we can see barely 50 yards because the headlamps are reflecting off the swirling snowflakes. Socks continues to do yeoman duty, pushing through fresh snow sometimes up to his chest.

The trail sweeps are important to every musher running in the back of the pack. Often they use their big snowmachines to re-pack trails and to help mushers as far as the rules allow.

Soon the snow is falling so densely we can't even see 30 yards. Every few minutes we have to stop, set our snow hooks, and go ahead on foot to try to find the next marker. The heavy, wet flakes are sticking to everything. We're completely soaked right through our parkas and cold-weather gear, and the extra exercise of stomping through the deep snow on foot adds oceans of perspiration to our discomfort.

After an hour we're so involved in slogging ahead and then moving the teams forward we don't realize we haven't seen any more markers for maybe 10 minutes. Again we fan out on foot to try to find the trail, but to no avail. Without hesitation we turn around and go back to the last marker we passed.

Our tracks are already fading under the thickly falling snow as we reach the marker. Now we move out on foot again, this time feeling for the packed trail underneath the snow. After half an hour we realize the trail turns at the marker; we had gone straight on without thinking. By repeated stomping forays we determine the trail's new orientation, but we still can't see any markers in the new direction.

I notice part of our problem: the snow is sticking to the reflective tape of the stakes, making them difficult to see even in the direct beam of a headlamp. Since it's near dawn we decide to wait for first light, which should improve our visibility and allow us to see the wooden tripods. After another half hour the snow lets up for a few minutes and I pull out my powerful reserve headlamp to try to spot a marker.

Sure enough, the lithium-powered sealed beam reveals a faint reflection in the direction we've determined the trail should be headed. We immediately pull the hooks and Socks takes us unerringly to the marker. By the time we reach it I see the next one, and then a tree line appears ahead out of the swirling snow: we're dropping back onto the river. Socks has brought us off the tundra and back to concrete reality.

We greet the river like a long-lost friend. In the glimmering dawn I direct Socks down the wandering channel as the still-obscured trail jumps from side to side to avoid icy patches and overflow areas; he responds crisply to my commands like the pro he is. After a few miles a snowmachiner pulls up alongside us; he says we're only five miles from Unalakleet and he'll be glad to break the trail on into town for us.

I let Andy and Lisa pass; Socks has been breaking trail for almost five solid hours in abysmal conditions and has never missed a beat. He and I have been working as a team in a sense I never imagined possible. It's almost as if we can read each other's minds, and it's a good feeling. We happily follow Lisa's team along the newly opened trail while Socks takes a well-deserved break from his duties as the point man in our expedition.

The snow tapers off markedly as we near Unalakleet. The people at the checkpoint probably didn't have much idea what we were going through as we struggled in from the east. It's typical of the weather out here: a few miles can make all the difference in the world. By the time we skate across the frozen lagoon to the windswept, treeless spit on which Unalakleet perches it's been almost 23 hours since we left Kaltag—on a run which normally takes 12 to 15.

We made excellent time over the first 50 miles to Old Woman cabin, but battled for 12 hours to cover the last 40 in from there. Even if we'd left earlier we'd still have had problems: the half-dozen other tail-enders who left Kaltag shortly after we arrived there yesterday took 18 hours.

Interestingly, we never saw any sign of their tracks even though they left only 10 hours ahead of us, which is an indication of how rapidly conditions were changing.

For the moment, though, we've made it to a safe haven. We're all still in good shape, if a bit tired and wet. Most of all, we've finally made it to the coast, and we've done it well under the five-day deadline. Jeff King roared through here four days ago on a fast trail under fair skies—a far cry from what we've encountered. Of course, nobody ever said the weather played fair out here, but if there's any justice, now maybe we've earned a couple of days of easy runs.

The trail arrives on the Bering Sea coast at the ancient village of Unalakleet, perched on its treeless spit at the mouth of the Unalakleet River. The "place where the east wind blows" has been has continuously inhabited for at least two thousand years.

March 14-15— The Iditarod: Unalakleet to Shaktoolik (40 miles)

The first thing we hear on pulling into the checkpoint is the checker telling us we need to get moving up the trail as quickly as possible. Ostensibly there is more snow coming and we must take advantage of what appears to be a 24-to-36-hour weather window. It would be a good idea, he says, to be across Norton Sound to Koyuk by the time things deteriorate. Nobody debates the wisdom of his suggestion, but we are beat. We're soaked to the bone and must get our gear dried out, and the dogs are plainly in need of a rest after their snowplowing marathon.

When we announce our collective decision to stay here for as long as it takes to put things in order, the checker responds by hinting he will send the trail sweeps on up to Shaktoolik in a few hours, and if we want to have a decent trail we'd better be moving by then. We don't appreciate the roust and Lisa takes matters into her own hands with a phone call to race officials in Nome for clarification.

The compromise result, agreeable to all concerned, is an eight-hour stay here in Unalakleet. We all concur a few extra hours won't make much difference if the forecast holds; we'll make Koyuk in plenty of time. Besides, I want the extra hours in the checkpoint to work on Buck, who's

In the makeshift kitchen in the Unalakleet checkpoint during the 1994 race, mushers Bob Ernisse (at table, left) and Ron Aldrich (right) grab a bite to eat and discuss the race with checker Doug Katchatag (center).

starting to show shoulder and wrist problems. By careful massaging with liniment and applying leg sweats I've been able to keep a couple of dogs in the team the vets thought I should drop. However, in my opinion only three or four hours in a checkpoint doesn't give enough time to bring a shoulder or wrist around. I want to keep Buck if I can because he's my main reserve leader—and now we're on the coast where you can never have enough leaders.

I notice Linda Joy's team is still here, as is her handler. Linda, running in the group ahead of us, came in last night with extreme swelling in her legs. She's been in the local clinic for observation, but there seems to be no change this morning and no one knows what's causing the problem. Everyone thinks the best course is to fly her to the hospital in Nome.

Unfortunately, this means she has been withdrawn from the race, and her handler says she's not in very good spirits right now. I feel badly for her; she's worked as hard as anyone I know to make this dream come true and has already gone through an incredible journey of her own just to get this far.

Some mushers change to lighter sleds once they reach the coast at Unalakleet to let their smaller teams go faster on the last 275 miles to Nome.

After a couple of hours to work on the dogs Lisa and I head over to the restaurant for a real burger. We're joined by Harry Johnson, the local airport manager whose beacon was our lodestone on the way in from Old Woman. His sister Harrilyn taught the fourth grade across the hall from mine while I was student teaching in Anchorage in the fall of 1994. Their brother Paul raced in 1986 and the family is well known in coastal mushing circles. As the saying goes, Alaska may be a big place, but it's a small world.

I wish we had more time in Unalakleet; it's the biggest town between Wasilla and Nome with 800 people, mostly Yup'ik Eskimos. (Fewer people are using the term "Eskimo" these days; it was once a derogatory term used by French-Canadian voyageurs and has been applied indiscriminately to half a dozen different Native peoples.) Nowadays the town is a major fishing center and the beaches which surround it on three sides are lined with all manner of boats hauled out for the winter.

We're ready to go by late afternoon. Old Buck looks fit and I'm thankful for the extra rest he got. There's been no word of any trail problems out to Shaktoolik. In any case, the trail sweeps are leaving ahead of us so we will again be the beneficiaries of their trail grooming.

Our only possible concern is for the polar bears reported by other mushers about 10 miles north of town near the fishing camp of Egavik. Jerry Austin, who lives in this area and ought to know a polar bear when he sees one, claimed he was charged by two of them a couple of days ago. There have been other reports as well, and it seems a sow and two big cubs have crossed 100 miles of ice from St. Lawrence Island to check out the hunting in this area.

Polar bears are definitely not common along this part of the coast and have never before been seen on the Iditarod. However, this has been a surpassingly strange winter and no one is discounting anything. Just in case, mushers have been urged to travel in groups if possible, especially during the evening. The potential danger lies in the fact that polar bears are the only bears which will intentionally stalk humans. What's more, they're huge—10 feet tall or better when standing, and weighing as much as 1,500 pounds, much bigger than the biggest blacks or grizzlies or even the monster Kodiak brownies.

Slim and the trail sweeps roar out ahead of us; they'll be in Shaktoolik later this evening. Andy pulls out not long after they do, followed an hour later by Lisa and me. The weather is clearing rapidly and the wind is blowing 15 miles an hour from the north, which usually means the front has passed and the snow is over. If the wind doesn't pick up too much, this will only be a six-hour run, followed by a short stop at Shaktoolik and a quick push on to Koyuk, 60 miles farther north across the ice of Norton Bay.

The trail basically follows the coast north from Unalakleet for 25 miles and then runs along a low-lying spit northwest for 12 miles to Shaktoolik. Enough of the coastline is rock-bound and cliff-lined to force the trail inland before it reaches the Shaktoolik spit. This necessitates about 10 miles of heavy climbing right up the spine of the Blueberry Hills in a series of several long grades.

The last climb is an endless pull up to the 1,000-foot crest of the hills, followed by a notorious three-mile downgrade to the beach. The screaming descent from the summit has devoured more than a few mushers over the years. In 1992 Lloyd Gilbertson broke a leg when he missed a twisting downhill turn. Last year Diana Moroney wrecked so badly she had to scratch at Shaktoolik, and the list goes on.

Before we get too far out of town Lisa and I stop to lock and load for our safari. She's carrying a .45 automatic and I've got my ancient single-action .44 magnum Virginian Dragoon, which is so big and heavy I'd probably get better results using it as a club.

Musher Steve Adkins runs along the coast of Norton Sound during the 1994 race. Coastal trails are some of the toughest on the race because they are completely exposed to the wind, and because the emptiness can sometimes cause teams to hesitate.

As we make our last checks and put the pistols where we can find them in a panic, we realize even this artillery would only annoy a polar bear. Indeed, someone in Unalakleet reminded me to make sure the front sight of my hand cannon is filed down so it won't hurt so much when the bear takes it away from me and sticks it up my nose.

We enter the alleged bear territory in an hour or so. The trail comes back down to the beach after skirting inland around a hill, passes an old building at the fish camp, crosses Egavik Creek, and then heads back up a steep hill. As we move toward the building the dogs seem to be nervous, but we don't see anything which might resemble a bear nor do we see any tracks. We have the distinct feeling of being watched, though, and we decide not to go looking for an *Ursus maritimus* just to say we saw one.

The brush-lined creek has a 50-foot stretch of overflow and the dogs balk, requiring us to stop and lead them across. We are not at all comfortable being stalled in such a vulnerable position and move on with unseemly haste. A few hundred yards later we lose the trail in a windswept area and again have to dismount and lead the dogs back to the markers. We still haven't seen any sign of the bears, but we've both got a strong feeling they're not far away, almost certainly watching us. The dogs are jumpy and looking around and we're intensely relieved when we start back up to the open ridgeline.

Once up on the ridge we have a more immediate problem: the wind. It's apparently been blowing quite hard up here for some time. This isn't the promised new snowstorm, but a persistent wind can be just as troublesome and maybe even worse. With all the new snow on the ground from last night to move around, the gale has already piled drifts across anything it can reach, including the trail.

I know the trail sweeps came through here not an hour or two ago, and Andy has been here even since then, but I can see only the faintest signs of their passing. In places Andy's sled tracks are covered by foot-deep drifts. It seems our run over the Blueberry Hills to Shaktoolik won't be as easy as we'd hoped.

Fortunately the trail is well marked and Socks is able to find his way as darkness falls. Whenever we drop into the lee of the ridge and have a chance to look around, we can see it's a beautiful moonless night with stars almost bright enough to illuminate the trail by themselves.

After an hour or so of slogging up hills, breaking through drifts, and careening back down into intervening valleys, we see Andy stopped ahead in a sheltered grove of trees. He says the wind and drifts were tiring his dogs and he had to rest for awhile. We wait while he gets his team up and then move on with him in the lead.

It's slow going as his leaders break trail and we make frequent stops. After a steep climb up an exposed 100-foot slope in howling wind which requires us to break through hip-deep drifts on foot so the dogs can follow, he says his team has had enough leading. It's time for Socks the Wonder Dog to do his thing.

I move out front with Socks in the lead. We are by now running mostly along the treeless ridgeline, steadily climbing, but with occasional surprise drops into ravines. The trail is marked well, but the wind is gusting to more than 50 miles an hour and at times I can't even see the front of my team in the swirling snow, much less the markers.

Socks pushes resolutely forward, feeling out the trail and heading for the markers when we spot them. Between gusts I scan among the drifts to find the intermittent snowmachine tracks of the trail sweeps. Occasionally Socks misses the trail and I have to redirect him; all I can do is shout "GEE!" or "HAW!" at the top of my lungs and hope he hears above the screaming wind.

Finally we catch glimpses of the lights of Shaktoolik out on the flats to the west and we know we're nearing the top of the Blueberry Hills. Although the lights are barely 15 miles away they seem impossibly far, a tiny island of amber sodium-vapor light in a vast sea of darkness, a cluster of stars fallen from the glittering sky above. It's already taken us eight hours to cover 20 miles from Unalakleet; I don't want to guess how long it will take us to cross the black windswept snow desert to the golden oasis hovering in the distance.

After fighting through a final mile of blasting wind and drifting snow across the barren mountaintop, the hurricane suddenly calms as we come to what appears to be the edge of the earth. Christopher Columbus would have appreciated this; I wonder what he would have told his superstitious sailors to convince them to push on into the unknown.

Of course, our crewmen don't need any urging, and there's the rub. The trail drops abruptly down a steep slope into the tree line and our dogs will try to do it at warp nine if we let them. It looks like the entrance to the world's most dangerous luge run and we're about to try it in the dark with rocket-powered sleds.

Lisa has been here before and suggests we spread out and go down the long hill at least 10 minutes apart. This will give each of us time to recover from any spills and get moving before the next juggernaut comes hurtling through the forest. The dogs will be moving at 15 miles an hour, so we should reach the bottom easily within half an hour.

We agree this sounds like a plan and Lisa disappears over the edge. I wait nervously for another 10 minutes, pondering where the wind has gone and estimating my chances of reaching the beach intact. Finally I give Socks the okay and hold on for dear life.

The dogs obviously appreciate the rest they've just had and respond by trying to drag the sled and me through the sound barrier. Whatever other problems I may have, I don't think I need to worry about their strength and spirit. We hit the tree line at better than 15 miles an hour despite my booted foot jamming the brake so hard we're leaving a rooster tail of snow behind us. I barely scrape through several turns lined with heavy brush and spruce trunks as the trail plunges down the mountainside.

If this continues I'm going to miss a cue somewhere and imitate Linda Joy's dances-with-trees routine. In one singularly fascinating series of switchbacks I graze one spruce, kick away from another, and take a face full of willow branches within about five seconds. Just as I'm about to intentionally spill the sled to try to regain control of the situation the trail levels out briefly and the brake begins to take effect. The dogs have blown off their excess steam and I'm able to get them slowed to a fast trot.

Now I can drop into my Dalzell Gorge mode and concentrate on basic sled driving. The trail is actually in good shape after its recent fresh snow and packing by the trail sweeps. When taken at a velocity slower than a speeding bullet the curves aren't all that bad. However, like the Gorge, there are more than enough hazards waiting to ambush an inattentive driver and abruptly end someone's Iditarod.

We reach the bottom of the hill in about 20 minutes; at least for this little stretch of the trip we've gone as fast as the front-runners. As the trees scatter out and the terrain levels I see Lisa stopped ahead. We're back in a windswept area and she's lost the trail. Andy thunders up in a few minutes and we all fan out to try to find a trail marker. After our experience on the tundra outside of Unalakleet we're getting good at this and I locate a tripod and then a reflector within 15 minutes.

I point Socks at the marker and we're off. The wind picks up again as we leave the shelter of the hills. We pass a deserted cabin, cross what looks to be frozen overflow, and then pull up a 20-foot rise. Suddenly Socks disappears over a steep bank and I slam on the brake. After I set the hook and walk up to see what's happened, I'm shocked to find we've run right over the barrier dune and onto the beach. My headlamp shows nothing but jumbled slabs of sea ice.

As I lead Socks back from his beachcombing excursion Lisa and Andy have found the trail leading along the slough which runs behind the dune. It's already heavily drifted and the wind is picking up. We know we're only 12 miles from Shaktoolik and decide to push on, taking turns breaking trail up the slough. It is tortuously slow and laborious going, each of us making only 100 yards or so before yielding the point position to give the dogs a rest.

With every yard the wind seems to increase. After a couple of hours of banging through the drifts it is howling from the north at 40 miles an hour or more, creating a vicious ground blizzard which reduces our visibility to 50 yards. If we only had to contend with the wind I have no doubt Socks could get us to Shaktoolik. Teams in the front and middle of the race managed to get through here with winds as bad as we are experiencing. However, with fresh snow to shove around, the wind has obliterated the trail and constructed a virtually impassable jungle of drifts; the darkness compounds the problem.

The slashing gale is inescapable; there is no shelter out here. The slough is completely exposed to the north wind and there are no trees of any consequence. At one point I stop and climb over the barrier dune to see if conditions are any better in its lee, but the beach is choked with drifts and if anything the wind is stronger. And the sea ice is a nightmare of upended floes jammed onshore by south winds earlier in the season.

Finally we come to a particularly nasty series of drifts. The wind is screaming and the driven snow stings our faces when we try to peer up the darkened slough to see the next marker. Socks simply stops and looks back at me. I know it's time to go back to the cabin we passed and wait this out. Besides, I'm worried the dogs will become hypothermic in the wind and I want to get them sheltered from it as quickly as possible.

Lisa and Andy turn their teams around without difficulty. As I lead Socks back, however, the other dogs anticipate me and begin a retreat from the maelstrom on their own, causing an instant tangle. In the mess, Silvertip and Bear decide to chew on Yankee. I pull them apart and with steadily mounting frustration start to undo the Gordian knot.

I'm cold and tired and my hand is hurting fiercely and I'm finally out of patience. I shout at Lisa for help so we can get moving back to the cabin. In a daze I begin to undo snaps and lines. As Lisa starts to work with me I'm becoming so upset I don't notice when I inadvertently unhook Yankee's neckline and tugline and he wanders away from the confusion.

When I realize he is loose I bolt toward him, shouting at Andy to try to intercept him. This only spooks the normally gentle giant, who turns and flees up over the barrier dune toward the sea ice with me chasing clumsily in my heavy gear. I watch in paralyzed horror as Yankee vanishes over the snow-crusted dune in the black, gale-swept night.

The image sears itself into my mind; as long as I drive dogs I know I will never forget it. I am overwhelmed by a wave of total desperation. If I can't catch Yankee I'm out of the race. Worse, there's no way he can survive out there on the ice in the piercing wind and cold with no food. Everything has come unglued with frightening swiftness and is spinning out of control. This is my absolute worst nightmare come true, far more terrifying than anything I experienced last year.

I keep plodding after him, hoping he will let me get close enough to capture him. I can only see him when he turns to look at me and my headlamp catches the flickering blue gleam of his frightened eyes. He runs out into the jumbled maze of floes; I stumble after him, shouting. I'm chasing yet another ghost, by far the most important specter of my whole mushing career.

Suddenly I come to my senses and stop. I call Yankee's name as gently as I can and he turns and looks at me. I kneel down and call him again and he slowly shambles toward me, head down, almost apologetic. When he finally comes up and sniffs my outstretched hand and lets me wrap my arms around him I am almost in tears with relief and affection.

I hug him for what seems a long time in the howling wind and enfolding night and slowly the world comes back into focus. As I lead him back to the team the events of 10 minutes ago are already ancient history. We've got work to do, and quickly. We must return to the cabin we passed and get the dogs out of the wind and get warm food into them. We need to get a fire going for ourselves and we must prepare to push on out to Shaktoolik once daylight evens up the odds with the wind.

As I crest the dune Lisa has finished unsnarling my team and I hook Yankee back into his slot. Andy leads the way as we retrace our tracks for what I now see is a very short distance: we worked for three hours and probably didn't even break a mile of trail through the drifted slough.

We discover the cabin to be an under-construction plywood shack, barely 10 feet square. It has no door and is strewn with lumber and boxes, but it has a wood stove with a ready supply of split wood. As far as we're concerned, it's the Hilton and we check in.

The sky is brightening as we bed down the dogs behind whatever windbreaks we can improvise. I use a shovel I find in the cabin to dig holes in a snowdrift for my team and then stick fragments of plywood in front of them to further deflect the insistent wind. We set up our alcohol cookers on the cabin's tiny porch and pack them with wind-hardened snow for hot water.

As our designated pyrotechnic expert, Lisa gets a fire started in the wood stove. Unfortunately she doesn't have any more atomic fire logs so she has to do this one the old-fashioned way. We discover the flue has no damper and most of the heat is going up the stack, but the fire still goes a long way to warm up the cabin's frigid interior.

As I sit semicomatose in front of the stove I realize I've become mildly hypothermic myself and spend some extra time inside warming up. I don't want to think what our situation would be if we'd kept pushing toward Shaktoolik and gotten stalled somewhere in the open.

Within a couple of hours of our decision to turn around the dogs have had a hot meal and are resting. Andy and Lisa and I have decided to wait several more hours to give the dogs—and ourselves—a chance to recover from the long cold night. If Slim and his trail sweeps come back to look for us, we'll follow their tracks in to Shaktoolik. If not, we'll resume our trailbreaking efforts later in the morning and punch our way through somehow. We're not about to be denied our trip to Nome by a little breeze.

About mid-morning we hear the sound of snowmachines above the wind. A few minutes later Slim and his cohorts materialize from the direction of Shaktoolik. They roar to a stop in front of the cabin as we step outside to greet them. It's as happy a reunion as I've seen since Yankee came back last night.

Slim says everyone has been worrying about us since yesterday evening. The wind in Shaktoolik blew 50 miles an hour or more all night and they feared we'd been caught up in the Blueberry Hills and wandered off the trail. The tempest died down somewhat this morning and they headed back to find us.

Their best hope was that we'd stop at this shelter cabin if we got this far. To say they were relieved when they saw smoke coming from the chimney would be an understatement. This has been the kind of unexpected windstorm which kills people in this part of the country. And it's not over: we need to get moving and on out to Shaktoolik before the wind comes back up this afternoon.

Lisa and I are hooked up and moving in 45 minutes. Andy says he'll be along shortly. Shortly after we're back on the slough Lisa and I discover we still don't have a trail to follow: the snow has already completely drifted over the snowmachine tracks. We hope Andy is moving behind us because it's getting worse and he runs the risk of getting stuck all over again.

After an hour and maybe two miles Lisa's leader won't go any farther through the drifts on the slough, which are just as bad as last night. The only difference is now we can see everything, and the revelation isn't reassuring. I knew this country was bleak, but out here in the middle of it I wish I was back in the relative lushness of the Farewell Burn.

We decide to move up onto the barrier dune and try to run along it until we can pick up what Slim said is a less-drifted part of the trail closer to Shaktoolik. Once we're up on the dune we find it varies from 30 to maybe 60 yards wide. There are numerous patches where the scouring wind has left a surface of hard-crusted snow.

I start to work Socks from patch to patch, zigzagging back and forth across the top of the dune line as we inch our way ever closer to Shaktoolik. He never falters as I give him a constant stream of commands: "Gee; haw; little gee; okay; over haw; okay, go on; little haw; go on...."

Periodically we must turn into the teeth of the wind or plow through wind-packed three-foot drifts which collapse as the team clambers over them. Sometimes we must skirt stunted clumps of willow bushes or thread between driftwood snags sticking up out of the snow or retrace our steps when we reach a dead end. But Socks remains as steady as the wind itself, following my commands as if we did this kind of thing every day.

After two hours of the most intense command work I've ever done with a team I see trail markers ahead on the dune. As we break through one last drift I see an open trail, actually a narrow road for ATVs, stretching ahead toward a shadowy cluster of buildings on the horizon which must be old Shaktoolik, two miles this side of the new town. I turn and shout to Lisa, who's following 50 yards behind me. We've broken our way through and Shaktoolik is only five miles ahead over a fast trail.

We don't even notice the 30-mile-an-hour quartering head wind as we accelerate down the road. We've just beaten—at least temporarily—an implacable, impersonal adversary which had every intention of destroying us if it could. It's an exhilarating feeling and the dogs seem to understand what we've accomplished. We'll certainly have more battles to fight but we've won this one.

The outline of old Shaktoolik, abandoned when the new village was built in 1967, grows steadily closer. Like many Native villages, the actual townsite has changed many times over its 1,000-year history, although it has remained in the same general area. Old Shaktoolik dates from the 19th century; it, in turn, replaced an earlier village somewhere close by, but still near the mouth of the fish-rich Shaktoolik River with access to the fishing grounds of Norton Sound. It is now a ghost town, although it sees much traffic from its nearby successor.

We are approaching the two dozen buildings of "Old Shak" end-on as we run the track up the barrier dune. Perched on a low rise, they float above the haze of the ground blizzard. From our viewpoint they appear to coalesce into a single structure looming like a castle above the featureless expanse. I know it's an optical illusion aided and abetted by fatigue and stress, but it seems like we are knights of old charging home toward Camelot after a grueling quest.

Soon enough the shining castle resolves itself into shabby, weathered wooden buildings with windows broken and doors ajar. One or two houses seem to be occupied and Socks tries to turn us into their yards; I urge him back onto the road to the new village, now visible a couple of miles farther on. I estimate the wind is gusting to more than 40 miles an hour and I want to get into the checkpoint without delay.

As we pull out of the old town, I am startled to see three six-dog teams materialize out of the blowing snow ahead. They are making almost 20 miles an hour and rocket past my surprised workhorses before they even have a chance to react. The drivers wave as they pass, and I return their greeting. I've heard Shaktoolik has rediscovered dog mushing in the past couple of years and these must be village teams.

It's only fitting: the Natives in this region are Malemiut Inupiats, who over the centuries developed a hardy breed of work dog bearing their name—the Malemute. These are the first non-Iditarod teams I've seen since the race started. They certainly look good as they vanish into the blizzard, heading back the way we just came.

In a few more minutes we enter Shaktoolik's single street. It is ridged by semipermanent four-foot drifts, the result of a winter's worth of north wind whistling between the houses. The drifts would be worse if not for the half-mile-long, eight-foot-high windbreak fence paralleling the slough

Old Shaktoolik sits abandoned on its low line of dunes next to the Bering Sea. The town moved to a new location a few miles west in the 1960s.

to the north, protecting the entire village. This is probably the windiest checkpoint on the race, and no one likes to spend any more time here than necessary for fear of being delayed when the gales come up—as is happening now.

It's been more than 20 hours since we left Unalakleet, and most of that time has been hard work breaking trail, fighting the wind, and banging through drifts. We've spent almost five hours just on the last 12 miles into Shaktoolik. The dogs will require some rest here before we tackle the 60 miles up to Koyuk across the ice of Norton Bay, all of which will be into a nasty head wind. So much for our goal of making it to Nome in time for the big banquet Sunday afternoon; we've lost a full day to the whims of Mother Nature since Kaltag.

The checkpoint is in the local National Guard armory; the teams are parked behind it, out of the direct wind. There is only one team here: rookie Mark Black scratched just before we arrived. He was running with the group ahead of us but got delayed leaving Unalakleet. By the time he pulled out yesterday morning, just before we got in from Old Woman, the wind was already increasing and he had a rugged 15-hour trip through the Blueberry Hills. He had to do it on his own and didn't get in until midnight.

His team apparently didn't want to buck the wind this morning, so he felt he had to scratch. Lisa and I are sorry for him and wish we'd had a chance to talk him out of it; we've both been there and know how easy it is to fall into the mental black hole. We agree he would have been a perfect candidate to join our slow freight to Nome, and we could have used the company.

For the moment our concern is for Andy, who didn't keep up with us as we were working our way over from the shelter cabin. Slim says the village teams who roared by us are part of a local race; they will check on his progress. In the meantime I busy myself with getting the dogs fed and as comfortable as possible.

As I'm walking back to the checkpoint with a bucket of water for the cooker another team comes in from the direction of Koyuk. I see immediately it's not a village team, which means it's an Iditarod team which has turned around. The driver gives me a "Hi, how are you?" as he passes and parks his team beside mine behind the armory. I spend the next 15 minutes getting my cooker going and then head into the checkpoint to see who the returnee is.

As I come through the door I'm shocked to see the driver who so casually greeted me a few minutes ago stretched out on the floor, looking very, very ill. He's surrounded by an agitated cluster of people headed by the vet, who is a volunteer from Australia. This is well beyond my scope and I stay out of the way, but I hear muttered words like "heart attack" and "stroke" along with "medevac."

The musher is Bob Bright; he's a marathon runner from Chicago who finished the race in 1985. He left late this morning and got seven or eight miles toward Koyuk before he decided something was badly wrong and decided to turn around. If he'd continued he would likely have died of exposure in the increasing wind. Apparently his good judgment saved his own life, and the race organization has him on a plane to the hospital in Nome within a couple of hours.

Later in the afternoon we hear Andy is on his way in. He apparently left right behind us but lost our trail in the drifts. He's had even a worse time than we did crawling across the wasteland and we are extremely glad to see him. By the time he pulls in the wind is up to 40 miles an hour with higher gusts and the snow is like tiny bullets when it hits exposed skin. Even sheltered behind the armory it's all we can do to feed the dogs and keep their straw where it will do them some good.

No matter how bad the weather, we can't bring a dog inside a building, not even a remote shelter cabin. The dog must be dropped and the musher may have to scratch—as happened to Andy last year

New Shaktoolik stretches along its single street, sandwiched on a spit between the Bering Sea and a slough of the Shaktoolik River. The massive snow fence behind town offers some protection from the incessant north wind. This area is consistently the windiest on the entire race. The trail to Koyuk exits through a gap in the snow fence.

within sight of Nome. We're nowhere near that extremity but I doubt the team is getting quality rest in the swirling gusts. I pile more straw around the most exposed dogs and drag some unopened bales over for extra windbreaks.

The only exception to the no-dogs-inside rule is if a vet wants to bring a dog in to work on it. Yankee needs a couple of precautionary stitches as a result of his set-to with Bear and Silvertip last night and the vet decides it would be better to bring him into the armory for a few minutes to do it. It's the first time I've ever had a dog inside a checkpoint and I'm sure it's a new experience for Yankee, who is strictly an outside dog even back home.

The fun begins when the vet produces his suture needle and 75-pound Yankee, my biggest and arguably my strongest dog, decides he'd rather be in the great outdoors. I'm working to hold him steady but it's like trying to restrain a rodeo bull. I'm actually more worried I'll get stitched instead of him as the vet hovers and strikes like a cobra.

The vet, however, seems completely unconcerned and neatly closes the cut in his bobbing target, somehow missing the various parts of my anatomy in close proximity. Once the deed is done Yankee almost demolishes the door on his way out with me hanging on. I don't think I'll have to worry about his being pulled from the race because of being inside; I just hope I can get him in the airline kennel to ship him back from Nome.

Late in the afternoon we receive word four drivers who left Shaktoolik early this morning finally straggled into Koyuk after a nine-hour crossing. Three of them—Aaron Burmeister, Rob Carss, and Ararad Khatchikian—had already had a rough 15-hour trip from Unalakleet. They were stuck here in Shaktoolik for 15 more hours waiting for a break in the storm-force winds.

The fourth driver, Dave Branholm, had been here for almost two days after his leaders had a meltdown coming up from Unalakleet. He tried to follow several groups to Koyuk but had to turn back each time. Finally his leaders condescended to follow Aaron's group and he made it across with them. It was no picnic, with 30-mile-an-hour winds and blowing snow, but they made it. Now they're out of the wind zone with clear sailing to Nome. They even have a good chance to make it to the banquet on Sunday; we'll just have to follow when we can.

We remaining exiles decide to get some rest so we can try to leave tonight when the wind is supposed to die down a bit. About seven p.m. I wake up and look outside. The checker walks over and says to go back to sleep because the wind is pushing 60 miles an hour and isn't forecast to abate until tomorrow morning. I don't even wake Lisa and Andy; we are pawns of the weather god and may as well make the best of our extended stay here by catching up on sleep.

The wind howls around the armory all evening. We get up and feed the dogs again about midnight and it's brutal outside. The dogs are doing okay but the wind chill in the open is 110° below zero. Despite my best precautions I refreeze the tips of a couple of fingers I froze back in the Klondike 300 in January. Of course, the flash-frozen digits are the only ones still working on my broken hand. Now when I try to pick something up it's like using chopsticks because the fingertips have no feeling. I wonder to myself if I can apply for some kind of disability when the race is over, because I'm going to have a hard time even signing my name for a month.

March 16—The Iditarod: Shaktoolik to Koyuk (58 miles)

The wind finally begins to die down after sunrise. We've enjoyed the local hospitality for more than 20 hours and it's definitely time to move on. Lisa, Andy, and I are ready to go by mid-morning and we head out of town against a mere 15-mile-an-hour breeze. We cross the slough behind the village and pass through what is locally called the Gate, the only gap

Looking back to Shaktoolik from the trail to Koyuk, the village's few dozen buildings form a thin line along the ice-bound shore of the Bering Sea. There is not so much as a shrub for 60 miles north across the ice of Norton Bay.

in the endless Great Wall which fends off the north wind.

As we move out onto the blinding white expanse beyond the wind-break we must look again like a trio of armor-clad knights sallying from the safety of the shining castle on a great and uncertain crusade—and that's just about how we feel, given the events of the past few days. Koyuk is 60 miles away and the wind is going to come up again during the afternoon; our crusade today will probably be a long one.

The wind stays mercifully light as we work the 15 miles across the low-lying peninsula behind Shaktoolik to Island Point, a 200-foot rock jutting up from the edge of Norton Bay. We pass the old shelter cabin on the point and shortly drop down a 30-foot embankment to the ice of Norton Bay. Andy is in the lead but his leaders falter as they start out onto the drifted and utterly flat expanse of the sea ice. Lisa's team balks as well, leaving Socks to be our guide across the void.

The old master doesn't even hesitate as he trots up the blown-in trail at his usual stately pace into the now-increasing wind. Lisa and Andy fall in line astern as we marshal our oceangoing convoy for the voyage to Koyuk. Although we will be miles from land on salt water, we're not exactly adrift on the deep sea because we can easily see the hills and mountains which virtually surround the bay. We can clearly make out the low mountain dead ahead under which lies Koyuk, 45 miles distant. At night the red light on a radio tower above town is said to be visible almost from Shaktoolik.

Koyuk is another Malemiut Inupiat village of 100 people which has been here at the mouth of its river since before the Russians. Around the turn of the century it became a major supply point for gold mines on the Seward Peninsula. There was even a coal mine in the area which supplied Nome for many years. Today there aren't any booms underway and the village residents maintain a largely subsistence lifestyle buttressed by a few jobs, mainly with various government agencies.

The 50-mile expanse of open sea ice across Norton Bay from Shaktoolik to Koyuk is utterly featureless. Mentally, this is probably the toughest leg of the race for the dogs.

As we trek across the bounding main the wind picks up to 30 miles an hour or so but Socks continues his metronomic 10-minutes-a-mile pace. I put down the seat on my sled and settle in for a long ride. By sitting, I'm also helping the team by ducking out of the wind and cutting the drag, yielding a welcome extra mile an hour or so. For the next six hours we watch the hill behind Koyuk rise above the horizon with maddening slowness. I doze off repeatedly but Socks never misses a beat; he's racking up more steak dinners than he can eat in a year.

Eventually the wind dies down and I stop for a break. Andy has been keeping up with me and Lisa has dropped a ways behind. As Andy and I chat and toss some snacks to our dogs while Lisa catches up, we notice something on the trail in the distance behind her team, which is still almost a mile off. As the team comes closer we start to make out the object in the distance: it is Lisa, apparently on foot. Her team is chugging unconcernedly along without her.

In other circumstances this would be a cause for alarm, but now it's just something else to break the monotony, and is even a little funny. I ask Andy to watch my dogs and I mosey back down the trail toward Lisa's oncoming team. Brains dutifully pulls the team up to me, stops, and waits patiently while I turn everyone around. Then I drive them the mile or so back to Lisa, who is casually hiking up the trail after her wayward puppies.

She laughs as I pull up and sheepishly admits she dozed off and got deposited on the sidelines when the sled hit a bump. Of course, the team wasn't going to do anything out here on the ice except follow Andy and me, so she was never in any danger of losing them. This is another advantage of hanging together back here at the tail end when we're not at our effervescent best.

The sun sets behind Mount Kwiniuk on the run across Norton Bay to Koyuk. The 2,000-foot mountain is on the coast near Elim, 60 miles southwest of Koyuk. The trail passes directly beneath its steep flanks.

Besides, I'm glad for the opportunity to repay her—at least in part— for her help the other night when I almost lost Yankee. I hop onto her sled bag for the ride back to my team, where we all have a brief celebration: we're within striking distance of Koyuk and we've finally left the heavy winds behind, for awhile anyway.

Even after we finally make out the individual buildings of Koyuk it still takes an hour to cover the last miles. We pull into the checkpoint on the beach at sunset. Our plan is to rest for several hours here and then head southwest down the coast, stop briefly in Elim, and then run over to White Mountain. The total distance is under 100 miles and we hope to be in White Mountain tomorrow night. From there it's only 77 miles to Front Street and the end of our journey.

We are the only ones here. The four teams in Aaron Burmeister's group that escaped Shaktoolik yesterday are already at White Mountain. They will be in Nome tomorrow in time for the banquet, which starts at four in the afternoon. The checker suggests we leave as soon as possible while we have good weather and a good trail in front of us and for once we agree. The run over to Elim promises to be fairly innocuous and we intend to be on the road after midnight.

As we work on the dogs some of the village kids are hanging around. They are interested in candy and the charcoal hand warmers which seem to have become a popular item everywhere along the trail. Unfortunately I don't have any of either to spare because one of my bags was rifled here a few days ago along with nine others, including one of Andy's. It's the only place this has happened on the race and the village elders are much

The village of Koyuk and its gravel airstrip hug the north shore of Norton Bay. The State of Alaska maintains airports at more than 200 bush villages and towns to support the air "highway system" on which much of Alaska depends.

embarrassed. Luckily we can make do with what we've carried from Shaktoolik, so the damage is more symbolic than severe.

After we take care of the dogs and head up into the village to the checkpoint we're ready for a nap. I have another fax waiting for me, this time from Bert, who is already in Nome. He says we need to keep moving because a major storm is gaining strength in the western Aleutians.

By his estimation, which is usually pretty good since he flies in the Aleutians and the Bering Sea for a living, we have no more than 48 hours before unpleasant things start to happen between here and Nome. If we're not through the gauntlet by then, we could be stuck for several days.

I know what happens when one of these late-winter weather systems moves through this region and it can be truly biblical. Aside from lousy weather which can include everything from freezing rain to blinding snow, the pressure gradient can trigger hurricane-force winds all along the coast, such as the ones which trapped Andy in front of Nome last year and have nearly killed mushers in previous years. If we get caught, it will be a fight every inch of the way to Front Street, far worse than anything we've already endured.

We catch a nap while a local teacher who's helping the checkers dries some of our gear in the school dryer. I don't get much sleep worrying about the weather: it's good now, but in this part of the country, at this time of the year, the only time it's good is just before it gets bad.

A team pulls into the Koyuk checkpoint. The dogs will be lined out on straw, examined by vets, fed warm food, and allowed to rest for several hours. The driver may also have enough time for a nap and a bite to eat.

March 17—The Iditarod: Koyuk to Elim (48 miles); Elim to White Mountain (46 miles)

We move out on schedule after midnight. This is where Lisa scratched two years ago when her leaders wouldn't go any more; she insists on going first. As her team moves smoothly out of the checkpoint I can see her relief and I know exactly how she feels. She has finally exorcised her demon. Now she can look forward to the run up Front Street without the ghost of races past hovering over her.

The trail is mainly hard and fast and the dogs are in nighttime high gear. We cruise southwest along the shore ice for 15 miles and then dive inland across a low divide behind Bald Head, a prominent mountain at the tip of a peninsula we could see all the way up from Shaktoolik. By dawn we're past Bald Head and crossing a series of inlets to Moses Point.

This area has been known to blow hard and was doing so a few days ago, but it's only whispering now. As the persimmon sun rises above the mountains on the east side of Norton Bay we reach the long spit separating Kwiniuk Inlet from the ocean. Strung out along the narrow strip of sand is the old village of Elim, an eerie collection of ramshackle houses, huts, and fish drying racks. The new town was built a couple of decades ago 20 miles down the coast on high ground and this ancient place is now used as a summer fish camp.

We're running on the lagoon side of the spit; this lets the slowly rising sun outline each house in turn as we pass. The warm pinks and golds of the sunrise contrast dramatically with the weathered tints of the buildings

The trail between Koyuk and Elim runs along the shore ice in places. Winds can jam ice floes onto the shore in jumbled heaps, or just as easily push them back out to sea, leaving open water.

and the monochromatic whites and grays of the shadowed snow and sea ice. It's a continuous series of scenes any photographer would kill for and is another well-earned reward for us; I wish the dogs could appreciate is as much as I do.

Once more I bemoan the demise of my pocket camera, which expired a few days into the race. I have only a handful of pictures to document what we've been through and I'm sure I'm going to regret it later. On the other hand, I've found photographs to be woefully inadequate to capture especially important events; often they are better left untaken. The memory is sometimes a better camera. One thing is for certain: there's no way I'll ever forget the incredible flood of images recorded in my mind over the past two weeks.

Past the old village we make a slow five-mile run on a very soft and punchy trail across the lagoon to the abandoned Moses Point FAA station. This is a relic of the pre-World-War-II buildup of Alaska's aviation network. At one time its 5,000-foot runway, hangars, and terminal building hosted dozens of planes a day enroute to and from Nome. Its cluster of trim government houses was home to a dozen families manning this outpost of modern civilization.

The 9-mile state highway from Moses Point to Elim is left unplowed in the winter. The town of Elim and its new airport are at the foot of the hill. The coast around Elim supports a thick forest, one of the very few wooded areas on the Seward Peninsula.

The airport and its buildings are derelict now; the only sign of activity is a radio beacon in its hermetically sealed blockhouse with its generator softly putt-putting above the rustle of the wind. As a pilot, I find scenes like this depressing; too many airports are closing around the country, even in Alaska where airplanes are vital necessities. But I understand what happened here: when the village moved and a new airport was built adjacent to it there was no longer any justification to keep this one open. In some cases progress has a certain rationality to it.

The remaining nine miles into new Elim are on a state-maintained (but unplowed) road which climbs several hundred feet to skirt the bluffs punctuating the coastline from here to Nome. We roll into the checkpoint late in the morning and discover my old friend Jasper Bond is running things, having transferred here after he finished more than three weeks in the wilderness at Rohn.

As usual he's got everything well organized, right down to finding a convenient source of hot water. Within half an hour the dogs are fed and resting in the warm sun; this is the first true out-of-the-wind rest they've

Checker Jasper Bond looks over teams at Elim while mushers take a break inside the nearby checkpoint. (Jasper usually works the Rohn checkpoint earlier in the race.)

had since the Yukon. We'll wait out the heat of the afternoon and then push on in time to get over the mountains to Golovin by dark. In the meantime Jasper's crew has sandwiches and hot soup ready for us inside the spacious state maintenance garage being used as the checkpoint.

After a good nap we get ready to leave about mid-afternoon. Jasper and his people are closing up the checkpoint; the plane is already on the way to take them to Nome for this afternoon's banquet. I jokingly ask Jasper (who resembles a pro football lineman and is known to have a healthy appetite) to save some food for our arrival tomorrow.

We all leave Elim about the same time; the trail runs alongside the airport and we watch the Iditarod Air Force plane take off as we head out of town. Two years ago I was flying the plane that pulled the last volunteers out of Elim for the banquet; I'm certainly getting a different perspective on things today.

Once we're past the airport, the race route out of Elim this year doesn't follow the sea ice for the first 10 miles as it usually does. The strange weather this winter has resulted in open water just offshore from here to Nome. Instead, we're using the old mail trail, an overland detour we heard about a few days ago but which didn't sound like anything to cause undue worry. It's a little longer but the villagers have told us it's quite a beautiful run, so we're in the cruise mode.

Like everyone else, we consider the main challenge on this leg to be crossing the mountains between the coast and Golovnin Bay. From an abandoned coastal cabin at Walla Walla 10 miles south of Elim, the trail turns inland, to the west. Then it climbs directly up and over a series of 1,000-foot ridges which culminate in Little McKinley, a 1,200-foot summit overlooking the village of Golovin.

Many mushers consider Little McKinley the toughest climb on the race. It's even worse than Rainy Pass because its succession of brutal climbs probably totals 5,000 feet or more, all within only eight miles, interspersed with steep downhills which don't give the dogs a chance to recover. Additionally, the weather is often abominable because the entire overland stretch is completely above timberline and exposed to the almost incessant wind.

Little McKinley will be hard work for the dogs, but they're well rested. In fact, my team is getting stronger and stronger as we work toward Nome. After 1,500 miles of training and 1,000 miles on the Iditarod, the dogs are superbly conditioned and trail-tough and could probably run the remaining 100 miles to Front Street nonstop if I asked them. They're working as a single coordinated unit and showing the intuitive trail savvy of seasoned Iditarod veterans. I modestly consider the 11 I've been running since Kaltag to be the best dog team I've ever driven, even if they're not very fast.

After the first mile out of Elim we decide we shouldn't have been leaning forward so much to Little McKinley because we've got trouble right here in River City. The allegedly innocuous mail trail is turning out to be not your average dog trail: it's a narrow, roller-coaster, mogul-marred cliff-hanger through heavy forest requiring every ounce of skill and attention we can muster, and then some.

It repeatedly climbs abruptly hundreds of feet to snake along the tops of dizzying bluffs and then plunges down steep tree-choked chutes which threaten to wear out our brakes. Several times I get ambushed by cleverly concealed low-hanging branches that nearly wipe me off the sled. We spend an inordinate amount of time angling along hillsides so steep I don't even want to look down them.

At one point we run for 50 yards along a ledge not more than three feet wide with a rock wall on the uphill side and a 300-foot drop to the beach on the other. It's so tight I'm worried if one of the dogs sneezes we'll become the blue-plate special at Chez Raven down on the rocks below.

This trail is genuinely terrifying. I'm glad I didn't know about it beforehand or I might have had second thoughts. Dalzell Gorge and the Blueberry Hills were only warm-ups for this monster. I'm profoundly thankful I didn't waltz blithely into this at night.

After a thrill-packed hour and a half I finally ease the team off the flanks of Mount Kwiniuk and onto the beach at Walla Walla with all of our various appendages and appurtenances still in their appropriate places. The country has been beautiful and the scenery spectacular, but I don't think the Elim mail trail will ever make it into the *Guide Michelin*.

I've been so busy maintaining my death grip on the handlebar I haven't noticed I've outrun Lisa and Andy. I stop the team to wait for them and feed some frozen beef while I try to coax my adrenaline level back into its normal operating range. Fifteen minutes later Lisa pulls up; she's still shaking from her E-ticket ride over the mail trail and also calls a temporary halt to the festivities.

We wait for Andy for quite awhile, growing more and more worried something has happened to him. Finally we hear a snowmachine coming from the direction of Elim. We flag down the rider and ask him if he's seen a team on the trail behind us. To our immense relief he says a musher returned to Elim just before he left and is back at the now-closed checkpoint. Lisa and I don't know if Andy has given up or is just resting his dogs as he's done earlier on the race. In any event, he's on his own now; besides, we're not sure we'd survive the trip back to Elim to check on him.

We thank the snowmachiner, who's on his way to White Mountain on an everyday 50-mile afternoon trip in the Bush, and shortly follow our fellow traveler up the first of the interminable grades leading to Little McKinley. After two miles of steady uphill slogging I'm glad I've got a lot of big males on the team. Nobody's really even breathing hard and I only need to assist with a perfunctory pump once in awhile. Lisa, however, is having more difficulty with her smaller team and is doing a lot of walking, so I periodically stop and wait for her to catch up.

As we gain the top of the first hill we're well above timberline; stretching to the west I can see the series of ridges we're about to cross.

Surprisingly, there's not a breath of wind up here and the temperature is almost above freezing. The clement weather is unusual but certainly not unwelcome; this upland stretch is known for its extremes and we're thankful for a lucky break after our tribulations around Unalakleet and Shaktoolik.

After another hour and a half of by-now-routine ups and downs we power up the final incline to Little McKinley itself and stop just before the steep three-mile downgrade to take in the view. Ice-covered Golovnin Bay lies below us, probing 20 miles northwest past the village of Golovin on its rocky point to our goal of White Mountain, nestled far inland under its wooded namesake hill alongside the Fish River.

Unlike the heavily forested eastern side of the mountains, the slopes below us and to the west as far as we can see are bleak and barren except for scrub. The only real trees from here to somewhere in Siberia are much further inland, limited strictly to sheltered slopes and river valleys.

The sun is just about to set over Topkok Head 35 miles to the west and the rich late-afternoon light gilds everything around us. On the western horizon beyond Topkok we can barely see the hazy outline of Cape Nome,

The author with Pullman (left) and Socks (right) atop Little McKinley in the 1996 race. Nome is less than a hundred miles ahead over a fast trail. (Photo by Lisa Moore)

now only 60 air miles away with Front Street and the burled arch only a few miles further on.

We hold a quick meeting of the tail-enders' club and officially decide we can start to have fun now. For the first time since leaving Anchorage I really relax. We're actually going to make it even if we have to hole up somewhere to wait out the approaching storm, of which we've so far seen no sign.

As the sun sets over the Russian Far East—only a couple of

hundred miles away—we plunge down the hill toward Golovin. Shortly we pass the shelter cabin at the mouth of McKinley Creek and turn up the ice of the bay toward the village. The sky is crystal clear and the wind is dead calm; the temperature begins to plummet toward zero as the sun disappears. The trail is hard and fast and the lights of the village beckon invitingly.

Golovin is a small Inupiat Eskimo settlement of slightly more than 100 souls. The village was already old when Captain Golovnin of the Imperial Russian Navy sailed through this area in the early 1800s. The bay as well as the lagoon behind the town still retain the correct spelling of his name; the name of the village has been subtly changed over the years. Golovin was a full-fledged stop on the early Iditarods but now it is only a sign-in checkpoint and few mushers, at least in the front end of the race, spend much time here.

Lisa and I decide to stop in town to get into some warmer gear. I ask the checker about a place to change clothes and she says to wait a minute. Shortly she helps us park our dogs and then ushers us into her aunt's house, where we are plied unmercifully with coffee, tea, hot chocolate, sandwiches, soup, cookies, offers of places to rest, and good conversation.

Here in Agnes Amarok's snug home we find the warmest display of hospitality either of us has yet seen on the race. We are completely taken with the wonderful people of Golovin, several of whom stop through to say hello and offer encouragement and trail information.

We spend a couple of hours relaxing in this unexpected but completely welcome haven. As we chat it develops Lisa went to high school in Nome with the checker, and a couple of the older residents remember Ron from his early Iditarods; once again the big-state-small-world paradox manifests itself.

The awards banquet in Nome is still going on and we listen to it on the radio while munching sandwiches and sipping hot coffee. We figure this is a fair exchange for not making the party ourselves; we'll take some extra time here and attend the banquet vicariously via KNOM radio.

Eventually we realize we must leave to get on to White Mountain, an easy 18-mile run across Golovnin Lagoon. Our hosts duly warn us about a potential problem which snared Martin Buser and DeeDee Jonrowe. It seems an inviting side trail leading to a hunting camp was marked similarly to the Iditarod before the race. Martin and DeeDee got confused and took it, costing them an extra hour and a half, and slipping DeeDee a place in the final standings.

We get specific instructions to avoid this: take the trail heading directly

356

for the White Mountain airport beacon, easily visible for the entire run from Golovin. We figure this is about as simple as it gets and move out, promising to spend some time in Golovin on future Iditarods.

I take the lead out of town, carefully avoiding the false turnoff. Once out on the ice, the trail across the lagoon is ideal in every respect: straight as an arrow, well-marked, perfectly groomed, and utterly level. The temperature is perhaps 10 below zero and the dogs accelerate immediately to nighttime cruising speed.

In my headlight I can see an endless line of golden reflectors pointing northwest, precisely at the rhythmic green-and-white strobe of the White Mountain beacon on the horizon. Mariners throughout history have navigated by lighthouses just as we are using the beacon flash. This is also how pilots found their way at night up until the 1930s, following airway beacons just like this one across the darkened landscape before instrument flying was developed.

The sense of voyaging is inescapable. Socks and Pullman are up front and are following the well-defined trail as if they are on rails. The rest of the team is pulling so quietly and smoothly I almost don't realize they're there. We are on full autopilot, leaving me with nothing to do but ride along and keep myself amused.

My headlight is just a nuisance on this trail so I turn it off. When I do I gasp in awe. Here in the middle of the flat, five-mile-wide expanse of the lagoon, the clear moonless sky arches overhead in an incandescent blaze of stars. The evening star hovers in the west—over Nome—with a brilliance unmatched even by the powerfully focused beacon ahead.

And in the east, the entire sky is dominated by a northern lights display the likes of which I have never seen. I can see a huge section of the circumpolar arc of the aurora, its curvature clearly visible. It resembles nothing so much as a line of summer thunderstorms in eastern Oklahoma, continuously illuminated from within by lightning which rips through the cloud tops and dances behind the veils of rain. I can even follow individual swirls in the auroral arc as they spin along the shimmering curtains, touching off glowing cascades of green, red, and even purple as they pass from horizon to horizon.

The celestial panorama is almost too much to absorb. I rig out the sled seat and simply sit and watch as the team pulls silently on, the only sound the swish of the runners over the packed snow. For two hours my magic carpet glides serenely across the lagoon. Every half hour or so I flash my headlamp back at Lisa, who is holding steady a mile behind, and then return to my musing.

This is beyond perfect, the most extraordinary run I have ever experienced. It is a most sublime reward, and is an especially exquisite counterpoint to the bleak despair of watching Yankee disappear over the barrier dune not 72 hours ago. Everything has come full circle; the world is in harmony, at least from my perspective, and I see no reason it should not remain so until we pull under the arch in Nome tomorrow evening.

I'm almost disappointed when I must break the spell and maneuver Socks into the White Mountain checkpoint. It's a bit past midnight and we've been 10 hours since leaving Elim. This is bog-slow for a mere 46 miles, but we spent at least a couple of hours waiting for Andy and another two or more at Golovin. We have nothing to be ashamed of, especially since our main goal now is just to finish in good order tomorrow; the exact time is no longer of consequence.

The author pauses while working on his team at the White Mountain checkpoint, 77 miles from Nome. Mushers must take at least an 8-hour layover here, although many would as soon push on to Nome.

We have to take a mandatory eight-hour layover here, which means we can leave around 10 in the morning on the 77-mile jaunt into Nome. We break out the cookers for our last run-through of the now-automatic checkpoint routine. We have become so proficient over the past two weeks that the dogs are fed and asleep on their straw within 45 minutes.

The checkpoint is in the municipal building just up the hill. We hang our outer gear in the boiler room to dry and then toss our sleeping bags in the back of the library. The building also houses the local National Guard armory and I notice a large-scale military map of the Norton Sound area on the wall. This is the first accurate chart I've seen since the race started and I try to trace our course from Unalakleet to Shaktoolik and on to here.

Despite my best efforts I simply cannot pinpoint where we were for many stretches. I eventually fall asleep wondering where we crossed the Blueberry Hills, all the while realizing I will probably never know exactly, short of physically doing it all over again. Perhaps this is as it should be, always leaving enough uncertainty to preserve the mystery of the trail.

March 18—The Iditarod: White Mountain to Safety (55 miles)
Safety to Nome (22 miles)

We're up and running within an hour after our layover expires. Before we leave we get a great piece of news: Andy is moving again. He left Elim about 8:30 after almost 24 hours there. Knowing how fast he can move once he gets rolling, I expect he'll be in here within six hours and then on

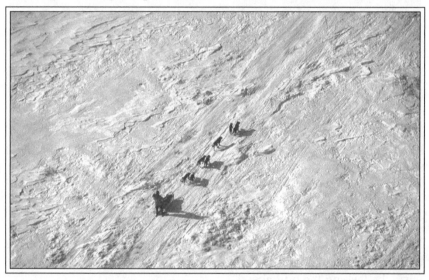

By the time they reach the bleak expanse of the Bering Sea coast, teams can be down to barely half of their starting strength. In 1994, eighteen-year-old Aaron Burmeister, here making the long climb to Topkok after leaving White Mountain, had only seven dogs all the way from Kaltag to Nome. (Five dogs is the minimum number to finish.) Aaron was a top Junior Iditarod competitor.

into Nome sometime tomorrow morning. But the big thing is he's on the trail; he hasn't tossed in his cards. He's still going to chase his ghost. We back-of-the-packers will prevail after all.

As Lisa and I move steadily toward Topkok in the bright morning sunlight, the only possible disruption to the positive energy flow is an ominous swirl of cirrus clouds slowly moving up from the southwest. This is the harbinger of the storm Bert warned us about.

If it's moving as fast as some of these monsters have been known to do, it could be close enough to Nome to trigger the Solomon blowhole just this side of Safety by the time we get there in four or five hours. And I'm worried about Andy; his margin will be much thinner than ours and he runs a real risk of getting caught in the same kind of tempest which robbed him of his dream last year.

We push on with all due haste, devouring the series of 300-foot ridges leading to the final push up Topkok. My superdogs don't even break stride on the steep hills and by three in the afternoon we're making the final

From an abandoned A-frame shelter cabin at the east foot of Topkok Head to the windswept summit is only a few miles, but they can be some of the most difficult and dangerous on the entire race when storms roaring in from the Aleutians strike the exposed promontory.

assault on Topkok. We stop at the summit to admire the view out to Cape Nome. I am also scanning for any sign of a ground blizzard between us and Safety; even though winds are light up here, a 50-knot gale could easily be lashing the trail ahead.

Seeing nothing but clear sailing, we push on. We reach the shelter cabin at the west foot of Topkok by four o'clock and stop to feed the dogs. From here to Safety is a 25-mile run along the beach, with the last 12 along an unplowed state highway, part of a local network of roads radiating from Nome. As we head across the now-quiet Solomon blowhole, I remember what a fearful toll this natural wind tunnel has exacted from mushers over the years, and especially from tail-enders like us.

In 1992 I was waiting in Nome to meet Bob Ernisse, a friend who was running with a group near the back of the pack. I had just flown over them on my way back to Nome after closing down the checkpoint at Unalakleet. Bob's group was trapped by a hurricane-force ground blizzard in the exact area we're now traversing. He almost died of hypothermia before fellow driver Bob Hickel, son of the former and then-current governor, found him and kept him from sinking further. I finally met Ernisse after he had been evacuated to the hospital in Nome; it had been a very close thing and he looked worse than a survivor of Stalingrad.

In 1994 I watched tail-ender Beth Baker make the climb up Topkok from my plane. She was heading into a ferocious but highly localized blizzard with winds of 80 miles an hour I had personally clocked with the Global Positioning System in my airplane. She was being escorted by a snowmachiner but later got lost when her leader took the team onto the

The Nome Kennel Club maintains a snug shelter cabin at the west foot of the rugged Topkok Hills. Located in the middle of one of the worst wind areas on the trail, this cabin has saved more than a few snowmachiners and mushers over the years.

sea ice in a complete whiteout. She was within a few hundred yards of open water when she got stopped. A massive search failed to find her until the next morning. She had to scratch after spending most of the night on the ice in wind chills of minus 130 and badly freezing her hands.

But today the blowhole is a toothless tiger and I have plenty of time to take in the scenery as we glide along the beach trail. After 12 miles we reach the Bonanza Ferry bridge and the Nome-Council Road. The history in this area is hard to miss; buildings and relics are everywhere. The remnants of the old city of Solomon, once a roaring boom town to rival Nome, are a mile inland. The bridge is flanked by the Last Train to

Nowhere, the remains of three steam locomotives used during the early 1900s on the short-lived railroad from Solomon to Council.

Council, 35 miles northeast of Solomon and 15 northwest of White Mountain, had its own gold rush a year before the discoveries at Nome. John Wayne's "North to Alaska" was filmed partly on location at Council. The movie's theme song by Johnny Horton celebrated the gold "beneath that old white mountain just a little southeast of Nome." The mountain was supposed to be Cape Nome, but nobody's ever worried much about his geographic license.

From here to Nome the shoreline is strewn with old cabins now used as summer fish camps. The very beach over which we're running was the magnet which drew thousands of miners to the area between 1898 and 1900. While gold abounded in placer deposits inland, mining it was expensive and difficult. When the precious metal was discovered in the sands of the beach itself, anyone who could wield a shovel and run a crude sluice box descended on Nome from around the world.

Nome is much closer to Tokyo and many cities in Asia than to many points in the United States. This signpost is a standard stop on all tours of downtown Nome.

This was what made Nome so different from other gold rushes: would-be miners could literally step from their ships onto the beach and look for their pay-streak with virtually no equipment or experience. Most went home broke in a few months, but a few made fortunes before the easy beach gold played out after a couple of years.

The harder-to-get placer gold was abundant, however, and the area is still a gold-mining center. One of the biggest mines in Alaska operates in a huge pit a mile north of downtown, just off the end of the airport's main runway. In the summer dozens of small mines are reopened and hundreds of latter-day stampeders work claims from the beach to the mountainous backbone of the Seward Peninsula. There's still lots of gold here; its lure has not dimmed over the years.

Nome has an aura unlike any other city in Alaska, or in the country, for that matter. It boasted more than 20,000 people in 1900 and was the largest city in Alaska. The town was wide-open 24 hours a day and sported the most notorious saloon row north of San Francisco; the legendary Wyatt Earp ran one of these establishments. In fact, the City of the Golden Beaches was probably the last hurrah of the Old West and was populated with many other refugees from the vanishing frontier down south.

In many ways the 1900s never ended out here. The town has an omnipresent look and feel of living with one foot in the past, combined with a civic outlook on life which can best be described as different if not

Rookie Sonny King emerges from a relatively mild 50-mph ground blizzard between Topkok and Solomon in the 1997 race. The poles are trail markers. The Solomon blowhole has nearly killed mushers in past races, almost within sight of Nome. A natural wind tunnel, it can hurl 80-mph winds and blinding whiteouts.

downright zany at times. It's likely there's not another town in Alaska that collectively enjoys a good joke as much as Nome. This slightly warped sense of humor manifests itself all year in a series of goings-on which sometimes befuddle visitors who don't understand it takes special people to live here, and a good laugh is one of the strongest weapons to fight off the wind, weather, and isolation.

Nome is the perfect place to finish the Iditarod, an ideal foil for too-urban, self-conscious, often-pretentious Anchorage. Nome is the Last Frontier's last frontier town. As the dogs trot past the cabins lining the snowy road to Safety I realize the Iditarod is really the ultimate flight from modern civilization, requiring a complete break with many of the premises and assumptions which govern life in a nine-to-five world of cable television and home pizza delivery.

It's nearly sunset as I approach the Safety Roadhouse standing by itself alongside the bridge across the frozen entrance to Safety Sound. As I pull into the drifted parking lot alongside a handful of snowmachines I know this is the beginning of the end of the journey. Nome is barely 20 miles up the road and the weather is perfect. Besides, I've been listening to KNOM radio on my Walkman and I know we're expected.

The theme song of John Wayne's *North to Alaska* celebrated the gold "beneath that old white mountain just a little southeast of Nome." The mountain was really Cape Nome, between Safety Roadhouse and the city of Nome. A musk-ox herd forages atop the headland during the winter.

Lisa arrives in a few minutes; her mother, Barb, whom I've met before, has been waiting anxiously. When Lisa finishes in a few hours they will be the first mother and daughter to have completed the race. I'm glad to have been part of it. I throw my dogs some well-earned chunks of beef and head inside for a steaming bowl of chicken soup and hot coffee. Most drivers don't spend more than a minute or two here, but we're in no hurry. Nome isn't going anywhere. Besides, I've become so enmeshed with the dogs and the trail I want to enjoy every minute I have remaining.

When we leave an hour later Lisa and I agree she will go first down Front Street. For her it's a homecoming; for me it doesn't matter where I finish—just getting here has been my only goal. I take the lead as we head to Cape Nome; we'll swap when we get closer to town. Inevitably a couple of lines from the last verse of Hobo Jim's Iditarod anthem roll through my mind: "Just pulled out of Safety, on the trail all alone...." Maybe I don't fit his scenario exactly, what with Lisa on the road a half-mile behind, but it's close enough for me.

For the last few miles into Nome, the trail runs along the shore of the Bering Sea before climbing the seawall to Front Street.

Watching the dogs pulling smoothly and powerfully in front the sled, I almost wish we could go another few hundred miles. Unlike the front-runners who have no choice but to push their dogs, my guys are only now peaking. I'd give anything if I could start the race next year with these same dogs in exactly the condition they're in right now.

Now I understand how Ron Aldrich and Del Allison could run their teams on up to Barrow after they finished the Iditarod in 1979. For them it was just a continuation of the trail and I almost wish I could do something like it. Ron says he wants to run again next year for the big 25th Anniversary race and maybe we'll do just that.

As we climb around Cape Nome the wind starts to blow, as it always does here, but it's nothing we haven't seen before. I stop and wait for Lisa, who shortly pulls up. There's been some confusion about how the trail is marked through a construction project up ahead and we proceed carefully past a six-foot excavation in the middle of the road. The road is plowed beyond this point and we can't run on the icy gravel surface, so we look for alternate trails.

I work my way for a couple hundred yards up the shoulder to the point where the marked trail departs the road and heads down to the beach. When I look back I don't see any sign of Lisa. I take my team down the trail for a quarter mile, thinking she's taken a shortcut, but I can't see her headlight anywhere. I stop the team and walk back up to the road, where I hail a passing motorist to help me search in the 30-mile-an-hour wind and blowing snow.

The end of the trail is in sight at last at the far end of Front Street, Nome's main avenue. (This is the author's team at the finish of the 1997 race.)

Eventually I find tracks heading down to the beach; Lisa has obviously moved on ahead. A couple of miles on up the trail I catch her. Her headlight burned out as she skipped the gravel and headed for the beach, so she couldn't signal me. We've lost 45 minutes while I looked for her and she groped along the moonless trail. I loan her my spare light and we both get a good laugh. The trail god had to throw us one last curve ball to remind us not to get complacent.

For several miles we run within sight of the road, accompanied by a steady stream of cars. We're listening to KNOM on our Walkmen; the radio station has a spotter car out looking for us just like big-city stations have traffic reporters. We stick to our plan to have Lisa go in first, which means I have to periodically stop my by-now-faster team to let her pull ahead. When I'm running close behind her I also turn off my headlight to avoid distracting her dogs. This apparently causes no end of confusion to the watchers on the road, and the radio reporter never does figure out exactly who is who or where we are.

Finally we pull up a steep bank onto Front Street, where our police escort is waiting with lights flashing. The finish line is 10 blocks ahead. As we work up the legendary thoroughfare in a tight two-team convoy we're swamped with shouts and honking horns. I'm amazed at the number of people out here even though it's past midnight and we're not exactly Jeff and DeeDee.

As we near the arch I stop to let Lisa go the last couple of hundred yards by herself. After a minute or so I give Socks his final "Okay!" of the race and he charges up the last block in a blaze of speed I wish he'd shown back on the trail. As we pull into the chute Jack Niggemyer gives me a high-five and Bert and Bobby Lee and Joanne Potts and Lois Harter and Steve Adkins and most everyone else I've worked with on the race over the years are waiting under the arch. I only wish Ron could have been here, but he couldn't make it; I know he's here in spirit, though, and that's good enough.

Once we stop I run up and hug Socks. This has been his race at least as much as mine, and I don't know how I—or Lisa or Andy, for that matter—could have made it without him. Amid the shower of congratulations and hugs and handshakes (each of which reminds me my hand is still broken) and the traditional radio interview, I slowly start to register it's really over. I'm actually here under the arch after two interminable years. It's been a long wait, but it's been everything I'd hoped and a universe more besides.

As much as I'd like to stay here all night and celebrate, the accumulated fatigue of two weeks won't be denied and I almost nod off while I'm talking to someone. We have to get the dogs settled in the dog lot and then I'm going to go get something to eat. And then I'm going to go to sleep for the first time in a fortnight without having to worry about getting up in a few hours to get out of the checkpoint.

March 19—The Iditarod: Nome

After sleeping the sleep of the near-dead in a real bed in my hostess' house (her name is Holly Aldrich, but no relation to Ron, we've discovered) I get up to meet Andy. As I expected, once he got moving he made bullet-train time from Elim to White Mountain and on into Nome. He pulls in just before 10, in 49th place with red lantern in hand. Quite a crowd is waiting for him under the arch, including Slim and the trail sweeps, who have finally finished their own eventful trips from Anchorage.

With Andy safely home we can celebrate our collective victory, because Lisa and Andy and I have shared it in more ways than we ever anticipated. We each fought through our own problems and chased our own ghosts, but it took all of us to give each other the chance to do it.

Amazingly, we're the fastest tail-end in the history of the race: Andy's red-lantern time is 16 hours faster than the old record. Indeed, his trip of just under 16 days would

The last musher to make it to Nome always goes into the Iditarod record books as the winner of the fabled Red Lantern. The tail-end driver is given the symbolic lantern as he enters Front Street and carries it with him to the finish line. After he crosses under the burled arch at the finish, he extinguishes a similar lantern (called the Widow's Lamp) that has been burning under the arch for the duration of the race, signifying that the Iditarod is finally over.

have made him a contender little more than a decade ago.

After an afternoon to recuperate we assemble for the Red Lantern banquet. It's completely sold out, with at least 200 people jammed into the Nome race headquarters. Several of the back-of-the-packers who finished ahead of us didn't get to say much at the real banquet so they get their open mike tonight. It's about as relaxed a party as I can remember and everybody has plenty of tales from the trail.

When Lisa takes the stage, she mentions she promised Socks a steak if he got us through the blizzard outside Unalakleet. Then she pulls a choice sirloin out of a bag and her mother brings up Socks, who has been hiding under a table at the back of the room. To the cheers of the crowd our real hero calmly devours his just reward. It's only fitting: Socks gets his steak even before we do—and I fully intend to see he has a chance to earn lots more next year.

After the banquet I have a little time before Bert and I are to meet Lisa and her mother at the Board of Trade saloon for a quiet celebration. I wander the streets for awhile, the solid weight of my newly awarded finisher's belt buckle tugging at my pocket. The burled arch and the chute leading to the finish line have been taken down and Front Street has reverted to its workaday self. The long-promised storm is starting to make its move and the wind is beginning to whip through the streets; another day and we'd have been facing its wrath out by Topkok. But we're safe here in Nome; the storm can do its worst.

Without question these have been the most eventful two weeks of my life. I've ridden a physical and emotional roller coaster which soared to the summits and plunged to the depths and back again so many times, and

The author stands under the burled arch at the finish line in Nome after completing the Iditarod. The arch is moved from its normal resting spot in front of the Nome City Hall to the middle of Front Street for two weeks every year during the Iditarod. (Note the Widow's Lamp hanging from the right side of the crossbar.)

in such a short period, I still don't fully comprehend everything that's happened and maybe never will. Driving a dog team to Nome may be a mundane matter for the professionals, but the first time for me has been beyond words.

Preparing for the race and running it has changed my outlook on more things than I would have thought possible. My concept of time and space founded on years of flying and other motorized travel has been irrevocably altered. The world has become a startlingly large and three-dimensional place, full of alternate but perfectly valid realities. Having now actually traversed Alaska on the ground at a respectful pace, I have an appreciation for its vast size and many different faces I could have gained no other way.

And I have learned that even at the pace of the old sailing ships a huge world can be conquered with a little patience and determination. Indeed, my perspective of just about everything has been remolded over the past two years and fired in the furnace of the last two weeks. I know it's trite to say I'll probably never look at anything again the same way, but it's true. Most of all, I regret the race is actually over; part of me wants it to go on and on, to find more new trails to explore. But that will have to wait for the future.

I end up in the dog lot at the foot of Front Street. My guys seem to know I'm coming and are watching me as I walk up. I stand for a moment to admire them. We've learned volumes about each other over the past couple of weeks. I walk back to dignified old Buck, indestructible Rocky, ever-forgiving Yankee, half-goofy Bear, and moody Wild Thing and give them all a hug.

The huge dog lot at the west end of Front Street in Nome is the end of the trail for hundreds of weary dogs after their 1,200-mile treks from Anchorage. From here, teams are trucked to the airport for their rides home.

I continue along the line, thanking each one: dapper Kisser, one-eyed Steel, stalwart Pullman, still-playful Silvertip, and crazy little Maybelline, whose bouncy attitude and wraithlike appearance, I now know, conceal cast-iron toughness. I wish Lucky, Bea, Batman, Panda, and Diablo could be here, too; they did their best and deserve just as much.

My team has become more than a family to me. We've shared adventures I couldn't have imagined even a month ago. My dogs have shown everyone they can run the toughest race on earth. They have demonstrated incredible strength, indomitable courage, and total loyalty. They have done everything I've asked of them and more. I don't know of anything I can do to reward them sufficiently. This hasn't been my triumph, but theirs.

Finally I stop in front of Socks. He casually yawns, stretches, and puts on his best world-weary-traveler expression as if to say, "Been there, done that. So what else is new?" At the end of it all, it's the old master who brings me back down to earth. He's done this more times than I probably ever will and he's not swayed by anything we've been through. Indeed, it's as if he's reminding me we haven't really gone through anything worse than most of the mushers and teams that finally make it to Nome.

At that moment, gazing into Socks' wise eyes, all the abysmal trails, broken hands, sleepless nights, windswept tundra, freezing fingers, treacherous overflow, and endless little frustrations—all the things which drove me to distraction and led me to the brink of tossing everything away—are swept into the insignificance they so richly deserve. It really was fun. We've got to do this again!

I plop down beside Socks and we wrestle in the straw as he tries to lick my face. If anyone is watching at this late hour, I'm sure they think I'm quite mad. And you know, they just might be right.

Don Bowers and Socks.

Epilogue

Kim Hanson did indeed make it to Nome in the 1998 Iditarod, with Pullman leading the way up Front Street. Socks helped lead most of the way but Kim had to drop him at Elim because his age was finally starting to slow him down as the remainder of the team began the final push for Nome. However, the Iditarod Air Force gave him a free flight to Nome and the Big Dog Lot one more time, where he was waiting in Nome for Kim and his teammates. He is now a comfortably retired couch potato at Bert's house in Anchorage and is always glad to tell his tales of the trail to anyone who will toss him a dog biscuit.

Linda Joy finally made it to Nome in 1998—on her third try. It's hard to imagine anyone who worked harder for a ride up Front Street and a stop under the burled arch. I wasn't as fortunate in my own 1998 run. Maybelline injured her foot and my other main leader, Polar Bear (who went to Nome with Ron in 1994) developed a bad internal infection. Moreover, I was sick most of the time. Everything finally reached the breaking point and I finally had to scratch at Nulato. As it turned out, I had walking pneumonia and wasn't able to shake it for three miserable months.

For the 1999 Iditarod, I put together a very strong team designed specifically to get me to Nome no matter how badly I screwed up. Maybelline went again, along with Polar Bear and my new main leader, Cutter, whom I bought from John Barron in the summer of 1998. I even leased a backup leader, Harley, from Lynwood Fiedler. Behind them was a tough crew including Iditapups Bonnie, Clyde, and Squeaky. Iron Dog, from my 1997 team and arguably one of the best sled dogs I've ever seen, was the team's elder statesman at almost 9 years old.

The 1999 race turned out to be the hardest race I have ever run. Even Jeff King said it was the toughest he'd seen in more than a decade. We began with minus-100 chill factors heading up to Rainy Pass, and continued with open water and slick ice coming out of Rohn, followed by bitter 50-below temperatures that forced one musher to scratch at McGrath with severe frostbite. We ran into more 50- to 60-below cold on the way to Iditarod, and then punched through a storm on the way to Shageluk.

After a blizzard heading out of Kaltag, the temperature dropped to 50 below again at Old Woman. Then things really got interesting out on the coast, with howling ground blizzards and bone-numbing cold. Our small group of tail-enders got into a particularly bad storm on the way from Shaktoolik to Koyuk, with 60-mph winds directly in our teeth the whole way, accompanied by near-zero visibility out on the sea ice.

We had to rope teams together to keep them from wandering off the trail. It was the worst situation I've ever been in, and potentially lethal. But

The author's long-suffering volunteer handlers pose before the restart of the 1996 race. Left to right are Julie and Mike Pannone, Doug Grilliot, Don Bowers, Jeannette Keida, Lindsey Hanson, Kim Hanson, and Misty Hammond. Kim Hanson will be the youngest woman to run the Iditarod when she heads to Nome in 1998.

Dr. Jim Lanier, a pathologist from Anchorage and a seasoned Iditarod veteran, worked his leader flawlessly through the storm and led us all to safety. It took us 18 hours to go 45 miles.

The rest of the way to Nome was mostly through screaming wind and drifted trails, with rarely a sight of a trail marker. The Solomon blowhole was roaring full throttle when I got to it, as a sort of a final insult from the

Trail God. However, Cutter turned out to be a worthy successor to Socks, plowing through drifts and finding markers every bit as well as the Old Master. Maybelline did her usual bulletproof job, and Iditapups Squeaky and Clyde matured into solid Iditarod leaders.

By the time we got to Nome, all of us back of the packers and our dogs were more than ready for a rest. In spite of the sometimes unimaginable conditions I still ran my fastest race, finishing in 44th place in barely thirteen and a half days.

Old Iron Dog ran in wheel without a complaint every step of the way, pulling hard and even barking to go faster on the way up Front Street. In his own way, he was every bit Socks' equal. However, he was just too old to take the long way to Nome again and I decided to give him and seven other older dogs, including Pullman and Lucky and Bear and Ben and Maggie and May, to a friend in Fairbanks as a ready-to-go recreational team. At last report they are enjoying all the fun runs they want and are receiving more attention and affection than any fifty dogs. (And I still get to visit them whenever I want.) As happy as I am for them, it was hard to see them go, along with other older dogs I've given to friends over the past year. But it was the only fair thing to do. They still want to run and I've got to move on and bring in new dogs. I've got plenty of youngsters who deserve their chance, including four two-year-olds from Socks and Josephine, and three of Squeaky's grandkids (which makes them Socks' great-grandpups). And most recently, I finally got three fine pups from Maybelline, born last summer. Little Screamer, Taffy, and Earless may well get a chance to run to Nome with their mother in a couple of years.

I signed up for the 2000 Iditarod, but received an offer to go on the Serum Run with Colonel Norman Vaughan and a dozen other mushers instead. It's only 700 miles to Nome by the 1925 relay-team route, and the longest daily run is only 60 miles. Every night is spent in a village or cabin and there's plenty of time to meet people and look around. It's a chance to travel across Alaska by dog team in the grand old manner—and is a lot less expensive than the Iditarod. Besides, who could pass up the opportunity to go on an 18-day mushing adventure with a living legend?

I may or may not be able to put everything together for the Serum Run, but I do plan to be back in the 2001 Iditarod—and with a well trained, competitive team. I've finally got some good dogs and enough young ones coming up to keep the team sharp for the next five or six years. Now the team's limiting factor is me. There's no question the back of the pack is fun, but I want to see if I can move up a bit and maybe even break the top 20. And after that, well, there's always the Yukon Quest....

Appendix
Iditarod Background

Booms and Busts

Gold rushes were a major part of Alaska history beginning in the 1880s. Strikes near Juneau in 1880, Klondike in 1896, Nome in 1898, and Fairbanks in 1902 helped define Alaska's very nature and directly resulted in the founding of three of the state's largest cities (Fairbanks, Juneau, and Nome).

These bonanzas were only the best known of more than 30 serious gold rushes in Alaska from 1880 to 1914. In fact, the last full-scale, old-fashioned, frontier-style gold rush in the United States roared into life in 1909 at Iditarod, 275 air miles west of the future site of Anchorage and almost halfway to Nome. By the next year, Iditarod eclipsed Nome and Fairbanks to briefly become the largest city in Alaska with 10,000 inhabitants. It boasted several banks and hotels, electric power, telephones, and even a newspaper, all supplied by regular stern-wheeler service up the Innoko and Iditarod Rivers, tributaries of the Yukon.

Many gold districts in Alaska could be served by steamboats plying the many rivers lacing the Alaska interior. Nome, on the coast, had regular oceangoing steamship service. However, there was virtually no way to travel to any of these places when freeze-up stopped river and ocean traffic from October to May. By 1910, the need for year-round mail and freight service to miners in western Alaska led the Federal government to survey and construct a 900-mile winter trail from Seward to Nome for use by dog sled teams.

The original Iditarod Trail started at Seward, or more properly, about 50 miles north at the end of the under-construction Alaska Central Railroad, which later became the Alaska Railroad. From the end of track, the trail wound along Turnagain Arm through what is now Girdwood, over Crow Pass, and down the uninhabited Eagle River Valley to Knik Arm and the tiny trading post of Knik, largest settlement on Upper Cook Inlet until the railroad town of Anchorage was founded in 1915. The Iditarod Trail never actually passed through Anchorage, since the beginning of the trail was moved to Knik when Alaska Railroad reached the area.

From Knik, the trail arrowed west through the wooded valleys of the Susitna and Yentna Rivers and climbed tortuously over Rainy Pass through the massive Alaska Range. West of the Range, the trail drifted across the vast Kuskokwim Valley to the hills west of McGrath and the town of Takotna, supply point for the Innoko River mining district and its chief settlement of Ophir, another classic boom town already ebbing from its glory days of 1907.

From Takotna, the trail rolled southwest through the ridge-and-valley country of the Kuskokwim Mountains to the bustling towns of Flat and Iditarod. Swinging northwest from Iditarod, the trail pushed across the trackless swampy wilderness of the lower Innoko River valley to the mile-wide, frozen expanse of the Yukon River and the Koyukon Athabaskan village of Kaltag. At Kaltag, the trail angled back southwest along the 90-mile Kaltag Portage, known for centuries to Eskimos and Indians as a shortcut through the low coastal mountains to Norton Sound and the Bering Sea. The western end of the portage was anchored by the ancient Yup'ik Eskimo village of Unalakleet, whose name means "place where the east wind blows."

From Unalakleet, the trail swept north and then west around the rugged shore of the Seward Peninsula, passing old Inupiat villages with names like Shaktoolik, Elim, and Golovin. Fifty miles before Nome, the trail dropped down onto the beaches which had caused the rush to Nome a decade before. After almost 1,000 miles, the Iditarod Trail opened onto Front Street in Nome, the site of northern North America's most notorious saloon row, whose proprietors at one time included such notables as Wyatt Earp.

Travelers on the Iditarod ranged from individuals with light sleds and a handful of dogs to freight drivers with a score of strong huskies pulling as many as three sleds laden with a ton or more of everything from gold dust to passengers. All of these mushers followed in the ancient tradition of Alaska Natives, who mastered the fine art of using dogs for winter transportation many centuries ago.

When Russians and eventually Americans arrived in the North

Country, they quickly discovered dog teams were the only way to reliably move across long distances in Alaska when rivers were frozen. Dogs have always been ideally suited for winter travel for a number of reasons, not the least of which is that pound for pound, the sled dog is the most powerful draft animal on earth.

In fact, the old freight mushers calculated their cargos based on 150 pounds per dog, or well over a ton for a team of 16 or 20. As a matter of interest, single dogs have pulled more than half a ton in the canine equivalent of a tractor pull. As late as the 1960s, Yup'ik Eskimos of Nelson Island moved much of their town—including entire houses—to a new site two dozen miles away with 100-dog teams.

The boom town of Iditarod was the largest in Alaska in 1910, with more than 10,000 people. It has been deserted for half a century except for the occasional trapper and, more recently, the biennial influx of mushers and race support people. Today only a few old buildings remain standing.

Dogs can easily keep up with horses over the long haul; even the old freight teams could average several miles an hour, and lighter teams could go considerably faster. Dogs require virtually no shelter and can easily withstand conditions which would kill horses or oxen. Even better, dogs can be fed from the land with moose, fish, or caribou in winter, while horses require expensive hay or grain. Perhaps most important, heavy draft animals simply cannot use the snow packed winter trails which lace much of the north country.

Early mushers used a mixture of breeds. Over the centuries, different Native peoples had bred dogs for their particular needs. For instance, the Malemiut Inupiat people of the Seward Peninsula developed a particularly hardy sled dog which today bears their name: the Malamute. The teams on the Iditarod Trail included everything from Native working dogs such as Malamutes and Siberian huskies to various domestic breeds imported from the Lower 48. Some mushers even used wolves—some full-blooded but mostly mixes—although these eventually fell into disfavor as more suitable dogs became available.

By 1900, dog teams were as common in Alaska as cars, ATVs, and snowmachines are today. Almost every winter photograph of early Alaska includes a dog team of some kind. These ranged from small family work teams to massive freight teams used for long-distance movement of supplies, mail, and even passengers. The Iditarod Trail and many other winter trails around Alaska (such as the famous Yukon Mail Trail which ran the length of its namesake river) were built and maintained primarily for the freight and mail mushers, who occupy a special place in Alaska history. They manned Alaska's winter lifelines in the days before airplanes and modern communications.

Freight drivers would start out from Knik with 20 or more dogs pulling up to three sleds laden with food and gear for the isolated mines and villages as soon as the river crossings were frozen. Traffic was heavy. In November of 1911, for example, 120 teams headed west across the Alaska Range on the Iditarod, and over an average winter many hundreds of teams would travel part or all of the trail.

Each evening the drivers would stop at roadhouses located about a day's travel apart. Some roadhouses were in villages and towns, but some, such as Mountain Climber Roadhouse, Rohn Roadhouse, and Pioneer Roadhouse, all located on the lonely trail across the forbidding Alaska Range, were isolated way stations not much different from Old West stage stops of half a century before. Mushers could get a meal (two dollars) and a warm bed (two dollars more), along with food for their dogs and a place to wait out the storms which periodically swept the trail.

The elite of the Iditarod, and throughout Alaska, were the mail drivers. With their large, well-trained teams, they operated on rigid schedules in all kinds of weather and were often trailbreakers for other travelers. They limited their loads to 50 pounds per dog and tried to make at least 25 miles per day regardless of conditions. They were accorded great respect and always got the best food and accommodations wherever they stopped.

A trip to Nome could take three weeks or more. Mostly the teams hauled cargo, but passengers were sometimes carried in the long sleds. (Most people who did not plan to winter over probably had taken the last steamboat out in the fall when "termination dust" coated the mountaintops.) Dog teams sometimes hauled out the season's gold on the return trip to Knik. According to Ron Wendt in *Hatcher Pass Gold*, 2,600 pounds of gold arrived at Knik on December 10, 1911, hauled by four teams. In December of 1916, no less than 3,400 pounds of the precious metal came out behind 46 dogs.

The Iditarod Trail was used every winter through the World War I era and well into the 1930s, with parts of it being used as late as World War II. By the mid-1930s, Alaska had more than 7,000 miles of maintained winter trails, mainly for dog teams, stretching from the Canadian border to the Bering Sea and from the Gulf of Alaska to the Arctic Ocean. Even as the Pennsylvania Turnpike and the autobahns were being built elsewhere in the world, Alaska's extensive winter trail system was still in daily use.

The inevitable end for the Iditarod and other long-distance winter sled trails in Alaska, though, was the airplane. In the late 1920s and 1930s, air freight became economically feasible with the advent of reliable engines and sturdy, easily maintained airplanes capable of using short bush airstrips and sandbars. At the same time, the gold mining which had provided much of the freight for the dog teams dwindled as strikes played out; Iditarod itself was a ghost town by end of the 1930s.

Even as the freight traffic waned, mail continued to use sled trails. However, the airplane soon began to usurp this hallowed domain of the dog team as well. The first airmail in Alaska was flown from Fairbanks to McGrath in early 1924 by legendary aviator Carl Ben Eielson. The first regular air mail contract was given to Harold Gillam in 1931. By 1938, airplanes had won most of the long-haul mail contracts in the territory.

Once the mail teams vanished, the roadhouses began to disappear and thousands of miles of trails that had so admirably served the territory for half a century were abandoned. Alaska went directly from the steamboat and the dog sled to the airplane, without the road-and railroad-building era which led to the dense road and rail networks of the Lower 48.

But the dog teams had one last taste of glory in early 1925 when a diphtheria outbreak threatened isolated, icebound Nome. The nearest serum was in Anchorage, and the first thought was to fly it to Nome. However, the only pilot in the Territory considered capable of braving the unpredictable weather was Eielson, who was on a trip in the Lower 48 and was not available.

Instead, a Pony Express-type relay of dog teams was quickly organized. The serum was loaded on the newly completed Alaska Railroad and rushed to Nenana, where the first musher took it westward down the frozen Tanana River to the Yukon. Every village along the route offered its best team and driver for its leg to speed the serum toward Nome. The critical leg across the treacherous Norton Sound ice from Shaktoolik to Golovin was taken by Leonhard Seppala, the territory's premier musher, and his lead dog Togo. Gunnar Kaasen drove the final two legs into Nome behind his leader Balto through a blizzard hurling 80 mile-per-hour winds.

The serum arrived in time to prevent an epidemic and save hundreds of lives. The 20 mushers and their teams had covered almost 700 miles in little more than 127 hours (about six days) in temperatures which rarely rose above 40 below zero and winds which were sometimes strong enough to blow over dogs and sleds. The serum run gained worldwide press coverage and the mushers received special gold medals from Congress. A statue of Balto, Kaasen's heroic lead dog (who actually belonged to Seppala) was erected a year later in New York's Central Park, where it still stands.

But the day of the dog team as an integral part of Alaska's long-range transportation system was almost over. The bush pilots were in the ascendant, learning how to fly the air routes now taken for granted by Alaskan aviators. Within a decade of the serum run, pioneer flyers like Noel Wien, Mudhole Smith, and Bob Reeve had fashioned the foundation of a far-flung network which today serves nearly as many scheduled destinations as all Lower-48 airlines together.

Even after airplanes took over the territory's long-haul work, one remarkable dog-team trip captured national attention, although it is surprisingly little remembered today. In his book, *Northwest Epic*, about the building of the Alaska Highway, historian Heath Twichell relates how early proponents of a road link from Alaska to the Lower-48 decided to help a sourdough gold miner named Slim Williams run his dog team down the proposed highway route. Williams left Copper Center in November of 1932 with a team of eight wolf hybrids, intending to mush all the way to the Chicago World's Fair.

Had his journey been scripted by Hollywood it could not have been more incredible. He nearly drowned in half-frozen rivers and lakes. One of his dogs was killed by wolves in remote northern British Columbia. He was forced to negotiate trackless mountain terrain where no one had ever taken a dog team. He had to put wheels on his sled when he returned to the road system in southern Canada and ran out of snow. And to keep his dogs from overheating he ended up running mostly at night as he crept along the highways of the Great Plains.

Williams gained publicity with every mile and he and his team were treated royally by every town they passed through. By the time he finally mushed his dogs into Chicago in September of 1933 he was a national hero, at a time when the Great Depression was deepening and real heroes were few and far between. After a month and a half in the limelight representing Alaska at the World's Fair, he drove his team on to Washington, D.C., where he was invited to dinner with President and Mrs. Roosevelt.

However, the popularity of Williams and his dogs could not stop the decline of long-distance dog mushing, although dog teams continued to be used for local transportation, mail delivery, and day-to-day work in Native villages and remote areas. Even the little-publicized but vital roles played by mushers and their teams in World War II in Alaska were not enough to arrest the inexorable decline of long-haul dogs.

After the war, short-haul freight and work teams were still common in many areas of Alaska. Even as President Kennedy announced the United States would put a man on the moon, the mail was still being delivered by dog sled in a few isolated parts of the new state. During the 1960s, however, it was not space travel but the advent of the "iron dog" (or snowmachine, as it's called in Alaska) which resulted in mass abandonment of dog teams and the loss of much mushing lore.

The Iditarod Trail Sled Dog Race

To help save some of Alaska's fast-vanishing mushing heritage, Dorothy Page, a planner for the 1967 Alaska Centennial celebration, conceived of the idea of a dog race over the Iditarod Trail, which by then had been disused for many years. Local mushers' groups, with the leadership of Joe Redington, Sr., and retired Air Force Col. Norman Vaughan, threw themselves into the project. Col. Vaughan was in charge of Admiral Byrd's dog teams on Byrd's famous 1928-1930 Antarctic expedition, on which Byrd made the first flight over the South Pole. Vaughan later used dogs for search and rescue work in Alaska and Greenland during World War II.

With much volunteer labor (the start of a fundamental Iditarod tradition) the first part of the trail was cleared and short races over the Susitna Valley portion north of Anchorage were held in 1967 and 1969. Finally in 1973, with the Army helping clear portions of the trail not already in use as winter snowmachine trails, and with the support of the Nome Kennel Club (Alaska's earliest sled-dog racing association, founded in 1907) the race went all the way to Nome for the first time. The winner, Dick Wilmarth, took almost three weeks to finish; the last musher spent more than a month on the trail.

While the race officially commemorates the 1925 Serum Run to Nome, it is really a reconstruction of the freight route to Nome. The mushers travel from checkpoint to checkpoint much as the freight mushers did 80 years ago, and even carry a packet of mail in honor of the intrepid mail drivers. However, modern mushers like Doug Swingley, Martin Buser, Jeff King, Susan Butcher, and Rick Swenson move at a pace which would have been incomprehensible to their old-time counterparts, making the trip to Nome in under 10 days.

Since 1973, the race has persevered despite financial ups and downs, and is now famous enough to allow the best mushers to receive tens of thousands of dollars a year from corporate sponsors. Dog mushing has recovered to become a north-country mania in winter, and a few people now make comfortable livings from their sled-dog kennels. Dog mushing has even been officially designated as Alaska's state sport.

Alaska is the world mecca for sled dog racing, which has developed into a popular winter sport in the Lower 48, Canada, Europe, and even Russia. (There are even mushing clubs in Australia and South America.) Mushers from more than a dozen foreign countries have run the Iditarod, and Alaskan mushers routinely travel Outside to races such as the John Beargrease in Minnesota, the Big Sky in Montana, and the UP200 in Michigan. Even the Winter Olympics are considering adding sled dog racing as an event, and several sled dog races were held in Norway in conjunction with the 1994 games.

While the Iditarod has become by far Alaska's best-known sporting event, there are a dozen other major long-distance races around the state every winter, such as the grueling 1,000-mile Yukon Quest, the Kobuk 440, the Kusko 300, the Klondike 300, and the Copper Basin 300. And, there are many short-distance (or sprint) races run as well, including the prestigious North American in Fairbanks and Fur Rendezvous in Anchorage. In a revival of tradition, entire villages and towns in rural Alaska become swept away in the frenzy of sled dog racing, and sled dogs are once again common in many rural areas where they were eclipsed by "iron dogs" only a few decades ago.

Although the Iditarod's fame causes many people to think of the Iditarod Trail when they think of traveling to Nome, the trail is actually impassable during spring, summer, and fall. Moreover, its routing is far from a direct course, taking more than 1,150 miles to cover the 600 or so airline miles from Anchorage to Nome, largely thanks to the race committee's massaging of the race route to pass through a number of towns and villages missed by the original trail. Additionally, the race has adopted a northern route for even-numbered years to include more villages along the Yukon.

Checkpoints for the first half of the current race are Anchorage, Eagle River, Wasilla, Knik, Yentna Station, Skwentna, Finger Lake, Rainy Pass Lodge (Puntilla Lake), Rohn Roadhouse, Nikolai, McGrath, Takotna, and Ophir. In odd-numbered years, the middle part of the race loosely follows the original trail, from Ophir through Iditarod to Shageluk and then Anvik on the Yukon, then up the mighty river to Grayling, Eagle Island, and Kaltag. In even years, the trail swings north from Ophir down the Innoko to Cripple, then northeast to the Yukon at Ruby (heart of another old mining district), and then down the river to Galena, Nulato, and Kaltag.

Shageluk, on the southern route of the Iditarod, is the chief village of the Ingalik people; its name means "place of the dog people." It is typical of many isolated, mostly Native villages in the Interior of Alaska.

From Kaltag, the home stretch is the same every year: Unalakleet, Shaktoolik, Koyuk, Elim, Golovin, White Mountain, Safety Roadhouse, and Nome. True to their predecessors, the mushers run up Front Street past the still-notorious saloons to the burled arch. Every team's arrival is heralded by the city's fire siren and each driver is greeted by a crowd lining the "chute," no matter the time of day or night, or if he or she is first or fifty-first across the line.

The Drivers and Their Dream Machines

On the first Saturday in March, anywhere from 50 to 80 mushers leave the starting gate on Fourth Avenue in Anchorage. Of these, at least half have no real hope of winning or even seriously competing: their main goal is simply to finish in the best time they can—and in some cases, just to finish. Crossing under the famous burled arch at the finish line in Nome with their dogs is more than victory enough.

Running the Iditarod is a grueling test of dogs and drivers which can last as long as three weeks and can involve head-on encounters with some of the most forbidding weather and terrain on earth. Nevertheless, any musher worth his (or her) salt wants to run the Iditarod some day, just as runners want to do the Boston Marathon, even if there is no chance of winning.

Drivers who run the race cover a wide spectrum. Mushers have included teenagers and octogenarians, well-to-do adventurers and backwoods trappers, executives and laborers, teachers and students, storekeepers and factory owners, lawyers and Maytag repairmen. A few can be considered professional dog mushers who make their livings from their dogs, while most are part-timers who must hold down a "regular" job to keep their teams afloat.

But the most striking feature of the Iditarod is that everyone competes equally: men and women, young and old, amateur and professional—there are no separate men's or women's divisions, nor is there a senior class or a special amateur bracket. About 20% of mushers are female, and women have won the race five times (all within the past 12 years). The top 20 finishers in every race routinely include several women. Age is no barrier, either: most Iditarod winners are older than 30 and two mushers have finished the race at 80 or more years of age.

Of course, not everyone completes the trip: on average, one of every five mushers will scratch somewhere along the trail. Not surprisingly, the Iditarod Official Finishers Club is one of the most exclusive in the world, with under 500 members. (More people have climbed Mount Everest than have finished the Iditarod.)

Because of its difficulty, the Iditarod places strict qualifying restrictions on people who would take the long road to Nome. Naturally, anyone who has previously finished the race is eligible to sign up. Rookies, however, must finish one or two approved mid-distance races totaling at least 500 miles within the previous two years. (The term "rookie" can be misleading: some so-called rookies have finished or even won major races such as the Yukon Quest; they have little difficulty qualifying for the Iditarod.)

Training for the race usually begins in summer of the preceding year, when dogs are hooked up to all-terrain vehicles (ATVs) for short runs of three miles or so. These four-wheeler runs may lengthen to 10 or 15 miles by the time snow falls in mid-October. Once sleds are hooked up (which pull much more easily than the ATVs), the runs rapidly increase to 30 and 40 miles; some mushers will have their teams routinely making 50-mile runs by Christmas.

The first "mid-distance" races (meaning anything between 200 and

500 miles in length) are in late December and early January. Most Iditarod mushers will try to run their teams in at least a couple of these races for the good training; some better drivers, of course, also have an eye toward prize money. By the time the Iditarod rolls around in March, most of the dogs will have 1,500 miles or even more behind them. Since the training is usually done with smaller teams, mushers themselves may have more than 2,500 miles on the runners.

The basic setup of a dog team is fairly simple. Long-distance racing sleds weigh no more 50 pounds and can be built of traditional materials such as birch or ash, or of modern lightweight plastics and composites. The eight-to nine-foot-long runners are built to accommodate special plastic bottoms which can be slipped off and quickly replaced when they wear out. The musher stands on the rear part of the runners, behind the basket (or body) of the sled.

The rear part of the sled basket is the handlebar, which is the driver's only hold on the sled—and on the team. Some mushers attach themselves to their sleds in case they inadvertently depart for some reason. (Losing a team is a major sin for a musher—and additionally usually makes for a long, cold, embarrassing walk.)

In the sled bag is an assortment of items. Mandatory gear for the Iditarod (and most other races) includes basic survival gear: snowshoes, an ax, an arctic-quality sleeping bag, at least two pounds of food and two sets of booties for every dog, and an alcohol stove with a three-or-four-gallon pot (for melting snow and making hot water for dog food).

Mushers will also include warm clothing items (temperatures can range from 40 above to 60 below), food for themselves, spare lines and snaps, and a small tool kit. A Thermos of drinking water is critical: dehydration is a major threat in the cold, dry climate. Most drivers will also include a camera and a Walkman with their favorite cassettes to help fight the interminable hours of boredom on the long, wide-open stretches of the trail.

Dogs are hooked up in pairs on either side of a central gangline of heavy braided rope with a cable core, which in turn is attached to the sled bridle with carabiners. Gangline is made in two-dog sections with loops on the ends; the loops allow the sections to be linked together to handle as many dogs as are required. A 16-dog team stretches 70 to 80 feet from the leader's nose to the musher on the back on the sled—as long as a highway 18-wheeler.

A stout tugline connects the rear of each dog's harness to the gangline. Each dog also has a neckline hooked to its collar to keep it from straying too far away from the gangline. The thin neckline is designed to break if the dog should get wrapped around a tree or other obstacle which might cause choking.

On very cold days or on rough trails, the dogs will usually wear booties of tough fabric to protect their feet. Thin-coated dogs may also be fitted with special warming blankets. Sled dogs are never muzzled and are free to jump back and forth across the gangline as the sled cuts across sharp bends.

Each Iditarod team is limited to 16 dogs, of which at least five must be on the gangline at the finish. This constitutes an incredibly powerful pulling machine, fully capable of dragging a pickup truck with its brakes set on packed snow. The musher's only real control of this juggernaut is voice commands to the lead dogs (the drag brake on the sled is often only marginally effective). This cleverly takes advantage of the dogs' wolf heritage: a dog team is basically a pack, and a pack always follows the leader, who in turn follows the commands of the driver.

Most mushers run a pair of leaders up front (one of which is usually primary), while a few run a solo leader. Iditarod mushers will include as many leaders as possible in their teams, rotating them to take advantage of each dog's particular strengths as the trail conditions vary. Regardless how many leaders are in the team, the "pack" will always follow the dog(s) in the actual lead position.

Lead dogs (like all good sled dogs, for that matter) are superbly bred and trained, and tend to be smarter than average. Some dogs will run in lead but don't know commands very well; they are sometimes called "trail leaders" and can be very important to help set a team's speed. Other leaders are especially good at following commands under all conditions; they are called "command leaders" and are very valuable in bad weather and on tight or confusing trails.

Usually a trail leader will be paired with a command leader, although trail leaders can run by themselves quite satisfactorily in many cases. The basic commands for the leaders are "Gee" (turn right), "Haw" (turn left), "On by" (pass or go straight) and "Whoa." The usual command to start the team is "Hike" or "Okay." Only Hollywood believes dog drivers shout "Mush!" at their dogs. ("Mush" is from the French "marchon," which means to move.)

The dogs just behind the leaders are called the swing dogs; they are often leaders in their own right. Just in front of the sled are the wheel dogs; they are very important to help guide the sled through turns. The other dogs are team dogs, although most of them can handle swing or wheel or even lead when needed. Indeed, most Iditarod mushers try to load their team with as many leaders as they can.

There is no special type of dog used on the Iditarod. Some mushers run specific AKC-recognized breeds such as Malamutes and Siberians, but most sled dogs are called by the generic term "Alaska husky," which usually means any critter with four legs and a tail capable of pulling a sled.

Over the years, mushers have mixed all sorts of breeds trying to find the perfect sled dog; some have been quite successful. When referring to

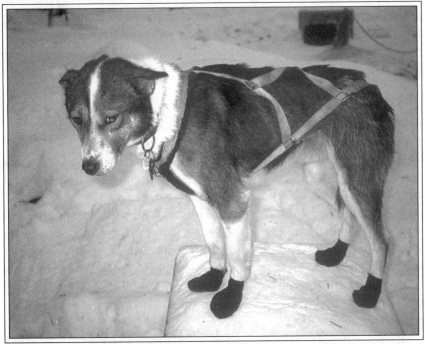

The harness is an all-important item of gear. It must fit properly and allow the dog to run comfortably while still pulling smoothly. On most races, including the Iditarod, dogs usually wear their harnesses from start to finish.

sled dogs, most mushers don't talk about what breed they are, but from whose kennel and what lineage they descend, such as "That's a Buser dog," or "This one's a Victor grandson." The average Iditarod sled dog is basically a mutt—albeit a carefully bred and highly prized one.

The chief distinguishing characteristics of a good long-distance sled dog are extreme endurance and almost unbelievable aerobic efficiency. Studies have shown the so-called Alaskan husky to be among Nature's most extraordinary athletes. Long-haul sled dogs can directly metabolize fat and sometimes use 10,000 calories a day on extended races. They are quite literally born and bred for the trail, and can travel for more than 100 miles nonstop at better than 10 miles an hour if conditions are right—and do it again and again as long as they get sufficient rest and food.

The dogs can easily outlast their human drivers and routinely do so on long races. Fortunately, a good team can run virtually on autopilot once underway, almost always choosing the correct trail. Indeed, the musher's job on long runs often involves long hours of merely monitoring the team's progress and making commands only when needed—and perhaps grabbing a short nap here and there on open stretches. Regardless, there is usually plenty of time for the driver to enjoy the scenery and appreciate the smooth workings of the finely tuned living machine that is an Iditarod dog team.

The Race Behind the Race

Although the Iditarod Trail Sled Dog Race is now incorporated, it's a nonprofit organization (in more ways than one) and still relies on volunteers and donations to make it work. It has only a tiny permanent staff. In an average year, it takes a multi-million-dollar budget and a couple of thousand volunteers to stage the race.

When considering the scope of the Iditarod and what's required to put it on, it's important to remember there are no roads or railroads west of the Anchorage-Fairbanks "railbelt," and the only way to get to Nome in winter is by airplane or snowmachine—or dog sled. Because of this, the race logistics effort, including grooming the trail and handling the myriad of details in Anchorage and all of the enroute towns and villages, is similar to a major military operation.

It's also crucial to keep in mind a central premise of the race: mushers must generally be on their own for the trip to Nome. They must feed and care for their own dogs, and all dogs must be kept and fed in a common area at each checkpoint. They cannot add or replace dogs and must generally rely on what they have carried with them or sent ahead—just as in the old days when they had to rely on whatever was available at the roadhouses and villages. Mushers can help each other, of course, and often do on the trail, but they cannot otherwise receive outside assistance.

Meals are usually available for the drivers at the checkpoints, including some notably sumptuous spreads provided by certain towns. Mushers are free to visit friends and even grab a beverage or a shower if they can find one and time permits. If necessary, they can even buy supplies in local stores or repair their sleds with locally available materials and tools. The goal is to make the race as much an individual effort as possible—within reason.

While the enroute towns and villages provide some support, the vast bulk of food and other items used by the teams and the volunteers must be shipped from Anchorage before the race. Every musher must provide a specified amount of food for his or her dogs at 20-odd checkpoints along the route (usually a total of about a ton or so). Each must also carry a required amount of equipment in the sled at all times, much of which is survival gear because the mushers are completely on their own between checkpoints, some of which are more than 90 miles apart.

After climbing the seawall from the beach, teams must thread their way along Nome's Front Street. Sometimes the snow has melted from the roadway and the dogs must run on the sidewalk.

Each driver's food and supplies for the checkpoints are shipped out of Anchorage by the race organization so as to be in place when the teams arrive. This provides the equivalent of an old-time network of roadhouses along the trail. A typical musher's "food drop" shipment includes several 50-pound sacks for each checkpoint; the color-coded bags contain frozen dog food, "people food," booties, spare lines and snaps, batteries, and other miscellaneous items necessary for what is, in effect, a major wilderness expedition.

Additionally, the race sends several dozen bales of straw to every stop along the route, plus food and equipment for the volunteers ranging from food to tents to fuel. For a field of 75 mushers, 100 or so on-the-trail volunteers, and maybe 1,200 dogs, the total can be more than 200,000 pounds.

Getting this mountain of goodies out to the checkpoints is a story all by itself. A few of the checkpoints are good-sized towns (good-sized for Alaska, anyway) with major airports; some are Native villages with small airports; a couple are ghost towns; several are conveniently located frozen lakes with a lodge or cabin; and some are just wide stretches of snow-covered river in the middle of nowhere with nobody around for miles. The resulting delivery system is truly Alaskan and definitely unique.

First, all but about a half-dozen checkpoints have regular mail air-freight service, thanks to the U.S. Postal Service. The race organization ships truckloads of mailable supplies to every checkpoint with a zip code west of the Alaska Range. All told, it's cheap to use the U.S. Mail to ship goods to the Bush, thanks to the subsidies given to Alaskan air carriers. The system isn't very cost-effective for the taxpayer, but without it many Alaska Bush communities would have no air service at all.

The main intake point for this continuous flood of packages is the mammoth Anchorage International Airport Post Office, which is open 24 hours a day, 365 days a year. It's worth a visit all by itself to watch people carting in things like refrigerators and engine blocks to ship to some remote Bush village. One can only wonder what Carl Ben Eielson and other early airmail pilots have thought if they knew where their pioneering efforts would lead.

For checkpoints without mail service, a slightly different method is used. Some checkpoints (McGrath, Unalakleet, Nome, and also Galena in even-numbered years) have major airports with regular passenger and air cargo service. The bundles for the boonies are mailed to the nearest of these "hubs" for onward shipment. Also, items which can't be shipped through the mails (such as big disassembled tents, perishable vet supplies, and 30-odd cases of Heet to every checkpoint for use in mushers' alcohol cook stoves) are airfreighted to the hubs.

From these staging points, everything is entrusted to the "Iditarod Air Force" for movement to the outlying checkpoints. The IAF consists of volunteer pilots using their own planes, some on skis, some on wheels, some on both; the race committee pays for (or arranges donations of) gas, oil, and insurance, and provides food and warm places to throw a sleeping bag at night. This is far cheaper than an equivalent amount of charter airlift (estimated at more than a quarter of a million dollars), which the always strained race budget cannot afford.

Flying for the race can be a lot of fun, but it is even more work—and is sometimes dangerous because of the places and conditions which are an inherent part of the race. In the history of the IAF and its tens of thousands of hours in the air, a few airplanes have been damaged or lost, but no IAF pilots or passengers have ever been seriously injured—which is just short of amazing, considering the abysmal conditions which often prevail. In any case, the informal selection process usually limits the IAF to experienced Alaskan pilots.

Some of the loads in IAF planes run to the truly eclectic: everything from trail marking stakes to snowmachine fuel to tent stoves and the tents they go in. Sometimes this even includes the proverbial kitchen sink (in the form of portable camp kitchens). Packs and sleeping bags

An army of airline kennels holds dropped dogs waiting at Galena for an airplane ride back to Anchorage. Dogs with serious problems are given special flights directly to veterinary hospitals in Anchorage as quickly as possible.

stuffed to the ceiling and dogs on passengers' laps aren't uncommon (and these aren't even the really challenging loads!).

Canines make particularly interesting passengers. A Cessna 185 or 206 with the seats removed can hold 18 or even 20 dogs, and race pilots have developed unique tricks and techniques to ensure harmony during flights which could otherwise be, well, eventful.

One ubiquitous commodity in IAF planes is dog food. The dogs dine like kings on the race, wolfing down 5,000 to 10,000 calories each day. Their food includes lots of protein, fat, and other high-energy stuff. Some mushers make their own concoctions from ingredients like fish, moose, caribou, and seal meat. (One musher from the Bering Sea coast likes to stuff seal carcasses in his bags—skin, hair, flippers, and all—because that's what his dogs normally eat.)

Fortunately, the "dog food" is stored outside and is normally frozen solid. Now and again, however, a harried IAF pilot forgets what he's hauling and turns up the cabin heat, resulting in a near in-flight emergency as acrid, eye-watering fumes from fish or seal oil waft forward from the thawing bags. (Yes, you can fly with your window open at 20 below zero if you have to.)

At each checkpoint along the trail, there are numerous race personnel with specific functions. The first person the musher sees on pulling into a checkpoint will usually be the checker, often a local resident who is a musher himself. The checker will record the official times and count the dogs, and may formally inventory the sled for the required gear. The checker often has one or more assistants who help him keep track of the official arrival and departure times for each team, and make sure each musher's pre-positioned food and supplies are readily available.

A musher is automatically disqualified if he or she does not physically have every dog that left the previous checkpoint. If a dog becomes tired, sick, injured, or worse, it must be still be carried to the next checkpoint, which will usually be manned by at least three veterinarians (also volunteers, from the International Sled Dog Veterinary Medicine Association). Every dog on every team is given a quick exam at every checkpoint.

The first concern is for the dogs. If a vet believes a dog is not fit to go on, or if the musher does not want to continue with a dog, it is dropped. The vet can also treat a dog on the spot and let it continue the race, if appropriate. Dogs dropped at outlying checkpoints are cared for by the vets until they can be flown by the IAF back to a hub, from which they are returned to Anchorage on donated air cargo runs.

"Communicators" (amateur radio operators) are at the checkpoints; they run the race communications net using radios, telephones, or even fax machines. Operating at some locations in tents with generators and batteries, the hams pass arrival and departure times, relay logistics information along the trail, and handle personal messages. The communicators have saved lives on the trail by calling in emergency airlift to mushers—and dogs—who have had serious accidents or medical problems.

Logistics staffs are located at the major hubs (Anchorage, McGrath, Unalakleet, Galena, and Nome). These can include half a dozen people, ranging from a logistics coordinator to dog handlers. The race pilots also base out of these hubs, which provide fuel, communications, and a safe place to tie down airplanes in the face of rapidly changing weather.

A staff of race judges, headed by the race marshal, works the entire trail. These are selected mushers who have previously run the Iditarod. They decide questions of race rules and conduct and can impose a broad range of penalties, including disqualification if necessary.

A dropped dog waits for a plane ride home. Tired, sick, injured, or unneeded dogs can be dropped at Iditarod checkpoints. They will be cared for by race vets and handlers until they return to Anchorage.

There is also an overall race manager, who is the single person most responsible for the staging of the race; he is selected a year ahead of time and becomes one of the tiny cadre of full-time race employees. During the race, he and the race marshal usually have dedicated IAF airplanes to move them wherever they need to go along the trail.

A highly select team of several volunteer trailbreakers gets one of the more enviable jobs of the entire race: riding high powered snowmachines from Anchorage to Nome at race expense. While some parts of the trail are routinely used for village-to-village snowmachine traffic during winter, many other segments must be groomed for the race or even built from scratch. Mushers could break the trail if required (and must sometimes do so in any case), but the lead mushers would be penalized for it by wearing out their teams. To keep it all fair, and to add to the safety margin, the race organization breaks and marks the trail.

The trailbreakers use special long-track snowmachines towing big freight sleds to pack the trail and to carry trail-marking supplies (usually four-foot wooden stakes with reflective tape which the mushers can see at night with their headlamps). On occasion, they also must build temporary bridges over open streams and clear brush and trees.

They try to stay no more than six hours or so ahead of the lead teams; any farther ahead and the wind could drift the trail shut behind them. On the other hand, they can't drop so far back they hinder the mushers, although weather sometimes gets so bad trailbreakers and mushers alike must hole up and wait it out. A team of trail sweeps brings up the rear of the race, picking up trash and dropped equipment and often shepherding the "red lantern" (last-place) musher along the trail.

At the Anchorage end of the race, a volunteer staff hundreds strong does things like staging various pre-race banquets and social events, dealing with the media, sorting mushers' food for shipment, picking up and caring for dropped dogs returned from the checkpoints, manning public information booths and hotlines, operating concession stands and souvenir shops, purchasing supplies, soliciting donations, coordinating with sponsors, working with city and state agencies, running a taxi service for race personnel, acting as trail guards for sections of trail in populated areas, and dozens of other functions associated with a major sporting event.

At Nome, a large staff of volunteers does all of the million and one things needed to bring the race to an orderly and enjoyable conclusion. This includes handling the worldwide media blitz and running the massive dog lot at the west end of Front Street where teams which have finished wait for their airplane rides home.

Nome volunteers also put on the sumptuous Awards Banquet in the Nome Convention Center, routinely attended by 2,000 people or more, where every musher gets a chance to speak and the awards are given out. Every finisher is entitled to a banquet and a chance at the podium to receive the coveted belt buckle and finisher's patch. Since not all of the mushers are finished by the time of main banquet, the volunteers also put on a smaller but no less popular Red Lantern Banquet for latecomers.

Because the race lasts more than two weeks (only the top teams make it in under 10 or 12 days), the turnover of volunteers is continuous. In keeping with the nationwide and multinational flavor of the race, volunteers come from all over the Lower 48 and abroad. To accommodate individual schedules, people filling positions along the trail must be periodically moved ahead to high-traffic areas or into the hubs for their ride back to Anchorage as the race progresses.

The IAF runs what amounts to a mini-airline before, during, and after the race, moving 100 race volunteers from

Joe Redington, Sr., the "Father of the Iditarod," takes a break at Kaltag in the 1997 race. He finished a very respectable 36th at the age of 80.

checkpoint to checkpoint. Even within the IAF, pilots rotate back to their regular jobs during the race, so there are never more than 10 or a dozen airplanes actively working the trail at any given time.

It can safely be said no other single event (not even politics) captures Alaskans' enthusiasm so completely and enlists their support so wholeheartedly as the Iditarod. Indeed, the race and everything about it constitute one of the few things which can unite Alaska's normally fractious and independent-minded people for a single purpose, if only for a few weeks each year.

No one who has ever run the Iditarod—or even part of it—would ever trade the experience for anything else. The volunteers who make everything run smoothly year after year against daunting obstacles would echo this sentiment. It is truly a voyage of personal discovery, even for veterans and perennial contenders, and every year is different in a thousand significant details. It is truly the
Last Great Race on Earth.